THE CH'OL MAYA OF CHIAPAS

The Ch'ol Maya of Chiapas

Edited by
KAREN BASSIE-SWEET

with

ROBERT M. LAUGHLIN, NICHOLAS A. HOPKINS,
AND ANDRÉS BRIZUELA CASIMIR

University of Oklahoma Press : Norman

Also by Karen Bassie-Sweet

From the Mouth of the Dark Cave: Commemorative Sculpture of the Late Classic Maya
   (Norman, Okla., 1991)
At the Edge of the World: Caves and Late Classic Maya World View (Norman, Okla.,
   1996)
Maya Sacred Geography and the Creator Deities (Norman, Okla., 2008)

Publication of this book is made possible through the generosity of Edith Kinney Gaylord.

Library of Congress Cataloging-in-Publication Data

The Ch'ol Maya of Chiapas / edited by Karen Bassie-Sweet, with Robert M. Laughlin, Nicholas A. Hopkins, and Andres Brizuela Casimir.

   pages   cm.
Includes bibliographical references and index.
ISBN 978-0-8061-4702-4 (hardcover : alk. paper) ISBN 978-0-8061-9307-6 (paper)
1. Chol Indians—Mexico—Chiapas—History. 2. Chol Indians—Religion. 3. Chol Indians—Antiquities.

   4. Chiapas (Mexico)—Antiquities. 5. Chiapas (Mexico)—Religious life and customs. I. Bassie-Sweet, Karen, 1952–
   F1221.C57C56 2015
   972'.7500497428—dc23   2014036546

The paper in this book meets the guidelines for permanence and durability of the Committee on Production Guidelines for Book Longevity of the Council on Library Resources, Inc. ∞

Copyright © 2015 by the University of Oklahoma Press, Norman, Publishing Division of the University. Paperback published 2023. Manufactured in the U.S.A.

In memory of J. Kathryn Josserand

CONTENTS

PART III: ANCIENT AND CONTEMPORARY DEITIES OF THE CH'OL REGION

ILLUSTRATIONS

Maps

PREFACE AND ACKNOWLEDGMENTS

Karen Bassie-Sweet

This volume contains research from two separate but closely related projects in the Ch'ol Maya region: the linguistic research of J. Kathryn Josserand and Nicholas A. Hopkins, and the Joljá Cave Project directed by Karen Bassie-Sweet, Robert M. Laughlin, and Andrés Brizuela Casimir. Josserand and Hopkins began their field work in the Ch'ol region in 1978 and continued this research until the untimely death of Josserand in 2006. I first met Kathryn and Nick at the 1978 Palenque Mesa Redonda. They had just started their collaboration with Ausencio "Chencho" Cruz Guzmán, a native of the Tulijá Valley who was then living in Palenque and working with Merle Greene Robertson. One of the tales Kathryn, Nick, and Chencho recorded and subsequently published in the proceedings of the Mesa Redonda describes a cave god called Don Juan who lives on the high mountain behind Palenque. They also recounted to me several other unpublished stories about Don Juan that sparked my interest in cave deities and began my fascination with Don Juan Mountain and the modern Ch'ol Maya.

In the late 1950s, the Protestant missionary Wilbur Aulie was shown a cave located on Tumbalá Mountain across the Tulijá Valley from Don Juan Mountain and near the village of Joloniel. In the cave was a series of paintings, which Aulie recognized contained ancient Maya hieroglyphic writing. A few years later, the photographer Gertrude "Trudy" Duby Blom photographed the murals, and copies were sent to J. Eric Thompson, who subsequently published several of them (Thompson 1975). After visiting the cave in January 2000 with Alfonso Morales and Julie Miller, I initiated the Joljá Cave Project to properly document the cave paintings and to record the contemporary beliefs about this sacred location and its relationship to Don Juan. My co-directors were Robert M. Laughlin and Andrés Brizuela Casimir. Chencho was our Ch'ol translator, and his exceptional community skills and knowledge enhanced the project in endless ways beyond mere translation. Other project members included

Christina Halperin and Jon Spenard, who mapped the cave and conducted archaeological field work; Jorge Pérez de Lara and Gene Ware, who photographed the murals using multiple techniques; and Marc Zender and Stanley Guenter, who studied the hieroglyphic texts of the paintings. Alfonso and Julie provided the project with logistical support and with a home base in Palenque. It is an irreplaceable and tragic loss to the field that these fine archaeologists are no longer working at Palenque.

We would not have been able to carry out our research at Joljá without the permission and support of the Joloniel community that owns the cave. We are deeply thankful for the honor of conducting research there. We were directly assisted in our work by numerous members of the Joloniel community, and we acknowledge in particular the contributions of Domingo Pérez Moreno and his wife Carmen, Eulalio Pérez Moreno, Manuel Torres Peñate, Antonio Pérez Méndez, and the *tatuch* Felipe Pérez Montejo. In Tumbalá, Javier Solís has been a staunch supporter of our project, providing us with important information, contacts, and logistical support. Javier's father, Domingo, provided us with critical historical and ethnographic material. Javier's mother, Agustina, warmly welcomed us into their home and made us feel like family members. Her untimely death in 2012 deeply saddened us. We also wish to acknowledge the support of Dr. Enrique Florescano, Etnólogo Sergio Raúl Arroyo García, the late Dr. Alejandro Martínez Muriel, Dr. Laura Pescador, L.A.E. Juan Antonio Ferrer Aguilar, Dr. María Teresa Franco, Antropólogo Hector Álvarez Santiago, Dr. Susanna Ekholm, Karl Herbert Mayer, Fabiola Sánchez, Marcia Bakry, and the late Jan de Vos. Many thanks also to the University of Oklahoma Press editors Alessandra Jacobi Tamulevich, Emily Jerman Schuster, and Katrin Flechsig for their diligence and skill.

Funding for the Joljá Cave Project was provided by the Foundation for the Advancement of Mesoamerican Studies, the National Geographic Society, the National Speleological Society, Joel Skidmore, Mary Ciaramella, and Karen Bassie-Sweet. Josserand and Hopkins received financial support from Centro de Investigaciones Superiores del INAH and its successor, Centro de Investigaciones y Estudios Superiores en Antropología Social; National Science Foundation; National Endowment for the Humanities; Foundation for the Advancement of Mesoamerican Studies; and the Council on Research and Creativity, Florida State University. Any opinions, findings, and conclusions or recommendations expressed in this publication are those of the authors and do not necessarily reflect the views of the funding institutions.

INTRODUCTION

Nicholas A. Hopkins

On the slopes of Tumbalá Mountain in the Ch'ol region of Chiapas, the headwaters of the Ixteljá River gush from a cave on the white cliffs and tumble down a steep gorge to the lush valley below. Known as Joljá, "head of the water," the mountain cliff contains three separate cave passages. On the walls of one of these cave passages are ancient Maya paintings documenting Early Classic period rituals that were conducted in the cave. Caves are relatively common in many areas of the Maya zone, and there is significant evidence of cave rituals in these sacred spaces as early as the Pre-Classic period. The modern Ch'ol regularly make pilgrimages to Joljá (also spelled Jolja') to petition a deity called Don Juan who is thought to inhabit these caves (Joljá Cave Project field notes). They take with them an image of their patron saint and wash the saint with the waters of the cave. In their world view, Don Juan is a powerful spirit who works in unison with Christ and the saints. He owns the earth and all of its wealth. It is thought that abundant rain, essential for a successful corn harvest, will only come if Don Juan releases it from his caves. Contemporary Ch'ol culture is a hybrid of pre-Columbian beliefs and Spanish Catholicism. As will be discussed in this volume, the origin of Don Juan is rooted in the religion of the ancient Maya.

Maya civilization, with its many fascinating achievements in art, architecture, literature, math, and astronomy, has been the subject of scholarly research for well over a century, and it has captivated the attention of the public for an equal amount of time. Less study and attention have been directed at the modern Maya, particularly in the Ch'ol region. Although some researchers of ancient Maya society overlook or disregard contemporary culture as a source of information about the past, it affords a wealth of material that illuminates many important aspects of ancient life. In a similar vein, contemporary Ch'ol culture could not be put into perspective without knowledge of its pre-Columbian history. The focus of this book is on the history, religious beliefs, and world view of the Ch'ol and their direct ancestors, the ancient Maya. It is an attempt to understand the continuities and changes of this remarkable and resilient culture over the centuries. The book is divided into three parts. Part I (chapters 1 and 2) is an introduction to the region and its history. Part II (chapters 3, 4, and 5) is concerned with the archaeology of the region with special emphasis on the ritual caves of Joljá. Part III (chapters 6, 7, and 8) is a discussion of the ancient deities and their contemporary parallels.

Our volume begins with a general overview chapter on the history of the Ch'ol region. During the Classic period, this region was a frontier zone between the rival cities of Palenque and Toniná. One of the ancient footpaths between these two powerful cities traversed the Ch'ol area and was still in use well into the twentieth century. Not surprisingly, many of the pre-Columbian towns in the region were adjacent to this route. Due to a lack of archaeological research in the Ch'ol area, little is known about the Pre-Classic, Classic, and Postclassic periods, but a number of colonial documents provide some insight into the Late Postclassic. The most fascinating of these records involves the Postclassic ruler called Votan. Votan was likely a Chontal merchant who migrated into the area and established a community. His interests in this highland region may have been centered on trade in quetzal feathers, amber, and green stone, which are found in the vicinity. Writers in the late nineteenth century speculated that Votan originated from Egypt, Jerusalem, or Atlantis, and New Agers still try to promote such groundless notions.

Colonial documents indicate that the Ch'ol area was rich in agricultural resources and had a significant population base. At the time of the conquest, Tila was the principal Ch'ol town, and its ruling elite received tribute from the neighboring Tzeltal community of Petalcingo. Despite the fact that the Ch'ol initially capitulated to Spanish rule without a fight, Tila and the adjacent Tzeltal communities were subjected to Spanish raids for slaves. It was a brutal time. The Lacandón Ch'ol, who lived in the lowlands to the south, did not yield to the Spanish and repeatedly attacked highland communities that had. Their futile struggle is an extraordinary story.

The second chapter covers the colonial and post-colonial periods. It examines the many attempts to convert the Ch'ol to Catholicism and explores the exploitation of the Ch'ol population by the Catholic Church, government authorities, and foreign companies. Two of the most intriguing episodes of this period were the establishment of the cult of the Black Christ in Tila at the beginning of the eighteenth century and the indigenous rebellion of 1712, when natives from the Tzeltal, Tzotzil, and Ch'ol regions purged their towns of their Spanish and ladino overlords. The popularity of the Black Christ continues today with tens of thousands of pilgrims annually visiting the church shrine. Indigenous devotees also climb the mountain in front of the church to worship a stalagmite idol in a sacred cave and to obtain medicinal clay from a nearby source.

Chapter 3 describes the ancient footpath between Toniná and Palenque and reviews the pre-Columbian sites and the ritual caves located between these two powerful cities. The three so-called Tila stelae, which actually originate from a site called Ujaltón near Petalcingo, are discussed. The inscriptions on these Ujaltón monuments record Period Ending events in A.D. 685, A.D. 692, and A.D. 830. Period Endings are the most frequently illustrated ceremonies in Classic period art. The famous explorer John Lloyd Stephens took the Toniná-Palenque route when he journeyed from Ocosingo to Palenque in 1840. Because he used native carriers traveling on foot to transport his luggage, their travel time is an excellent indication of how long a journey between Toniná and Palenque took. The sites of Chilón and Ujaltón are one and two days' journey from Toniná, respectively. The location of these communities at these specific intervals surely cannot be a coincidence.

Although the modern Ch'ol believe that the deity Don Juan inhabits a number of caves in the region, he is particularly associated with a cave—like the Joljá caves, on a white cliff—located on a mountain that bears his name. Don Juan Mountain overlooks the coastal plain, and the ancient site of Palenque is nestled at its foot. Literally millions of people have visited the site of Palenque, but few are aware that on the east peak of the mountain is an ancient site that includes a temple and ballcourt, or that the Cueva de Don Juan contains Classic period ritual remains. Even fewer people realize that the modern Ch'ol still perform ceremonies at this white cliff cave, which is adjacent to the Toniná-Palenque route.

Chapters 4 and 5 deal with the caves of Joljá, which are situated across the Tulijá Valley from Don Juan Mountain and adjacent to the Toniná-Palenque route. These chapters describe the caves in detail and analyze the figures and hieroglyphic texts painted on the cave walls. Like the Ujaltón stelae, the paintings refer to Period Ending ceremonies. However, unlike the Late Classic rites of Ujaltón, the Joljá rituals occurred as early as A.D. 426 and A.D. 435. These paintings confirm the presence of Maya elites in this region during the Early Classic. The caves of Joljá are on the property of Joloniel, a Ch'ol hamlet located a kilometer downstream from the caves. In the late 1950s, Wilbur Aulie, an American evangelical Protestant, visited Joloniel as part of his mission to convert the Ch'ol to his form of Christianity. The villagers took Aulie to Joljá and showed him the paintings on the wall of their cave. Aulie immediately recognized the wall paintings as ancient Maya art, and he quickly contacted various authorities requesting they do something to protect them from vandalism and theft. It is ironic that Aulie had such high regard for the Joljá paintings, given that his goal and that of his fellow missionaries was to eradicate Ch'ol religious beliefs.

Chapters 6 and 7 contain an introduction to pre-Columbian genesis stories and world view, with an overview of the principal Classic period deities, including the family of creator deities and the thunderbolt and meteor gods. A primary focus is on Itzamnaaj, supreme creator deity and paternal grandfather of the hero twins, and God L, their maternal grandfather. The contemporary deity Don Juan shares many traits with these two grandfather deities, and we submit that they were the precursors of Don Juan. Lightning plays a prominent role in both ancient and contemporary Maya religion, and anyone who has witnessed the intensity of lightning storms in the Maya region can appreciate why this powerful spectacle would be viewed with awe and reverence. There is significant evidence that the Maya categorized meteors as a type of lightning. Rulers and other community leaders often dressed in the costume of these thunderbolt and meteor deities, and thus, were transformed into these beings. In addition, it was thought that certain powerful leaders had these phenomena as part of their souls.

The last chapter explores the contemporary deities that are identified with caves, mountains, lightning, and meteors. As in ancient times, humans are thought to have supernatural co-essences who share their soul and destiny. The co-essences of spiritually strong individuals are thought to have the form of thunderbolts and meteors. The parallels between ancient and contemporary beliefs are striking and demonstrate the great time depth of these convictions. This chapter also concentrates on the deity Don Juan and the important role he plays in agricultural abundance, rain, fertility, and health. Despite the best efforts of evangelical missionaries to characterize him as a manifestation of the Christian devil, traditional Ch'ol still regard Don Juan favorably, and in times of crisis, even converted Protestant Ch'ol are known to petition him. The chapter concludes with a discussion of several Ch'ol folktales and the many elements from these stories that parallel ancient legends. The appendix contains a number of modern folktales about Ch'ol deities that exemplify their characteristics and attributes.

Geography of the Ch'ol Region

The Ch'ol region is situated in the Chiapas municipalities of Tila, Tumbalá, Salto de Agua, and Palenque. It lies in the valleys and foothills of the Don Juan, El Sumidero, Tumbalá, and Cordón Jolvit mountain ranges (map 1). The area is bounded on the north and east by the Tabasco coastal plain and the lower Usumacinta River drainage. To the southeast is the Cojolita mountain range and river valleys that lead to the upper Usumacinta River and Petén lowlands. The area is bounded on the south by Ajcabalna Mountain (2,470 meters) and Sierra Anover (2,070 meters).

The main rivers of the region are the Michol and Chacamax Rivers, which run along the northern side of Don Juan Mountain, and the Tulijá River, which runs along its southern side. On the opposite side of the Tulijá river valley from Don Juan Mountain are the El Sumidero range (440 meters) and the much larger Tumbalá range (1,630 meters). The major river on the northeast side of the Tumbalá range is the Ixteljá, which separates the El Sumidero and Tumbalá ranges. After cutting through the El Sumidero range, the Ixteljá empties into the Tulijá.

On the west side of the Tumbalá range is the Tila Valley and Cordón Jolvit range. The south side of the Tumbalá range is demarcated by the Río Grande–Hidalgo River, which begins at the northern end of the Tila Valley, flows down the valley to the Tzeltal town of Petalcingo, skirts around the southern base of Tumbalá Mountain through a deep gorge, and also eventually joins the Tulijá River to the east. Directly south of the river is the massive Ajcabalna Mountain and Sierra Anover.

Michol River

Salto de Agua •

Palenque Ruins
•

Chacamax River

N

Don Juan
Mountain

San Pedro •
El Sumidero

Ixteljá River

Tulijá River

Cordón Jolvit

• Tila

• Tumbalá

Petalcingo •

Río Grande–Hidalgo River

Ajcabalna
Mountain

Yajalón
•

Sierra
Anover

• Chilón

```
0          5          10 mi
0     5     10    15 km
```

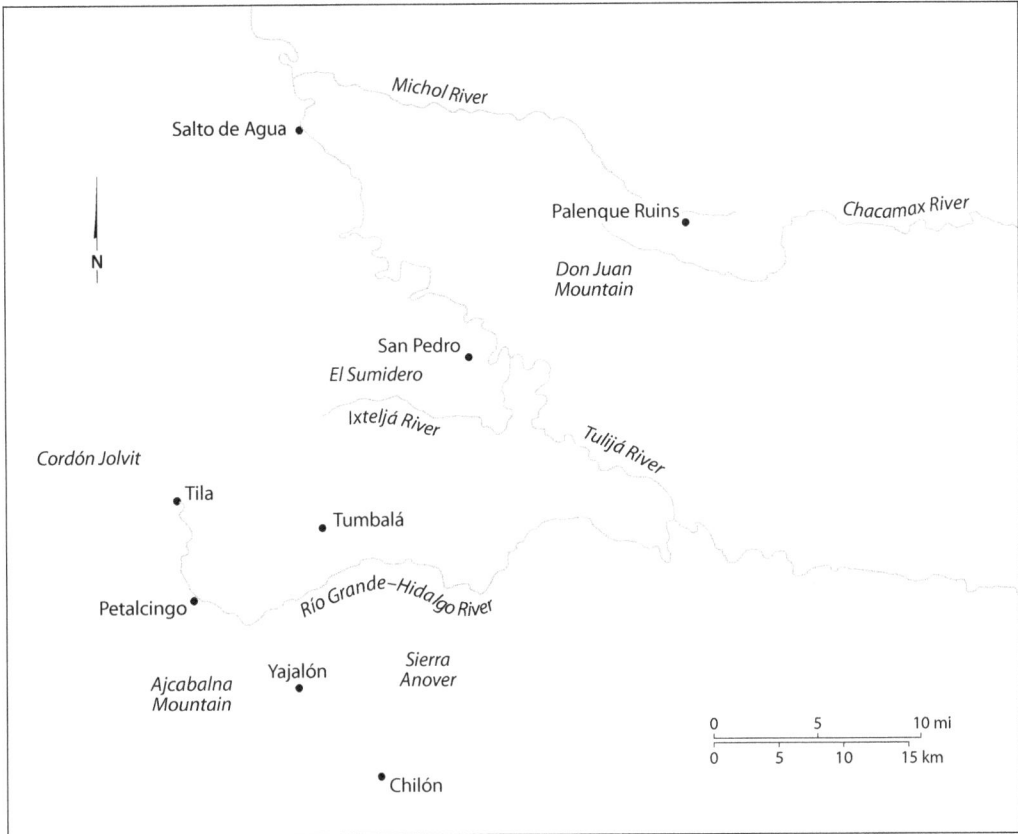

Map 1. Ch'ol region. Map by Bill Nelson, based on a map by Marcia Bakry. © 2015, University of Oklahoma Press.

Between these two great mountains is a series of valleys that lead to the Tzeltal communities of Yajalón, Chilón, and Bachajón and eventually to the Ocosingo Valley of central Chiapas, where the Classic period site of Toniná is located.

The municipal capitals are the towns of Tila at the northern end of the Tila Valley, Tumbalá on the southern end of Tumbalá Mountain, Salto de Agua near where the Tulijá River emerges onto the coastal plain, and Palenque at the base of the north side of Don Juan Mountain. About six kilometers from the town of Palenque on a foothill ridge of Don Juan Mountain is the ancient site of Palenque.

The Mayan Languages

In the early sixteenth century, at the time of the arrival of the Spanish in Mesoamerica, speakers of the Cholan languages (a subgroup of Western Mayan) occupied a continuous area that stretched from the Gulf coast of modern Tabasco to western Honduras and El Salvador (map 2). To the south were the territories of many other Mayan groups, including the other Western Mayan languages Tzotzil, Tzeltal, and

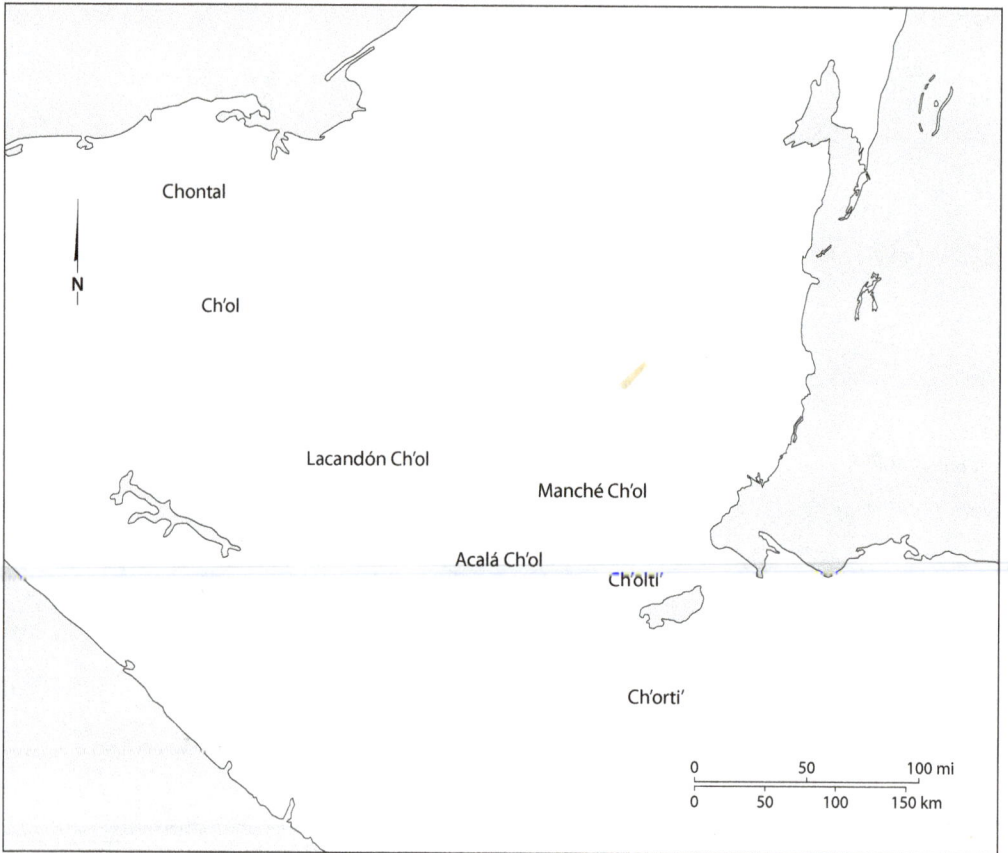

Map 2. Mayan languages. Map by Bill Nelson, based on a map by Marcia Bakry. © 2015, University of Oklahoma Press.

Tojolab'al (Tojolabal) in the modern state of Chiapas, and the various languages of the Cuchumatán Mountains in northwestern Guatemala, as well as the Eastern Mayan languages of the Mamean and Quichean branches of the Mayan family. Overlapping territorially with the Cholans and extending beyond Cholan to the north were languages of the Yucatecan subgroup of Mayan: Lacandón Maya, Itzaj (Itzá), Mopan (Mopán), and Yucatec Maya proper. Thus the territory of the Cholans included all of the area occupied by lowland Classic Maya culture except the more northerly regions.

The pre-Columbian Cholan region apparently constituted a dialect chain, a series of language variants, each relatively like its adjacent neighbors, with the ends of the chain somewhat distinct. However, there is little or no information about most of these variants, and following colonial period extinctions and resettlements, there are extensive data on only four varieties of Cholan:

Chontal, along the Gulf coast
Ch'ol, in the northern highlands of Chiapas (but now having spread to a much larger area)

Ch'orti' (Ch'ortí), along the Guatemala-Honduras border

Ch'olti' (Choltí), an extinct colonial language of southeastern Petén, Izabal, and Alta Verapaz, Guatemala (the main Ch'olti' population in the southeastern Petén during the colonial period is referred to as Manché Ch'ol)

Chontal and Ch'ol are classified as Western Cholan; Ch'orti' and Ch'olti' are classified as Eastern Cholan. Prior to European contact, other varieties of Cholan extended along the Usumacinta, Lacantún, and Chixoy/Salinas drainages; they are variously known as Palencano Ch'ol (around what is now the town of Palenque), Lacandón Ch'ol (the towns of Pochutla, Topiltepeque, Lacam Tun, Sac Bahlán, Peta, and Map), and Acalá Ch'ol (the piedmont and lowlands north of Cobán). Whether these various groups were Western Cholan or Eastern Cholan speakers is uncertain. Robertson, Law, and Haertel (2010) have argued that these groups spoke dialects of Ch'olti' (Manché Ch'ol) and therefore were Eastern Cholan speakers, but we do not find the scant evidence conclusive. Furthermore, they state that the two translators used by Franciscan priest Antonio Margil de Jesús in the conversion of the Lacandón Ch'ol people were Ch'olti' speakers, and therefore, the Lacandón Ch'ol must have been Ch'olti'. As Margil's own letters indicate, these translators were actually Acalá Ch'ol from the San Marcos barrio of Cobán (Leutenegger 1976:66, see chapter 1, this volume). From July to October of 1694, Margil and his companion Fray Pedro de la Concepción studied the language of the Manché Ch'ol in order to work in that region. Yet the following year, while trying to convert the Lacandón Ch'ol in the town of Sac Bahlán, Margil expressed his frustration at not being able to communicate with the Lacandón Ch'ol. In one letter, he commented that he and his fellow priests would try to "learn the words of their language as best we can" until the Acalá Ch'ol translators arrived (Leutenegger 1976:56). In another letter, he notes that he and his fellow priests were trying to learn the language, but "in most cases the Indians do not understand us" (Leutenegger 1976:66). Such statements suggest that Lacandón Ch'ol and Manché Ch'ol were separate languages.

In the Ch'ol region today, two major dialects have emerged, related to the two major Ch'ol *municipios*, Tila and Tumbalá. A third, minor dialect is associated with Sabanilla to the west (see Aulie and Aulie 1978, and Warkentin and Scott 1980, for notes on these varieties of Ch'ol). The dialects are mutually intelligible, and speakers are usually familiar with the characteristics of dialects other than their own and have no difficulty communicating (Hopkins 1983; De la Torre 1994). The Tila and Tumbalá varieties of Ch'ol are sometimes referred to as Western Ch'ol and Eastern Ch'ol, respectively. As Ch'ol-speaking populations have expanded out of these highland municipios in modern times, these varieties have been carried to hundreds of small pioneer settlements, with considerable dialect mixing as people from different dialect areas settle together to form new communities.

Most scholars, following Thompson (1938, 1980), consider the Cholan languages (Chontal, Ch'ol, Ch'olti', and Ch'orti') to be closely related to the language recorded in Classic period hieroglyphic inscriptions, although opinions vary as to whether or not one or more of these languages has greater claim to more direct descent from Classic Maya (or Epigraphic Maya, as it is sometimes called). In any case, the relationship of Cholan to the inscriptions is supported by epigraphic and linguistic evidence (Josserand, Schele, and Hopkins 1985; Josserand and Hopkins 1988; Houston, Robertson, and Stuart 2000; Lacadena and Wichmann 2002). Early historical documentation of these languages is sparse. The major source for Ch'olti' (either the colonial ancestor of modern Ch'orti' or an extinct close relative) is a later copy of a grammar sketch and dictionary dating to about 1625 (Morán 1935). The primary source for colonial Chontal is the Paxbolón papers, 1612–14 (Scholes and Roys 1948), and the sole colonial source for Ch'ol is a word list recorded in 1789 (Fernández 1892; Hopkins, Cruz Guzmán, and Josserand 2008). However, there are many documents in civil and ecclesiastical archives, and a number of ethnohistorians have published on the area (e.g., for the Western Cholan area, Scholes and Roys 1948; Calnek 1970, 1988; Klein 1970; Gerhard 1979; De Vos 1980b, 1988; Watson 1982, 1983; Breton 1988; Alejos García and Ortega Peña 1991; G. Lenkersdorf 1993).

ORTHOGRAPHY

In 1987, the Guatemalan government, in consultation with the Academia de las Lenguas Mayas de Guatemala and other indigenous organizations, issued a decree, Acuerdo Gubernativo Número 1046-87. The decree established new orthographic standards for the indigenous languages, including the spelling of their names, some of which were distinct from traditional usage. These new standards are a work in progress. A second decree in 1988, Acuerdo Gubernativo 129-88, corrected errors in language names in the first and added letters that had been omitted (Instituto Indigenista Nacional 1988). A major collection of articles on Maya linguistics published two years later introduced further changes in language names (England and Elliott 1990), as have other publications.

The process that is underway responds to the increasing participation of educated speakers of indigenous languages in scholarly pursuits. Many are well-trained in linguistics, but such decisions are made by a relatively small number of people and occasionally without adequate consultation with speakers of the languages involved, who may later introduce distinct preferences. For instance, Jakalteko (Jacalteco) is now Popti', Itza' (Itzá) is now Itzaj, Wasteko (Huasteco) is now Teenek. Only linguists refer to the native language of Yucatán as Yukateko (Yucateco), and its speakers prefer the indigenous name Maya. Even though there is not yet a universally accepted standard, Mesoamerican scholars in general have accepted the proposed changes, and have extended the orthographic norms to other languages and language names. The innovations in language names are also accepted here; traditional language names are given in parentheses at first mention. Nonetheless, while we refer to the language names using the suggested changes, we have not extended the changes to include ethnic names, place names, and the names of earlier stages of languages and language families. Thus we may refer to the K'iche' language as a Quichean language spoken by the Quiché in the Department of El Quiché.

All decisions with respect to orthography are compromises, responding to linguistic, historical, cultural, and political factors. The same is true here. We have chosen to adopt the new conventions for the language and ethnic name of the group we are most concerned with here, the Ch'ol (Chol), in order to emphasize that the name is not related to the word *chol*, "milpa, cornfield," a misunderstanding well-embedded in the literature. By the same token, we adopt the parallel versions of the names of their relatives, the Ch'orti' (Chortí) and Ch'olti' (Choltí), but preserve Chontal, since this name is of Nahua origin.

PART I

THE CH'OL REGION
AND ITS HISTORY

1

HISTORY AND CONQUEST OF THE PRE-COLUMBIAN CH'OL AND LACANDÓN CH'OL

Karen Bassie-Sweet, Nicholas A. Hopkins, and Robert M. Laughlin

The information about the Ch'ol and Lacandon Ch'ol regions discussed in this chapter is from a variety of documents written primarily from the perspective of Spanish conquistadors, administrators, politicians, and priests. When the Spanish first arrived in Chiapas, various indigenous groups possessed pre-Columbian manuscripts that were related to divination, healing, history, and genealogy (Calnek 1962:15). Although some of these documents survived the initial conquest period, many of them were later confiscated and destroyed by Francisco Núñez de la Vega in his efforts to eradicate pagan beliefs (Núñez 1988). As bishop of Chiapas from 1682 to 1698, Núñez claimed to have burned more than thirty native manuscripts. It is likely that his actions forced the owners of other manuscripts to hide them. The highly regrettable result is that no pre-Columbian documents from Chiapas have survived. In certain areas of the New World, the Spanish had a policy that indigenous lords and their descendants were entitled to retain their administrative functions within their own communities and to receive certain privileges if they yielded to Spanish authority. Consequently, many documents were created by indigenous leaders to verify their status and to support their claims for preferential treatment. Fortunately, these certifications often included information on ancient histories and customs.

PRE-COLUMBIAN CONFLICTS

The magnificent site of Palenque and its rival site of Toniná were the major pre-Columbian settlements in the Lacandón area. The site of Palenque is well known for its artistic achievements and the extensive hieroglyphic narratives found on its public monuments. Its inscriptions refer to a long line of kings beginning in the Early Classic period (A.D. 430) and extending to near the end of the Late Classic period (A.D. 800). Palenque's narratives refer to military conflicts with the powerful site of Calakmul located 250 kilometers to the northeast and the communities in between these centers, such as Pomona, Santa Elena, and Moral-Reforma. Palenque also extended its influence to the southeast and consequently infringed on the territories of such communities as Piedras Negras, La Mar, Anaite, Sak Tz'i', and Bonampak that were located along the Usumacinta corridor. Sixty-five kilometers due south of Palenque, in the Ocosingo Valley, is the highland site of Toniná. Like Palenque, Toniná's inscriptions relate a long history of kings and military conflicts. Toniná was likewise interested in encroaching on the Usumacinta corridor communities and engaged in a number of conflicts there. Toniná's access route to these sites was along the valleys of the upper Jataté, Perlas, and Santo Domingo Rivers, and later Spanish expeditions used these same routes when they journeyed from the Ocosingo Valley to the east.

War events between Palenque and Toniná are recorded in the inscriptions of both cities. For example, the Palenque ruler K'inich Kan Bahlam II apparently captured Toniná Ruler 2 in A.D. 687, and Toniná subsequently captured the next Palenque ruler, K'inich K'an Joy Chitam II (Martin and Grube 2008:181). Scholars have argued that the Palenque-Toniná conflicts were centered on their mutual desire to control the Usumacinta corridor, and most of the archaeological work has been focused on this lowland zone. In contrast, our volume concentrates on the pre-Columbian sites that are located on the ancient mountain route between Palenque and Toniná that passed through the Tila and Tumbalá region, as well as the sites west of Palenque.

The population levels in the lowlands dropped dramatically after the decline of elite society in the Late Classic period (A.D. 800–A.D. 900). Our knowledge about the time period between the Terminal Classic period and the Spanish conquest in the Ch'ol and Lacandón Ch'ol regions is limited, but it is likely that at least some population remained in the area, particularly in the rural zones. At the time of the first Spanish contact in the sixteenth century, there were indigenous towns in the region that were ruled by caciques and groups of principal lords. Despite the waves of European pandemics that preceded the actual arrival of the Spanish, there was a significant population base and resilient culture. This chapter is an overview of the Ch'ol and Lacandón Ch'ol areas from the Late Postclassic period through the conquest period. We include a detailed discussion of the Lacandón Ch'ol conquest because the events that affected these towns also impacted the Tila and Tumbalá Ch'ol region.

Three Votan and the Late Postclassic Period

While Núñez was in the Soconusco region, he acquired a native manuscript written in Tzeltal and titled the "Probanza de Votan." A *probanza* was a statement of claim verifying the status of a family. The Votan probanza detailed the history of a Postclassic ruler named Three Votan and his descendants. At the time, there were still two hundred Tzeltal families living at the town of Teopisca who claimed to be descendants of Three Votan, so it is not surprising that such a document existed. Núñez quoted from the probanza when he wrote his *Constituciones diocesanas del Obispado de Chiapa.* The canon Ramón de Ordóñez y Aguiar of San Cristóbal de Las Casas (1739–1825) claimed to have been in possession of the same Votan probanza almost a hundred years later (Ordóñez y Aguiar 1797, 1813, 1817; Brasseur de Bourbourg 1866; Megged 1996:24–25). Given Núñez's predilection for destroying native documents, it is possible that Ordóñez had unknowingly acquired a different copy. In any event, the Ordóñez copy was subsequently lost, but Ordóñez and his contemporary Pablo Félix Cabrera described its contents in their writings. The abbot Brasseur de Bourbourg, who collected and copied many important colonial documents during his time in Chiapas and Guatemala, obtained copies of Ordóñez's writings and wrote about Three Votan as well. All three of these men speculated wildly that Three Votan and the ancient Maya originated in Egypt, Jerusalem, or Atlantis, and that Three Votan had founded the city of Palenque. Despite not having the original probanzas to consult, some reliable information about Three Votan can be deduced from the writings of Núñez and these later authors.

In the Maya calendar system, the 260-day tzolk'in cycle was composed of twenty day names combined with thirteen numbers. A survey of the tzolk'in day names used by the various Mayan language groups indicates that while some day names or their cognates were common to all groups, a number of these day names were different (Thompson 1950:66–103). The third day name in the Yucatec, Ixil, K'iche', and Pokom calendars is Ak'bal. This word derives from the word *ak'ab'*, which means "night" in virtually all Mayan languages. This meaning is found in hieroglyphic writing where *k'in* "day" is often paired with *ak'ab'* "night." The equivalent day name in the Tzeltal, Chuj, and Popti' (Jacalteco) calendars is Votan. In Mesoamerica, it was a common practice for deities and people to be named after the tzolk'in day on which they were born. The etymology of Votan is unclear, but in the context of the Postclassic ruler Three Votan, it is obvious that he was named for the day he was born (Calnek 1962:17; 1988:9–10).

Although the etymology of the name Votan has long been a mystery, it may have been a Nahuatl loanword. Karttunen's dictionary of Central Mexican Nahuatl reports the term *cuauhtlah* (*kwaw-tlah*) "mountain, wilderness, forest (*montaña, arboleda o bosque*)," from the entry *quauhtla* in Molina's 1571 vocabulary (Karttunen 1983:64). This is a locative noun, a variant of *kwawi-tlah*, literally "tree-place." A cognate term in a Salvadoran variety of Nahuat is *cuhtan* (*kuh-tan*) "*monte, campo*" (Geoffroy Rivas 1961). From these two forms we postulate a Gulf Coast Nahuat term *kwohtan,* intermediate between the Central Mexican term and the Salvadoran one. (An asterisk marks the form as a hypothetical reconstruction, a form not attested directly but hypothesized on the basis of attested data.) It is reasonable to imagine *kwohtan (or a similar form) being loaned into Mayan as *wotan,* i.e., Votan. Our hypothesis is that this name may refer to the earth lord, who goes by many names, including Chuj Witz-'Ak'lik "Mountain-Grasslands" (i.e., Earth); Kekchí Cuul Taq'a "Mountain Valley" (also Earth), and Chol Yum Witz "Mountain Lord," among others (see chapter 8 for a discussion of earth lords).

The Votan probanza indicates that Three Votan was a member of a lineage called Chan and that he was born on an island off the coast of Yucatán at a place called Valum Chivim (Nine Chivim). Place names that include the number nine are common in the Maya area. The lineage name Chan had a wide distribution and appears in documents from Tumbalá (Ch'ol), Acalán (Chontal), northern Yucatán, and the Petén (Maya of Yucatán) (Roys 1940:39, 44; Calnek 1962:121). Calnek has observed that the island of Three Votan's birth was probably Cozumel, an important trading center located off the east coast of Yucatán, where the Chan family held prominent political positions at the time of the Spanish conquest (Calnek 1962:16–17; 1988:10). It is likely that Three Votan had a Chontal Maya heritage.

Three Votan and his followers are said to have ascended the Usumacinta River from Laguna de Términos and established a town called Na Chan at the base of the Tumbalá mountains. Calnek (1962:121) noted that the names Nachan and Chivim appear in sixteenth-century Catholic baptism records from Yajalón, which suggests there were intermarriages between Tzeltzal from Yajalón and Ch'ol from Tumbalá. How and when Three Votan moved from this Ch'ol area into the Tzeltal and Soconusco regions to the south is not indicated, but the probanza refers to conflicts with other foreign groups that had subsequently moved into the highlands. After resolving these issues, Three Votan is said to have divided Chiapas into provinces and established order. These events are paralleled in the life of the Chontal ruler Auxaual, whose name is likely Aj Ux Ajwal (Lord Three Ajaw). Auxaual came from Cozumel, ascended the Usumacinta, and founded a town called Tanoche (near present-day Tenosique) sometime in the mid-fourteenth century (Scholes and Roys 1948:79, 383–85). Auxaual's descendants then moved to the northeast and were in control of the entire Acalán region by the time the Spanish arrived in 1519. Whether Three Votan arrived before or after Auxaual or was his contemporary is unknown.

The Chontal Maya were merchants. Three natural products found in the Tumbalá mountains that would have attracted the attention of the Chontal were quetzal feathers, amber, and green stone. Quetzals were common in the region until the middle of the twentieth century, and according to the former president of Tumbalá, they were still found on Tumbalá Mountain well into the late twentieth century (Domingo Solís López, personal communication 2002). The amber deposits at Simojovel and the green serpentine deposits at Chalchihuitán are just thirty kilometers southwest and south of Tumbalá, respectively. The importance of two of these three products is reflected in the indigenous name for Tumbalá, which is K'uk'Witz "quetzal mountain," and Chalchihuitán, which derives from the Nahuatl term for green stone.

At the close of the Late Classic period, the cultural horizon extending from Morelos and Puebla to the Gulf Coast and the Yucatán Peninsula included such sites as Tula, Cholula, Cacaxtla, El Tajín, Xochicalco, and Chichén Itzá. The wind and morning star deity called Quetzalcoatl (Kukulcan in some of the Maya areas) played a dominant role in the religion of the time (Ringle, Gallareta Negrón, and Bey 1998; Ringle and Bey 2012). This deity was analogous to the Classic period deity One Ixim and his Postclassic K'iche' counterpart One Hunahpu (Florescano 1999; Bassie-Sweet 2008:298–300). Rulers not only used these deities as role models, but were thought to embody these gods. Consequently, we often see Maya depictions of their past rulers and cultural heroes with the qualities of these deities. Such was the case with Three Votan. For example, Three Votan was said to have come from the east. An eastern affiliation for founding ancestors is a common theme in Mesoamerican mythology, and such statements occur even when a group's actual migration was from a different direction. The reason for this connection rests in the identification of the ancestor with the morning star deity. In the Maya region, east is defined as the place where the sun rises. When Venus first appears as morning star, it rises close to the rising sun, so the arrival of the ancestor from where the sun rises is like the arrival of the morning star. Núñez (1988:237) described how Three Votan left behind relics that were to be honored by his descendants. To house these relics, it was said that Three Votan created a cave simply by blowing; thus he had the powerful wind attribute of the morning star deity.

Three Votan assigned a female ritual specialist to guard and maintain his shrine, and then he mysteriously departed. His departure parallels the Popol Vuh story of the primary lineage head Balam Quitze of the K'iche', who gave his people a sacred bundle that represented him, and then he and the heads of the other three K'iche' lineages miraculously disappeared (Christenson 2007:253–55). The Three Votan cave was located near Huehuetlán (modern Huehuetán) in Soconusco. When Núñez made his inspection of this town in 1691, he discovered the cave shrine was still guarded by a female ritual specialist and that the natives continued to venerate Three Votan. Núñez confiscated the relics and publicly destroyed them in the main plaza of the town.

There is little evidence to indicate where Three Votan established his first community of Na Chan at the base of the Tumbalá mountains. The extensive archaeological and epigraphic studies of Palenque history demonstrate that Ordóñez's belief that Nachan was the site of Palenque is simply wrong. Regrettably, little archaeological work has been conducted in the region of the Tumbalá mountains that would facilitate the identification of a Postclassic town. Even so, it would be most difficult to link such a site to Na Chan, given the meager description of its location. There is, however, a mountain in the Tumbalá region that might have been identified with Three Votan.

At the foot of the Tila Valley is Ajcabalna Mountain (2,470 meters) with the highest elevation in the region (see map 1). With its steep sides, this mountain has the shape of a great pyramid, and it is frequently shrouded in clouds. The contemporary Ch'ol believe that the deity who resides inside Ajcabalna provides rain for the corn and causes earthquakes and thunder. After a serious earthquake in the 1950s, ritual specialists journeyed to the mountain to petition this lord to stop the aftershocks (Joljá Cave Project field notes). It has been reported that the cave on this mountain contains pre-Columbian idols, burials, polychrome ceramics, figurines, and jade ornaments, which indicates that it had a long history of ritual use (Blom 1961; Piña Chan 1967:47). Given that Three Votan was likely of Cholan ancestry, his calendar name in that language would have been Three Ak'bal (Three Night). The Maya believe that mountains are manifestations of their gods, and they identify their founding ancestors with these deities. It is, therefore, possible that Ajcabalna, which literally means "night house" in both Ch'ol and Tzeltal, was thought to be the mountain manifestation of Three Votan.

The Spanish Conquest of the Ch'ol and Lacandón Ch'ol of Chiapas

At the time of the Spanish conquest of Mexico, Ch'olan speakers inhabited an area in Chiapas extending from the town of Tila in the north to the towns of Pochutla, Topiltepeque, Lacam Tun, Sac Bahlán, Peta, and Map in the south (map 3). The Spanish referred to the people of the southern communities as the Lacandón. This name likely derives from the place name Lacam Tun, the largest of these settlements. The term Lacandón was eventually applied to the Yucatec Maya speakers who moved into the region after the demise of the Ch'olan populations (Sapper 1907; Thompson 1938; Scholes and Roys 1948:45; Villa Rojas 1961; Hellmuth 1977; Bricker 1981:52, 330; Palka 2005). To distinguish between these two groups, the Ch'ol speakers are referred to as Lacandón Ch'ol while the Yucatec Maya speakers are referred to as Lacandón Maya. While Lacam Tun, Sac Bahlán, Peta, and Map are the Ch'ol names for these settlements, Pochutla and Topiltepeque are Nahuatl names that were assigned to these settlements by the Spanish. The Spaniards often employed Mexican place names in the Maya area (for example, towns that end in "tenango," such as Huehuetenango or Chichicastenango, are Nahuatl names).

From what little documentation exists about the southern communities of Pochutla, Topiltepeque, Lacam Tun, Sac Bahlán, Peta, and Map, they appear to have had reciprocal and cooperative relationships with each other (De Vos 1980a, 1980b). Their association with the Ch'ol communities to the north is unknown, but they maintained close ties with the Acalá Ch'ol (their southeastern neighbors) using overland and river routes (Feldman 2000). They also mined salt at Nueve Cerros on the Chixoy River on the edge of Acalá Ch'ol territory.

The region to the north and east of the conjunction of the Salinas and Pasión Rivers was occupied by a number of Yucatec-speaking groups including the Itzá, Kowojs, Kejaches, Mopáns, and Xocmos (Jones 1998). The Itzá were centered at the western end of Lake Petén Itzá, located eighty-five kilometers northeast of the conjunction, and were the most powerful in the region. The Lacandón Ch'ol communities had longstanding conflicts with the Itzá, who frequently raided and even burned the Lacandón Ch'ol communities, and the Lacandón Ch'ol responded in kind.

The Spanish pacification of the Western Ch'olan communities began soon after the conquistador Hernán Cortez defeated the Aztecs in 1521, but their final subjugation did not occur until the eighteenth century. The following is a summary of the major events of this subjugation (Sapper 1907, 1985; Means 1917; Ximénez 1929–31; Remesal 1932; D. Stone 1932; Chamberlain 1948a, 1948b; Scholes and Roys 1948; Cogolludo 1955; Saint-Lu 1968; Fuentes y Guzmán 1969–72; Calnek 1970; Gerhard

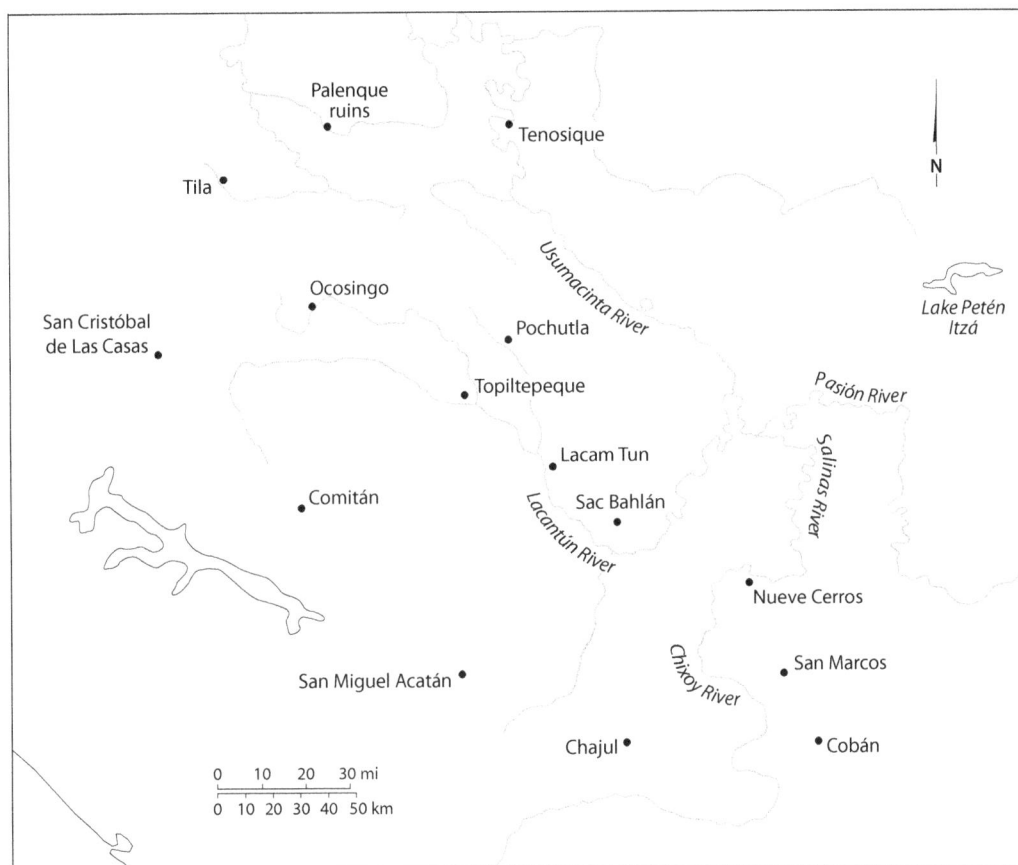

Map 3. Lacandón Ch'ol area. Map by Bill Nelson, based on a map by Marcia Bakry. © 2015, University of Oklahoma Press.

1979; Sherman 1979; De Vos 1980a, 1980b; Villagutierre 1983; Cano 1984; Lovell 1992; G. Lenkersdorf 1993; Feldman 2000).

Once he had conquered the Aztecs of Central Mexico, Cortez wasted little time in extending his domain and consolidating his control. He sent various military expeditions to adjacent areas with instructions to subdue the various indigenous populations and establish Spanish towns. Further expeditions were then launched from these satellite towns into neighboring areas to expand the conquest. One of Cortez's officers, Gonzalo de Sandoval, founded such a satellite town (Espíritu Santo) near the mouth of the Coatzacoalcos River, while another officer, Juan de Vallecillo, established another Spanish town (Santa María de la Victoria) at the mouth of the Grijalva River near the Chontal Maya community of Potonchan (Scholes and Roys 1948: 124; Gerhard 1979:36).

The Spanish used a method of control in their conquered lands called *encomienda*. In this system, an *encomendero* was given trusteeship over a community of conquered natives. Although they allegedly retained their land rights, the natives were required to pay tribute and provide labor to the encomendero, who was supposed to maintain the peace and provide instruction in Catholicism in return. The initial encomenderos were usually the officers who had distinguished themselves in the military campaign. A lack of accountability allowed the encomenderos to ruthlessly exploit their native charges, and abuse was widespread (Sherman 1979). Another major form of enrichment for the Spanish was slavery. The Spanish policy was to enslave any indigenous persons who resisted their authority, and expeditions for the sole purpose of obtaining slaves were common and highly profitable.

Under the authority of Cortez, encomiendas were first granted in the Tabasco region to residents of Espíritu Santo in 1522 (Gerhard 1979:36–38, 150–58). In the same year, Bernal Díaz del Castillo (another one of Cortez's officers) was awarded encomiendas at Teapa (a Zoque community) and Potonchan. An attempt to implement the encomienda system in the areas adjacent to Espíritu Santo began when the Spanish residents of the town demanded that the Chiapas communities to the southeast pay them tribute, despite the fact that this region had yet to be conquered by the Spanish military. Efforts to impose jurisdiction were met with predictable resistance, so Captain Luis Marín was sent to engage the powerful Chiapanecs of eastern Chiapas, who controlled all the major trade routes in their region. After the defeat of the Chiapanecs in 1524, many of the adjacent Zoque, Tzotzil, and Tzeltal communities capitulated, but when a Spanish officer made unauthorized demands for gold, Tzotzil Chamula and Tzeltal Huehuistan were soon in revolt. After Marín quelled the rebellion, he chose to return to Coatzacoalcos without establishing a Spanish settlement in the conquered zone, probably because he simply did not have the resources to do so.

While Marín was battling the Chiapanecs, Cortez also dispatched military expeditions into Guatemala and Honduras to expand his territories. Pedro de Alvarado was sent overland to subdue the Soconusco region on the Pacific Coast, as well as the various groups in Guatemala, while Cristóbal de Olid was sent by sea to conquer Honduras. From 1524 to 1530, Alvarado subjugated both Soconusco and the major Maya groups of the central highland zone of Guatemala, and he established a Spanish town in Guatemala. On the other hand, Olid seized the opportunity to form an alliance with one of Cortez's political rivals in Cuba and declared himself governor of Honduras. In response to this betrayal, Cortez sent a naval force under the command of Francisco de las Casas to Honduras, and he personally headed the land expedition to deal with Olid. This arduous and costly mission that began in October of 1524 took Cortez through Espíritu Santo, Tabasco; the Chontal area of Acalán; and the Kejach and Itzá area of the central Petén to Honduras (Means 1917:26–38; Villagutierre 1983:32–42). When Cortez finally arrived six months later at his destination, Olid had already been deposed and Cortez's authority restored. The journey provided the Spanish with a rudimentary knowledge about the terrain and communities of the interior, but accomplished little else.

Back in Chiapas, the various native leaders who had been conquered by Marín had no motivation to pay their tribute without a Spanish military presence in the area, so a second expedition under Diego de Mazariegos was dispatched from Espíritu Santo to deal with them (Gerhard 1979:150, Bricker 1981:45–46). Mazariegos successfully defeated the Chiapanecs in early 1528, but he was immediately presented with another issue. Competition among the Spanish military leaders for territories and the subsequent wealth those territories might supply was intense. Pedro Portocarrero (one of Pedro de Alvarez's officers) brought a force from Guatemala to the Comitán area to extend Alvarez's boundary into Chiapas. Fortunately, Mazariegos was able to avoid a confrontation by bribing Alvarez's soldiers with encomienda grants. After more political maneuvering, Mazariegos established a permanent capital called Villa Real that was later renamed Ciudad Real (present-day San Cristóbal de Las Casas) and began administering the new town.

Various soldiers were awarded encomiendas for the communities in the immediate vicinity of Ciudad Real. Although the Tzeltal and Ch'ol zones northeast of the city were, for the Spanish, economically marginal, they were likewise placed under the jurisdiction of encomenderos living in Ciudad Real and Espíritu Santo, and they apparently paid their tribute without military intervention. People in these smaller settlements were well aware of the events happening around them, so it is not surprising that they would submit to Spanish tribute demands once the larger indigenous centers had been subdued. Being under the protection of an encomendero, however, did not necessarily protect an indigenous community from other Spaniards. For example, Julián Pardo of Espíritu Santo held the encomienda for Tila in 1528, but Pedro de Guzmán (the *alcalde* of Espíritu Santo) raided Tila for slaves. Tila would be subjected to a similar raiding expedition eight years later. In 1529, Mazariegos lost his political appointment at Ciudad Real and was replaced by Juan Enrique de Guzmán.

While these events were taking place in Chiapas, the crown authorized Francisco de Montejo to pacify the Yucatán peninsula and named him Adelantado and Capitán General of this northern zone (Chamberlain 1948a). Montejo's initial attempts on the eastern coast of the peninsula in 1527 were failures, but he soon changed his tactics and decided to move to the Tabasco region, which he believed would be an easier conquest as well as a strategic base to launch an assault on Yucatán. Montejo was subsequently named *alcalde mayor* of Tabasco, and he used Santa María de la Victoria as a base for his expeditions into the unconquered Tabasco interior. It was a hard-fought campaign that left Montejo and many of his men in ill health. As they were nearing the end of the campaign near Teapa, they encountered Guzmán, who was leading an expedition from Ciudad Real to subjugate the same zone. Both forces were fatigued and battle weary. The two leaders amicably decided on a boundary between their territories and agreed to collaborate.

Montejo's next goal was to subdue the Acalán region to the east of Santa María de la Victoria. Although it was a highly circuitous route, Guzmán suggested that Montejo proceed to Ciudad Real and approach Acalán overland from there. Montejo's health was so poor that he could not continue, so he directed his lieutenant, Alonso Dávila (also known as Alonso López de Ávila), to command the expedition (D. Stone

1932:230–35; Chamberlain 1948a:83–88; Villa Rojas 1967–68; De Vos 1980b:49–51). The force marched to Ciudad Real, where Guzmán resupplied and reinforced their ranks. After resting, they set out in the spring of 1530. The precise route that Dávila took is unknown, but after thirty leagues his guides from Ciudad Real turned back because they were not familiar with the road beyond that point. The expedition then continued on a difficult path that led them to a large lake with a town on an island. From the description, this could only have been Lacam Tun on Lake Miramar (map 3). This was the first direct contact that the Spanish had with the Lacandón Ch'ol.

The Spanish forces lashed together four canoes they found at the edge of the lake and tied two horses to the raft. A party of soldiers then boldly crossed the lake on the raft with the two horses swimming behind and quickly assembled in front of the Lacandón Ch'ol warriors who had gathered on the shore of the island. The warriors hesitated in attacking the Spaniards, and their indecision gave Dávila enough time to move more troops to the island, forcing the inhabitants to flee their town in canoes. The Lacandón Ch'ol strategy of withdrawing into the forest when an enemy appeared at their community would be successfully repeated many times in the future.

The Spaniards described Lacam Tun as a town of rich Indians; merchants and warriors. Dávila captured one of the slaves of the Lacam Tun cacique, and during her interrogation, she told him that the ruler had twelve *cargas* of gold. Given the Spanish obsession with this precious metal, it is highly likely that the terrified woman was merely telling Dávila what she thought he wanted to hear, for the Lacandón Ch'ol had little or no gold. In hopes of finding the cacique's treasure, Dávila pursued the Lacandón Ch'ol along the lakeshore but only caught some who were trying to flee with bundles of feathers. The Spaniards described the feathers as rare and highly prized by the natives, which indicates that they likely included the tail feathers of the male quetzal. To the Maya, these were far more valuable than gold.

The Spanish remained at the abandoned community for several days while they plundered the town's food supplies, and then pushed on for Acalán. Using several captured Lacandón Ch'ol as guides, Dávila marched to the northeast through difficult terrain of high ridges and swampy valleys before emerging on the banks of the Usumacinta. With canoes seized from a small community near the river, the force traveled downstream, braving several sets of rapids before wearily arriving at the indigenous town of Tanoche (present-day Tenosique). The fleet of soldiers and horses paddling down the canyons of the Usumacinta in dugout canoes must have been remarkable to see. From Tanoche, Dávila moved toward the north and eventually found the remnants of the road created by Cortez six years earlier, and from there he proceeded to his goal of the Acalán area of the Chontal.

In the same year as Dávila's entrada, Pedro de Alvarado successfully petitioned the Spanish king to have Chiapas placed under his authority, and he subsequently installed his own deputy at Ciudad Real to oversee the region. In 1536, he ordered a military expedition to proceed from Ciudad Real to Pochutla and establish a Spanish town from which the surrounding area could be pacified and controlled (Chamberlain

1948b:181–82; Sherman 1979:60–63; De Vos 1980b:53–55; 1990:49–52). The force was under the direction of Francisco Gil Zapata, who had served under Alvarado in Guatemala. Alvarado's choice of commander had dire consequences for the indigenous population of the region, because Gil had his own agenda and planned to use the occasion to acquire captives for his slaving enterprise. Although the majority of the Pochutla population fled into the forest, Gil captured some natives and sold them to a slave merchant. He then marched farther north beyond the limits of Alvarado's territory and founded a Spanish town at the by then deserted village of Tanoche on the banks of the Usumacinta. From this location, Gil moved his force one hundred kilometers southwest to the Tila area, where he began a reign that can only be described as sheer terror.

Colonial period documents indicate that Tila was still governed by its indigenous ruler at this time, and that the nearby Tzeltal community of Petalcingo paid Tila tribute. Both towns were under the jurisdiction of the encomendero Francisco Ortes of Ciudad Real, and one assumes that the two communities sent annual payments to him. The communities of Yzcatepeque (near Yajalón) and Tuni (near Bachajón) also made payments to Ciudad Real encomenderos. Gil attacked these peaceful encomienda towns starting with Tila and proceeding to Petalcingo, Yzcatepeque, Suteapa, and Tuni for the sole purpose of obtaining captives that could be turned into slaves. As in Pochutla, the citizens of Tila had the good sense to abandon their town and flee to the countryside. Those who were captured or enticed to return were branded and enslaved. Gil and his second in command, Lorenzo de Godoy, executed many of the captured caciques and principal men when demands for more slaves were not met. As a message to those who would resist him, Gil sent one lord back to his people with his nose and hand cut off and strung around his neck. Rather than submit more of their people to enslavement, Petalcingo and Tuni burned their towns and fled into the mountains. Gil and his men finally returned to Tanoche.

Despite being denounced by the Ciudad Real encomenderos for the destruction of their livelihoods, Gil apparently suffered no real consequence for his actions. He would likely have continued his slaving activities in the region were it not that Tanoche was in Tabasco and consequently under the authority of Francisco de Montejo. Although Montejo was away, raising resources for another Yucatán expedition, his son (Francisco de Montejo the Younger) had been left in charge. When Montejo the Younger learned that Gil had trespassed on his territory, he took a small force to Tanoche from his base at Santa María de la Victoria and confronted Gil. Gil was forced to relinquish his command, turn his soldiers over to Montejo, and return to Ciudad Real.

When Montejo the Elder subsequently became governor of Chiapas (1539–44), he authorized military force to reestablish the encomiendas in the Pochutla and Tila regions (Chamberlain 1948b:182–84; De Vos 1990:52–53). Pedro de Solórzano, who ostensibly held the Pochutla encomienda, successfully led an expedition against Pochutla, Tila, and Petalcingo in 1542. Pochutla briefly paid tribute to Solórzano, but as soon as the Spanish forces withdrew to Ciudad Real, the community revolted again. The leaders of Pochutla later attempted to make peace directly with Solórzano by sending emissaries to Ciudad Real with tribute payments of jewels, feathers, and slaves. Unfortunately for them, they had to travel through territory controlled by Christian natives who had been previously harassed by Lacandón Ch'ol raiding parties. The Christian natives took the occasion to seek revenge, and they killed the emissaries.

Meanwhile, in Guatemala, the lack of immediate riches in the rugged, unconquered northeastern Guatemalan highlands and the bellicose nature of its inhabitants had given Pedro de Alvarado and his followers little incentive to extend their conquest into these zones. The Dominican order successfully petitioned the crown to give them exclusive control over the area in order to convert the indigenous populations and obtain their submission to Spanish authority peacefully (Remesal 1932; Saint-Lu 1968). The crown agreed, and Spanish settlers and encomiendas were banned from the zone. From 1537 to 1547, the Dominicans established tentative Spanish authority and congregated much of the indigenous population into newly founded Christian towns. The Dominicans induced the local caciques to convert and accept Spanish rule by giving them gifts and promising that they would retain their high status and authority within the native community. Undoubtedly, there was also a strongly implied threat of military intervention if the caciques resisted.

In Alta Verapaz, Christian towns were established at Cobán, San Pedro Carchá, San Juan Chamelco, San Cristóbal Verapaz, and Santa María Cahabón. From their base at Cobán, the Dominicans proceeded into the lowlands to try to congregate and convert the Acalá Ch'ol and Manché Ch'ol communities to the north and east, respectively (see Feldman 2000 for an overview of these conversion attempts). By 1550, the Dominicans had baptized some of the Acalá Ch'ol living directly north of Cobán along the Río Icbolay (a tributary of the Chixoy). They congregated these Ch'ol at a community near the modern village of Yaxcabnal and named the town San Marcos.

The Dominican strategy of congregation was also used in Chiapas, although the Dominican priests in this region were in constant rivalry with the Ciudad Real political authorities and encomenderos as well as with their Franciscan colleagues for control of the native population. Existing highland towns, including Tila, Petalcingo, and Ocosingo, maintained their integrity or were moved short distances to more accessible locations; other indigenous communities were centralized in *cabeceras* (head towns); some communities were merged. The Lacandón Ch'ol region to the southeast, however, remained unpacified.

In 1552, Lacandón Ch'ol from Pochutla and Lacam Tun made raids on frontier Christian native communities, sacrificing and killing a large number of people and burning several towns (Sherman 1979:216; Villagutierre 1983:44). In response, Bishop Tomás de Castillas set out from Ciudad Real for Pochutla hoping that he could convince the Lacandón Ch'ol to accept Christianity and Spanish rule (Chamberlain 1948b: 184). Castillas sent a small party ahead with a message of reconciliation, but the Pochutla warriors responded by killing them. Believing that further peaceful overtures were futile, Castillas and his entourage were forced to return to Ciudad Real. Although he implored the Spanish authorities to do something to protect the Christian communities, no military intervention was ordered, because the crown had endorsed the Dominican plan of peaceful conversion. The Lacandón Ch'ol thus continued to harass not only the Christian towns in Chiapas, but also those to the south in the Cuchumatanes and Alta Verapaz without consequence. The failure of the Dominicans in the Acalá Ch'ol area would, however, soon change that situation.

In 1555, Domingo de Vico, who was the Dominican prior of Cobán, accepted an invitation from the Acalá Ch'ol of San Marcos to visit their community (Sapper 1907, 1985; Remesal 1932, 2:265–67, 370–378; D. Stone 1932:243; Villagutierre 1983:45–50; Feldman 2000:37–54). Vico, a fellow Dominican, and their Christian Kekchí assistants were accompanied on their three-day journey to the town by the Christian cacique of San Juan Chamelco, named Matal B'atz', and a party of armed Kekchí guards (Chamelco is located just seven kilometers southwest of Cobán). Although he was aware of conflicts between the converted and unconverted Acalá Ch'ol, and despite repeated warnings from Matal B'atz' that the pagan Acalá Ch'ol were planning some kind of treachery, Vico imprudently sent the Kekchí ruler and his men back to Chamelco once the expedition arrived at San Marcos. In collusion with the Lacandón Ch'ol, the Acalá Ch'ol subsequently killed almost everyone in the Vico party. Later Spanish expeditions to the Lacandón Ch'ol towns of Lacam Tun and Sac Bahlán found articles belonging to Vico that implicated the residents of these specific towns with Vico's murder.

The response by the Spanish authorities in Cobán to the slaughter of the Vico party was swift and deadly. They sent a military expedition composed of both Spaniards and Christian Kekchí to San Marcos and pursued the fleeing Ch'ol as far as the lower Icbolay region, executing all they were able to capture. After that initial, bloody retaliation, the Dominicans intervened and then persuaded some of the remaining Acalá Ch'ol to return to San Marcos in hopes of reestablishing the Christian town. Frequent attacks on the community by the pagan Ch'ol began soon after. Lacking the military ability to protect the San Marcos population and fearing that it would once again apostatize, the priests resettled the San Marcos population in an eastern barrio of Cobán.

The removal of lowland Ch'ol to the highlands was a common Dominican strategy. A similar removal happened in the Manché Ch'ol region in 1685. The Manché Ch'ol were taken from their lowland homeland and resettled in the Urran Valley in Baja Verapaz (Santa Cruz El Chol, also known as Belén) (Feldman 2000:187). The distance between the Manché Ch'ol region and Belén made it impossible for the Ch'orti' to return to their fields to work. The Acalá Ch'ol fared better. Though residing in Cobán, they were able to continue to farm and harvest forest products such as cacao and achiote in their homelands in order to support themselves and pay their tribute fees to Spanish authorities. Nevertheless, both groups were eventually assimilated into the local non-Ch'ol population.

After the massacre of the Vico party and the continued attacks on Christian towns by the Lacandón Ch'ol, the Spanish authorities finally decided to send a military force, under the direction of Pedro Ramírez de Quiñones (judge of the high court of Guatemala), to deal with Lacam Tun, Topiltepeque, and Pochutla (D. Stone 1932:244–45; Sherman 1979:216; De Vos 1980b:81–88; Villagutierre 1983:52–59). The initial Dominican plan was to capture the inhabitants of these communities and transport them to an area to the west of Ciudad Real where they could be resettled and controlled. The Spanish authorities stressed that Ramírez should use all possible means to pacify the Lacandón Ch'ol before resorting to military force. The expedition was given permission to make slaves of any natives captured in war, which was a great incentive for the Spaniards to disregard diplomatic solutions. The opportunity to acquire slaves and booty attracted numerous Spaniards from Chiapas and Guatemala as well as nearly two thousand indigenous warriors and bearers from Chiapas and highland Guatemala. The cost of the expedition was mostly borne by the participants, who hoped to be well compensated with plunder and slaves.

In 1559, the Chiapas contingent gathered together and marched all the way to the Guatemalan capital, where they were joined by the Guatemalans. With great pomp, the army then turned around and marched back to Comitán to begin their assault. It took the heavily laden army fifteen days to struggle though the ninety kilometers of mountainous forests that separated Comitán from Lacam Tun. After building a brigantine for transportation, the army crossed the lake, and the population of Lacam Tun prudently abandoned their community and tried to escape. When the Spanish entered the town, they found the murdered Friar Vico's cloak as well as several Christian images. More than 150 natives were captured, including the ruler and high priest, but a large group of fugitives was able to make its escape down the Lacantún River to the southeast. Their fate was sealed, however, when they encountered a contingent of Christian Kekchí soldiers from San Juan Chamelco who had come to join the Spanish in their attack. Their leader, Matal B'atz', hanged eighty of the Lacandón Ch'ol whom he deemed responsible for Vico's death, and he enslaved the rest.

After looting the town and burning it, the army moved on to Topiltepeque some forty kilometers to the northwest. Their advance party did not remain vigilant while en route, and a band of a hundred Lacandón Ch'ol was able to surprise them with a hail of arrows in a narrow canyon. Before the Spanish could engage them, the Lacandón Ch'ol melted into the forest. After regrouping, the Spanish pushed on to Topiltepeque, only to discover that the entire population had already fled into the forest. It is probable that the canyon attack was a diversionary tactic to delay the Spanish long enough for the town to evacuate. The army looted the town of its food supplies and other items of value, and moved on to Pochutla, which lay twenty-five kilometers to the northeast. Like Lacam Tun, this settlement was situated on an island, and the Spanish immediately began to build rafts to cross the lake. The Chiapanec soldiers, who were accomplished swimmers, towed the Spanish across the water. The Pochutla warriors launched their canoes and engaged them, but their arrows were no match for the superior power of the Spanish firearms, and they were soon routed. When the Spanish entered the town, they discovered that it was empty. The Pochutla women, children, and possessions were already hidden in the mountains.

Although many of the Spanish and their native allies had acquired little of value so far during the looting of the three towns, Ramírez decided that the army would return to Guatemala rather than pursue the Lacandón Ch'ol further. Ramírez's motivation is unstated, but he surely must have recognized that supplying such a large force once the Topiltepeque supplies were exhausted would have been extremely difficult, and that the additional effort of chasing small bands of Lacandón Ch'ol through heavily forested areas would have had diminishing returns. His actions indicate that he was not interested in pursuing the Lacandón Ch'ol relocation plan of the Dominicans. The army returned with more than 190 captives destined for slavery, but once in Guatemala many of them managed to escape and eventually return to their homeland. Some of the Topiltepeques accepted the invitation of the Dominican priests to move to the Cobán area, and eventually they settled in the barrio of the San Marcos Acalá Ch'ol at Cobán. They were joined there by the prisoners that Matal B'atz' had brought back to Cobán. Other Topiltepeques who did not want to make the arduous journey to Cobán apparently moved to Ocosingo, just sixty kilometers northwest of Topiltepeque, where they formed a separate barrio from the Tzeltal inhabitants of the town.

An interesting aspect of the Ramírez expedition was that Ramírez had ordered the alcalde mayor of Yucatán to send a contingent of soldiers to the Acalán region of Tabasco to attack the Lacandón Ch'ol simultaneously from the north. Captain Francisco Tamayo Pacheco and forty soldiers were dispatched to Acalán, but before the group could set out, they received word that Ramírez had completed his conquest, so they stayed in the Acalán region to deal with an uprising of natives there. The Pacheco expedition is described in the probanza of the Chontal Maya cacique Pablo Paxbolón and his Spanish son-in-law, Francisco Maldonado. The probanza states: "the oidores of Guatemala had summoned them to go to take the province of the Lacandón and Popo, and they remained here in Tixchel because they learned that Licenciado Ramírez, who was going as captain of this expedition, had returned, for he had taken the land and the people of the Popo" (Scholes and Roys 1948:398). The original Chontal text in these probanza papers refers to the Poo instead of Popo. After the conquest of the southern Lacandón Ch'ol communities, the inhabitants of Peta and Map were congregated at a new town called San Ramón Nonato. The name Ah Poo "he of Poo" appears as the name of an individual in the 1697 census for this community, so it is likely that Poo was another name for the Lacandón Ch'ol population.

The main sign of the Toniná emblem glyph is a T687 *po* sign. Emblem glyphs are Classic period royal titles that refer to a particular kingdom. The Early Classic version of this sign is composed of two T687 signs that suggest a reading of *pop* or *popo*. This raises the slim possibility that the Lacandón Ch'ol called Poo were descendants of the people of Toniná (Martin and Grube 2008:179).

The lack of a permanent Spanish military presence in the region after the withdrawal of Ramírez allowed the fugitive Lacandón Ch'ol to return to their communities and rebuild. The Dominicans persisted in their attempts to peacefully congregate the Ch'ol as well as the Tzeltal. The most successful priest in this endeavor was Pedro Lorenzo de la Nada, who arrived in Chiapas in 1560 (Ximénez 1929–31, 2:150; D. Stone 1932:245–46; De Vos 1980a; 1980b:89–102). After studying the indigenous languages in Ciudad Real, Fray Pedro began an almost single-handed campaign to convince the natives to leave their more remote communities and settle in centralized towns. His first foray to Pochutla in 1563 was unsuccessful, but the following year, one of the Pochutla lords and his followers agreed to move to Ocosingo, and they settled in a new barrio. Although some remained at Pochutla, it is likely that this significant loss of inhabitants presaged the end of the community.

In 1564, Fray Pedro worked in the highland valleys to the northwest, moving the Ch'ol town of Tila to a new location at the head of its valley, establishing the Ch'ol town of Tumbalá, and congregating Tzeltals to form the towns of Yajalón and Bachajón. After growing impatient with his superiors in San Cristóbal, the padre went rogue and twice proceeded alone into the Lacandón Ch'ol forest to try to convince the Lacam Tun community to accept Spanish rule and avoid more bloodshed. After failing at this mission, he moved a hundred kilometers north and gathered the Ch'ol speakers living in this zone to form the town of Santo Domingo Palenque, where he took up permanent residence himself.

Fray Pedro's next goal was to convert the Itzá, who were located at Lake Petén Itzá two hundred kilometers southeast of Santo Domingo Palenque, and he petitioned the governor of Yucatán to assist him. The governor responded by sending Feliciano Bravo to Tabasco to organize an expedition. Fray Pedro gathered together Christianized Ch'ol natives from Santo Domingo Palenque to accompany him as well as Christianized Lacandón and Pochutla Ch'ol. As Scholes and Roys (1948:492) noted, these latter Ch'ol must have been from the Ch'ol barrio of Ocosingo. In 1573, the Bravo expedition moved overland from Tenosique to the Río San Pedro Mártir and proceeded upstream by canoe in search of the Itzá. After five days on the river, the expedition arrived at the edge of Itzá territory but could not find the trail to the lake. With food supplies running out, the expedition returned. While the Bravo expeditionaries did not succeed in reaching the Itzá, they were told that a band of two hundred warriors from Pochutla and Lacam Tun had recently attempted to raid the Itzá, and all but twenty of the Ch'ol were killed. Whether the Lacandón Ch'ol were trying to retaliate against the Itzá for a prior raid on their own communities is not known, but such a disastrous loss of able-bodied men must have had significant repercussions for the viability of the Lacandón Ch'ol communities.

A second Bravo expedition to the Itzá area was organized in 1580 and set out from Tenosique again. This group included a "cacique of Lacandón and Pochutla" named Cenuncabenal and his followers (Scholes and Roys 1948:497). Given that Lacam Tun was still occupied by hostile pagan Ch'ol, this leader and his men were likely from the Ocosingo Ch'ol barrio. The expeditionaries followed the Río San Pedro Mártir past the point where they had previously turned around, and they found signs of milpas and habitation. From here, they planned to move inland to the Itzá capital of Nojpetén, but Fray Pedro fell ill and was unable to walk. The expedition once again turned back. Some of the expedition climbed to a high point of land where Cenuncabenal pointed out to the Spaniards the sierras surrounding Lake Petén Itzá, which demonstrates that the Lacandón Ch'ol knew this territory well.

The submission of the Pochutla and Topiltepeque communities to Spanish authority did not deter Lacam Tun from raiding. After they boldly attacked two Christian settlements near Comitán, an expedition headed by Juan de Morales Villa Vicencio was dispatched from Comitán to Lacam Tun in 1586 (Morales 1936; De Vos 1980b:97–113). When Morales demanded that the island town surrender to Spanish authority, the Lacam Tun inhabitants again responded by fleeing into the jungle. Morales pursued them with a vengeance, killing and capturing as many as he could. He also razed their town, milpas, gardens, and orchards, leaving nothing unburned: "and said rocky island is presently totally destroyed and burned under orders of the Lord Captain in such a manner that not a wooden pole remained . . . and all the foundations of the houses were ruined and everything else that could be destroyed was so . . . in such a manner that the island is presently nothing but barren rock" (Hellmuth 1977:424). Whether those who escaped returned and tried to rebuild after Morales withdrew is unknown. One of the Lacam Tun captives told Morales about another Lacandón Ch'ol town called Cabenal (Sac Bahlán) some ten leagues away, so it is possible that the Lacam Tun inhabitants moved to that town, which was more remote from Spanish settlements. The Spanish did not return to the lake for more than ninety years, and at that time, Lacam Tun was abandoned.

Despite the apparent demise of the Lacam Tun community, the Lacandón Ch'ol raids did not cease. In the mountains of the Cuchumatanes to the south of the Lacandón Ch'ol territory, the towns of San Mateo Ixtatán, Santa Eulalia, and Chajul were the targets of raids between 1586 and 1593 by the community of Sac Bahlán. In 1608, the Lacandón Ch'ol attacked the Ixil town of Chajul (Lovell 1992:82; Feldman 2000: 112–15). Although they sacrificed all those whom they captured, they did spare a young boy who then lived with them for the next twenty-two years. The reason given was that one of his relatives was a Lacandón Ch'ol. One has to wonder how a union between a Lacandón Ch'ol and an Ixil had come about. As an adult, the boy returned to Chajul, where he was interviewed by the Verapaz governor Martín Tovilla in 1630. Tovilla learned that the Lacandón Ch'ol had two towns called Culuacan and Cagbalan (Sac Bahlán), separated from each other by eight leagues, and that these Lacandón

Ch'ol were often at war with the Itzá. He also discovered that they traded with the natives of Tabasco for axes, and that such a trip to the coastal zone took thirty-five days. To reach Tabasco, the Lacandón Ch'ol could have gone overland to the north or by canoe on the Usumacinta. The overland route would have likely passed by a lake called Nohha "great water" that was situated just twenty-five kilometers north-west of Pochutla.

A Spaniard named Diego de Vera Ordóñez de Villaquirán had grand plans to conquer the Lacandón Ch'ol and Manché Ch'ol areas (D. Stone 1932:251; Scholes and Roys 1948:45; López Cogolludo 1955; Thompson 1970:69; Villagutierre 1983: 109–10). In 1647, Villaquirán began his campaign with an ill-fated expedition from Tenosique to the Nohha lake. At the lake, the expedition found an indigenous town that appeared to have been recently formed by both heathen and apostate natives who spoke a variety of Mayan languages including Yucatec. Villaquirán named the town El Próspero and left one of his officers, Captain Juan de Bilbao, in charge of the community. Villaquirán then marched on, only to have most of his men desert him. He returned to Yucatán and died the following year before he was able to mount another expedition.

When two Franciscan friars arrived to minister to the inhabitants of Nohha–El Próspero, they discovered that Captain Bilbao had been illegally extracting tribute from the natives in the form of cacao, achiote, and tobacco. Although Bilbao had conducted Catholic services for the community, he had pragmatically allowed the natives to retain their pagan ceremonies and idols. To the horror of the friars, he had even participated in a number of indigenous rituals. The friars also learned from the Nohha residents that there was a group of Ch'ol speakers called the Locen who lived nearby in eight villages. Whatever became of the Locen or exactly where their villages were located is a mystery. It is apparent, however, that there were more Ch'ol settlements in the Lacandón Ch'ol region than just those visited by the Spanish.

In addition to trading with their northern neighbors in Tabasco, the Lacandón Ch'ol also interacted with the Acalá Ch'ol to the south and mined salt at Nueve Cerros. In 1620, Dominican priest Gabriel Salazar made an excursion north from Cobán to the old site of San Marcos on the Río Icbolay (Feldman 2000:35–52). Salazar knew of two Spanish entrepreneurs who had traveled even farther north to Nueve Cerros. Their intent was to extract gold from the hills, but they withdrew when they saw the Lacandón Ch'ol. How they even knew about Nueve Cerros is uncertain, but both lowland Ch'ol and highland Christian Maya were known to come to the area to obtain salt and to gather cacao, achiote, cotton, and chile. No gold sources existed in this region, though.

In 1626, the Lacandón Ch'ol penetrated all the way to San Pedro Carchá near Cobán, where they brazenly sacrificed two young children and kidnapped seven farmers on the outskirts of the town (Feldman 2000:113–18). Several months later, an expedition headed by Juan de Santiago Velasco set out from Cobán to explore the region to the north to find a feasible route to Yucatán and to capture the offending

Lacandón Ch'ol if possible. The party was composed of a company of forty Spanish officers and soldiers, a number of native warriors, and the Cobán prior Francisco Morán. Following the trail of the Lacandón Ch'ol toward the north for three days, the group made its way to a point on the Chixoy River. After the construction of two canoes, Velasco sent four Spanish soldiers, Morán, and a number of natives down the river to see if it was navigable. After three days, the small party arrived at Nueve Cerros. The Lacandón Ch'ol, who were at the mine processing salt, saw them approach and hid across the river. The unsuspecting Spanish party sent a message back to Velasco informing him of their progress and waited for their main group to arrive. The Lacandón Ch'ol party numbered more than 140, but they retreated, fearing that the Spanish expedition was larger. Meanwhile, the heavy rains, the shortage of supplies, and the mounting illness among his soldiers had convinced Velasco that he should terminate the mission and return to Cobán.

Letters penned to the central authorities in Antigua by Verapaz governor Bartolomé Flores and various Dominican priests indicate that in 1654 there were at least four hamlets of non-baptized or apostatized Ch'ol in the forests north of Cobán including one hamlet at the old site of San Marcos on the Río Icbolay. During one of their Manché expeditions in 1676, the priests Francisco Gallego and Joseph Delgado were told of a Ch'ol-speaking Axoyes town in the Acalá area. On returning to Cobán, Gallego sent a message to the Axoyes leaders asking that they visit him. After interviewing them, he discovered that the older males had been baptized in Cobán sometime in the past, and that they knew and allegedly practiced the Catholic doctrine to some degree. The Axoyes held an annual achiote fair at their town: "Here, near the banks of the river of Sacapulas, are forty houses and a river filled with canoes. Using them, the Lacandons go to the lands of the Verapaz and those of the Verapaz go to the lands of the Lacandon. It is here that they make the achiote fair of Verapaz, and to it come the Lacandon, Ahitza, and many other nations of Indians" (Feldman 2000:177). Fairs that specialized in specific products were conducted in many parts of Mesoamerica.

There are limited possibilities for the location of the Axoyes town, given that it was situated near the mouth of a Chixoy tributary that provided canoe access down the Chixoy (the river of Sacapulas). The most likely candidate is Roknimá "foot of the river" (i.e., the mouth), which is located at the confluence of the Chixoy and Copalá Rivers, and which is near the head of navigation on the Chixoy during the dry season. The river route from Roknimá to the Lacandón Ch'ol and Itzá areas is quite straightforward. Canoes destined for Itzá territory simply went downstream until reaching the conjunction with the Río Pasión. They took that river upstream to another tributary called the Subín that took them close to Lake Petén Itzá. Canoes heading to the Lacandón Ch'ol area went past the conjunction with the Pasión River to the conjunction with the Lacantún River and took that waterway upstream.

The Lacandón Ch'ol also had trade relations with the highland towns in the Cuchumatanes mountains of northwestern Guatemala. In 1685, Fray Diego de Rivas, the provincial of the Mercedarians in the region, learned that the natives of Santa Eulalia and San Mateo were friendly with the Lacandón Ch'ol, and he prevailed upon these natives to conduct him to Lacandón Ch'ol territory for the purpose of converting the pagans (Villagutierre 1983:115–19. Although some at Santa Eulalia were willing, San Mateo resisted. It is likely that they were trading metal tools, quetzal feathers, and their locally produced salt for Lacandón Ch'ol cacao and achiote. Their reluctance to assist the Spanish may have reflected their desire to continue this trade without Spanish interference. It took a considerable amount of coercion, and finally, the intervention of the district governor, before they complied with Rivas's request.

The expedition set off north for the lowlands from Santa Eulalia. After five days of difficult travel, it reached lowland milpas that the people of Santa Eulalia had cultivated in the past. The governor and Rivas believed that a Spanish town could be founded in this rich agricultural area and that it could be used as a base to pacify the Lacandón Ch'ol. The next day, they encountered signs that the Lacandón Ch'ol were farming in this area. The governor was of the opinion that an encounter with the Lacandón Ch'ol would result in an armed conflict, so they withdrew back to Santa Eulalia. On their return, they implored the president of Guatemala to act on their recommendation to establish a town, but nothing was ever done.

In 1691, Franciscan priests Antonio Margil de Jesús and Melchor de López were sent to Cobán to assist the Dominicans with their conversion of the Manché Ch'ol (Ximénez 1929–31, 3:4–5; Leutenegger 1976; Villagutierre 1983:130–32). The two priests entered the Manché Ch'ol region from Cajabón and began congregating the Ch'orti' into new communities. After working in this region for eighteen months, they were asked by the Verapaz alcalde mayor to convert the Lacandón Ch'ol. Setting off from Cobán in August of 1693, the pair descended the piedmont into the Acalá Ch'ol region, guided by Christianized Cobán natives who were so fearful of encountering the fierce Lacandón Ch'ol that they deliberately misdirected the expedition until it ran out of supplies. Undeterred, the two Franciscans sent the guides back for more provisions. When the guides returned, they continued the journey, only to run out of food again. The priests remained beside a river while the guides were once again sent back to Cobán for more supplies. After waiting five weeks, it was apparent that the guides had permanently abandoned them. Luckily for the priests, a Christianized native traveling by canoe on the river stopped and gave them some corn to eat.

With Melchor too weak to travel, Margil set off in the canoe with the native in search of help. They soon arrived at some cornfields that were being worked by a cacique and his followers from Cobán's San Marcos barrio. At this point, Margil and Melchor had been wandering in the jungle for an astounding five months, even though a trip between Cobán and the Lacandón Ch'ol region can be made in less than two weeks. It is clear that their Cobán guides had been leading them in circles around the Acalá Ch'ol area to avoid entering Lacandón Ch'ol territory.

Fortunately for Margil and Melchor, the Acalá Ch'ol cacique and his men agreed to guide the priests to the Lacandón Ch'ol settlements. After rescuing Melchor and allowing him to regain some strength, the expedition pushed on and arrived at the Lacandón Ch'ol town of Sac Bahlán in February of 1694 just before Ash Wednesday. This town, consisting of more than one hundred households, was located on the north side of the Sierra Chaquistero, which runs parallel to the Lacantún River. The Lacandón Ch'ol accepted presents from the priests but treated them with contempt. It is likely that they did not simply kill the priests and their guides because they feared Spanish military reprisal. At some point during their exchanges, the Lacandón Ch'ol showed the priests some Catholic vestments that their ancestors had taken from San Marcos after they had participated in the 1555 Vico massacre. The deaths of Vico and his entourage were clearly still part of the oral history of the Lacandón Ch'ol 140 years after the event.

The Lacandón Ch'ol tried several strategies, including intimidation and threats, to get the priests to leave their community, but the two Franciscans carried on with their preaching. They finally convinced the Lacandón Ch'ol to send a delegation to Cobán to experience the sincerity of the Christians and make a peace treaty. Leaving Melchor and their guides behind as hostages, Margil set off with a group of twelve Lacandón Ch'ol dignitaries. On their arrival in Cobán, they were warmly welcomed and lavishly feted by the Dominicans. The delegation appeared poised to accept Spanish authority, but disaster struck when ten of the Lacandón Ch'ol fell ill and died, likely from some illness contracted in Cobán. When Margil and the remaining two Lacandón Ch'ol arrived back at Sac Bahlán, the inhabitants of the town predictably reacted with outrage to the news of the deaths and beat the priests. Fearing retribution from the Spanish, the Lacandón leaders allowed the Franciscans and their guides to leave. When they returned to Cobán in April, the two Franciscans recommended to the Spanish authorities that a military expedition be launched against the Lacandón Ch'ol to force them to convert. They then turned their attention back to the Manché Ch'ol region.

While they were away conducting their Lacandón Ch'ol mission, Melchor had been appointed President of the Missions. He returned to the Guatemalan capital to assume his duties, and he sent Margil and his new companion, Fray Pedro de la Concepción, to Belén (Santa Cruz El Chol in Baja Verapaz) to learn the language of the Manché Ch'ol in preparation for further work with this group. As noted above, Belén was populated with Ch'olti' who had been removed from the Manché Ch'ol region and had been resettled at this highland town. The two priests spent three months studying under the direction of Fray Ángel, who was fluent in Ch'olti'.

As the close of the seventeenth century approached, the Spanish were in a precarious situation. The English had dominated the Tabasco and Campeche coasts since 1558, when British pirates first occupied the Isla del Carmen (West, Psuty, and Thom 1985: 261). It was of great concern to Spanish colonial authorities that the English not be able to form an alliance with the Maya and link their work camps in Tabasco and Campeche (where they were taking out dyewood, the first stable black dye and a boon to the English fabric industry) with their colonies in Belize and along the Central

American coast. With pirates regularly plundering the coastal communities and making sea trade around the Yucatán peninsula a dangerous undertaking, the Spanish recognized that an inland route between Mérida and Guatemala was a partial solution to their problem. The time had come for such a venture that would also put an end to the attacks on Christian frontier towns by the various lowland Maya and facilitate Spanish conquest. The acting governor of Yucatán, Martín de Ursúa y Arismendi, and the president of Guatemala, Jacinto de Barrios Leal, finally decided to conduct a joint conquest. Nicolás de Valenzuela, who accompanied Barrios, wrote an extensive description of the expeditions, and Villagutierre (1983:157) quotes from him extensively (see also Ximénez 1929–31, 3:6–15, 23–47; D. Stone 1932:272–80; De Vos 1980b:134–89; Cano 1984). The Ursúa expeditions are summarized by Jones (1998; see also Means 1917). The initial plan called for Ursúa to attack the Itzá at their stronghold of Lake Petén Itzá from the north while Barrios attacked from the south. Regrettably, there was more competition than cooperation between the two leaders. Ursúa was the one who eventually succeeded, although Barrios organized his expedition first.

The Dominicans were primarily concerned with the conversion of the Manché Ch'ol, Mopán Maya, and ultimately the groups living around Lake Petén Itzá. They wanted Barrios to focus his attention on these eastern areas, which they correctly judged to be the most important, and to bring these groups decisively under permanent Spanish control. In contrast, the Franciscan, Margil, argued for a dual campaign that would attack both the Lacandón Ch'ol and the Itzá. After much consultation and many machinations, Barrios decided on an ambitious plan that had first been suggested by a military commander, Juan de Mendoza, in 1689 and endorsed by the Spanish crown. In this plan, the military forces would be divided into three groups that would simultaneously enter the pagan regions from different directions on February 28, 1695. From a logistical perspective, it was a flawed plan that was doomed almost from the start.

Barrios sent two companies of Spanish and Christian native soldiers under the authority of Juan Díaz de Velasco to Cobán with instructions to proceed through the Manché Ch'ol and Mopán Maya areas to Lake Petén Itzá. Two more companies, directed by Melchor Rodríguez were to descend into Lacandón Ch'ol country from San Mateo Ixtatán and proceed to Sac Bahlán. Barrios and his five companies would enter Lacandón Ch'ol territory through Ocosingo with the objective of Lacam Tun. After subduing Lacam Tun, they would proceed to Sac Bahlán, join with Rodríguez, and advance to Lake Petén Itzá. Each group was accompanied by priests who were supposed to attempt to pacify the natives peacefully before any use of force was employed. The Dominican, Fray Agustín Cano, who had worked in the Manché Ch'ol region, traveled with Díaz. Rodriguez was accompanied by Margil's Franciscan companion, Fray Pedro de la Concepción, and by the Mercedarian, Fray Diego de Rivas, who had made the journey down the piedmont to Lacandón territory in 1685. Margil, who had become Barrio's personal confessor, traveled with him.

The Díaz expedition moved quite easily through the Manché Ch'ol region and within a month had arrived in the middle of Mopán territory. Both the Manché Ch'ol and Mopán Maya were willing to accept the gifts of the Spanish and submit to their authority. After congregating these groups and sending a letter to the authorities in Guatemala detailing his success, Díaz marched to the Chaxal River on the Itzá frontier. Several engagements with fierce Itzá hunting parties convinced Díaz that the Itzá would not submit without a fight. With no sign of Barrios or Rodríguez, Díaz was in a precarious position, for he did not have the manpower to intimidate or overcome the Itzá. With his supplies running low, his men falling ill, and the rainy season beginning, Díaz decided to retreat to Cahabón at the beginning of May. Although he was initially condemned by the Spanish authorities for his decision, it was a wise choice, because the contingents from Chiapas and San Mateo never arrived. Had Díaz stayed, it is highly likely that he and his men would have been annihilated by the Itzá.

In the meantime, the Rodríguez expedition descended down the steep Cuchumatanes foothills from San Mateo into Lacandón Ch'ol territory. It took the expedition nineteen days to cut a horse trail to the shores of the Lacantún River, and another eighteen before the advance party led by Fray Pedro de la Concepción located Sac Bahlán on the other side of the Sierra Chaquistero. Fray Pedro renamed the town Nuestra Señora de los Dolores. The Lacandón Ch'ol fled to the forest before the main body of the expedition arrived, so the army took up residency in the vacant town. For the next ten days, Rodríguez and his men scoured the area looking for any signs of the Lacandón Ch'ol or Barrios, without success.

Barrios and his five companies entered Lacandón Ch'ol territory through Ocosingo and proceeded to Nohha, where Barrios had sent an advance party to establish a camp. After finding no signs of Lacandón Ch'ol in the area, the army marched south through extremely difficult terrain, slowly making their way toward Lake Miramar, where they expected to find the main Lacandón Ch'ol town. They stopped and camped for eight days to wait for supplies and stopped again for six days to celebrate Holy Week. In all, it took them forty-five days to travel the mere seventy kilometers from Nohha to Lacam Tun, only to find, much to their surprise, that it had long been abandoned.

While they debated what to do next, one of the scouting parties came across four native hunters and captured one of them. Oddly enough, no one could understand the language of the captive. Through the use of sign language, Barrios concluded that the Lacandón Ch'ol captive was from Sac Bahlán or at least knew where it was located. The captive then guided the army south to the Lacantún River. As Barrios and his troops were preparing to cross the river, Rodríguez found them and guided them the short distance to Sac Bahlán. The Spanish decided to send the captive into the forest with a peace message for the inhabitants of Sac Bahlán. Once he was released, they never saw him again. It is possible that the captive was not from Sac Bahlán and that he had led the army to this town rather than his home community.

Three days after settling in at the town, Barrios received a message from Guatemala indicating that Díaz had successfully pacified the Mopán. In response to this positive news, Barrios decided that he would leave a garrison of soldiers and some of the priests at Sac Bahlán and try to march on to Lake Petén Itzá to join Díaz. Before he was able to depart the area, five Lacandón Ch'ol were captured in the woods and brought to him. Although it is unclear how they could now communicate with the Lacandón Ch'ol, the Spaniards apparently convinced the new captives that they would not harm them, and two of them were sent into the forest to bring back the Sac Bahlán inhabitants. These two returned with the ruler Cabnal and a large number of Lacandón Ch'ol. It was decided that Barrios would remain at Sac Bahlán to entice the remainder of the population to return, while a company of soldiers under the command of Auditor General Bartolomé de Amézuita would go downriver to look for Lake Petén Itzá.

Although the Lacandón Ch'ol indicated to the Spanish that they only traveled downriver during the dry season, they provided Amézuita with two guides. One group of men followed the shoreline while another paddled down the river in canoes. At the direction of the guides, the expedition made numerous excursions inland from the river but found nothing. It became increasingly apparent that the guides had no intention of taking them to the lake. When the guides finally deserted and the rainy season started in earnest, Amézuita and his men were forced to return to Sac Bahlán. It is unknown how far down the river they went, but they were gone for a total of eighteen days. Knowing that the lowland rivers would continue to swell with the heavy rains and soon cut off their supply lines, Barrios had to return with his army to the highlands. He departed Sac Bahlán, taking the much shorter route back through San Mateo. He left behind a group of priests including Margil and a small garrison of soldiers to continue the congregation and conversion of the Lacandón Ch'ol. The enormous cost of the two expeditions to the Lacandón Ch'ol area only resulted in the subjugation of one small town, Sac Bahlán. Barrios had squandered his opportunity to conquer the Itzá.

While the residents of Sac Bahlán wanted the gifts of metal axes, machetes, and trinkets that the Spanish provided, they were reluctant to forgo their customs, and they often actively resisted and mocked the Spanish priests. A frustrated Margil sent for two Acalá Ch'ol from Cobán who had acted as guides and translators on his previous trip. They arrived in early August and apparently made some progress teaching the Lacandón Ch'ol the Catholic faith. Shortly after their arrival, Margil and his Franciscan colleagues Lázaro de Mazariegos and Blas Guillén sent Barrios a report on Lacandón Ch'ol religion, politics, and economics. The document and the report of Valenzuela, who was with the Barrios party, provide the only substantial accounts of this culture (Hellmuth 1977:425; Tozzer 1984).

During their interrogations of the Lacandón Ch'ol, the priests learned of two Ch'ol towns called Peta and Map in the vicinity of Sac Bahlán, and that all the Lacandón Ch'ol towns were in constant fear of Itzá raiding parties. With information supplied by the Lacandón Ch'ol, the priests created a map of the territory between

Sac Bahlán and Lake Petén Itzá to assist the expedition that was being planned by Barrios for the coming January. The Lacandón Ch'ol consistently told them that it was possible to reach Itzá territory by river in seven days, which, in fact, it was.

Barrios, who had been in ill health, died in November before being able to mount his second campaign. His replacement, José de Escals, continued on with his pacification plans. Escals directed Jacobo de Alzayaga to take a contingent to Sac Bahlán via San Mateo and to proceed to Lake Petén Itzá from there. Amézquita was instructed to take a second contingent to the lake using the Manché Ch'ol–Mopán Maya route used by Díaz the previous year. The Amézquita expedition ran into supply problems that delayed their advance from Cahabón. When they finally arrived in Mopán, they received news from Guatemala that Alzayaga was already at Lake Petén Itzá, as was a contingent that had arrived via Yucatán. With this false news, Amézquita decided that his entire group need not immediately proceed to the lake, and he dispatched a party led by Díaz to proceed six leagues past the Chaxal River and prepare the road to the lake for the supply mules. In fact, Alzayaga was not anywhere near the lake, and the Yucatán contingent had been wiped out by the Itzá. Disregarding Amézquita's orders, Díaz advanced to the lakeshore and tried to ascertain the situation. Some Itzá came out from their island and invited the Spanish to get in their canoes and cross to the island. The Spanish understood that they were vulnerable to attack on the water if they accepted, but finally they saw what they thought were the two Franciscan priests of the Yucatán contingent waving them over from the island. With this enticement, they all entered the canoes. Unfortunately for the Spaniards, the Itzá had merely dressed two men in the robes of the slain priests. As they approached the island, the Itzá attacked and killed everyone in the Díaz party. They also killed all the Christian natives who had been left to guard the mules and supplies. When Amézquita and his contingent arrived at the lake, he soon realized that the Díaz party had likely been killed, and he wisely withdrew to the Chaxal River. Further harassment by the Itzá forced him to retreat to the Mopán area and eventually abandon the entire enterprise.

Meanwhile, Alzayaga arrived at Sac Bahlán to discover that more than five hundred Lacandón Ch'ol had congregated at the community. He immediately began to assist Margil and the other priests in locating the adjacent Lacandón Ch'ol towns. Expeditions into the forests to the northeast located both Peta and Map, and plans were made to congregate the inhabitants of those communities at a new town called San Ramón Nonato. With the Lacandón Ch'ol region under tentative Spanish control, Alzayaga decided to proceed to Lake Petén Itzá to join Amézquita. He built fifteen boats to transport his men and supplies down the Lacantún River, and they set out on March 3, 1696, investigating both sides of the river as they made their way downstream.

When they reached the conjunction with the Usumacinta, the colonial document referring to this expedition states that they proceeded upstream but could not find Lake Petén Itzá despite a diligent search of the shorelines and excursions into the forest. At one point, members of the expedition saw the remains of a site:

> At another spot where some soldiers landed they came upon a site which they knew must have been inhabited long ago, because of the many stone foundations and very old building ruins they discovered—more than a league in circumference. In all of this navigation and searching, both on land and water, not even by climbing to the tops of the tallest trees of the forest or those on the highest banks, could they discover a lake, nor indications of where it might be, nor any paths which might lead to it. (Villagutierre 1983:229)

Maler (1903:107) and Morley (1937–38, 1:41–42) both suggested that Villagutierre was mistaken and that the expedition actually went downstream when it reached the Usumacinta. They believed the expedition members saw the ruins of Yaxchilan, which is sixty kilometers downstream from the conjunction of the Lacantún and Usumacinta. It seems more likely that the Amézquita expedition did indeed go upstream but did not find the lake because they apparently did not realize that they had to follow a small tributary of the Río Pasión called the Río Subín, and then proceed forty kilometers overland to the lake (Ron Canter, personal communication). The mouth of the Río Subín is easily missed, and it is impossible to see the lake from the river. After many weeks of fruitless exploring, the Spanish were forced to return to Sac Bahlán. In all, the expedition had been away for fifty-seven days and had accomplished little. With the onset of the rains, Alzayaga was ordered back to Guatemala by the newly elected president Sánchez de Berrospe.

In 1697, Ursúa was finally able to mount an effective campaign against the Itzá from the north and conquer the towns around Lake Petén Itzá, but the conquest of the Itzá brought prosperity to no one (Jones 1998). Within a year, an epidemic swept across the newly subjugated areas, killing off large numbers of natives and Spanish alike. The disease spread to the Lacandón Ch'ol region, and although the census of 1698 indicates that Sac Bahlán had grown to a town of eight hundred souls, just three years later it had lost more than 40 percent of its inhabitants. The decision to construct the royal road from Guatemala to Lake Petén Itzá via the Manché Ch'ol region rather than the Lacandón Ch'ol territory permanently turned the latter area into a marginal zone. Under the protection of a Spanish garrison, the Dominicans continued their work with the Lacandón Ch'ol until the authorities decided that the financial cost of maintaining this arrangement was too high. In 1721, the residents of Sac Bahlán were moved to the Jacaltenango area and were soon assimilated into that highland population (De Vos 1980b:190–211; Bricker 1981:52).

The final defeat of the Lacandón Ch'ol brought the conquest era to an end, but the indigenous population continued to resist and defy colonial authorities. The following chapter reviews the timespan from the colonial period to the modern era in the Ch'ol region and discusses the conditions that led to several indigenous rebellions. It also includes an overview of the methods used by the Catholic Church to convert the natives and the establishment of the Black Christ cult in Tila.

2

THE COLONIAL TO
TWENTIETH-CENTURY PERIOD
IN THE CH'OL REGION

Nicholas A. Hopkins, Karen Bassie-Sweet, and Robert M. Laughlin

The military conquest of the indigenous population of Chiapas was a protracted but relatively straightforward endeavor, given the superior weaponry and resources of the Spanish and their indigenous allies. In comparison, the subsequent administration of the indigenous population and its conversion to Catholicism was a far greater challenge that the authorities struggled with for centuries after the conquest. This chapter presents a historical overview from the post-conquest period to modern times, and details the religious and political events and circumstances that shaped Ch'ol communities. It begins with a brief discussion of the methods used by the Spanish priests in their attempts to transform the Maya into Christians.

The Conversion of the Maya

The strategies used by the Catholic Church to convert the Maya were varied. The church took the position that all of the ancient deities were manifestations of the Christian devil who had deceived the indigenous population into worshipping him. Consequently, it was a great sin to make offerings to these ancient gods. Nevertheless, some merging of Christian and Maya beliefs was at first tolerated and even encouraged by the Church as a method of conversion. It was not a novel approach. The Catholic Church had quite successfully used this strategy in the past, merging pagan European religions with its own. Maya and Catholic religions had certain traits in common that allowed for such integration. For example, attributes of the Christian God are easily seen in the supreme creator god Itzamnaaj-Xpiyacoc, while traits of Christ are found in both the corn god One Ixim-One Hunahpu and the youthful sun god One Ajaw-Hunahpu (see chapter 6 for an overview of Maya gods). These latter amalgamations are still apparent in the contemporary Maya's identification of Christ with corn and with the sun. In a similar manner, the Virgin Mary became identified with the moon and with the childbearing and healing characteristics of the primary Maya goddesses.

Bishop Francisco Núñez de la Vega stated that each town in Postclassic Chiapas had possessed a unique patron deity in addition to the primary deities who were thought to have brought the earth, sky, and humans into existence and who were recognized and worshipped over the whole region (Calnek 1988:45–47). In Mesoamerica, many occupations also had specific patron gods. As an example, the first sons of the deity One Hunahpu were the patron gods for artisans (Christenson 2007). With this long-standing tradition of patron gods already in place, the Spanish easily introduced Catholic patron saints for each town. Tila, Tumbalá, and Palenque (the three main Ch'ol towns) were assigned San Mateo, San Miguel, and Santo Domingo, respectively.

In the early years of conversion, the Spanish priests founded *cofradía* organizations to sponsor the festival of the patron saint and other religious events during the year. The cofradía organization was based on Spanish military order, with the highest-ranking members being called majordomos and lesser officials called captains and corporals. In addition to the expenses for ceremonies, the cofradía members were responsible for paying the fees to the Spanish priests and for the costs of maintenance and renewal of sacred images and paraphernalia. This situation was not unlike the Postclassic tradition in which community leaders had sponsored various festivals and feasts (Tozzer 1941:140–49). Despite the change of the religious structure of the community to Catholic norms, cofradía members often continued various ancient practices alongside their newly acquired Catholic rituals—much to the distress of the Spanish clergy. The Spanish simply did not have the manpower or resources to effectively monitor or control these activities of the population.

In many instances, when it came to establishing Catholic places of worship, ancient temples and shrines were ripped apart and the building material used to construct the new churches and chapels. The placing of a Catholic structure on a location that already had sacred associations sent a powerful message of dominance, but in many cases, the Maya simply used these new spaces to continue to worship their old gods. Time and again, the Spanish priests would find evidence of what they considered "idolatry" within their own churches. For example, the Tzeltal of Oxchuc worshipped two pre-Columbian deities called Hicalahau (*ik'al ajaw* "black lord") and the meteor deity Poxlon during the late seventeenth and early eighteenth century (Megged 1996:154) (map 4). Hicalahau was described as looking like a ferocious black man, and he was identified with a sacred mountain near Oxchuc. During his inspection of the region in 1687, Núñez discovered that the community had images representing Hicalahau, Poxlon, owls, and vultures in the church and was worshipping them (Núñez 1988:274–75). Although Núñez denounced such activities and destroyed the effigies, the veneration continued, and Hicalahau Mountain remained a sacred location for indigenous worship. During the 1712 rebellion, discussed later in this chapter, the Oxchuc leaders fled from the advancing colonial forces with the community's books and cofradía paraphernalia, and hid them in a cave on Hicalahau Mountain.

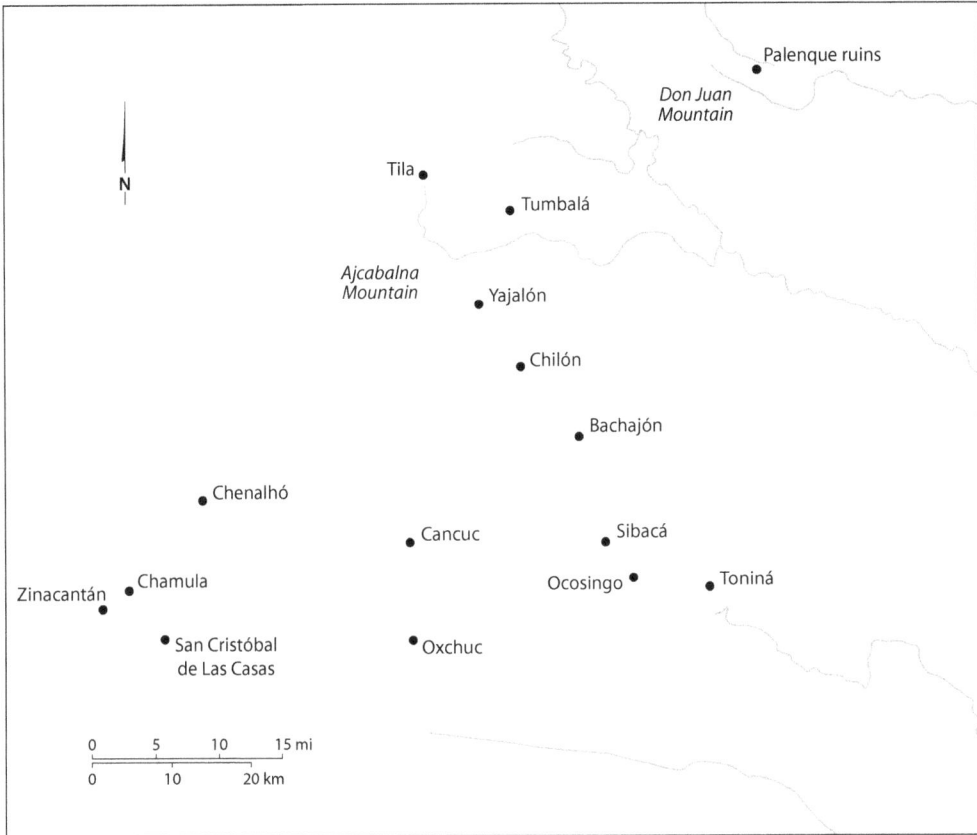

Map 4. Colonial towns. Map by Bill Nelson, based on a map by Marcia Bakry. © 2015, University of Oklahoma Press.

Fray José de Ordóñez y Aguiar sums up the commitment of the Maya to both religions when he states, "The Indian is no less devoted in the Church, pouring out his tears at the feet of a holy Christ, than when he joyfully offers incense in a cave to the demons" (Laughlin 2003:89). On the whole, the Maya were quite tenacious in maintaining certain parts of their world view, particularly their customs involving agricultural practices. Despite the best efforts of the Spanish to eradicate indigenous beliefs, the religion of the Maya was transformed into an amalgamation of Catholicism and ancient beliefs.

The Colonial Period

Although the subjugation of the main Lacandón Ch'ol towns drastically reduced the attacks on highland Chiapas communities, these nominally Christian towns were hardly tranquil, affluent settlements. The second census of Chiapas, taken in 1611, reported that the Ch'ol area had abundant maize and other crops and was exporting large quantities of *zarzaparrilla* root (*Smilax,* English "sarsaparilla") to Spain via the ports of Tabasco and Veracruz (Standley 1920:104; West, Psuty, and Thom 1985:259). The dried sarsaparilla root was used as a purgative and cure for venereal disease, and exports continued into the nineteenth century, when it was used mainly as a flavoring for soft drinks. However, despite its agricultural richness, the region's economy weakened and its population base decreased as a result of a series of epidemics, locust plagues, and droughts throughout the seventeenth and eighteenth centuries. Of even greater consequence was the fact that the majority of the indigenous population of Chiapas was exploited and abused by its Spanish overlords from the very beginning of the conquest (Calnek 1970; Gerhard 1979; Sherman 1979; Watson 1983; Gosner 1984). Within a short period of time following the military conquest, church officials used their own systems to exact revenue and accumulate wealth at the expense of the natives. Competition between the various Spanish authorities and church officials for control of the native population was intense. Native groups were often caught in the middle and had to pay the brutal consequences.

Despite the famines and reduced population, the Spanish did not lower the levels of tribute required. Unrest was mounting and reached a critical degree in August of 1712 when the newly installed bishop increased the church service fees as well as the amount of goods and services that the communities had to provide to their clergy. A group of indigenous leaders used miraculous appearances by the Virgin Mary to rally Tzeltal, Tzotzil, and Ch'ol towns to purge their Spanish and ladino populations. Cancuc, with its new shrine to the Virgin Mary, became the center of the rebellion (Bricker 1981:55–69; Gosner 1984, 1992).

The rebels organized themselves according to the civil, military, and religious institutions used by the Spanish. New indigenous priests were ordained by the leaders, and they began to carry on the former duties of the Catholic priests, including administering the sacraments. The insurgency leaders ordered all rebel communities to strip their churches of their paraphernalia and send this wealth to Cancuc (map 4). For example, the Catholic priest at Tila discovered the town officials and other citizens sacking the church, taking crosses, candles, and vestments to be sent to Cancuc. The priest fled to Tabasco; others were not so fortunate. All non-indigenous men who were unable to flee the area were murdered. Some non-indigenous women and children were spared to be used as servants, while others survived by consenting to marriages with native men. Communities that did not join the movement or that questioned the authority of Cancuc were attacked, their leaders executed and replaced with more compliant individuals. As an example, the Cancuc leaders amassed a good deal of wealth from the estates, cofradías, and churches in the surrounding communities. A group of community leaders led by Juan López from Bachajón protested this hoarding. Although Cancuc relinquished some goods, Juan López was executed for questioning Cancuc's supremacy.

At first, the rebel troops enjoyed victories at Chilón, Ocosingo, and Chenalhó (map 4), but their success was short lived. With reinforcements from Guatemala, the Spanish authorities won successive battles at Huistán, Oxchuc, San Martín Obispo, and Cancuc itself. Over the next months, Sitalá, Chilón, Yajalón, Bachajón, Ocosingo, and Sibacá were defeated. A Tabascan force under the direction of its alcalde mayor Juan Francisco de Medina Cachón subdued Los Moyos, Huitiupa, Petalcingo, Tila, and Tumbalá. Finally, Dominican priest Joseph Monroy convinced the remaining rebel towns to submit. Many of the rebel leaders were executed, but some were sent to exile in Guatemala. The Franciscan priest Antonio Margil de Jesús noted in a letter in 1717 that "the Royal Audiencia of Guatemala took the main Indian popes and bishops from their towns and placed them in the monasteries in the City of [Antigua] Guatemala and in our College, where with charity we instructed them in the truth and gave them the enlightenment they needed to prevent them from deceiving their people again" (Leutenegger 1976:237).

Following the rebellion, few non-natives remained in the highland Ch'ol towns, and the ladino population did not fully reestablish itself until the end of the nineteenth century after German coffee-growers arrived. The Ch'ol, on their part, continued to struggle to survive under heavy taxation and exploitation by both political and religious authorities.

Outside the Ch'ol region, the tenure of diocesan priest José de Ordóñez y Aguiar at the Tzotzil town of Chamula is a poignant and well-documented example of the post-rebellion abuse of natives (Laughlin 2003:85–90) (map 4). Fray José of San Cristóbal de Las Casas had replaced the Dominican priest of Chamula in 1763. Public whippings, excessive tribute demands, and forced labor were the norm. As was a common practice, Fray José required women to produce large quantities of textiles for his own enrichment. The priest's ventures were in direct competition with the local political official, who wanted the indigenous workforce for his own business enterprises. In particular, this official used Chamulans as porters to transport his tobacco and straw mats to markets on the Tabasco coast. Each man accused the other of abuse, but little was done to improve the lot of the Chamulans.

To a certain degree, the physical isolation of the Ch'ol region buffered some of the indigenous population from abuses. In 1737, the priest of Tila complained to a colonial official from Ciudad Real that families hardly came to mass, he had not heard a confession in nine years of service, and to avoid Christian burial, deaths were not reported to the church (Breton 1988). The population still lived in dispersed settlements, in defiance of orders to concentrate in an easily controlled location. An official sent to assess compliance in 1740 reported that settlements were scattered at intervals of five to eight hours' distance from one another, and that in the midst of milpas and cacao groves were "many Indians who live in total liberty, and without any subordination to their superiors, sheltering all those who enjoy the same barbarous liberty or who flee to those places from oppression" (Watson 1983:103).

The first documentation of the Ch'ol language did not occur until 1789 when King Charles III sent a royal decree ordering that reports on indigenous languages be sent to him. Juan Jossef de la Fuente Albores, the Catholic priest at Tila, responded with a list of several hundred words in the Tila Ch'ol dialect (Josserand and Hopkins 1988).

It was during this period that the first official notice of the archaeological site of Palenque was recorded (Brasseur de Bourbourg 1866:3–5; Laughlin n.d.). In 1746, Fray Antonio de Solís was appointed resident priest for the Tumbalá region, and he spent six months in the town of Santo Domingo Palenque. As was the custom, Solís was accompanied by his extended family, who visited the Palenque ruins during a jungle outing and was astonished by its size. The family's time in Santo Domingo Palenque was cut short when Fray Antonio unexpectedly died. His young nephew José de la Fuente Coronado was sent to study in San Cristóbal, where he met his young cousins José and Ramón de Ordóñez y Aguiar. Coronado's stories of the jungle ruins intrigued the young Ramón, and he longed to visit the site. Ramón grew up, joined the priesthood like his older brother, and rose to the position of canon of the San Cristóbal cathedral. His strong interest in native history continued, but time and financial limitations prevented Fray Ramón from leading his own expedition to investigate Palenque. Instead, he asked his brother Fray José and a group of friends to make the journey, which they did in 1773. Ramón then sent a report of their findings to Luis de Roca, the Dominican provincial, urging that the site be mapped and excavated and that the artwork and inscriptions be drawn. Roca, in turn, sent the report to José de Estachería, the president of the Royal Audiencia. In 1784, Estachería ordered José Antonio Calderón, the alcalde mayor of Santo Domingo Palenque, to explore the ruins, and thus began the early investigations of Palenque (see Stuart and Stuart 2008:35–85 for an overview of subsequent investigations).

The rugged terrain of the Tzeltal and Ch'ol area and the lack of an adequate road system limited the movement of trade goods and hindered the economic development of the region. In 1787, the *subdelegado,* or mayor, of Ocosingo, Sebastián Fulgencio Solórzano, tried to open a new road to the northeast between Bachajón and Santo Domingo Palenque because he had landholdings in the area and wanted a direct route to his export market on the Tabasco coast (Solórzano 1787). Solórzano expressed concern that the "Lacandóns" would attack the road workers. Given that any pagan native was at that time called a Lacandón, it is difficult to know whether he was referring to Ch'ol- or Yucatec Maya-speaking natives. The fear of pagan "Lacandóns" persisted well past the time they were any real threat. The modern Ch'ol refer to the Lacandón Maya as *kichañob* "our mother's brothers," and this term is also applied to a class of demons who live in the deep woods, behave like savages, and are cannibals (Josserand et al. 2003). But even in the eighteenth century, pagan Ch'ol and Lacandón Maya came to Santo Domingo Palenque to trade with the Christian Ch'ol who lived there. In 1786, Lacandón Maya even attended the festival of Palenque's patron saint.

In 1794, the Ch'ol living in the lower Tulijá Valley were congregated at the newly established town of San Fernando de Guadalupe (Salto de Agua). One of the purposes of the settlement was to provide a way station on the trade route between Tumbalá and the coast. In 1805, Solórzano's road was finally open between Bachajón and Santo Domingo Palenque. The route passed through the valleys of the Paxila, upper Tulijá, and Bascan Rivers. The path was not maintained and soon fell into disuse, while the road through Tumbalá and the lower Tulijá Valley remained the primary route (see chapter 3).

THE POST-COLONIAL PERIOD IN THE CH'OL REGION

By the beginning of the nineteenth century, a new wind was sweeping through the highlands. A national independence movement was growing, and in 1812 an army of insurgents threatened the colonial establishment in Chiapas. Fearing insurgent forces, Bishop Andrés Ambrosio de Llano y Valdés fled San Cristóbal in the night and escaped to Tila (Laughlin 2003:109). One assumes he sought refuge at Tila because of its remoteness. In 1824, shortly after the colonies gained their independence, Chiapas seceded from Guatemala to join the new Republic of Mexico. The positive effects of these political changes were minimal in the Ch'ol areas. The lack of a good road system in the rugged mountains continued to hamper trade with adjacent regions. Merchants and ranchers in the Tumbalá region petitioned the government to improve the road between Tumbalá and Tabasco (via Salto de Agua) so that mules could be used to transport the goods that were currently being carried on the backs of indigenous men, but little was done to improve this situation.

In the late nineteenth century, the government was eager to increase its revenues and attract investment and development. It began to sell lumber concessions and deeds for the land that indigenous people had occupied for centuries (García de León 1979; De Vos 1988; Alejos García and Ortega Peña 1991; Alejos García 1994; Rus 2003). The forests of the Lacantún, Usumacinta, and upper Tulijá river drainages were turned over to a few large lumber companies that endeavored to strip the region of its mahogany. It was a labor-intensive venture, and indigenous men were coerced into joining the lumber operations. Once in the camps, they literally became slaves. Those who remained in the highland communities did not fare any better.

In the Ch'ol region, much of the land used by indigenous farmers for their milpas and cacao groves, including the communal lands of native communities, was sold by the state to ladinos and foreign investors, in particular German and American corporations. These new owners transformed the lands into coffee, sugarcane, rubber, *henequén,* and cattle *fincas* or exploited them for their lumber. Ladino merchants and traders who provided transportation to move these products to markets in San Cristóbal and Tabasco soon accumulated enough capital from their ventures to acquire land titles and create fincas of their own. In the remote Ch'ol and Tzeltal areas, a cheap labor supply for production and transportation was essential for the success of the finca operations. The deposed farmers, who had few options once their lands had been confiscated, were exploited and reduced to working for the plantation and lumber companies. Local government officials, schoolteachers. and parish priests often worked as labor recruiters in collusion with the plantation and lumber overseers, and forced natives under their jurisdiction to work on these operations against their will.

Indigenous workers were kept in a constant state of poverty and increasing debt. Workers were given a small wage and access to a tiny plot of land to grow corn in exchange for toiling on the finca for four to five days of the week and transporting the finca products to market. Their compensation was well below subsistence levels. The larger fincas had company stores that maintained monopolies on the staple goods needed by the workers and their families, and wages were often paid in currency only acceptable at the company store. Credit was extended to the workers, with the full knowledge that it could never be repaid. The sale of sugarcane liquor was a highly lucrative enterprise for the finca owners, who controlled its distribution and promoted its use among natives to increase their debt load (Bobrow-Strain 2007). Upon the death of a peon, his family members were obliged to continue working for the finca until his debt was paid. In reality, the family simply sank further into arrears with no hope of ever being free.

The most infamous finca in the Tumbalá region was El Triunfo (The Triumph), owned by the German American Coffee Company. Located just five kilometers north of Tumbalá, El Triunfo, with its company store, post office, jail, church, and large indigenous population, soon eclipsed Tumbalá in importance. At the height of its power, the El Triunfo estate incorporated forty-three thousand hectares and had three thousand workers. So great was its need for slave labor that it forcibly recruited natives from the Tzotzil and Tzeltal regions as well.

The indentured indigenous population had no legal recourse, and those who attempted to flee the estates were hunted down and severely punished or killed. An example of the horrific lethal punishment meted out to recaptured workers was the practice of burying them alive in anthills as a warning to others. The absolute power that the finca owners had over their workers included the use of rape, and some finca owners practiced the seigniorial right to have intercourse with indigenous brides before their weddings (Laughlin 2003:5–6, Bobrow-Strain 2007:64). These many abusive practices established and reinforced the subservient role of the peon. No one was ever held accountable for any of these crimes. As Frederick Starr (1902:73) noted, a small number of the Tumbalá Ch'ol were able to escape this situation by fleeing across the Tulijá Valley to the remote slopes of Don Juan Mountain or heading to Tabasco. Not surprisingly, the Tumbalá Ch'ol refer to the finca period as "the age of servitude" or "the time of slavery" (Alejos García 1994). The Mexican Revolution of 1910–17 did not alter this near-feudal situation, and the land reforms instituted after the revolution did not become effective until after the election of Lázaro Cárdenas (1934–40).

CH'OL EJIDOS IN THE TWENTIETH CENTURY

In the mid-twentieth century, the coffee estates, which had gone into steady decline after world coffee markets collapsed, were finally broken up and some of the land given over to the Ch'ol and Tzeltal who had worked them as virtual slaves (Alejos García

1994). A major dispersal of the Ch'ol began after some of the estate lands were shaped into collective farms, or *ejidos*. New Ch'ol ejidos were created in the Tulijá Valley and around the base of Don Juan Mountain. Ejidos spread eastward from there to the Usumacinta River and followed the river as far south as Boca del Lacantún (Torre 1994). With these expansions, western Ch'olans have effectively reoccupied some of the territories from which they were removed in the sixteenth and seventeenth centuries. In more recent years, the Ch'ol population has leapfrogged to the southern parts of the states of Campeche and Quintana Roo, where some two dozen Ch'ol-speaking ejidos have been established between Xpujil and the Guatemalan border. It is notable that earlier ejidos took Catholic names based on the saints, such as San Manuel and Santa María; but as the Protestant conversion of Ch'ols progressed, later ejidos took biblical names such as Babilonia and Jerusalén. Some ejidos took their names from historical people or dates, such as Belisario Domínguez or 20 de Noviembre. Some ejidos can be roughly dated by their names, taken from politicians prominent at the time of their establishment, such as López Mateos, Díaz Ordaz, and Frontera Echeverría (now Frontera Corozal).

The ejido system is an engine for producing new colonies. Each ejido is formed from a certain number of heads of household, each of whom shares in the collective landholding. An ejido is formed when pioneers identify a plot of unoccupied or surplus land that is suitable for colonization. They then approach land reform officials for permission to colonize, and they recruit colonists from older ejidos. Originally, land could neither be bought nor sold, and a share could only be inherited by one child of each shareholder. Because families tend to have more than one child, there is constant pressure to create new ejidos to accommodate those who do not inherit shares.

The ability to speak Ch'ol is a major factor in recruiting pioneers for a new ejido. Someone who speaks Ch'ol is assumed to share a common world view and common values, as opposed to the outsiders who come offering great benefits that somehow never manifest themselves. When the requisite number of pioneers is assembled and the final petition for land accepted, men go out to the new ejido to select settlement locations, clear land, and begin to plant crops. They bring their families and begin life in the new location. But Ch'ol ejidos are demographically peculiar. As the pioneers tend to be of a single generation, they do not bring elders with them, and the ejidos lose the thread of traditional knowledge that depends on multigenerational settlements. Consequently, ejido dwellers may speak Ch'ol fluently, but often they do not share the traditional lore that is common in highland settlements. Thus, while Ch'ol language has reoccupied the ancient territories, Ch'ol traditions are not present throughout. The highland communities in Tila and Tumbalá remain the best source of traditional knowledge; they retain customs (and traditional language) that are alien to the more progressive populations of the Ch'ol diaspora (Josserand and Hopkins 1996; Josserand et al. 2003).

In recent years, the Ch'ol-speaking area has been affected by yet another resistance movement. The federal government announced changes in the land reform laws that would allow shareholders to sell their land. This was a death knell for the ejidos. *Ejidatarios* knew that if they could sell their land, sooner or later they would have to when illness or some other family crisis struck (Hopkins 1995).

Furthermore, on January 1, 1994, the fledgling Ejército Zapatista de Liberación Nacional (EZLN) seized four municipal administrative centers, including San Cristóbal de Las Casas, and announced the beginning of a movement to restore autonomy to the highland indigenous communities (Collier and Quaratiello 1994). In a process similar to that of the 1712 rebellion, many Indian *municipios* have declared themselves autonomous entities no longer responsive to state and federal governments.

In the 1970s and 1980s, Chiapas had been host to thousands of refugees fleeing the Guatemalan civil conflict. Chiapas was well known to the international aid community, with offices of major agencies located in San Cristóbal and elsewhere in the state. The presence of these observers probably accounts for the relatively (but by no means completely) bloodless repression of the liberation movement. However, the highlands and adjacent jungle lowlands have been thoroughly militarized, and army bases are ubiquitous, with frequent checkpoints set up along major and minor routes to control the movement of people and goods. Extraofficial agents of repression abound, such as paramilitary death squads, and are responsible for numerous atrocities and acts of violence against suspected rebels and their communities. The highland Ch'ol towns are not exempt from this violence, and escape from the conflict is often cited as a reason for the migration of pioneers to the states of Campeche and Quintana Roo.

History of the Black Christ of Tila

The Black Christ of Tila, also known as the Señor de Tila, is famous throughout Chiapas and Tabasco, and pilgrims from all strata of Mexican society make journeys to worship and petition this image of Christ on the cross (Pérez Chacón 1988; Navarrete 2000; Monroy Valverde 2004; Josserand and Hopkins 2007). Before the completion of a proper road between Yajalón and Tila in 1995, these journeys were arduous. Even the Ch'ol who have migrated away from the area make annual pilgrimages or return during times of drought to seek his aid. The Black Christ plays a paramount role in the religious, social, and economic life of the Ch'ol.

As noted in the previous chapter, a Ch'ol town called Tila stood at the south end of the Tila Valley during the Late Postclassic period. While little was recorded about the town, stone remnants of an early Catholic church in a milpa near the hamlet of Misiljá (N17 14.983 W92 23.287) likely mark the town's general location (Bassie-Sweet, personal observation). In the sixteenth century, the Spanish moved the Tila community from the lower valley to a location near the modern village of Chulum Chico, some five kilometers to the northwest. It is possible that the Spanish moved the town to establish some distance between it and the Tzeltal community of Petalcingo, located just four kilometers to the southwest (Jan de Vos, personal communication). A second church was begun at Chulum Chico but was abandoned. The stone foundation of this church still remains (Bassie-Sweet, personal observation). A third church was constructed just a kilometer to the northwest near the base of a hill where the cemetery for the modern town of Tila is now located. The church walls remain intact, but its interior is now filled with graves. This church was then replaced with yet another at the very top of the hill. Bishop Núñez apparently provided the funds for this fourth structure. Although parts of the original atrium and a bell tower remain, a more recent Catholic church, which houses the Señor de Tila, now stands at this location, and it is the spiritual and physical center of Tila. A colonial-period watercolor in the San Cristóbal archives illustrates the town of Tila with the early version of the present church, a bell tower, and the abandoned cemetery church (Monroy Valverde 2004:104–108).

Tila acquired its Black Christ statue sometime after Bishop Núñez's 1687 pastoral inspection of the Tzeltal and Ch'ol region. Although there is no documentation of its origin, it is quite likely that the bishop himself sent the crucifix to Tila in the hope that it would take the place of the indigenous black idols. The tradition of Black Christ icons originated in the Chortí town of Esquipulas in eastern Guatemala (Borhegyi 1953, 1954). Esquipulas was known for its sulfurous springs and sources of clay used in indigenous healing rituals. In 1595, Esquipulas used profits from its cotton harvest to purchase a crucifix for its chapel. The carver was a well-known Portuguese artist named Quirio Cantaño, who carved his sculpture from dark wood, hence the nickname "Black Christ." Why Cantaño used dark wood is unknown, but the color resonated with native people, perhaps because it was similar to their own flesh tones. Indigenous people were already predisposed to dark ritual colors, for ceremonial participants were often painted black, and several important pre-Columbian deities were this color. The Esquipulas shrine became a popular pilgrimage destination after several episodes of miraculous healing were attributed to the power of its Black Christ. Even before the alleged miracles, other centers obtained Black Christ statues representing the Señor de Esquipulas, and by the end of the eighteenth century, some forty towns had Black Christ of Esquipulas shrines.

Unlike the Esquipulas carving, the Señor de Tila is not carved from dark wood. The first documented event concerning the Señor de Tila occurred in 1693 when Bishop Núñez was making a pastoral visit to Tila (Navarrete 2000:65; Monroy Valverde 2004). Apparently a considerable amount of grime from incense and candles had accumulated on the sculpture, so the bishop ordered that it be washed and renewed the following day. When the restorer arrived the next morning to perform his duties, he discovered that the statue was clean and had turned a pale color. Núñez questioned the indigenous leaders responsible for the church, and even under oath no one would confess to cleaning the crucifix. He then declared that it was a miraculous transformation. Today, the Señor de Tila has a dark finish with a lighter undertone where the finish has peeled (Bassie-Sweet, personal observation).

The lack of refinement of the Tila sculpture as compared with the Esquipulas sculpture has not diminished the level of devotion that pilgrims have for the image.

Diocesan archives in San Cristóbal indicate that pilgrims from Tabasco participated in Epiphany rituals at Tila as early as 1695, and Tabasqueños continue to make pilgrimages to the Señor de Tila to this day, particularly during the festival of Corpus Christi (Josserand and Hopkins 2007). In 1887, the vicar of Palenque noted that Tila was well endowed with funds provided by pilgrims from Tabasco and Campeche (Ruz 1994). The economic advantages for Tila are still evident. A steady stream of pilgrims visits the Señor de Tila all year long, and during the two major festivals held in January and June, tens of thousands of devotees make the trek to Tila to petition the Black Christ. The regional importance of the Black Christ is evident in the prayers that petition the Señor de Tila recorded at the Tzotzil community of San Pedro Chenalhó (Guiteras Holmes 1961:54–55), but he draws devotees from across Mexico. Tila ritual specialists are known throughout the region for their ability to cure difficult diseases and illnesses with the aid of the Black Christ.

A secondary object of the Black Christ cult is a natural stalagmite found in a nearby cave. While the Black Christ sculpture in the Tila church is the major focus of devotion, pilgrims also petition the Señor de Tila in this small rockshelter located near the top of their sacred San Antonio Mountain (Bassie-Sweet, personal observation 1994). The cave contains a stalagmite column that is believed to be a manifestation of the Black Christ. Although the column does not particularly resemble an anthropomorphic figure, the surface of the stalagmite is blackened with soot from the incense and candles burning before it. An outdoor chapel and huge cement cross have been erected just above the cave. During various festivals, such as the Day of the Holy Cross and Corpus Christi, a small Black Christ statue housed in the church is taken in a procession to the cave, reinforcing the Black Christ's association with the cave (see also chapter 8).

An indentation in the stalagmite collects water that is thought to have miraculous curative power, and healing rituals are conducted in the cave. Clay from a clay bed adjacent to the San Antonio cave is ingested during these healing rituals (Juan Jesús Vásquez, personal communication). Around the world, clay is used as a dietary supplement during pregnancy and as a remedy for a host of afflictions. At Esquipulas and several other Señor de Esquipulas shrines, clay tablets imprinted with the image of the Black Christ and blessed by a Catholic priest are sold to pilgrims for their own health or to take home to family and friends. The tablets are eaten or dissolved in water and drunk. Although such tablets are not sold at Tila, the San Antonio cave may have become specifically associated with the Señor de Tila because of the proximity of this clay source. In addition to the clay and water of the San Antonio cave, the residual wax from the candles burned for the Señor de Tila is thought to have curative properties and is used by shamans in their healing ceremonies (Heriberto Cruz Vera, Tila priest, personal communication). Miraculous qualities are commonly ascribed to materials associated with a sacred icon. For example, the Black Christ of Zinacantán is identified with salt, which was an important trade commodity for the

Zinacantecos. Like the clay of the Black Christ, this salt is thought to have curative power (Vogt 1969:170–71, 361, 513, 518–519: Laughlin 1977:200–201).

The identification of a god or saint with a cave is widespread in Mesoamerica. In Tzotzil Chamula, the patron saint, San Juan, has a senior and junior aspect (Gossen 1974:292; 1999:48–53). Both aspects of the saint were thought have built the Chamula church, but the senior San Juan then retired to his cave on Tzontevitz, a high mountain east of town. The Black Christ of Zinacantán was thought to have been found originally in a cave; numerous stories tell of the discovery of an image of a saint or the Virgin Mary in a cave (Vogt 1976:17; Laughlin 1977:201). In Joloniel, Chiapas, saints are said to appear from caves, and the statue of their patron, La Virgen del Carmen, was thought to have been discovered in a cave (Joljá Cave Project field notes). Some people believe that the cross of the Señor de Esquipulas came from a cave near the town (Brady and Veni 1992). The water of the river adjacent to this cave is thought to have miraculous healing benefits, and the cave is the site of healing rituals. It is quite possible that the original clay beds associated with the Señor de Esquipulas were near the Esquipulas cave, though today the clay for the Black Christ tablets is mined in the surrounding mountains.

Indigenous stories concerning the Señor de Tila are a mix of historical fact and folklore. He plays a prominent role in one tale concerning the founding of Tila (Pérez Chacón 1988). In this story, it is the Señor de Tila who directs the people to move their community from the Misiljá site at the south end of the Tila Valley to the various other locations. In the typical fashion of Chiapas saints, the Señor de Tila is unhappy with the locations first chosen by the people for his church because they are too wet or full of ants. Comparable tales are told regarding the founding of the churches of Santa María Magdalena and San Andrés Larráinzar in the Tzotzil region, where the patron saint is displeased with a particular site because it is too wet, rocky, or windy. In these stories, the patron saint is also portrayed as the founder of the town. The Tila version states that when people from San Cristóbal came to loot the Tila church, the Señor de Tila fled up San Antonio Mountain and hid in the cave. After staying in the cave for a number of years, he returned to the church with the help of Tabasqueños, but he left behind in the cave an image of himself (the stalagmite). The colonial reports of the looting of the Tila church during the 1712 rebellion do not specifically refer to the Black Christ statue, but it is possible that it was removed from the church and hidden on San Antonio Mountain. Given that it was the Tabasco alcalde mayor Medina Cachón and his troops who restored colonial rule at Tila, the oral tradition may stem from these events.

During conflict, hiding treasure and saints' images was a common strategy. The Chilón cofradía members, for example, buried their funds in the mountains rather than surrender them to the Cancuc cult in the 1712 war. A similar situation occurred at Tumbalá. A ritual cave known as the Cave of the Vulture because its mouth resembles a vulture in flight and vultures roost there is situated on a cliff face below the

Tumbalá cemetery (Javier Solís, personal communication, Joljá Cave Project field notes). Access is only possible using ropes to descend from above. During times of trouble, the saints' images in the church were hidden in the cave to protect them. Some believe that the cave is connected to the church by a cave passageway.

The notion that sacred places or communities are connected by cave passageways is common in Mesoamerica. The Tzeltal of Pinola believe that the numerous caves in the mountains that surround their town are inhabited by powerful deities and are interconnected by subterranean passages (Hermitte 1964). In the Ch'ol village of Joloniel, it is believed that when the Señor de Tila first arrived in the region, he traveled to Tila through Tumbalá Mountain by following a cave passageway starting in Joljá Cave 1 (Joljá Cave Project field notes). His arrival at Joljá was said to be announced by thunder. It is also thought that there is an underground passageway between Joljá and Don Juan Mountain. In Tila, it is believed that a cave at the edge of the town is connected to Palenque. The American traveler and diplomat John Lloyd Stephens was told by the residents of Ocosingo in 1840 that there was a cave near Toniná that he could take all the way to Palenque (Stephens 1841).

Even during times of religious upheaval, the popularity of the Black Christ did not diminish. Certain parts of the 1917 Mexican Constitution were intended to reduce the influence and wealth of the Catholic Church across Mexico. The governor of Tabasco, Tomás Garrido Canabal (1920–24, 1931–34) repressed the Church in his state and ordered the destruction of its churches. Churches in Chiapas were also closed or converted to other uses, and religious services were suspended. As a consequence, saints' images in the church at Tumbalá were destroyed. Perhaps because of the popularity and remoteness of the Black Christ of Tila, his cult continued. Quite naturally, the indigenous civil-religious hierarchy assumed more responsibility following the temporary withdrawal of the Catholic priests, and they continue to control church activities today.

The indigenous cargo system in Tila evolved from the early cofradía organizations. At the top rank of the Tila cargo holders are four majordomos, one for each of the principal images in the Tila church: the Black Christ, the Virgin Mary, the Blessed Sacrament, and Saint Matthew. In addition, there are twenty-one more majordomos who care for the lesser saints of the church. Under this top level of officials is a second and third tier of cargo holders called captains and corporals. Once a man has risen through this hierarchy and performed his duties well, he becomes a respected elder called a *tatuch*. These *tatuches* are often consulted during times of crisis and illness. They make pilgrimages to various shrines and caves to petition on behalf of individuals and the community as a whole. The term *tatuch* is related to the Tabasco Spanish term *tatoque* "powerful person, person in command" (Santamaría 1959:1015), in turn derived from a Gulf Coast Nahuat word for "ambassador, intermediary, treaty maker" (from *tatowa* "to speak"; cf. Nahuatl *tlatoani*). The role of these intermediaries was "to speak with the enemy in order to arrive at an accord," making this an appropriate term for a religious specialist who mediates between petitioners and potentially dangerous deities (Santamaría 1959:1015). The tatuches are not the only ritual specialists who attend to people's health. Curers are known by such titles as *xwujt, x'ilaj, tz'äkañ,* and *xlok' ch'ich'* (Josserand and Hopkins 1996:24). In addition, there are midwives called *xyoty'oñel* and female curers known as *xyojkoñel.*

Besides the Black Christ, the Ch'ol place great importance on petitioning the earth lord known as Don Juan (further discussed in chapter 8). In the mid-twentieth century, a number of Protestant missionaries began working in the Ch'ol region (Beekman 1957; Whittaker and Warkentin 1965; Aulie 1979; Scott 1988). Considering indigenous deities to be manifestations of the Christian devil, they preached not only against traditional Maya rituals, as the Catholics had before them, but also against the worship of Catholic saints. In Ch'ol world view, transgressions against Don Juan were thought to be one cause of illness. To regain health, petitions had to be made to Don Juan. The Protestant missionaries observed that the community shamans who made these petitions were leaders of the traditional world view, and that much of their prestige and power rested in their ability to treat illnesses. The missionaries characterized such healers as witch doctors who worked in collusion with the devil. To diminish the authority of the shamans and help win converts, the missionaries employed an effective health care strategy. They provided modern medical treatments to potential converts and linked the curative powers of those treatments to their version of the Christian god (Beekman 1957). The Protestant missionaries were relatively successful in the Tumbalá region but met strong resistance in the communities affiliated with Tila. A primary reason for this difference was that Tila had a robust civil-religious hierarchy of indigenous leaders whose power was centered not only on their roles as interceders with Don Juan, but on their positions in the cult of the Black Christ. It is ironic that the writings of these early Protestant missionaries provide some of the best documentation of twentieth-century Ch'ol beliefs.

The next chapter steps back in time to examine the pre-Columbian sites between Toniná and Palenque, and the road that linked them. Most of the routes between Classic period sites are unknown, but the Toniná-Palenque trail is a rare exception that remained in use into the twentieth century.

PART II

ARCHAEOLOGY OF THE CH'OL REGION

3

THE PRE-COLUMBIAN SITES
OF THE CH'OL REGION

Karen Bassie-Sweet, Robert M. Laughlin, and Nicholas A. Hopkins

Epigraphic research, that is, the interpretation of ancient Maya inscriptions, has generally concentrated on the dynastic histories of the various Classic period sites and the political and military relationships between them. These studies have focused on such topics as genealogy, marriage alliances, and war events (see Martin and Grube 2008 for an overview). Modern archaeological investigations tend to be concerned with the urban environment and settlement patterns of individual sites. Very few studies have investigated the land routes between polities, and the geographical and social factors that influence or dictate the choice of route. Ascertaining ancient land routes in the uninhabited lowland rainforest of the Ch'ol area is particularly challenging. Due to the ruggedness of the mountain terrain, the Toniná-Palenque road and many other routes in the region often followed the path of least resistance through the river valleys and have remained relatively unchanged well into the twentieth century. In 1781, Sebastián Fulgencio Solórzano (1785) sent a letter to the San Cristóbal authorities that included the distances between the major settlements along the Toniná-Palenque route, and parts of this footpath were still in use as late as the 1950s. Not surprisingly, the main pre-Columbian sites of the region are adjacent to this pathway. In this chapter, we give a detailed account of this route and its adjoining sites.

The Route

The American adventurer John Lloyd Stephens (1841) gives a rich description of the path from Toniná to Palenque as it existed in 1840 (map 5). Setting out in the early morning hours of May 5 from Ocosingo (near Toniná) with his companions, Frederick Catherwood and Henry Pawling, the trio rode northwest on their mules, while their Tzeltal carriers followed on foot bearing the expedition equipment and luggage on their backs. Climbing the ridge that forms the north side of the Ocosingo

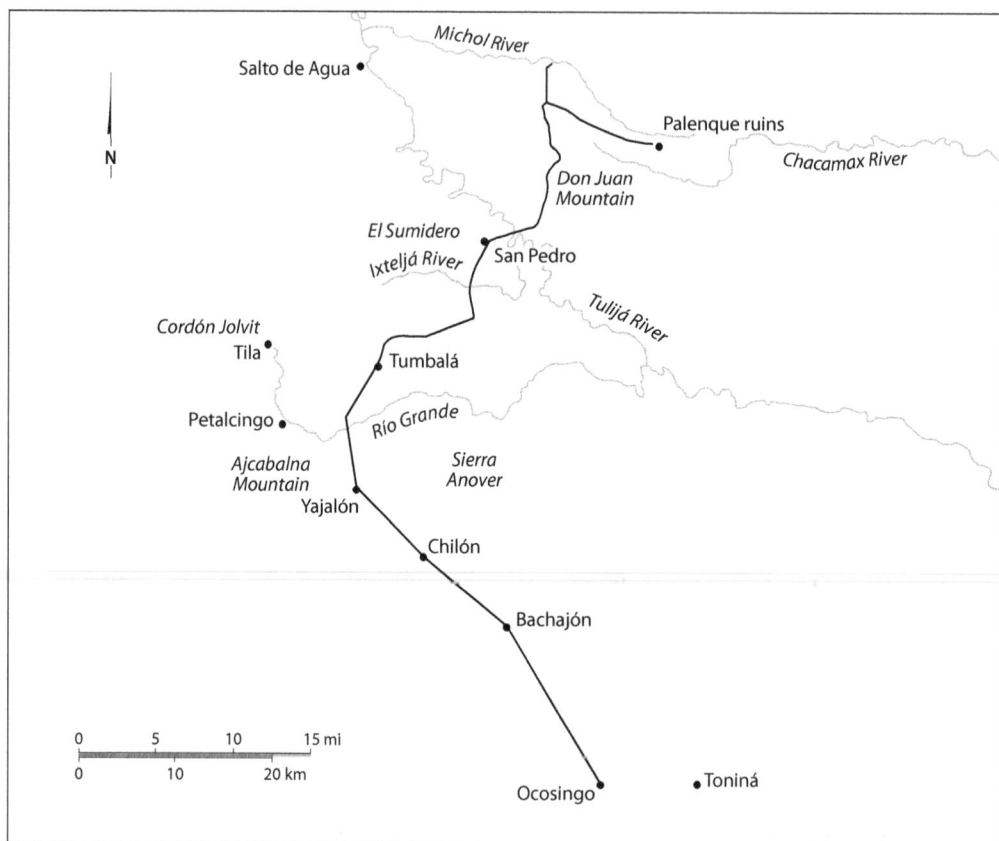

Map 5. Ancient road through Ch'ol area. Map by Bill Nelson, based on a map by Marcia Bakry. © 2015, University of Oklahoma Press.

Valley, they descended into the valley of Bachajón, arriving in the village of Bachajón at three in the afternoon. They continued along the valley to the northwest and ended their day at Chilón just after six in the evening.

During the era of Stephens's expedition, communities were required to supply dignitaries with men to carry their loads to the next town. The following morning at seven, therefore, the trio set out with Chilón carriers for their second day's destination of Tumbalá. Again they traveled northwest, following the valley between Ajcabalna Mountain and Sierra Anover, and within three hours they arrived at Yajalón. Their Chilón carriers were not required to transport their loads beyond this point, and Stephens was forced to find Yajalón carriers to continue on to Tumbalá. When Stephens's group reached the Río Grande at the southern end of the Tila Valley, they crossed the river and ascended the southwestern slope of Tumbalá Mountain to reach Tumbalá.

As noted in chapter 1, the indigenous name for the town of Tumbalá is K'uk' Witz "quetzal mountain," and the long green tail feathers of the male quetzal were one of the most important highland trade commodities. These birds only exist on mountains with elevations between 1,200 and 3,000 meters that have lower slopes with abundant wild fruit trees of the laurel family (*Lauraceae*). Most quetzal habitat in the Tumbalá region has been destroyed by agriculture, but the birds were common in the 1950s, and it has been reported that quetzals may still be found at Cerro San José on the north end of the mountain and Cerro Jolguitz in the adjacent range to the northwest (Domingo Solís López, personal communication 2002). There is no evidence of a pre-Columbian town in the vicinity of Tumbalá, but it is likely that any community near the top of the mountain was employed in the harvesting of quetzal feathers; hence the indigenous name.

Although Stephens arrived in Tumbalá when the town was preparing for the annual festival in honor of its patron saint, San Miguel Archangel, Stephens was able to procure carriers for the next leg of the companions' journey to San Pedro in the Tulijá Valley. Their route on the third day took them down the southeastern face of the Tumbalá mountain range, across the Ixteljá River, over the steep Sumidero foothills that run parallel to the base of the mountain, and into the Tulijá Valley and the village of San Pedro. The twentieth-century Protestant missionary Wilbur Aulie described this same path in a 1948 letter to his parents: "The trail was one of the worst I have ever seen. Impassable for a horse or mule, it winds up one forested slope and down another, now passing through a narrow cleft in a huge mass of rock and then by dark caves. Often there is no firm underfooting, for the trail goes over masses of tree roots and leaves which hide deep holes and, the Indians say, certain species of mountain cats" (Aulie 1979:10).

The route of the Tumbalá–San Pedro footpath is still known today by residents of Tumbalá. It went through the villages of La Sombra, Yuslumil, Chuchucruz, Cacahuatal, and Naranjil (Domingo Solís López, personal communication; Joljá Cave Project field notes). Solórzano does not refer to the village of San Pedro in his description, but rather mentions a rancho called Ixteljá. Such a hamlet is located just a few kilometers west of San Pedro. There are river crossings on the Tulijá adjacent to both of these communities, and they are likely where travelers crossed.

The massive Don Juan Mountain, which separates the Tulijá Valley from the Palenque plain, has two prominent peaks of almost equal height. On the fourth day of the Stephens expedition, the men crossed the Tulijá River and climbed up the mountain, skirting the western peak. Although Stephens wanted to spend the night in a thatched shelter near the summit, his Ch'ol carriers pushed the party on, and they descended the steep north side of the Don Juan Mountain paralleling the San Leandro River. They came off the mountain onto the plain near the present-day village of Agua Blanca. Both Solórzano and Stephens referred to the rancho at this location as Noj Pa' "big stream." The following morning Stephens's group traveled southeast along the base of Don Juan Mountain and the Río Michol to the village of Palenque.

A rudimentary 1933 United States Army map and a 1955 United States Air Force map both show the route over the western peak of Don Juan Mountain (Jan Rus and Robert Rands, personal communication). This western route was also mentioned by Karena Shields in her memoir about life on the San Leandro plantation (Shields 1959:41, 49, 174–75). Although it is no longer in use, the location of this footpath over Don Juan Mountain is still known to some older residents of the region (Joljá Cave Project field notes). Domingo Solís López (personal communication) noted that unencumbered men could cross the mountain in one day, as the Stephens expedition did, but normally the trip was divided into two days, particularly if the men were carrying full loads. The footpath began near Suclumpa at the southern base, ascended to Lote Ocho (La Gloria), and then went around the east side of the western peak of the mountain. The thatched shelter that Stephens referred to in his description is likely the place where most travelers spent the night. This is not the path of least resistance over the western end of the mountain, but the reason for this particular route will be discussed later in the chapter.

Although Stephens complained bitterly about the vertical nature of the western route and claimed that it was the worst mountain he had ever encountered, a path near the eastern end of the mountain would have been even more arduous. It would have traversed extremely uneven terrain and a second set of ridges on the north side of the mountain. The western route, on the other hand, took advantage of the natural break in the foothills on the north side of Don Juan Mountain where the San Leandro River exits the mountain and runs into the Río Michol on the plain.

Once on the plain, travelers could turn east to Palenque or west toward Salto de Agua and the Gulf Coast (map 5). At the turn of the twentieth century, several foreign-owned rubber and henequén plantations were established on the plain adjacent to the Río Michol, which flows along the northern and western base of Don Juan Mountain. The Chiapas Rubber and Investment Company had three fincas in this area at San Leandro, San Lorenzo, and Santa Isabel. The mule trail that connected Palenque with Salto de Agua and the Gulf Coast serviced these plantations and the local cattle ranches in the area.

The mule trail was located on the plain, but it was likely not the route the pre-Columbian Maya used when they journeyed through this area from Palenque to the coastal region. The natural break in the foothills at Agua Blanca provides access not only to the main mountain, but also to the narrow valley that extends along the base of the mountain from Agua Blanca to the valley of the Arroyo Agua Azul. Continuing westward along this valley brings one to the wide Bajo Grande Valley which extends almost all the way to Salto de Agua. Villagers from the Bajo Grande area still walk to Salto de Agua by this route. Travelers journeying on foot from Palenque to the coastal towns such as Tortuguero or Comalcalco, both in Tabasco, would have used this path to bypass the low-lying and often inundated terrain of the plain. The archaeological sites of Miraflores and El Retiro are located on this pathway, which suggests that the pre-Columbian Maya did use this route and not the plain.

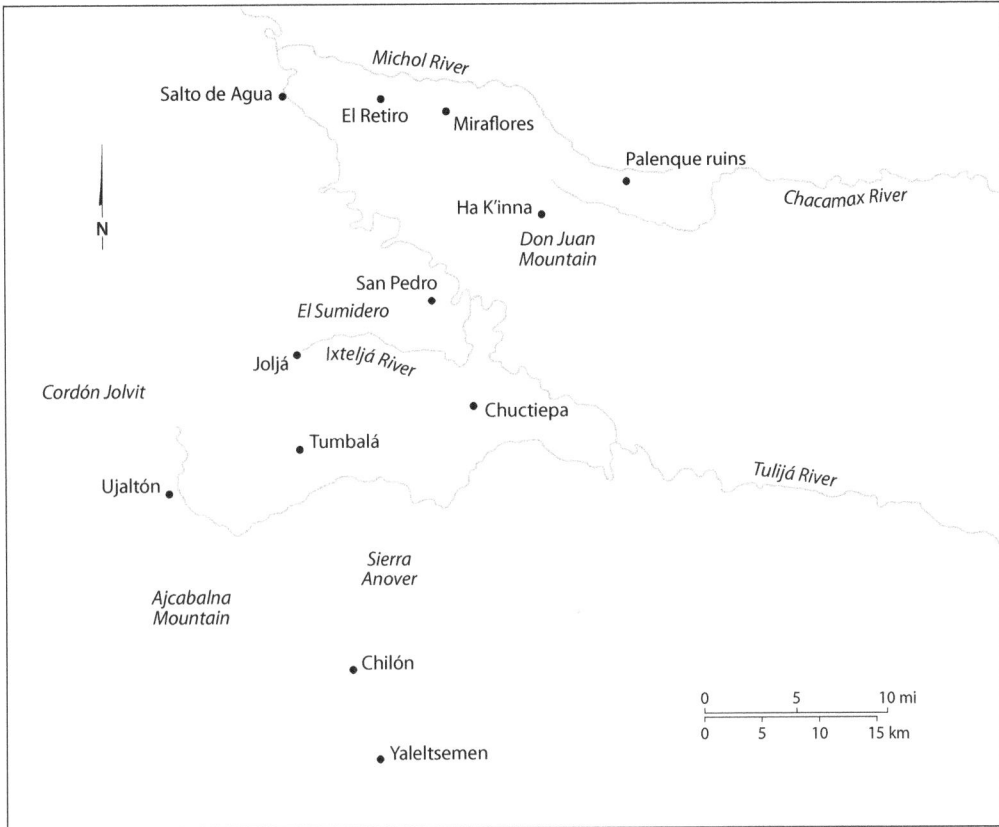

Map 6. Archaeological sites. Map by Bill Nelson, based on a map by Marcia Bakry. © 2015, University of Oklahoma Press.

SITES OF THE PALENQUE-TONINÁ ROUTE

In ancient times, an expedition setting out from Toniná to Palenque would have followed the same river valleys and ridges as Stephens. Given that Stephens's Tzeltal and Ch'ol carriers transported the expedition supplies on their backs, their travel time is an accurate indication of how long it would have taken ancient merchants carrying loads to traverse this same route. Like Stephens, they would have arrived in the vicinity of Chilón at the end of the first day of travel. On the ridges and hills above Chilón are the remains of a significant pre-Columbian town (Cordan 1963; Becquelin and Baudez 1979) (map 6). The site, which has never been systematically excavated, consists of several different architectural groups (designated as Bolonkin, Naxtenxum, Nachoj A, Nachoj B, and Mukana).

In addition to the Late Classic architectural decorations and hieroglyphs on the standing buildings of Chilón, beautiful Classic period murals decorate the interior walls of a structure at Bolonkin (Andrieu et al. 2012). These murals illustrate lords wearing the headdress of GI, which is composed of a motif called the Quadripartite Badge Monster (see chapter 7 for a discussion of this thunderbolt deity). The middle panel of the Palenque Temple of the Inscriptions indicates that the Quadripartite Badge Monster was the headdress of GI, and many Early Classic *incensarios* feature GI wearing the headdress (Hellmuth 1987). Based on the style of the k'in signs and ear spools of the Bolonkin headdresses, the murals have been dated to the period A.D. 554 to A.D. 652 (Andrieu et al. 2012). Stingray spines on the Bolonkin GI headdress have a squat shape, which accords with the stylistic dating of the k'in signs and ear spools. While Late Classic examples of stingray spines were depicted realistically—long and slender—earlier illustrations of stingray spines during the transition between the Early and Late Classic periods had the squat form of a shark's tooth.

Another site along the route from Toniná to Palenque is a ritual cave with a Late Classic painting on its wall. The cave, located seven kilometers southeast of Chilón and six kilometers west of Bachajón, is known locally as Yaleltsemen (map 6). Tzeltal natives from Bachajón took the missionary Marianna Slocum to this cave in 1963. Its spectacular entrance that includes a waterfall is located on the wall of a sinkhole near the top of a mountain (Bassie-Sweet, personal observation). Sometime in the distant past, a section of the passageway roof collapsed and almost completely blocked access to the back of the cave. A tortuous, narrow crawlspace snakes through the rockfall and leads into a large chamber at the rear of the cave. There, the elegant Late Classic depiction of a seated lord with a caption text was painted on a boulder (Thompson 1975:xxxvi; A. Stone 1995:91). The young lord was seated in a frontal pose, leaning to his right. Lords are frequently shown in similar poses on Late Classic pottery. The caption text of the Yaleltsemen painting indicated that the lord was from a site called Sibikte' (David Stuart, personal communication 2000). The Sibikte' place name also appears in the inscriptions of Joljá Cave 1 and Toniná (see chapter 5).

Archaeologists Carlos Navarrete, Eduardo Martínez, and Adolfo Muñoz visited Yaleltsemen in 1971 during their regional survey but have not published their results (Navarrete, personal communication). Members of the French archaeological project at Toniná also examined the cave during their own regional inspection and published a photograph of the painting (Becquelin and Baudez 1982:123). In 2002, it was discovered that the entire Yaleltsemen painting had been cut off the stone with hacksaws and, in the process, destroyed (Bassie-Sweet, personal observation). Whether this was an act of looting, evangelical fanaticism, or common vandalism is unknown.

From Chilón, the likely destination for ancient travelers on the way from Toniná to Palenque would have been the Classic period community of Ujaltón, located at the southern end of the Tila Valley (map 6). Ujaltón is one of the names the local Ch'ol use for this site. It is situated approximately 2.5 kilometers northwest of Petalcingo on a ridge owned by the Ch'ol ejido of Nueva Esperanza. It is currently used as a milpa, and its many buildings show evidence of numerous looting trenches (Bassie-Sweet, personal observation). The local Ch'ol consider Ujaltón a sacred location and make ritual offerings at the site during January.

Three Classic-period limestone monuments were recovered from the Tila Valley with calendar dates ranging from A.D. 685 to A.D.830 (Beyer 1926, 1927; Blom and La Farge 1926–27:511; Morley 1937–38, 4:371; Piña Chan 1967:83; Mayer 1984:9–10, plate 4; 1991:54–55, plate 206). There is clear evidence that these monuments came from Ujaltón, although no archaeological excavations have been conducted in this zone. The three monuments have been labeled in various publications as "stelae" and given alphabetic designations, but we follow Mayer and use the neutral term "monument" because at least one of these sculptures is likely a wall panel.

Beyer (1926, 1927) noted that Monument 1 was being used by the modern Ch'ol as a stone bridge over a small stream and that Fray Eleazar Mandujano, the Catholic priest of Tila, had arranged for the monument to be moved to his house to protect it (fig. 3.1a–b). Beyer could not determine the exact location of this stream, but he subsequently found Monument 2 on a hill he referred to as Cruz Tuin (fig. 3.2). When Frans Blom (1961) tried to ascertain the precise origins of these two monuments, he was given conflicting information by residents of Petalcingo, who thought they either came from Ujaltón or a site called Chulum. A local informant has confirmed that Cruz Tuin is another name for Ujaltón (Christian Heck, personal communication). Presumably Beyer went to Cruz Tuin-Ujaltón because it was the area where the priest had indicated he had recovered Monument 1. There is a small stream at the base of Ujaltón called Jilshibaquil, likely where Monument 1 was recovered.

Monument 1 is now in three fragments. The whereabouts of the upper portion are unknown, but the middle fragment resides in the *bodega* of the Museo Regional de Antropología e Historia in Tuxtla Gutiérrez, while the lower fragment resides in the Museo de Arte Prehispánico de México Rufino Tamayo. Monument 2 is now in two fragments. The upper portion of Monument 2 is on display at the Museo Regional de Antropología e Historia, but the location of the lower fragment is unknown.

An elderly local informant has indicated that as a young man he saw Monument 3 at Ujaltón (Christian Heck, personal communication). According to church records from Tila and Bachajón, Monument 3 was subsequently found near the village of Noj Já (Río Grande) just a kilometer downhill from Ujaltón in the late 1940s (fig. 3.3). The monument had been carried there and abandoned in some weeds beside the Petalcingo-Tila road. At that time, a tiny landing strip ran parallel to the road near Noj Já. We speculate that looters brought the monument to the airstrip for transport and for some unknown reason abandoned the attempt. Perhaps the weight was too much for the small planes that used the airstrip in those days. Monument 3 is currently on display at the Jesuit Mission in Bachajón.

A church record in the Jesuit Mission archive documents how this monument came to be in Bachajón and is worth quoting in full. We reproduce it with the permission of Fray Eugenio Mauer:

> The "Bachajón" Maya Stela: Why is this archaeological treasure here in Bachajón?
> Information provided by an elder of Tila, Chiapas, to Fray Amando Herrera
> Rios, S.J., January 13, 1964.

3.1a. Ujaltón Monument 1, middle fragment. Photo by Karl Herbert Mayer.

1. Between Petalcingo and Tila, at Noj-Já, very near the road, some visitors—tourists, investigators—discovered this "stone" half-buried among the weeds. They recognized with admiration that it was a Maya stela, but they could not explain why it was found there in total abandon.

2. These people informed the authorities in Tila about this important discovery and the archaeological value of said piece, and they suggested that, as the town authorities, they should arrange as soon as possible that the stela should be brought to the town itself for its protection, since it is part of the National Treasure.

3.1b. Ujaltón Monument 1, lower fragment. Photo by Annegrete Hohmann Vogrin, 1997, courtesy Karl Herbert Mayer.

3. This went on for several years without the authorities carrying out the task, so that it was necessary to urge the authorities, with more insistence, that they rescue the stela, and if they did not, they would have to answer to the state authorities.

4. Finally, after much time had gone by, the stela was carried to the town of Tila, with which an important step was taken in the rescue of such a valuable treasure. It remained, therefore, under the protection and vigilance of the municipal authorities.

5. There in Tila the stela remained for several years. Now the news reached the municipal authorities that there was a state museum in Tuxtla Gutiérrez, Chiapas, the capital of the state, where the stela should be placed. Therefore it would be necessary to make the effort to transport it to the capital, which would be in the public interest.

6. At this time, without any doubt, the museum in Tuxtla Gutiérrez already had received notice of the existence of the stela. The municipal authorities

3.2. Ujaltón Monument 2. Photo by Karl Herbert Mayer.

3.3. Ujaltón Monument 3. Photo by
Karen Bassie-Sweet.

aroused the interest of the town, and it was decided that the transfer of this treasure would be carried out as a public work.

7. The agreement is reached. It will not be possible to carry it by the direct road; it is very difficult, its weight and volume will oblige us to stop halfway. It is decided that it would be better to carry it by the big road, which, so it is understood, is a good part of what is now the highway. This is seen to be more favorable.

8. The agreement is made at a municipal level between the towns where the stela will pass, and it will take place in short stretches in order to facilitate the work. With time it was determined that the approximate weight of the stela is some 400 kilos.

9. First stretch: Tila-Petalcingo. Much fiesta, lots of people, music, fireworks, alcohol, etc.

Second stretch: Petalcingo-Yajalón. The same ambiance and enthusiasm, each municipality putting forth new elements to excite the people.

Third stretch: Yajalón-Chilón. The enthusiasm and optimism increases. What is notable, as always, is the participation of the women from the municipalities and the communities through which the stela passes. Abundant dancing. The stela didn't stay just one day in a place, but more time, according to the enthusiasm of the population. And the news of these happenings spread out to all parts.

Fourth stretch: Chilón-Bachajón. By now there is a world of people. Many are moved just to circulate among the multitude, without knowing what it is all about. A Maya stela? Who knows what that would be! The fact is that the town is in fiesta mode for several days.

Fifth stretch: Bachajón–Finca Hotol Já, property of Mr. Arnulfo Jiménez, halfway to Ocosingo.

Sixth stretch: Finca Hotol Já–Ocosingo. Up to here everything has functioned well. Probably something went wrong, for there were no longer any hands to carry the stela to Ocosingo. Thus for much time the stela stayed at the finca of Mr. Jiménez.

10. This did not go unnoticed. Thus every Sunday many people came to make fiesta, music, dance, fireworks, alcohol, etc. It is understood that this went on for some time, as Mr. Jiménez had to apply to the Municipal Agent of Bachajón to ask him to remove from his finca this "stone" (they still called it this), since he feared that some incident would take place and because the stela was on his property, he would be held responsible.

11. After some time, the Municipal Agent of Bachajón arranged for the return of the stela to the town. For a long time it was in the atrium of the church.

12. In 1954 the reconstruction of the church was completed, and the town decided to protect the stela in a designated place within the church.

Upon the arrival of the first Jesuit missionaries in 1958, in agreement with the town and its elders, the stela was moved to the place where it is now found, that is, the Convent of the Missionaries.

Monument 3 is highly regarded and well protected by the Bachajón community. It is mounted on a pedestal in a stone shelter that abuts the back exterior wall of the church within the courtyard of the Convent of the Missionaries.

Each of the three Ujaltón monuments refers to Period Ending ceremonies, which allows them to be securely dated. Monument 1 is a sculpture in the round similar to the type frequently found at Toniná. Although significantly eroded, the sculpture portrays a Maya lord. An inscription runs down the back. Though part of the inscription is missing, the Long Count date of 10.0.0.0.0 7 Ajaw 18 Sip (A.D. 840) can be reconstructed from the remaining glyphs. The inscription also refers back in time to the mythological 13.0.0.0.0 4 Ajaw 8 Kumk'u Period Ending event (August 13, 3114 B.C.) and mentions a pair of elderly deities known by the nickname the Paddler Gods. References to the mythological Period Ending ceremony and the Paddler Gods are found on other monuments as well. These references narrate that part of the Period Ending ceremony involved the changing or renewal of three hearthstones. This hearth was presumably that of the creator grandparents and was thought to be located at the center of the world (Bassie-Sweet 2008:241–46) (see chapter 6).

The name glyphs for the Paddler Gods have yet to be deciphered, but they were so-nicknamed because, on a series of bone carvings from Tikal Burial 116, they are portrayed paddling a canoe down a river (Freidel, Schele, and Parker 1993:90). Their name phrases refer to them as *mam k'uh* "grandfather gods" (Copan Stela 2) and Chahks (thunderbolt gods) (Jimbal Stela 1). On several monuments they hang from cloud symbols. A number of hieroglyphic texts including Monument 1 state that the Paddler Gods were lords of a place called Naah Ho Chan "house of five sky." The Paddler Gods are shown on Sacul Stela 1 carrying a title of office represented by a supernatural bird wearing a plain headband. No satisfactory decipherment of the headband-bird sign has been established, but secondary lords who were dressed in the accoutrements of Maya priests also held the office (Stuart 2005a; Zender 2005). Bassie-Sweet (2008:281–83) has argued that the Paddler Gods were parallel to the Popol Vuh deities called Xulu and Paqam, who were a pair of diviners closely identified with the river from which the hero twins were resurrected.

Monument 2 is the earliest of the three Ujaltón sculptures, and as noted by Mayer (1984:9–10), it was probably a wall panel. Its inscription includes the Long Count notation and tzolk'in position of 9.12.13.0.0 10 Ajaw (A.D. 685) as well as part of the Supplementary Series for this date. In Maya epigraphy, the Supplementary Series has not been completely deciphered, but we know it includes lunar information as well as information about the deities who were in power on the particular day. On Monument 2, the final glyph of the Supplementary Series, known as Glyph A, is missing, as is the 3 Sootz' month position for the date. It is apparent that there must have been an adjacent panel that completed the inscription. It is likely that the missing panel also included the verb stating the specific Period Ending action that was carried out on this date and the name of the ruler who performed this action. Hopefully, future excavations at Ujaltón will find this panel.

Monument 3 contains the k'atun ending date 9.13.0.0.0. 8 Ajaw 8 Woh (A.D. 692). The date is in pristine condition, with the exception of the top of the Initial Series Introductory Glyph (ISIG), which has been broken off. The ISIG contains the patron for the month. It is known from other monuments that the patron for Woh was a deity nicknamed GIII, and enough is left of the ISIG on Monument 3 to indicate that it indeed recorded the god GIII. Most Long Count notations for Period Ending ceremonies include a Supplementary Series between the tzolk'in date and month position. Like Monument 2, Monument 3 lacks the Supplementary Series. The inscription also employs the bar and dot notations for numbers rather than the more elegant head variants, which adds to its terse style.

Despite the lack of information on Monument 3, the date is a k'atun Period Ending, and there are many examples of these kinds of ceremonies in Maya art. They show that the ancient Maya conducted elaborate festivals at this time that included renewal rituals and feasts. They also made various offerings to the deities who would be in power in the upcoming k'atun, to ensure future good harvests and health. Divinations were an important aspect of the Period Ending ceremony. During these rites, the ruler and his priests made prognostications for the new k'atun period. While the three Ujaltón monuments do not refer to the people who performed the Period Ending rituals, they do indicate that a Late Classic elite population resided in the valley from at least A.D. 685 to A.D. 840.

Ujaltón was well placed to control not only the route to its east over Tumbalá Mountain, but also the route to its west along the Río Sabanilla to the Tabasco coastal plain. The amber deposits of Simojovel are just thirty kilometers to the southwest. Although the route between the Tila Valley and the Tabasco coast via the Sabanilla Valley has not been archaeologically surveyed, elaborate incensarios featuring the thunderbolt deities GI and GIII have been discovered in caves near the town of Tapijulapa, forty-one kilometers northwest of Ujaltón (Schmidt, Garza, and Nalda 1998:613).

As noted in chapter 1, an important ritual cave, perhaps associated with Three Votan, which contains pre-Columbian remains, is located at the base of Ajcabalna Mountain. The cave is near the community of San José Changuinic just six kilometers southeast of Ujaltón. Between Ujaltón and the modern town of Tila, a number of ritual caves such as Tumbuluch and Chulum Uitz contain pre-Columbian material (Blom Museum Archives; Manca 1995). According to Gertrude Blom's 1961 diary, she photographed pre-Columbian idols from Chulum Uitz. These pictures have not been located in the Blom Archives, housed in the Na Bolom Cultural Center in San Cristóbal de Las Casas. Blom noted that one of the idols had been smashed thirty-two years earlier by a local man who thought it might contain gold. She was told that the moment the idol was broken, the perfectly clear and beautiful sky turned into a raging storm with thunder and lightning. Eight days later, the local man died. Such cautionary tales are not uncommon.

We do not know what footpath the ancient Maya took from Ujaltón over Tumbalá Mountain toward Palenque, but the path may have circled to the north of the mountain summit, where the terrain is relatively easy, and emerged near the headwaters of the Ixteljá River (map 6). At these headwaters are three ritual caves known collectively as the Joljá caves. Although each cave contains pre-Columbian artifacts, Cave 1 also contains seven groups of pre-Columbian paintings from the Early Classic. The contemporary Ch'ol Maya continue to use the Joljá caves for ceremonies. They believe the deity called Don Juan inhabits these caves and several other caves in the region (notably that of Don Juan Mountain), and they dedicate annual cave ceremonies to him (see chapter 8).

From the Joljá caves, the path would have continued across the Tulijá Valley, crossed the river somewhere near San Pedro Sabana, and then followed the same route over Don Juan Mountain taken by Stephens. As noted above in this chapter, Stephens skirted the western peak of the mountain's two peaks and came down the steep north side. If, however, the travelers' destination was the Gulf Coast, they would have simply followed the Tulijá River west. The river is navigable from its junction with the Shumulá River to the coast with the exception of three small portages around two sets of rapids and a gravel bar (Ronald Canter, personal communication).

SITES OF THE TULIJÁ VALLEY

No significant sites are known in the Tulijá Valley, though it is possible that there were sites along the Tulijá River that over the centuries have been buried by silt (Liendo Stuardo 2011). The Classic period site of Chuctiepa (Cutiepa) is located in a small valley that runs parallel to the Tulijá Valley. It lies some fifteen kilometers down the mountainside to the east of Tumbalá, and it has an eroded altar and a stela in the round style most commonly found at Toniná. Frans Blom and Oliver La Farge (1926–27: 215) visited the site and mapped it along with several other sites on the upper reaches of the Tulijá River.

SITES OF DON JUAN MOUNTAIN

As noted in the introduction to this book, an important ritual cave is situated on the white cliff on the north side of Don Juan Mountain just below its western peak. The modern Ch'ol believe that this cave, known as Cueva de Don Juan, is inhabited by the mountain lord Don Juan, and they make pilgrimages to the cave to petition Don Juan for good harvest, hunting, and health. The ritual use of the Cueva de Don Juan by the Ch'ol was noted in an 1877 travel account of the region (Boddam-Whetham 1877:328). In 1952, three or more Classic-period flanged incensarios in the

Palenque style were removed from the cave by Ch'ol residents of the Tulijá Valley (Joljá Cave Project field notes). These incensarios likely featured portraits of the deity GIII. The Ch'ol placed these incensarios, which they considered to be images of saints, in community shrines at San Luis, San Pedro, and Trapiche. As late as the 1970s, these incensarios were still being venerated. One of the incensarios was destroyed when its shrine was accidently burned down, and the current location of the others is not known (see chapter 8 for a further discussion of the Cueva de Don Juan).

A schematic archaeological survey of the caves of Don Juan Mountain would provide unique insights into ancient Maya life, but sadly, only the looters have visited these locations. In 1964, Robert Rands (personal communication) attempted to reach the Cueva de Don Juan during his site survey on the northern slopes of Don Juan Mountain, but he was turned back when threatened by local bandits. Juan Antonio Ferrer, INAH director for Palenque, Bonampak, Yaxchilan, and Toniná, did reach the cliff area while conducting a walking tour of the area (Ferrer, personal communication). He noted that the northern approach to the cliff was extraordinarily difficult because of the intervening ridges and ravines. The Ch'ol access the cliff by climbing down from the western peak.

At the time of the conquest, Spanish priests noted that the Maya always made offerings to the mountain god whenever they journeyed over a mountain pass. With the conversion to Christianity, pre-Columbian shrines were often replaced with cross shrines. Stephens mentions such a cross that marked the summit of the Cordón Sumidero range that is located on the south side of the Tulijá Valley (Stephens 1841:270). In 1894, Karl Sapper noted that the custom of making offerings to the mountain god was still practiced, and he described the rituals his native carriers made at a mountain shrine between Tila and Sabanilla (Sapper 1897:271–74). It is, therefore, quite likely that a pre-Columbian shrine and later, a cross shrine, marked the summit of the Don Juan route near the western peak of the mountain. Such a shrine might have been near the thatched structure mentioned by Stephens, but a more likely candidate for this shrine is the Cueva de Don Juan, which is located just below the western peak.

As noted above, the ancient footpath over Don Juan Mountain that skirted the western peak is not the best route to Palenque. It is significantly easier to cross through Tiemopa and Actiepa Yochib on the far west end of the mountain. The obvious question is: why did they take the harder route? The most compelling answer appears to have been the need to make offerings to the mountain god to ensure a safe journey over the mountain.

The eastern peak of Don Juan Mountain, three kilometers from the western peak, in turn has a Late Classic site called Ha K'inna "house of the rising sun" at its summit (1,124 meters) (map 6). The Ch'ol ejido of Lote Ocho, which owns this section of the mountain, has converted the slopes around Ha K'inna to milpas. The site itself, however, is still covered in vegetation. In 1992, Juan Antonio Ferrer was informed of looting at Ha K'inna, and he sent archaeologist Gerardo Fernández to make a preliminary reconnaissance (Ferrer, personal communication). Its main temple is similar in layout to the Cross Group buildings at nearby Palenque, and like most unprotected buildings, large pits made by treasure seekers mar its interior (Liendo Stuardo 2011). The site also includes a ballcourt.

As to the nature of Ha K'inna, given its extraordinarily high and open location, it must have been subject to numerous lightning strikes. We suspect that the temple was dedicated to the deities GI, GII, and GIII, whom the ancient Palencanos identified with lightning. The site was also probably used as an outlook station for the defense of Palenque because it provides an almost 360-degree view of the surrounding territory. On the Michol Ridge on the plain just in front of Palenque is a building that probably had a similar defensive function. The Michol Ridge building affords a view up and down the northern foothills of Don Juan Mountain. There is an unobstructed view of Ha K'inna from this building.

Sites of the Northern Foothills of Don Juan Mountain

Two important pre-Columbian sites are found in the northern foothills of Don Juan Mountain. They are Miraflores and El Retiro, along the Agua Blanca to Salto de Agua route (Bassie, Miller, and Morales 2002; Liendo Stuardo 2011) (map 6). Miraflores is composed of three separate groups of buildings situated on the hills overlooking the valley of Arroyo Agua Azul. These groups of buildings are less than a kilometer apart. Starting at Agua Blanca, the first building one encounters is in Group I near the western end of the narrow valley that connects Agua Blanca and Arroyo Agua Azul. The building is a short distance up the steep southern slope of the valley. It has been extensively looted and damaged. Group II, composed of four buildings, is perched at the western end of the ridge that separates the narrow valley from the plain. Group II stands guard over the small break in the ridge where the Arroyo Agua Azul exits onto the plain, and it provides a panoramic view of the surrounding countryside. Group III is on the western slope of the Arroyo Agua Azul Valley above the modern hamlet of the same name. All three building groups are on private property.

In 1952, residents of Arroyo Agua Azul removed seven carved limestone fragments from Group I and placed them in their schoolhouse. At that time, an American woman named Karena Shields owned a finca at San Leandro just five kilometers away. When she heard about the fragments, she traveled to Arroyo Agua Azul and photographed them. In 1954, Heinrich Berlin also photographed the fragments in the Arroyo Agua Azul school, examined the temple in which they were found, and published a brief description (Berlin 1955; Mayer 1991:plates 28–31). At some point, the Miraflores fragments were stolen from the schoolhouse and taken to Macuspana to be sold on the black market. The fragment that Berlin denoted as Fragment A was eventually purchased by the Virginia Museum of Fine Arts in 1961, but not before it was trimmed of its upper glyph blocks and edges to make it more portable (Mayer 1980:plate 17; 1991:plate 28). The present location of the other Miraflores fragments is unknown.

Berlin's photographs are of poor quality. In the hopes of obtaining copies of the unpublished Shields photographs, Bassie-Sweet contacted Shields's daughter Lauren Essex, who was living in Atlanta, Georgia. By good fortune, Essex had retained some of her mother's photographs including the Miraflores ones, and at the request of Bassie-Sweet, George Stuart traveled to Atlanta in 2001 and obtained copies. David Stuart subsequently made a drawing of Fragment D from Shields's photograph and published it (Stuart and Stuart 2008:fig. 52).

The Miraflores fragments, as noted by Berlin, were likely part of a single composition. Fragment A illustrates an elegant Maya lord bedecked in jade jewelry and wearing a headdress highly reminiscent of the one worn by the Palenque ruler K'inich Ahkal Mo' Naab on the Tablet of the Slaves. The surviving portion of the Fragment A text names the lord as a *sajal,* or secondary lord, under the Palenque ruler K'inich Janaab Pakal. Pakal reigned from A.D. 615 to A.D. 683. While we do not know the precise function and duties of sajals, they act as warriors and ritual assistants who appear in a variety of military and ceremonial contexts.

Fragment D illustrates another sajal, although only his legs have survived. The surviving glyphs on this fragment state, in addition to the sajal title, that this lord was also a *yajawk'ahk',* literally "a vassal of the fire lord." Lords who held the office of *yajawk'ahk'* likewise had military and ceremonial roles. The presence of these sajal portraits at Miraflores indicates that it was under the control of Palenque during the early part of the Late Classic period.

Robert Rands collected pottery samples from the field adjacent to Miraflores Group III in 1964 for his regional ceramic study of the Palenque area (Rands, Bishop, and Harbottle 1978; Rands, personal communication and report in preparation). Juan Antonio Ferrer, Alonso Méndez, and Karen Bassie-Sweet made a preliminary map of the Group III buildings in 2001 that is on file with INAH. Also in 2001, members of the Joljá Cave Project were shown a recently looted limestone box found in a cave in the vicinity of Miraflores. This beautiful box and its lid were each carved from single blocks of limestone. The footed box measures approximately 36 cm tall by 29 cm long by 21 cm wide. Its well-fitted lid has a rabbeted edge to hold it securely in place. It was impossible to ascertain what the box once contained because its contents had been dumped in the cave.

The site of El Retiro is seven kilometers west of Miraflores. El Retiro sits atop a ridge that overlooks both the plain and the Bajo Grande Valley. The site is on the southern slope of the ridge and is oriented to the east with a view down the Bajo Grande toward Miraflores. It is on the property of the Corozal ejido, formerly the Bajo Grande ejido. Frans Blom and Oliver La Farge (1926–27:161–64) visited El Retiro in 1925 during their archaeological and ethnological survey of Chiapas. Rands collected pottery samples from El Retiro in 1964. Following Rands's indications, Bassie-Sweet, Julie Miller, and Alfonso Morales were able to relocate El Retiro in 2002 and visit the site in the company of Guillermo López Jimenes of the Corozal ejido (Bassie-Sweet,

Miller, and Morales 2002). Juan Antonio Ferrer subsequently visited the site with Morales. A recent survey of this area includes El Retiro (Liendo Stuardo 2011).

Blom and La Farge heard firsthand reports that a building at El Retiro contained a hieroglyphic panel, but just before their visit, a large cedar tree fell on the building and caused the central area to collapse. Blom and La Farge did not have the manpower to clear the fallen debris, so the panel remained buried. Based on the spaciousness and exceptional height of the interior rooms, Blom dated the building to sometime after 9.12.0.0.0 (A.D. 672), when such buildings were common at Palenque. The Blom and La Farge ground plan indicates that the building had a small inner sanctuary centered on the back wall, similar to the layout of the three Palenque Cross Group buildings. According to the Cross Group inscriptions, these three shrines were completed in A.D. 692, which fits with the time frame Blom suggests for El Retiro.

The front of the El Retiro building was divided into three doorways by two large pillars with the remains of stucco figures on them still visible in 1925, and the exterior walls were perforated by eight small windows. There were also the remains of a roof comb. Remarkably, the walls and roof of the rear room in the northwest corner of the building are still standing today, as is the lower portion of the exterior south wall (fig. 3.4). It is possible that the hieroglyphic panel is still buried under the building rubble. Remnants of the roof comb are evident, but the only other decoration remaining on the building is a stucco motif on an inner wall of the rear room. This building faces east with a clear view of the Bajo Grande and Don Juan Mountain.

Another pre-Columbian building is found south of El Retiro near the hamlet of Miguel Hidalgo. This unnamed site is on the opposite side of the Bajo Grande Valley on a plateau of rolling hills and in the middle of a cattle pasture. The site was first observed by Juan Antonio Ferrer during his 2001 inspection of Miraflores with Bassie-Sweet. More building groups probably exist in the vicinity, but thus far no archaeological survey of this area has been conducted.

A small site called Las Colmenas is on the plain north of El Retiro. It is located between the base of the El Retiro ridge and the Michol River. The 1964 Rands expedition collected samples at this site as well as at the Cueva del Conducto located partway up the El Retiro ridge. Five kilometers northwest of Las Colmenas is a large Pre-Classic site. It is located on the western part of a long, low ridge known as Cerro Limón on the coastal plain. Unfortunately, no archaeological work has been conducted at the site.

TORTUGUERO AND COMALCALCO

Although Tortuguero and Comalcalco are beyond the Ch'ol region, their relationship with Palenque in the Late Classic period requires a brief comment. Tortuguero is nestled at the base of a ridge overlooking the coastal plain about twenty-four kilometers west of Cerro Limón. Comalcalco, the westernmost Classic Maya site, is another

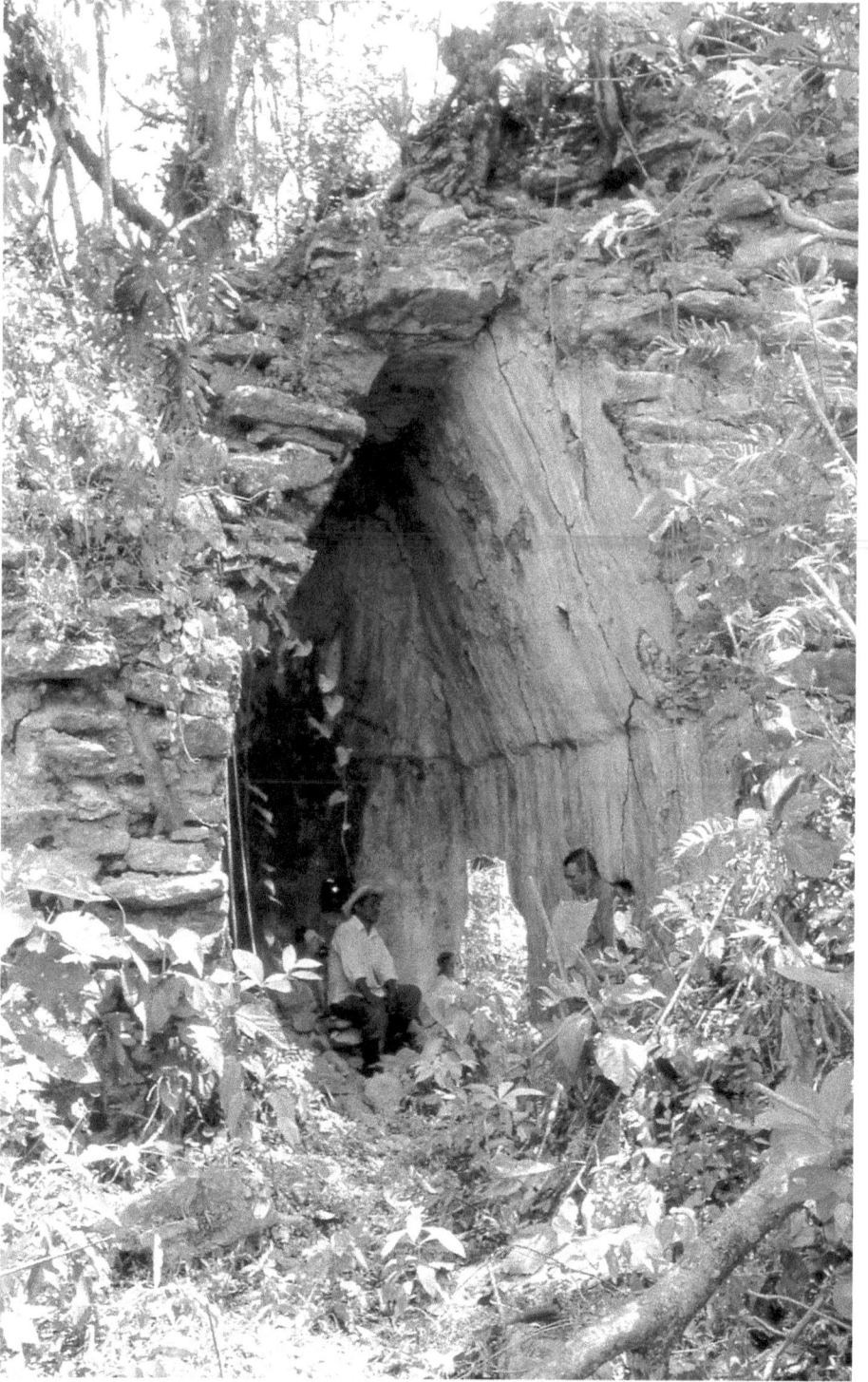

3.4. Ruined building at site of El Retiro. Photo by Karen Bassie-Sweet.

ninety kilometers beyond Tortuguero and just fifteen kilometers from the Gulf coastline itself. The Comalcalco area was an important production zone for high-quality cacao.

Tortuguero shares an emblem glyph with Palenque. What epigraphers refer to as an emblem glyph in the hieroglyphic texts is a title included in many personal names (Berlin 1958). Emblem glyphs are composed of the word *k'ul* "holy," a variable sign, and the word *ajaw* "lord." While the phonetic reading for many of these variable signs has been established, a subject of continuing debate is whether these glyphs are the names for polities, dynasties, or royal houses (Mathews and Justeson 1984; Houston 1986; Mathews 1991; Stuart and Houston 1994; Grube 2000; Martin 2005). The rulers of Palenque are all called lords of Baakal in their inscriptions, as is the Tortuguero ruler Bahlam Ajaw in his inscriptions (Gronemeyer 2006:37; Martin and Grube 2008:165). Whatever the Baakal emblem glyph designated, it is clear that the rulers of Palenque and Tortuguero claimed some specific, common background.

According to the Palenque inscriptions, the ruler K'inich Janaab Pakal married a woman from a site called Ux Te' K'uh in A.D. 626. Their son married a woman who was also from Ux Te' K'uh, as were two prominent secondary lords featured in ritual scenes in Palenque Temple XIX. As discussed by Zender (2004), these lords had priestly functions. The precise location of Ux Te' K'uh has not been ascertained, but the inscription on Tortuguero Monument 6 indicates that Balam Ajaw, who was a contemporary of the Palenque ruler K'inich Janaab Pakal, attacked the site of Ux Te' K'uh in A.D. 644 and A.D. 655 (Grube, Martin, and Zender 2001, pt. 2:19–21).

The story told on Monument 6 also refers to other sites attacked by Bahlam Ajaw, including Comalcalco and a site called Yomoop in A.D. 649. Like Ux Te' K'uh, the site of Yomoop has not been located, although looted monuments referring to Yomoop have appeared on the black market (Mayer 1995:26–28). For example, a close relationship between Ux Te' K'uh and Yomoop is seen on a looted wall panel that illustrates Lady Ok Ayiin of Yomoop. The caption text indicates the carver was a lord from Ux Te' K'uh. We can only speculate on the relationship between Palenque and Tortuguero, but given Palenque's familial and ritual relationships with the Ux Te' K'uh elite, it seems likely that Tortuguero and Palenque were competitors, not partners. All was not quiet on the western front.

The focus of the next two chapters is on the Joljá caves, located midway between Toniná and Palenque. An emblem glyph in the Joljá inscriptions refers to a lord of a site called Sibikte'. This place name occurs in the inscriptions of Toniná and of the Yaleltsemen cave near Bachajón. This suggests that Joljá was within the sphere of the Toniná polity during the Early Classic period.

4

ARCHAEOLOGICAL SURVEY OF THE JOLJÁ CAVES AND NUEVO MÉXICO CAVE

Christina T. Halperin and Jon Spenard

Many Mesoamerican scholars have emphasized the sacred nature of caves, whose potent symbolic meanings developed over a long history of human-cave engagement. Their creation as sacred places often involves mythologizing, consecrating, physically replicating, visiting, marking, and modifying them. Some of these processes leave physical imprints in the archaeological record, which we examine here with the Joljá caves in Chiapas, Mexico. In particular, we explore the archaeological features, artifacts, and spatial layout of the Joljá caves to contextualize the cave paintings found within them that will be discussed in the following chapter. These data derive from an archaeological cave survey by members of the Joljá Cave Project in March 2001 and May 2002.

Few Maya cave studies have had the opportunity to simultaneously examine archaeological evidence of prehistoric use and contemporary ceremonial practices from the same subterranean sites (cf. Andrews 1970; Brady 1991). Thus, because modern practices are undoubtedly informed by ancient ideas, rituals, and features, we are in the rare position to examine the modern ceremonial and spatial use of the caves to help inform our interpretations of the archaeological data. The contemporary practices at the Joljá caves generally support James Brady's (1989) spatial model of prehistoric cave use in which some entrances and light zones of caves were probably used for public ceremonies and rites, while dark zones of caves were probably used for more personal and private rituals. The contemporary data also underscore the significance of water and other natural cave features as integral components in rituals. The focus on water is not surprising, in that, for both the ancient and contemporary Maya, it is physically and conceptually tied to caves in a tripartite landscape complex of water, mountains, and caves (Bloch 1992; Brady and Ashmore 1999). At the same time, the archaeological features of the caves create a focal point and sense of legitimacy in contemporary rituals, such that the past continues to be used as a resource for the present.

Physical Location and Layout of Joljá Caves

The Joljá system is a group of three separate caves located at the headwaters of the Ixteljá River. Joljá "head of the water" is a Ch'ol phrase commonly used to describe the headwaters of a river. Cave 1 has also been referred to in the literature as Jolixteljá, Cueva de Don Juan (not to be confused with the cave by the same name on Don Juan Mountain), Cueva de Joloniel, and Cueva de Ixtelhá (Na Bolom Museum Archives; Thompson 1975; Riese 1981; Graham 1982:185; Meneses López 1986; Bonor Villarejo 1989; Alejos García 1994; A. Stone 1995; Pincemin Deliberos 1999). The caves are located on a white cliff-face approximately 900 m in elevation on the northeastern slope of Tumbalá Mountain, with all three cave mouths facing north. The Ixteljá River gorge and the caves are on property owned by the ejido of Joloniel, whose community center is located 1.45 km to the northeast and approximately 300 m below the cave.

Joljá Cave 1 is the easternmost in the system and is the only one to contain paintings. Cave 2 is located about 40 m to the west and slightly lower on the cliff than Cave 1. This second cave is located at the headwaters of the Ixteljá River, which cascades out of the cave entrance and down the mountainside into a deep gorge with waterfalls. Cave 3 is about 40 m to the northwest of Cave 2 and at about the same elevation as Cave 1. Thus, together they form a trio of caves along the mountain cliff with water emerging from the middle cave.

A fourth cave, called Cueva de Nuevo México by the inhabitants of Joloniel, was visited by the authors in 2002. Its entrance is located adjacent to the Ixteljá River, more than 1 km down the mountain from (and northeast of) both the Joljá system and the village of Joloniel (N17 21.603 W92 18.525). All four caves have evidence of prehistoric use and are also loci of ritual activities for the contemporary Joloniel community.

Chiapas caves have frequently been looted for their pre-Columbian artifacts. It is also commonly believed that they contain buried treasure from the Mexican Revolution. Consequently, cavern floors often have looter's holes and trenches, and the Joljá caves are no exception. In response to a looting attempt at Joljá Cave 1, the Joloniel community received funding from the Instituto Nacional Indigenista in 1998 to install a cinderblock and concrete wall, wire fence, and metal gate across the mouth of the cave to protect the paintings and prevent further destruction. Painted on the side of the concrete wall is "Patrimonio de Sitios Históricos Mayas, Grutas de Joloniel, Comité de Cultura, Feb. 1999." In 2001, the community received additional funding to build a stone walkway from the village to the cave mouth, making it possible for visitors to safely access the cavern. The Joloniel community is attempting to maintain the sacred nature of their cave while still allowing outsiders to view the precious works of art found within.

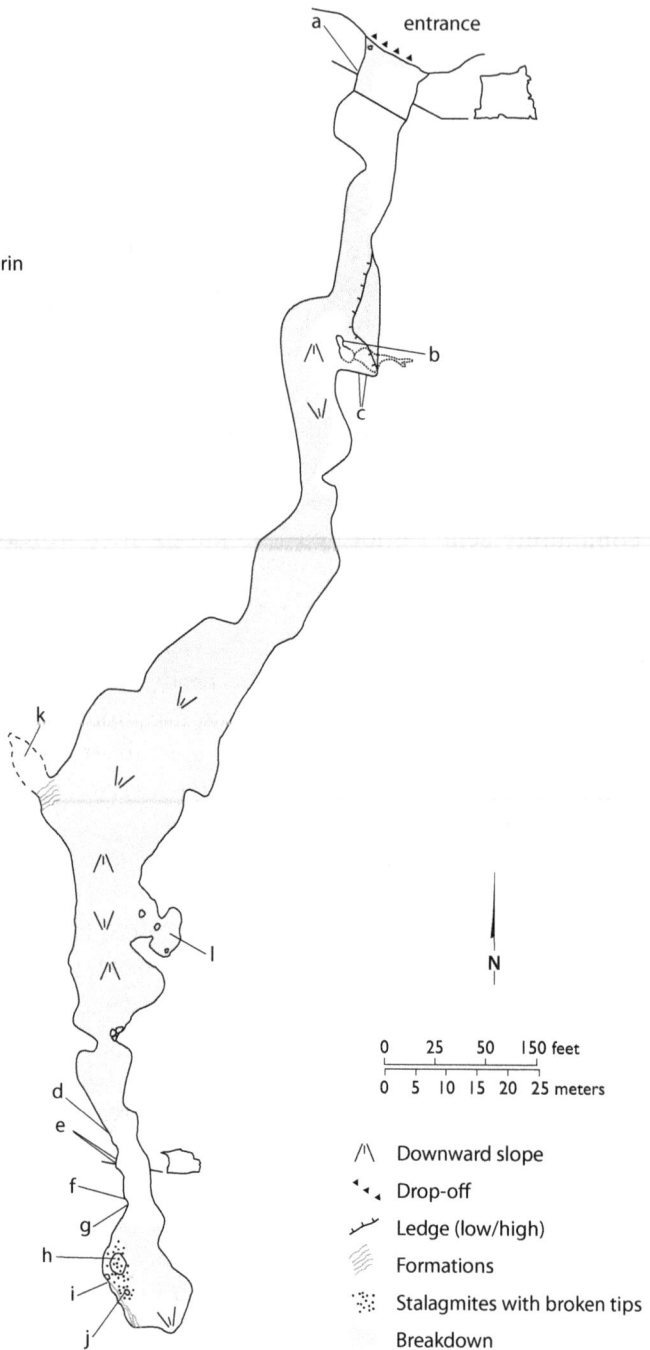

Plan of Joljá Cave 1
Municipio de Tumbalá
Chiapas, Mexico
Survey by
C. Halperin
A. Brizuela Casimir
R. Laughlin
C. Díaz Guzmán
A. Cruz Guzmán
E. Pérez Moreno
copyright Christina Halperin

entrance

a. Group 1
b. Acess to Chamber 1
c. Group 2
d. Group 3
e. Group 4
f. Group 5
g. Group 6
h. Large, oval formation
i. Group 7
j. Stalagmitic column
k. Chamber 2
l. Chamber 3

N

0	25	50	150 feet

0	5	10	15	20	25 meters

/\ Downward slope

◄ Drop-off

Ledge (low/high)

Formations

Stalagmites with broken tips

Breakdown

Map 7. Joljá Cave 1 plan. Map by Bill Nelson, based on a map by Christina Halperin. © 2015, University of Oklahoma Press.

JOLJÁ CAVE 1

The first cavern, Joljá Cave 1, is a single-conduit cave that measures 200 m long, 4–25 m wide, and approximately 1–20 m high (map 7). At the mouth of the cave, the Joloniel community constructed a long concrete bench perpendicular to the concrete wall, to be used for seating during rituals. The Group 1 painting is located across from this bench, and the remaining paintings are located in the interior semidark (twilight) and dark zones of the cave (chapter 5 discusses the paintings in detail).

The cave runs generally north-to-south and contains a spacious rectangular passage, most likely formed as a result of breakdown—collapsed rocks from the cave ceiling or ledges—from an elliptical tube passage (White 1988:73–75). The cave floor is almost completely covered with limestone breakdown, with rocks ranging between 5 cm and 2 m in diameter. The areas with limited breakdown rubble are where the prehistoric paintings are located. These areas may have been cleared intentionally or unintentionally (through repeated use of the space) for rituals in the past or present.

The Group 2 paintings are located on a north-facing wall about 50 m from the cave mouth (see map 7). The angle of the northern cave opening allows rays of sunshine to highlight the paintings, which creates an impressive framing device during certain parts of the day. Below these paintings is a passageway that descends to a small, dark chamber, designated as Chamber 1, where contemporary cave petitions take place (map 8). One meter to the east of the passageway opening to Chamber 1 is a one-foot-wide shaft that looks down into the chamber. Despite this small portal, and the descending passageway, a light source is required to enter the chamber. The bottom of the chamber floor is less than 2 m square, but the sloping sides of the chamber provide additional room for some participants to stand or sit during ceremonies. The other spectators remain outside, above the chamber. Three wooden crosses are permanently housed in the chamber and serve as central features for the rituals conducted there (fig. 4.1).

Two other small chambers, Chambers 2 and 3, are encountered farther inside Cave 1 but are not utilized in contemporary ceremonies. Chamber 2 is located 125 m from the entrance along the western cave wall. Smooth cave formations slope down at an azimuth of 320 degrees into a small, narrow chamber measuring approximately 8 × 4 m. The floor is devoid of breakdown material except for small rocks found at the chamber's constricted terminus. Chamber 3 is a small 4 × 6 m room located south of Chamber 2 just past the dark zone transition in the cave, where only a glimmer of light is present. One hundred and sixty-five meters into the cave, the passageway constricts to an opening 1 m high and 4 m wide. After this constricted zone, the passageway becomes larger again (but not as large as the first 165 m of passage) for the last 35 m of the cave. This dark inner zone contains the remaining groups of paintings along its western cave wall (Groups 3–7).

The wall where the Group 3 through Group 6 paintings are located is dry, but the end of the passageway is wet. The only active cave formations, such as stalagmites, found

4.1. Joljá Cave 1, front chamber with three ritual crosses. Photo by Karen Bassie-Sweet.

Map 8. Joljá Cave 1. Plan of Chamber 1. Map by Bill Nelson, based on a map by Christina Halperin. © 2015, University of Oklahoma Press.

in the cave are located here. The ceiling of this area is covered with hundreds of small soda-straw formations, and the south and west walls are covered in flowstone formations. On the floor is a large, oval flowstone formation that looks like a miniature hill (fig. 4.2). On and around this formation are two columns and about fifty small stalagmites measuring approximately 5–15 cm in height and less than 10 cm in width. The first column is found close to the wall, adjacent to Group 7. A small alcove containing a pool of water and broken speleothems (stalagmites, stalactites, or any other cave formation) is located along the southwest wall. Adjacent to the alcove is the second and largest flowstone column, measuring about 0.8 m in diameter. This column and the flowstone areas at the end of the passageway are the focus of individual water petitions during the Day of the Holy Cross ceremony. For example, during the ceremony in 2001, Bassie-Sweet noticed that lighted candles were placed in this area even though group gatherings were restricted to other parts of the cave. Old boxes of candles and soot marks on the formations are further evidence of these activities (see chapter 8 for a complete description of the ceremony).

4.2. Joljá Cave 1, back chamber, wet area with flowstone mound on floor. Photo by Karen Bassie-Sweet.

JOLJÁ CAVE 2

The entrance to Joljá Cave 2 is approximately 7 × 7 m (map 9). It is filled with large breakdown boulders, under which a river flows until it cascades over the cliff face at the edge of the cave mouth. The velocity and amount of water flowing out of the cave mouth serves as a gauge for rainfall in the immediate area. During the rainy season, water gushes out with force, but during the dry season, levels are significantly less. However, even during droughts, the cave water continues to flow. The entrance area serves as one of the gathering places for villagers to petition, pray, and burn candles during the Day of the Holy Cross, when the Joloniel community petitions the cave spirit Don Juan to release the rain for the coming season. Despite Cave 2's uneven terrain, men, women, and children find places to situate themselves on the boulders and ledges to watch the *tatuch,* the ritual specialist, and listen to the musicians.

To the east of this breakdown area is a side passage 15–20 m long that parallels the main tunnel. This parallel passage terminates at an elevated ledge overlooking the main corridor below. A waterfall 15 m high and 10 m wide is located at the southern end of the breakdown area. The water emerges from a crevice in the ceiling and cascades down onto a pile of breakdown rocks below. Some of these rocks appear to have been placed in a semicircular pattern to form a pool of water at the base of the waterfall. A tatuch collects a container of water from this pool on the Day of the

Entrance

Waterfall

X   Contemporary ritual deposits

▼ ▼   Drop off

←   Water and direction of water flow

ᴧ   Ledge (low/high)

Waterfall

N

0 10 20 30 feet

0   5   10 meters

Survey by C. Halperin, A. Brizuela Casimir,
and J. Spenard

River continues

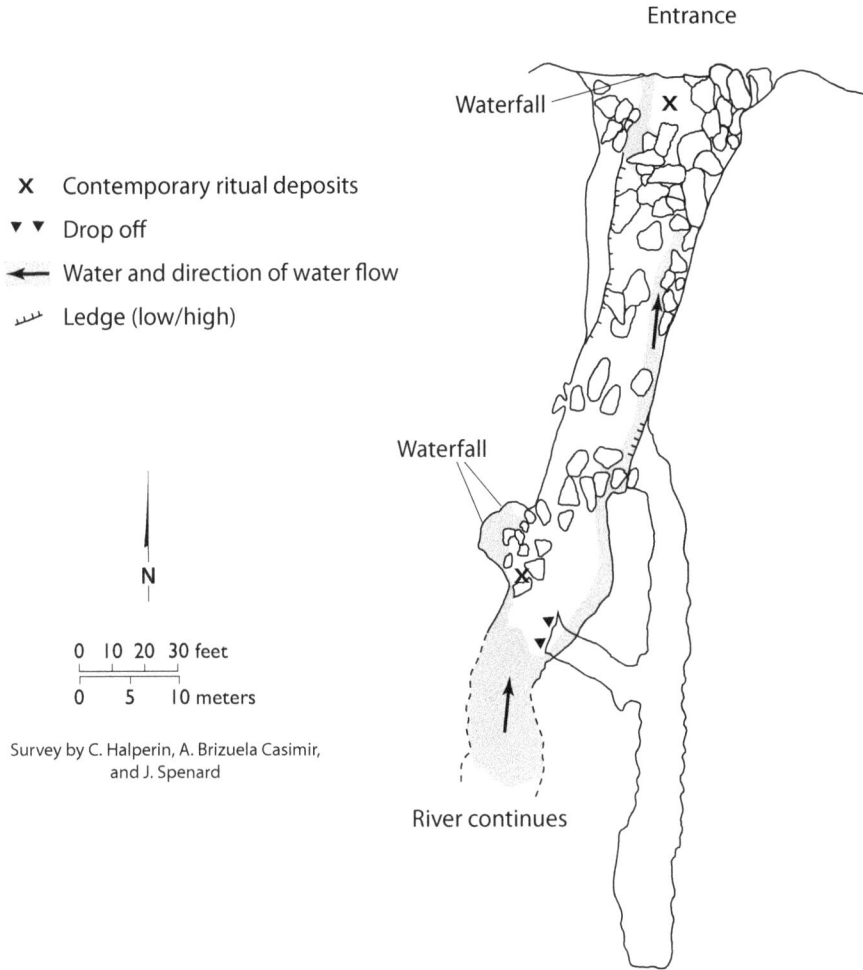

Map 9. Joljá Cave 2 plan. Map by Bill Nelson, based on a map by Christina Halperin. © 2015, University of Oklahoma Press.

Holy Cross and takes it into Joljá Cave 1 for ritual use. Candle remnants were found on these rocks during the 2002 survey.

Beyond the waterfall, the main cave passage continues southward. Because this area lacks breakdown, one is forced to enter the river, which is approximately 1–3 m high during the dry season, to continue into the cave. The cave forks approximately 100 m from the entrance. Both passages are submerged in water for at least 100 additional meters. We suspect that the main cave passage continues even farther as a large interior river without any ledges or dry areas.

Joljá Cave 3

The entrance to Joljá Cave 3 measures 19.6 m wide and 6.8 m high (map 10). The wide main cave passage has high, cathedral-like ceilings. The ground consists of an

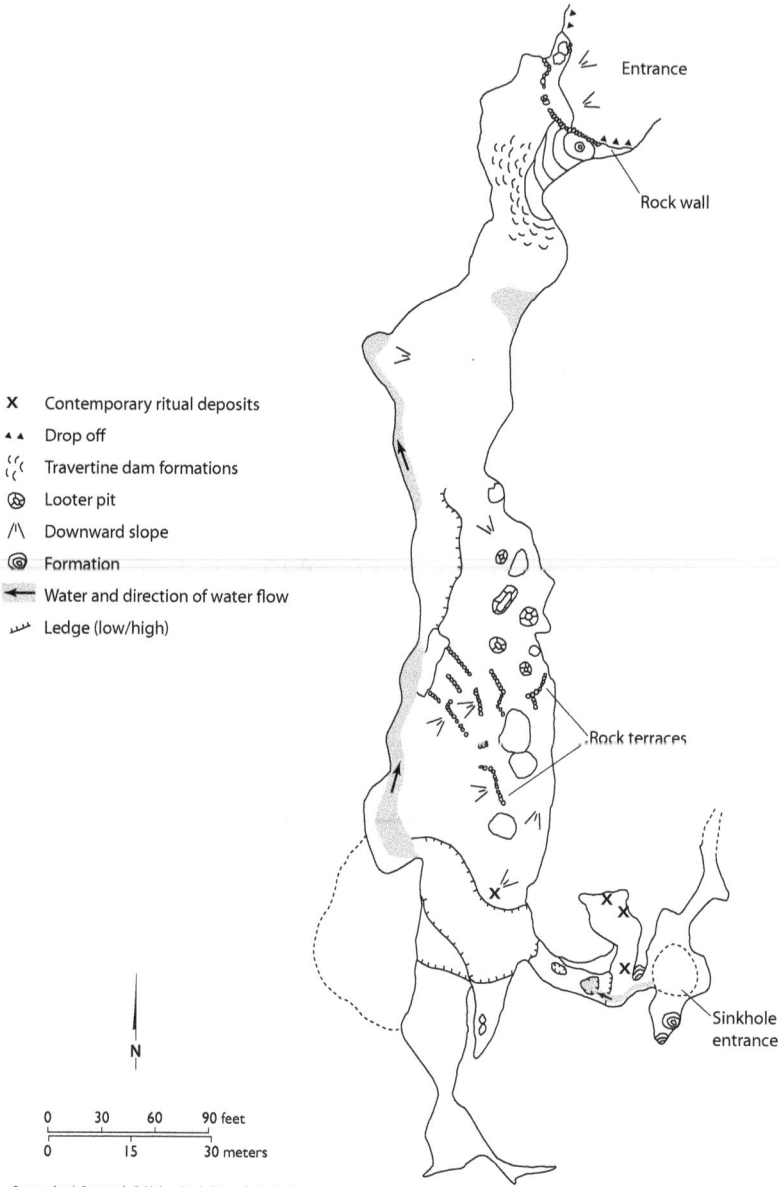

Entrance

Rock wall

| X | Contemporary ritual deposits |
| ▲ ▲ | Drop off |
| Travertine dam formations |
| Looter pit |
| /!\ | Downward slope |
| Formation |
| Water and direction of water flow |
| Ledge (low/high) |

Rock terraces

Sinkhole entrance

N

```
0    30   60   90 feet
0      15      30 meters
```

Survey by J. Spenard, C. Halperin, A. Brizuela Casimir,
N. Montejo Lopez, N. Pérez Moreno, and M. Angel Pérez

Map 10. Joljá Cave 3 plan. Map by Bill Nelson, based on a map by Christina Halperin. © 2015, University of Oklahoma Press.

alluvium of silty sand, scattered intermittently with large, boulder-sized limestone breakdown. In general, the cave slopes up and then down again, like a small interior hill, before reaching the back passage.

This cave has the largest dry surface area of the three caves in the system, even though it contains water seepage and a seasonally active interior stream. Water drips down the cliff face above the cave mouth, and small stalactites hang from the ceiling just inside the cave. A large flowstone column is situated along a southwest-facing slope at the entrance and has produced hundreds of small travertine dams that head down into the cave. The end of the Cave 3 passageway has a sinkhole opening in its roof approximately 30 m above the floor of the cave. During the rainy season, water enters the cave through the sinkhole opening and fills the streambed that runs through the cave and terminates at a pool close to the main entrance. The water system of this cave was dry during our two field seasons with the exception of the sinkhole area and the pool of water by the entrance.

The ceremony of the Day of the Holy Cross in Joljá Cave 3 occurs principally in the main passage on an elevated bank of the stream. Here the tatuch lights candles, conducts prayers, and makes offerings on behalf of the other community members, who gather around. Individuals make petitions in the back passage by the sinkhole entrance, similar to those in the inner alcove of Joljá Cave 1. In these back zones, candles are set into the ground or on top of stalagmites. Water from the sinkhole area is used to wash an image of the Virgin Mary.

NUEVO MÉXICO CAVE

Nuevo México Cave, a cave located near the Joljá cave system, is also visited by members of Joloniel and other nearby communities for ritual purposes. It has a small entrance, 5.78 m wide by 3.8 m high. The interior of the cave is split into two sections: a south branch and southwest branch. The south branch consists of a corridor with two ledges flanking its east and west sides. We followed the passage for 65 m, but a large pool of bat guano prevented further exploration even though the cave continued on. Bat guano may harbor the deadly fungus *Histoplasma capsulatum*. The western ledge contains numerous flowstone formations, most notably, two large stalagmites found about 20 m into the cave. The eastern ledge has fewer flowstone formations, and it contains numerous looter's pits. Small, non-diagnostic ceramic sherds were found scattered in and around the pits, indicating this area was used in antiquity. Evidence for contemporary cave use includes glass liquor bottles discarded on the flowstone formations at the northwest side of the entrance. In addition, at the base of the two large stalagmites on the western ledge were the remnants of burned candles. It was here that our guide placed two candles as votive offerings to the cave spirits for our safe entry and return.

The southwest branch is difficult to access due to the constriction for the first 8–10 m of the passage, which requires one to enter horizontally. Beyond the constricted area, the passage opens up to allow walking upright. This southwest branch of the cave travels underneath the Ixteljá River and continues for more than 100 m. No prehistoric or contemporary material remains were found here.

ARCHAEOLOGICAL REMAINS AND MODIFICATIONS

Many of the prehistoric remains and modifications of the Joljá caves correspond to Pre-Classic and Classic period cave practices recorded elsewhere in the Maya area. These include the removal of speleothems for use outside the cave, the construction of crude architectural features, and the discarding of goods used during cave visits and rituals. The painted inscriptions indicate that the caves were in use by the Early Classic period (Thompson 1975:xxxvi; A. Stone 1995:88–90; see chapter 5).

Prehistoric and Contemporary Speleothem Removal

The caves show indications of the extraction of stalactites, stalagmites, and other natural formations. Evidence of stalagmite removal was found in the back of Joljá Cave 1 where the paintings in Groups 3 through 7 are located. The majority of the stalagmites were sawed off or intentionally cracked, and both columns had broken speleothems at their bases. Many of the cuts on the stalagmites exhibit signs of regrowth, suggesting their modification took place in antiquity. In addition, at least one speleothem was modified into an idol and placed alongside several greenstone ax blades on one of the rubble piles in Joljá Cave 1, as a photograph by Alejos García (1994: photo 4) documents. This carved speleothem was missing by the time of our 2001 and 2002 visits.

The practice of breaking off and removing speleothems has been well documented in pre-Columbian times throughout the Maya area (Brady, Ware, et al. 1997; Brady, Cobb, et al. 2005; Lorenzen 1999:102; Rissolo 2001:357; McAnany et al. 2003:77; Peterson et al. 2005; Ishihara 2007:72–75; Spenard 2011; Spenard 2013). Broken speleothems are found on altars, in crude architectural constructions, and in burials, all within cave settings. Archaeologists have also noted the prehistoric practice of removing speleothems from caves for use in civic-ceremonial sites and settlements. For example, a large stalactite was used as a monument at the Classic period site of Yaxchilan (Maler 1901–1903, 2:159). Similar to their placement in caves, they are found on Classic and Postclassic shrines (Lorenzen 1999:102; McAnany et al. 2003:77), as building materials for shrines and other types of ceremonial structures, and in burials (Peterson et al. 2005:236–37). For example, one was found along with a spondylus shell fragment, and an infant cranium in a lip-to-lip centerline vessel cache in Structure 10 at Pacbitun, Belize (Weber and Powis 2013:160–61). Maya ethnographic research has documented the utilization of these natural cave formations on contemporary household altars, a finding that attests to the continuation of these practices into the present (Deal 1988:74; Brady, Cobb, et al. 2005:219).

In antiquity, speleothems were frequently carved into idols like the one photographed by Alejos García from Joljá Cave 1 (Pendergast 1970; Navarrete and Martínez 1977; Brady, Ware, et al. 1997:733; Brady 1999; Peterson et al. 2005:238–39:fig. 12.8). Regardless of whether speleothems were carved or not, however, ethnographic evidence suggests that the Maya often perceive them as animate and as embodying important natural forces such as deities, male and female anatomical parts, fertility, the earth, and water (Bassie-Sweet 1991; Garza et al. 2001; Brady, Cobb, et al. 2005). For example, one of the Joloniel villagers showed Bassie-Sweet (in 2001) a broken speleothem he had at his house and which he referred to as an *ídolo,* or idol, even though it had no visible carvings or modification. As mentioned in chapter 2, a large stalagmite is said to represent the Black Christ in a cave above the town of Tila (Navarrete 2000; Josserand and Hopkins 2007). Another large stalagmite from Río Frío Cave E, Belize, was the focus of Classic period ritual deposits and copal burning and may represent a prehistoric analog to the Tila stalagmite (Pendergast 1970). A cluster of broken stalagmites was likely thought of as the rain god, and was used for rain rituals from the Protoclassic through Terminal Classic periods in Actun Lak cave, Belize (Spenard 2014). Thus, the back chamber of Joljá Cave 1, the only wet part of this otherwise dry cave, held and continues to hold significant spiritual meaning, some of which has been tapped by removing parts of the cave for use elsewhere.

Cave Architecture

Pre-Columbian architecture has been documented at Joljá Cave 3 and Nuevo México Cave. Crude stone walls are located at the entrances of both caves. At Joljá Cave 3, the wall appears to have once stretched across the entire 19.6 m–wide entrance, although parts of it have since collapsed (map 11). The wall is composed of uncut limestone rocks with no visible mortar, with some spaces between the stacked rocks. At present, the wall measures approximately 1 m in height. Based on the low number of collapsed rocks at the base of the wall, it is unlikely that it was much taller than its current height. In fact, flowstone formations coat the side of some of the rocks, binding them together and attesting not only to the wall's low height, but also to the antiquity of the wall's construction.

The wall in Nuevo México also once spanned the entire entrance of the cave, although it is invisible from the outside because it is heavily covered by haphazardly placed limestone rocks. Nonetheless, at least six courses of limestone rock construction measuring 1.3 m in height are visible when viewed from the inside of the cave. In some areas, the wall construction fills the entrance from floor to ceiling. Based on the large number of collapsed rocks, it is possible that the entrance was once completely closed off.

Archaeologists frequently encounter crude walls that restrict cave entrances, chambers, and alcoves. Mexican examples can be found at Balankanché, Yucatán (Andrews 1970); Loltún Cave, Yucatán (Thompson 1897); and several caves in the municipio of Oxkutzcab, Yucatán (Bonor Villarejo and Sánchez y Pinto 1991). Guatemalan examples of walls can be found at Naj Tunich (Brady 1989:354); Cueva de las Pinturas, Petén (Brady, Ware, et al. 1997); various caves in northern Alta Verapaz and southern Petén (Carot 1989; Spenard 2006; Woodfill 2007); Balam Na Cave 4 (Garza et al. 2001); and Aguateca (Guerra Ruíz 2006; Ishihara 2007:70–72). Belizean examples of walls can be found at Las Cuevas or Awe Cave (Digby 1958), Flour Camp or

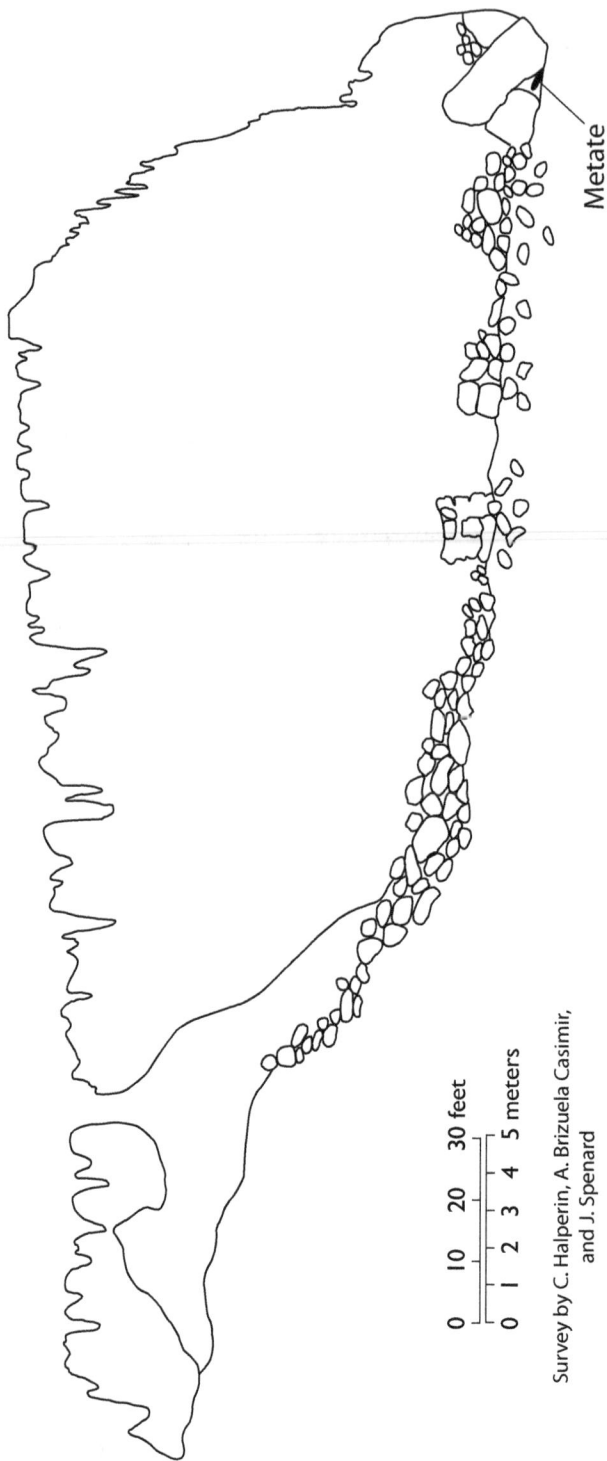

Metate

0   10   20   30 feet

0 I 2 3 4 5 meters

Survey by C. Halperin, A. Brizuela Casimir,
and J. Spenard

Map 11. Joljá Cave 3 profile of entrance and crude wall. Map by Bill Nelson, based on a map by Christina Halperin. © 2015, University of Oklahoma Press.

Black Rock Cave (Halperin, personal observation 2000), several caves in the Middle Sibun Valley (Kenward 2005), Eduardo Quiroz Cave (Pendergast 1971), Actun Balam (Pendergast 1969), Actun Dzonot (Spenard 2011), and Actun Lak (Spenard 2014). Numerous other caves in Mexico, Guatemala, and Belize contain similar walls (Guerra Ruiz 2006). The periods of utilization of many of these caves range from the Middle Pre-Classic through Postclassic periods.

A number of functions have been ascribed to these wall features. One of our Ch'ol guides informed us that the wall at Joljá Cave 3 is currently used by the Maya to trap *tepezcuintle* (Eulalio Pérez Moreno, personal communication 2001). Tepez-cuintle or agouti (*jalaw* or *te'lal* in Ch'ol) are small rodents that are prized for their meat. The Q'eqchi' Maya residents of La Caoba, Guatemala, offered the same reason to Spenard during his field work there in 2002, when they were queried about the large number of walls noted in the caves. In missionary Wilbur Aulie's correspondence with Gertrude Duby Blom, he described such walls a few meters inside the mouth of Cave 1, and he noted that they were used to trap tepezcuintle (Na Bolom Museum Archives). The use of crude cave walls for hunting is particularly interesting when considering that many Ch'ol and Tzotzil myths recount a story of a deity who lives in a cave with his corrals of animals, money, and other riches (Cruz Guzmán, Josserand, and Hopkins 1980; Vogt 1969, 1976; see chapter 8).

Other proposed functions for prehistorically constructed walls are suggested by their archaeological form and context. For example, some Late Pre-Classic and Early Classic period cave walls were constructed at alcove entrances to seal the burials placed inside, much like tombs (Brady 1989:353–55; Garza et al. 2001). Brady and Colas (2001:203, 348, 350) suggested that the Classic period peoples blocked off cave entrances and passages to ritually terminate the caves. They argue that the closing of caves and cave passages at the site of Dos Pilas marked a violent termination of these subterranean zones at the end of the Late Classic period, when the epigraphic record documents warfare at the site. The blocking off of cave entrances may have coincided with the ritual burning of the cave and the dismantling of nearby palace architecture. The Terminal Classic period Maya constructed a large earthen terrace outside of Actun Lak cave that spanned the entire entrance (Spenard 2014). The platform connected to a roughly built staircase that led downhill to another cavern. Collectively, the modifications transformed the two caves and the connecting hillside into a setting for a large-scale royal rain ritual (Spenard 2014).

The construction of architecture may also serve as a form of spatial appropria-tion by a community or a particular social group. We see this phenomenon most explicitly with the recent assembly of a concrete wall and metal gate at the entrance of Joljá Cave 1 by the community of Joloniel to protect their cave from vandals and unauthorized visitors. This construction indicates that access to the cave is a source of contention among differing interest groups. Thus, some prehistoric cave walls may have served to appropriate the landscape, delineate ritual space, and control movement.

Crude stone terraces are another type of architectural modification present at Joljá Cave 3. The five terraces are in the large open area of the cave that still maintains some light (the "twilight zone"). They form five different tiers of elevation and run perpendicular to a downward slope in the cave floor. They are crudely built up of uncut rocks of various sizes, and their construction involved little labor: they range from one to five stone courses per terrace. We suspect that, like the wall at the entrance, they were built in antiquity. Terraces are often used outdoors for creating level surfaces to plant crops, a function unlikely for the Joljá cave terraces because the ground surface has little organic content, and little light is available. The lower part of the terraced area in Cave 3 is near the bank of the streambed used as a gathering spot during Day of the Holy Cross ceremonies. The terraced slope may have helped form a stage for larger-scale communal ceremonies during pre-Columbian times. There is now mounting evidence that some caves indeed hosted such ceremonies during the Classic period (Brady 1989:405–407; Prufer 2002; Halperin 2005; Pugh 2005). Similar cave terraces in large open areas have been noted by the Western Belize Regional Cave Project at Actun Chapat (Ferguson 2001), in Actun Naj Che, both in western Belize (Spenard 2013, 2014), in the Candelaria caves in Alta Verapaz, Guatemala (Woodfill 2007), and at the entrances of rockshelters and caves in the Yalahau Region, Quintana Roo, Mexico (Rissolo 2001, 2005).

Prehistoric cave architecture is almost always crude in the materials and techniques employed. It contrasts with the formal architectural grammar of prehistoric settlement sites, which often incorporate cut stones and even linear stone placements (Seler 1901; cf. Brady 1989; Rissolo 2005; Guerra Ruiz 2006; Ishihara 2007). The choice to use crude materials and techniques, however, is not necessarily indicative of a lack of labor, skill, or resources on the part of the builders. For example, the chasm called the Grieta Principal at Aguateca was used by the site's Classic period elite inhabitants, who could have mobilized skilled labor to build architecture similar to the civic-ceremonial and settlement architecture just meters away. Instead, the walls within the Grieta were relatively crude and modest (Ishihara 2007). This contrast is also apparent among the Joljá caves, in that formal architectural constructions were not built at the cave despite the cave's apparent role in hosting noble peoples (see chapter 5). Prehistoric cave constructions thus appear to have conformed to a general cave aesthetic that was meant to preserve the wild, undomesticated quality of the underworld rather than giving them the attributes of the built environment in human settlements (A. Stone 1992; Taube 2003; Spenard 2014).

Artifacts and Ecofacts

Our exploration of the Joljá and Nuevo México caves involved only their documentation and the identification of their surface cultural features. Archaeological excavations were not undertaken, and few artifacts were found during our surveys in any of the caves. Nonetheless, the paucity of artifacts may underrepresent the intensity of prehistoric utilization, as artifacts are known to be buried by natural taphonomic processes, and some have been removed (Brady and Scott 1997:154–55). For example, archaeologist Carlos Navarrete removed several ceramic censers, figurines, and pottery samples from Joljá Cave 1 in the 1970s to be analyzed (Navarrete, personal communication with Bassie-Sweet 2002), and, as mentioned earlier, photographs taken of the cave in 1984 document the presence of a speleothem carved in the shape of an idol and several greenstone ax blades that are no longer present (Alejos García 1994, photo 4).

Artifacts and ecofacts were scattered throughout Cave 1. The floor of the cave entrance contained hundreds of freshwater snail shells (*Pachychilus* sp.), known locally as *puy*. These shells were also located throughout the strata of a small, 63 cm–deep looter's pit at the northwestern corner of the cave entrance, which suggests that they were deposited there in antiquity, and that buried artifacts are present. Many of the shells had been spire-lopped (modified at their distal end), presumably to extract the snails from their shells (see, e.g., Healy et al. 1990). The appearance of *Pachychilus* shells in Maya caves, particularly at cave entrances, is not uncommon during the Classic period and may represent offerings to earth spirits and deities (Halperin, Garza, Prufer, and Brady 2003). Some small ceramic sherds were also found at 23–27 cm of depth within the wall of the looter's pit.

Scatterings of ceramic sherds were found in a number of locations in Joljá Cave 1, but the largest concentration was in the back dirt of a looter's pit just outside Chamber 3. In his description of the cave, Aulie mentioned a stone block at the back of the cave. We found a limestone block in the shape of a cylinder (approximately 31 cm in diameter, 35 cm in height) placed alongside a broken speleothem near the Group 3 painting, which is likely the object Aulie mentioned. The cylinder's rounded shape denoted human workmanship. Both the top and bottom edges had signs of modification, and the side contained a 6 cm–diameter hole that was pecked into the shape of a small cone. The exposed, rounded side also contained inscribed alphabetic lettering such as a *V* and an *A*. If this object was modified and used during pre-Columbian times, it appears to have been subsequently modified in more modern times, as indicated by the inscribed alphabetic lettering.

Artifacts found on the surface of Joljá caves 2 and 3 and Nuevo México Cave were concentrated near their entrances. Artifacts included ceramic sherds in Joljá Cave 2 and ceramic sherds, an almost complete *metate* (mortar or grinding stone), and a fragment of an obsidian blade fragment in Joljá Cave 3. The metate was found next to the wall feature. One of our Ch'ol Maya guides reported finding two limestone metates approximately 15 m outside the entrance of Joljá Cave 1. The guide showed us the metates, one of which was complete with a restricted basin, the other a broken half of a metate with an unrestricted basin. Both were well-worn, with striations running lengthwise. While metates and other ground-stone artifacts are commonly found in Maya caves (Andrews 1970; Peterson 2006:171–73; Ishihara 2007:216–18), it is unclear whether their presence at the entrances to Joljá caves 1 and 3 follows a specific pattern of ritual deposition.

Conclusions

The Joljá caves and probably other caverns in the region, such as Nuevo México, were part of an ancient network of sacred landscape features whose prehistoric use included not only the painting of walls in Joljá Cave 1, but the construction of crude architectural features, the removal of speleothems, and the deposition of offerings or ritual refuse. The physical location of the caves on Tumbalá Mountain and at the headwaters of the Ixteljá River (Cave 2) or alongside it (Caves 1 and 3) suggests that the Joljá caves were conceived of as part of a tripartite landscape complex of caves, mountains, and water. This idea is further reinforced through the contemporary and ancient ritual use of water features in caves, including pools, waterfalls, and water-dripping speleothems. The cave-mountain-water complex is tied to creation and the supernatural world (Bloch 1992; A. Stone 1995; Bassie-Sweet 1996, 2008; Brady and Ashmore 1999). Mountains are accessed through caves, and all water that flows within is believed to be from the supernatural realm. The complex thus acts as a direct portal to the supernatural realm and the deities that reside there.

Contemporary practices at the Joljá caves appear to support prehistoric spatial models of cave use. For example, Brady (1989:402–405) has suggested that large, spacious cave entrances may have been used publicly by a wide range of prehistoric people, as they are analogous to public plazas in ceremonial sites. Alternatively, dark interior areas of caves were likely loci for ancient private rituals, as they are analogous to restricted areas of settlement sites, such as the interior spaces of temples. Similarly, a dichotomy of public and private rituals is apparent at the Joljá caves during the Day of the Holy Cross ceremony. At Joljá Cave 1, public ceremonial activities are focused at the entrance and in the open, twilight zone of the cave around Chamber 1, where the Group 2 paintings are located. Individual petitions to the cave deity, however, are made in the less accessible, dark back chamber of the cave. This dichotomy may be echoed prehistorically, in that the Group 2 paintings are primarily iconographic and were presumably "readable" by most audiences. On the other hand, the hieroglyphic writing in Groups 3–7, which could only have been fully read by a smaller section of the populace (i.e., literate, elite individuals), is located in the dark back chamber of the cave. This contemporary dichotomy of space is repeated at Joljá Cave 3, in that the large, open, twilight area of the cave serves as a focal point for public ceremonial activities, while individual petitions are made in a more spatially restrictive zone farther into the cave.

The contemporary practices also underscore the significance of water and other natural cave features as integral components in the production of rituals. These include the placement of candles around water-seeping cave formations, and at Joljá Cave 2, the ritual acquisition of water from a large pool at the base of an interior waterfall. The focus of contemporary rituals on specific water/cave features may be of considerable antiquity and, thus, have archaeological implications. In relation to Joljá Cave 1, the water-related features of the back of the cave—the only zone of the cave where speleothems are found—were undoubtedly focal points for the hieroglyph cave texts. Likewise, Andrews's (1970) research at Balankanché Cave in Yucatán, Mexico, documents the clustering of prehistoric artifacts plus the focus of modern-day ritual activity on bodies of water and large stalagmite formations inside the cave. In addition, Moyes's study of artifacts at Actun Tunichil Muknal in Belize using a geographic information system (GIS) demonstrates that the spatial proximity of artifacts with cave features such as pools of water and flowstone formations was statistically relevant and thus inferred to be socially meaningful (Moyes 2001a).

At the same time, the prehistoric Joljá cave features, the paintings in particular, may also create a focal point and lend a sense of legitimacy to contemporary rituals, such that the past continues to be used as a resource for the present. For example, the paintings in Joljá Cave 1 appear to dictate the spatial layout of present-day rituals conducted in the cave. The paintings, as markers of past ritual activities, may serve as a guide or memory device for successive rituals by linking the past with the present. The invocation of the past through material cues is well documented among many contemporary ritual practitioners, including the Lacandón Maya, who occasionally place their god pots on ancient mounds and ruins (McGee 1998). Similarly, highland Maya shamans and midwives collect prehistoric artifacts as part of their divining tools and personal *sacra* (Brown 2000). Another example is seen in the actions of Q'eqchi' Maya ceremonial practitioners who collect ancient jar sherds from the Cueva de las Tinajas rockshelter in Petén, Guatemala, on which they burn copal and candles during rituals known as *mayejac* (Spenard 2006). Thus, while we gain greater understanding of the prehistoric use of caves through the study of contemporary cave rituals, these modern ceremonies are simultaneously authenticated, renewed, and empowered by the prehistoric sanctification of such cavernous places.

5

THE PAINTINGS OF
JOLJÁ CAVE 1

Karen Bassie-Sweet, Marc Zender, Jorge Pérez de Lara, and Stanley Guenter

It is likely that the local Ch'ol population has always known about the paintings in the Joljá caves, given the long history of rituals there. Wilbur Aulie, a Protestant missionary in the 1950s, was the first outsider to see these works of art (Na Bolom Museum Archives; Edward Aulie and Lucas Arcos Tórrez, personal communication). While conducting his missionary work at the Joloniel ejido in the late 1950s, Aulie was taken to the cave by community members and shown the images. Recognizing the importance of the paintings to Maya cultural history, Aulie informed a number of civil authorities and scholars and requested that something be done to protect them. Professor Manuel Tipá Mota, president of Tumbalá and the director of schools at the time, examined Caves 1 and 2 and reported that only Cave 1 contained paintings. He apparently did not visit Cave 3, which contains no paintings.

The archaeologist Frans Blom and his wife, photographer Gertrude "Trudy" Duby Blom, who resided in San Cristóbal, were also among those whom Aulie contacted, and Trudy eventually decided to visit the cave and photograph the paintings. On April 26, 1961, Trudy, Wilbur Aulie, his young son Edward Aulie, and Lucas Arcos Tórrez (a Ch'ol resident of Tumbalá) journeyed on horseback from Tumbalá to Joljá. They followed the Tumbalá–Salto de Agua trail that passed just above the caves on the side of Tumbalá Mountain. Near the cave, they were joined by a dozen members of the Joloniel ejido. The expedition group spent several hours in the cave, during which time Trudy photographed Groups 2, 3, 4, 5, and 6 using large-format black-and-white film. Lucas Arcos paced off the cave to measure it, and Wilbur Aulie wrote a description (Na Bolom Museum Archives). Aulie noted evidence of recent digging at the mouth of the cave.

Frans Blom suggested that the inscription in Group 5 likely referred to the Period Ending 9.0.0.0.0 8 Ajaw 13 K'eh. In May of 1961, Frans sent copies of Trudy's photographs to Eric Thompson, who replied with comments about the paintings. He noted the early style of the glyphs and expressed regret that they could not be included in the new printing of his book on Maya hieroglyphs because it was already in press. Thompson eventually published examples from Group 2 and Group 5 in his introduction to Mercer's *Hill-Caves of Yucatan* (Thompson 1975). He suggested a date of A.D. 300 for the paintings, which in light of recent discoveries is probably too early.

Carlos Navarrete, Eduardo Martínez, and Adolfo Muñoz made a brief reconnaissance of Joljá Cave 1 during a survey of the region in 1971 (Navarrete, personal communication 2002). They created a preliminary map, photographed the paintings, and took several ceramic incensarios and figurines as well as pottery sherds from the cave. In a newspaper article, Navarrete described the cave and noted that several of the inscriptions had been damaged (*Excelsior* [Mexico City], April 8, 1974). More recently, Navarrete published a color picture of Group 2 Painting 2 (Navarrete 2000). Aulie mentioned the cave paintings and a stone altar in his dissertation (1979) and noted that the residents of Joloniel frequented the cave in order to speak to the spirits. Berthold Riese made drawings based on Blom's photographs and published them in a short *Mexicon* article (Riese 1981). The drawings included examples from Groups 2 through 6. José Alejos García visited Joljá in 1984 while conducting an ethnographic study of the Joloniel area. His black and white photographs include examples from Groups 2, 4, 5, and 6 (Alejos García 1994). A book on the history of Tumbalá, which includes stories about Joljá, also includes a color photograph of Group 2 Painting 2 (Miguel Meneses López 1986).

Andrea Stone (1987, 1989, 1995) reproduced three of Blom's photographs of Group 2. She also presented her own drawings of Groups 2, 4, 5, and 6 based on Blom's photographs and Riese's drawings. She discussed the Early Classic style of the paintings and correctly noted that the different groups were not contemporary with each other. Joljá is also mentioned in three other general surveys on Maya caves and rock art (Bonor Villarejo 1989:177; Pincemin Deliberos 1999:99–102; Mayer 2004–2005).

In 1998, Walter "Chip" Morris, at the time the director of the Na Bolom Museum, was awarded a National Geographic Society grant to organize the museum's photographic archives. As part of that process, the archivist Fabiola Sánchez; her husband, Ian Hollingworth; and anthropologist Alejandro Sheseña traveled to Joloniel to assess the condition of the paintings. They also made a preliminary map of the main passageway of Cave 1 and an audio recording of a cave petition made on their behalf by the Tumbalá tatuch Miguel Arcos Méndez (Arcos Méndez 2001). Sheseña (2002, 2004a, 2004b) has also published interpretations of the Joljá paintings.

In January 2000, Karen Bassie-Sweet, Alfonso Morales, and Julie Miller visited Joljá while touring the region. The Joljá Cave Project was initiated in the spring of 2000 in order to record the Joljá paintings and to recover as much information as possible regarding the nature of the pre-Columbian and contemporary uses of the caves (Bassie-Sweet, Pérez de Lara, and Zender 2000; Laughlin and Bassie-Sweet 2001; Zender, Bassie-Sweet, and Pérez de Lara 2001; Halperin, Spenard, and Brizuela 2003).

5.1. Joljá Cave 1, Group 2 paintings. Photo by Jorge Pérez de Lara.

Group 1 and Group 7 consist of glyph-like paintings that are encrusted in calcite deposit from the wet cave environment. Their age and subject matter can not be ascertained at the present time. The remaining paintings (Groups 2–6) can all be securely dated to the Early Classic period based on style and calendar notations, and they represent events that occurred at the cave over a range of time.

GROUP 2

Group 2 is composed of three paintings: Painting 1, Painting 2, and Painting 3 (fig. 5.1). These images are painted one above the other but on separate rock surfaces. The surface of the rock wall is uneven, and the paintings become significantly distorted when viewed from anywhere but immediately in front. A large percentage of the wall surface around the paintings is covered in a growth of green algae as a result of the moisture in the rock and the sunlight that strikes the wall.

Physical access to Paintings 1 and 2 is difficult because of their location high on the wall above a rock shelf. Their inaccessible location appears to have partially protected them from vandalism. The lower painting (Painting 3) is beneath the rock shelf and has not been as fortunate. A comparison of its present condition with the Blom photographs reveals that the lower right corner has been chiseled off.

Painting 1 is a glyph-like painting that did not appear in the Blom photographs because it is covered in algae growth. Infrared photographs reveal an Ajaw sign in Early Classic style (fig. 5.2). Painting 2 is 90 cm wide and just over 1 m tall. It illustrates two male figures flanking a 9 Ajaw day sign (fig. 5.3). The figures and day sign are executed in Early Classic style similar to that found on the earliest of Maya monuments (Proskouriakoff 1950; A. Stone 1995). Parts of the right figure are obscured by algae growth, but infrared photography has revealed portions of the face, upper body, and left arm (fig. 5.4). The right figure stands in profile and holds a donut-shaped object in his left hand and a torch in his right. The left figure is positioned higher on the wall and stands with his hands at his sides. He wears a feather headdress, and his face is decorated with white paint on the nose, under his eye, and on the crown of his head. His frontal pose, higher position, and feather headdress indicate that he is the principal figure.

The hands on both of the Painting 2 figures are formed using a black outline, while their bodies are solid black. Rather than merely representing human figures, this treatment suggests that the bodies of these two men were actually painted black (A. Stone 1989:330). The ceremonial use of black body paint is well known. For example, in the Postclassic period, ritual participants painted their bodies black when they fasted for a ceremony, as did warriors going into battle (Tozzer 1941:89, 152, 161; Cogolludo 1955; Avendaño y Loyola 1987). Carroll Mace noted that both the pre-Columbian and contemporary highland Maya painted their bodies black during rain rituals (Mace 1970:20, 108–109).

Between the Painting 2 figures, at the level of their feet, is the day sign 9 Ajaw with a wedge shape above it. Stone has suggested that this motif represents an altar

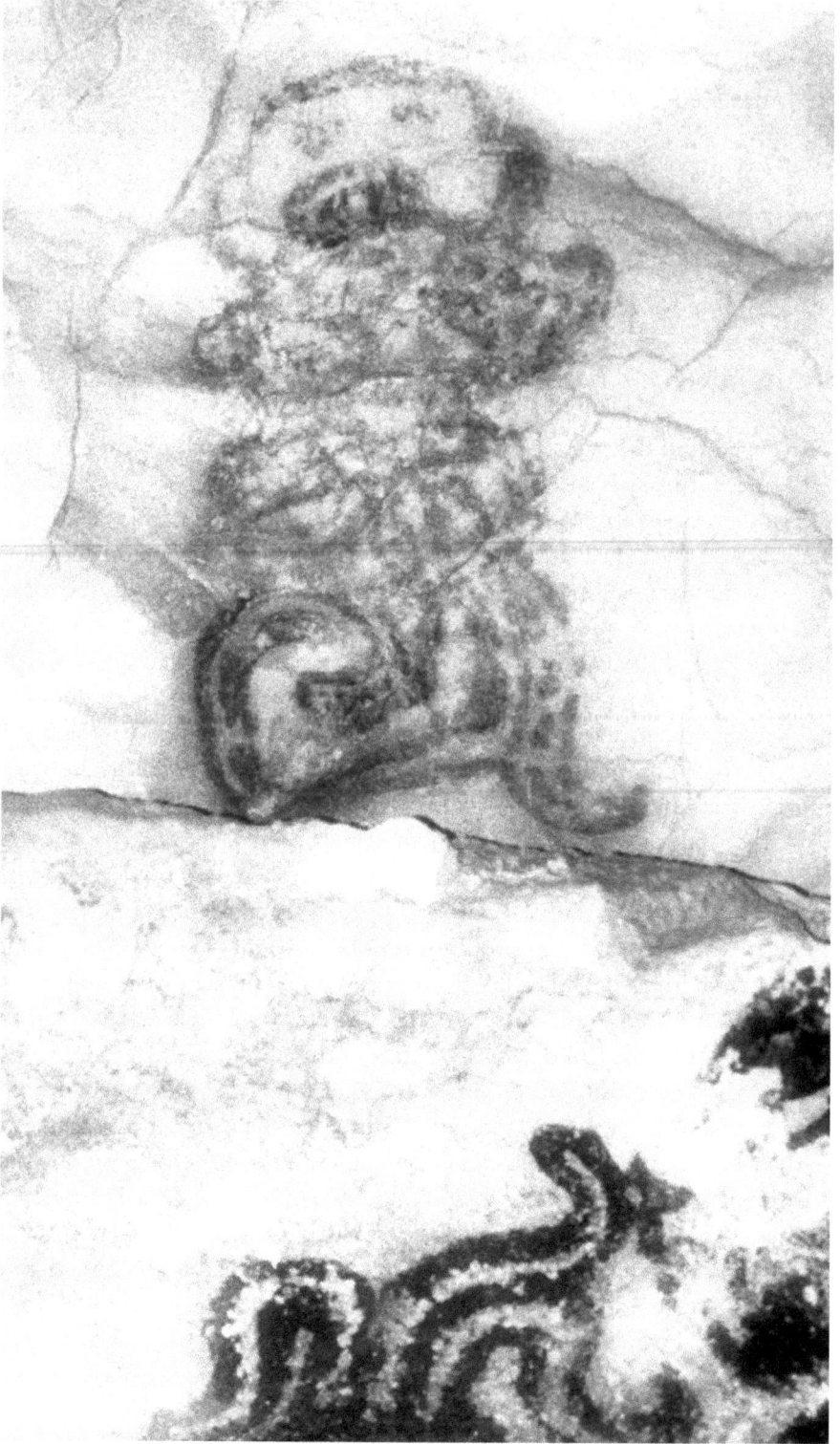

5.2. Joljá Cave 1, Group 2, Painting 1. Infrared photo reveals an Ajaw sign. Photo by Karen Bassie-Sweet.

5.3. Joljá Cave 1, Group 2, Painting 2 shows two figures flanking a 9 Ajaw sign. Photo by Jorge Pérez de Lara.

5.4. Joljá Cave 1, Group 2, Painting 2, detail with infrared photography. Photo by Karen Bassie-Sweet.

that is similar to Ajaw altars found at other sites. Such altars commemorated Period Ending events, and Stone has concluded that the Joljá scene represents such an event (A. Stone 1995:87–88). We concur with her conclusion.

In the Maya calendar, the Long Count calculations were divided into units of 360 days called *tuns*. All tun-ending events occurred on days that were named Ajaw. The most important Period Ending ceremonies were performed at the end of every *k'atun* (20 tuns). Although tun-ending dates that occurred on 9 Ajaw happened

5.5. Joljá Cave 1, Group 2, Painting 3, a zoomorphic head. Photo by Jorge Pérez de Lara.

approximately every thirteen years, the important Period Endings (fifth, tenth, thirteenth, fifteenth and twentieth) only occurred on 9 Ajaw dates four times during the first part of the Early Classic period:

8.13.0.0.0 9 Ajaw 3 Sac (December 14, A.D. 297)
8.13.13.0.0 9 Ajaw 18 Yaxk'in (October 8, A.D. 310)
8.16.5.0.0 9 Ajaw 3 Mak (January 8, A.D. 362)
8.19.10.0.0 9 Ajaw 3 Muwan (February 1, A.D. 426)

If the 9 Ajaw of Painting 2 is a k'atun date, it must refer to 8.13.0.0.0. Although this date is consistent with the early style, the Ajaw altars found at other sites such as Toniná commemorated fifth, tenth, and fifteenth tuns. This suggests the possibility that the Painting 2 date is a similar event. Joljá Group 5 contains calendar dates that refer to 8.19.19.7.7 3 Manik' 0 Woh (May 12, A.D. 435) and 9.0.0.0.0 8 Ajaw 13 Keh (December 11, A.D. 435). Given these two dates, it seems most likely that the 9 Ajaw date of Group 2 refers to the preceding 8.19.10.0.0 9 Ajaw 3 Muwan (February 1, A.D. 426) Period Ending, although it can not be unequivocally dated at present.

Painting 3 of Group 2 (62 cm × 26 cm) portrays a zoomorphic head (fig. 5.5). There are numerous examples of ritual participants standing on place name motifs that designate the location of the ritual (Stuart and Houston 1994). The position of the Group 2 zoomorphic head below the ritual scene suggests that it functions in a similar manner, that is, it is one of the ancient names for Joljá.

The eyes and nose of the Group 2 zoomorphic head are represented by three *u*-shaped elements in the center, while the mouth is the large inverted *u* shape on the bottom. The head has a large split on top with four eroded circles positioned over the split. The curls of the split are decorated with dots that are frequently found on the zoomorphic head used to represent a mountain (*witz*). On the right side of the Group 2 head is a bar and four dots representing the number 9. The left side has an eroded element. It is highly likely that the Group 2 head is an Early Classic variant of a well-known place name nicknamed the "nine blood footprint" place, conflated with a "mountain" glyph. The "nine blood footprint" place name refers to a mythical location that was often re-created by the Maya for various ceremonies (Kubler 1977; Friedel, Schele, and Parker 1993:269–70).

Another Early Classic cave painting that illustrates a Period Ending event has recently been discovered, and this work of art sheds additional light on these early cave events (Guenter 2007). This work was originally painted on a piece of flow-stone in a cave located somewhere in the northern Alta Verapaz region between Coban and Cancuen. At some point, looters sawed the stone off the wall, and the painting was displayed for a number of years in the Museo El Príncipe Maya in Coban. It is highly regrettable that the original context for this painting is unknown and that parts of it have been destroyed. Nevertheless, the remaining scene illustrates three figures performing a hand-scattering event on the date 9 Ajaw 3 Muwan. Such events were predominantly performed on Period Ending dates, which suggests that the calendar round date for this piece can be assigned a Long Count position of 8.19.10.0.0 9 Ajaw 3 Muwan (February 1, A.D. 426)—the same date posited for Group 2.

Two of the Alta Verapaz cave figures wear jaguar skin hip-cloths and have black body paint on their arms and legs. All three figures wear a soft cloth headdress that signifies a priestly office held by secondary lords nicknamed the banded bird office (Zender 2004b; Stuart 2005a:133–36). It is likely that this office was related to blood-letting duties, which were prominent activities conducted during the Period Ending ceremonies (David Stuart, personal communication).

Although there is little information in the Joljá Painting 2 scene to indicate what specific Period Ending actions the two Joljá lords were performing in the cave, or even who they were, an examination of the Period Ending rituals illustrated in other forms of Maya art shows that deity impersonation, dancing, music making, feasting, bloodletting, incense burning, and the giving of offerings to the gods were common. Divination was also an important component of these ceremonies.

The placement of the Joljá Group 2 paintings immediately above the entrance to Chamber 1 suggests that the Joljá lords may have utilized this space for their Period Ending rituals. As noted above, the right figure in the scene holds a torch. A torch is not needed during daylight hours in this section of the cave, as diffused sunlight comes from the cave mouth. Artificial light is needed in Chamber 1, however. Further-more, the baseline of Painting 2 follows the downward slope of the rock shelf below it, which gives the impression that the figures are standing on a slope. This position is just how ritual participants stand in Chamber 1. This circumstantial evidence suggests that the Painting 2 scene illustrates an actual Period Ending ceremony that was performed in Chamber 1.

The contemporary Maya believe that wind originates from caves, a belief based on the cool winds frequently blowing from the mouth of caves. A related phenomenon occurs in Chamber 1. The bottom of the chamber is a small space, and most of the participants in Day of the Holy Cross perch on the tiny ledges of the chamber walls. Although the heat from the bodies, incense, and candles should make the atmosphere in the chamber oppressive, the bottom of the chamber has a strong, cool breeze rising out of the lower crevices. During the Day of the Holy Cross ceremony, the shaman placed offerings in the largest of these wind crevices because this is where the cave spirit Don Juan is said to manifest himself. This air movement may have been one of the reasons why the ancient Maya chose this location for their rituals.

GROUP 3

Group 3 is located on the west wall in the rear chamber of Cave 1 (fig. 5.6). It is the first text encountered in this area of the cave. Sometime after William Aulie and Trudy Blom's visit, mud from the cave floor was intentionally smeared on this text, obliterating most of it. Blom's photograph indicates that it consisted of two glyph blocks representing the date 7 Kawak 5 Keh (fig. 5.7). This is an impossibility for a calendar round date because the day name Kawak can only occur with the month coefficients of 2, 7, 12, or 17 if it was a daytime event, and 1, 6, 11, or 16 if it was a nighttime event. Similar calendar mistakes are well known from other sites. From its style, it is an Early Classic inscription.

GROUP 4

Group 4 is composed of eight paintings situated near Group 3 in the rear section of Cave 1 (fig. 5.8). Six separate texts (Paintings 1–6) outlined in thick red paint are located at eye level on the west wall of the cave (fig. 5.9). In front of these texts is a stone slab lying on the cave floor (Painting 7; fig. 5.10). It is evident from fracture marks on the wall that the slab was chiseled from the area immediately below Paintings 1 to 6. This act of vandalism occurred just before Blom's visit, but the immense weight of the Painting 7 stone prevented its removal from the cave (Na Bolom Museum Archives). In his correspondence with Trudy Blom, Aulie mentioned the existence of another painted stone on the floor that was faded beyond recognition. Although we were unable to relocate this stone among the many in this area, we have given it the designation Painting 8.

A comparison of the layout and structure of the six upper paintings with other Classic period texts suggests that they represent personal names, and it is highly likely that these names represent individuals who visited the cave. Painting 1 (15 cm × 35 cm)

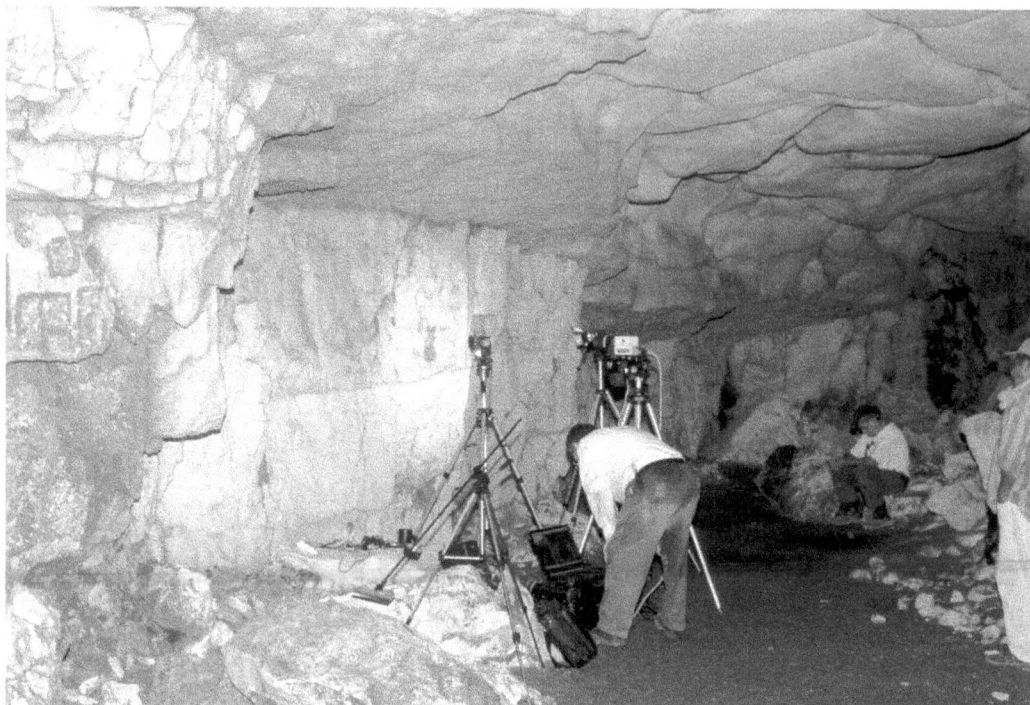

5.6. Joljá Cave 1, Group 3 location, showing Gene Ware and his multispectral imaging equipment. Photo by Karen Bassie-Sweet.

is composed of four glyph blocks that can be transcribed, transliterated, and translated as:

> u-ba-hi le le-ye HIX K'AK'-WITZ
> *u-baah leley hix k'ahk' witz*
> This is the image of Leley Hix K'ahk' Witz (Zender 2000)

Our present understanding of this phrase is that it should accompany an image of someone called Leley Hix K'ahk' Witz. It is possible that Painting 8 contained the image of this individual.

Painting 2 (11 cm × 18 cm) consists of two glyph blocks that provide the name and title of an individual, with little or nothing in the way of verbal or introductory elements. It reads as follows:

> AJ-ye-te b'a-KELEM
> *Aj-Yeet Baah-Keleem*
> It is He of *Yeet,* the Principal Youth

In this context, *Yeet* appears to refer to a toponym, but it is not a known place name.

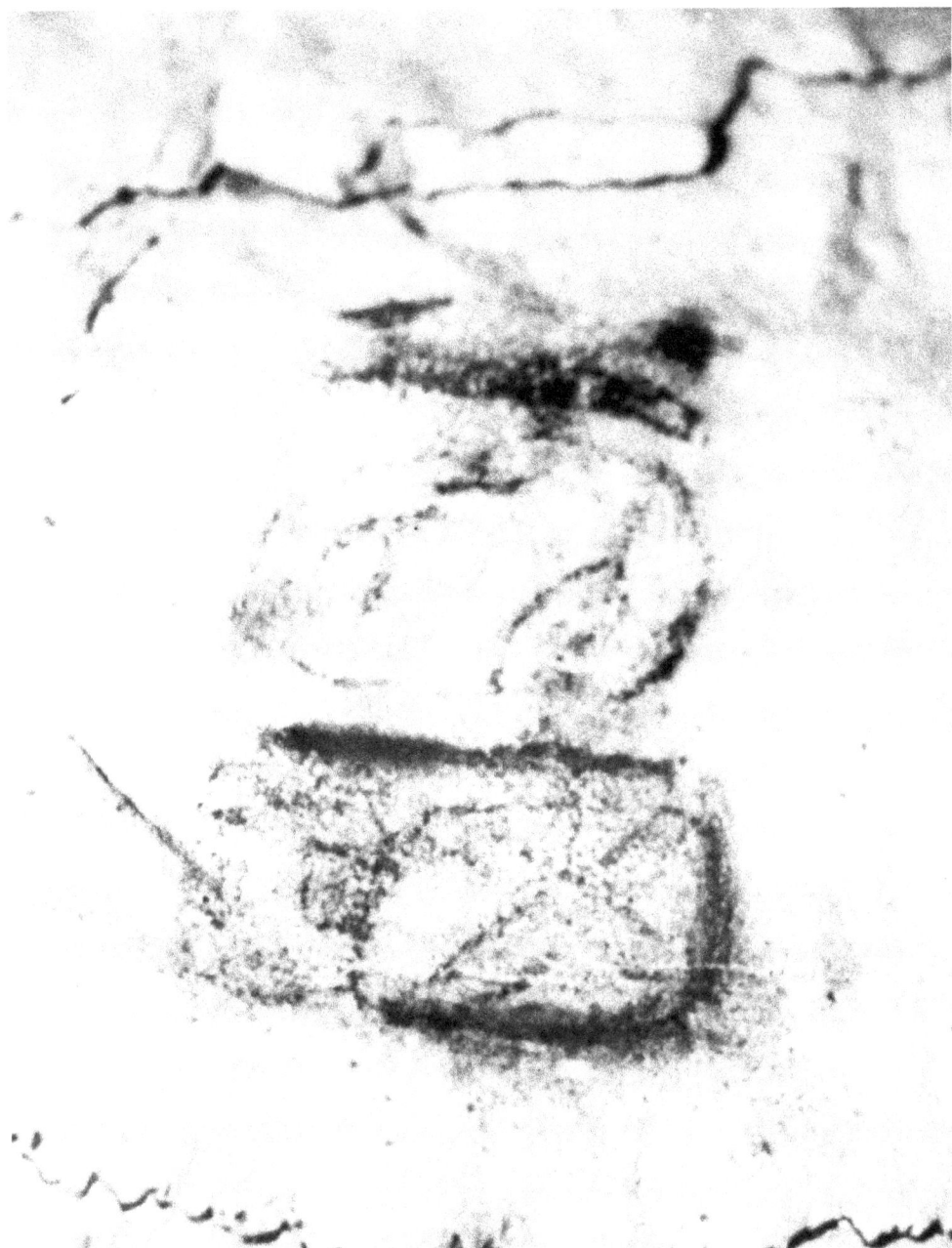

5.7. Joljá Cave 1, Group 3, showing date 7 Kawak 5 Keh. Photo by G. Blom, courtesy Na Bolom Museum..

Painting 3 (8 cm × 18 cm), Painting 4 (9 cm × 13 cm), and Painting 5 (9 cm × 9 cm) are each composed of two glyphs, but only the outlines of these glyphs are now visible. Their shortness and an absence of verbs suggests they also represented personal names. The attempted looting of Painting 7 destroyed the lower part of Painting 5.

5.8. Joljá Cave 1, Group 4 location. Domingo Pérez Moreno and Nicolas Pérez Moreno. Photo by Karen Bassie-Sweet.

The three glyphs in Painting 6 (14.5 cm × 27 cm) are clearer than the others, and this text begins with a compound sign that reads *u ts'ihb* "his writing" (A. Stone 1995:90). *U ts'ihb* phrases are used in other contexts to introduce the name of a scribe (Stuart 1987), and Painting 6 may well be the earliest known example of this kind of phrase. Unfortunately, the scribe's name is partially damaged.

Blom's photographs show that Painting 7 (43 cm × 90 cm) consisted of 32 glyphs in four columns (fig. 5.10). As in the upper texts, a thick red line encased the glyphs. While most of the glyphs are difficult to discern in Blom's photographs, there is a dedicational phrase involving fire (*k'ahk*). The only parts of Painting 7 visible today are small portions of the red outline.

Group 5

Group 5 (18 cm × 74 cm) is the next text encountered on the west wall of Cave 1. It is composed of at least eighteen glyphs arranged in two columns (fig. 5.11). A thick red band of semitransparent pigment is painted over the center of the two columns, overlapping the black text. This convention is also found on Early Classic pottery such as K5618 (Reents-Budet 1994:327). The painting style of Group 5 is

5.9. Joljá Cave 1, Group 4, personal names outlined in red. Photo by Jorge Pérez de Lara.

more refined than Group 4. The first nine glyphs of Group 5 are exceptionally clear, but the remaining ones are faded to the point that they are mere outlines.

The Group 5 text is somewhat disjointed in terms of its syntax, though whether this reflects its original state or is merely due to its washed-out lower half is difficult to say. The text refers to two separate dates. The first is given only as "the seating of Woh" (positions A1–B1 in the text) but can be reconstructed as 8.19.19.7.7 3 Manik' 0 Woh by virtue of the distance number of 10 *winals* and 13 k'ins (A2) connecting it to a Period Ending verb at A3. The signs at A3 represent a nominalized verb composed of a hand grasping a rod-like object above the "doubled-kawak" sign. This common Period Ending verb has been deciphered as *tzutz-pik* "bak'tun-ending" (Stuart 2001, 2006a:137), and it refers to the bak'tun ending date 9.0.0.0.0 8 Ajaw 13 Keh (A.D. 435). Similar Period Ending compounds in this style are found on a celt (Schele

5.10. Joljá Cave 1, Group 4, Painting 7. Photo by G. Blom, courtesy Na Bolom Museum.

5.11. Joljá Cave 1, Group 5. Photo by Jorge Pérez de Lara.

and Miller 1986, plate 22c) and on Tikal Stela 39, both of which date from the Early Classic period.

The Period Ending event is followed by the so-called "impinged bone" place name that has been interpreted to pictographically represent a cave (Bassie-Sweet 1996:64, 95–103) and to logographically represent the word *ch'een* "cave" (Stuart, in Stuart, Houston, and Robertson 1999, 2:15; Vogt and Stuart 2005). The *ch'een* "cave" glyph is used as a place name in many Classic Period texts, and in the Joljá context, it indicates that the Period Ending ceremony took place in the cave.

The next three glyphs in the Group 5 text appear to represent a personal name, though the exact syntactic relationship with the Period Ending verb remains unclear. The first glyph (A4) is the glyph for *mam,* "grandfather/grandson" (Stuart 2007a). This portrait glyph illustrates an old man with a large, round eye associated with deities and a long hank of hair falling in front of his face. In a variation of this sign found in other contexts, the man is replaced with a vulture with the same diagnostic features. When used as a title, *mam* also refers to elders who are held in the highest esteem. The next glyph (B4) is *tz'eh-k'ab* "left hand" (Stuart 2002), and it is followed by a portrait glyph bearing the characteristics of the Early Classic Chahk "lightning bolt" (A5). The overall sense may be something like "Left Hand of Chahk." Many Classic period lords incorporated the name of Chahk in their personal name. In all, these three glyphs probably name the individual responsible for conducting the Period Ending ceremony in the cave. The remaining glyphs may expand on this individual's name or explain the events that occurred on either of the two dates.

Group 6

Group 6 (16 cm × 46 cm) is located on the west wall to the south of Group 5 and is composed of sixteen glyphs in two columns, again with a semitransparent red band painted down the center (fig. 5.12). The text begins with the tzolk'in date 9 Ak'bal (at A1), but the corresponding month position of 11 K'ank'in does not appear until three glyph-blocks later at B2. The style of the glyphs suggests a Long Count position of 9.2.1.12.3 (January 6, A.D. 477) (Zender 2000; Martin, Zender and Grube 2002, 2:6). Between the Calendar Round glyphs is a unique phrase reading *hul-iiy t-u-ch'een* "he arrived at his cave" (MacLeod 1990; Stuart 2002; Vogt and Stuart 2005). The name of the person who arrived at the cave on this date is not immediately stated. It should be noted that Stuart first realized that the "impinged bone" glyph was the sign for *ch'een* after seeing a copy of Blom's photograph of the Group 6 inscription in the archives of the Corpus of Maya Hieroglyphic Inscriptions Program (Stuart, personal communication).

Following the month position is a verbal couplet (A3–B3) referring again to the arrival at the cave and the concomitant feasting (*uk' we'*) that accompanied the Period Ending ceremonies. The custom of ritual eating and drinking during ceremonies is well attested (Reents-Budet 2000; Zender 2000; Houston, Stuart, and

5.12. Joljá Cave 1, Group 6. Photo by Jorge Pérez de Lara.

Taube 2006:127–30). For example, the Paris Codex illustrates Period Ending ceremonies that include plates filled with tamales (Love 1994). The snail shell deposits
at the entrance of Joljá Cave 1 may indicate, at least in part, the repast on which the
ritual participants dined (Halperin, Spenard, and Brizuela 2003).

The name or names of the individuals who participated in the Joljá feasting are
eroded, but at B5 there is a relationship glyph (*yatan* "his wife") followed by a woman's
name at A6. The final two glyphs of the text refer to a Sibikte' Ajaw or "lord of
Sibikte'" (A8–B8). As noted in chapter 3, this title also appears in the Late Classic
text from the nearby cave site of Yaleltsemen and on Toniná Monument 171. The
inscription on Monument 171 states that a lord of both Toniná and the as yet uniden-
tified site of Sibikte' was the Late Classic ruler of Toniná named K'inich Ich'aak
Chapaat (Skidmore 2004). If Sibikte' does not specifically refer to Toniná, it may well
refer to an Early Classic polity of some note in the general region of both Yaleltsemen
and Joljá. A possible candidate would be Chilón.

CONCLUSIONS

The ceremonies recorded in the Joljá paintings occurred between A.D. 426 and A.D.
435. Those dates bring to mind several retrospective Late Classic texts at Palenque
that name the founder of the Palenque dynasty as a ruler called K'uk' Bahlam, who
came to the throne in A.D. 431. He is called a lord of Toktahn. His brief rule of four
years was followed by that of another Toktahn king who has been nicknamed Casper
because his name glyphs have yet to be deciphered. The Palenque Tablet of the Cross
relates the accession of Casper (A.D. 435) and the 9.0.0.0.0 Period Ending event
that occurred just sixty-four days later. This narrative states that the Period Ending
ceremony was performed at Toktahn. It is apparent from the text that these early
Palenque rulers were *not* lords of Sibikte' and therefore, not associated with the events
at the Joljá caves.

What can be surmised about the Joljá lords is that they either had priestly functions similar to those associated with the banded bird office or actually held this office.
The identity of the Joljá lords will, however, remain a mystery until further regional
inscriptions are found or until more archaeological research can identify the source
of the ceramics in the cave.

Despite the relative scarcity of inscriptions alluding to the 9.0.0.0.0 Period Ending
event, their geographical distribution indicates that Period Ending events were celebrated widely in the Maya region during the Early Classic period. Period Ending
ceremonies focused on the veneration of deities. The following chapters explore
some of the most important ancient Maya deities, their relationship to Period Ending
ceremonies, and how they are connected to the deities still honored by the contemporary Maya.

ANCIENT AND CONTEMPORARY DEITIES OF THE CH'OL REGION

6

THE FAMILY OF ANCIENT CREATOR DEITIES

Karen Bassie-Sweet and Nicholas A. Hopkins

In earlier chapters, we have drawn on ethnographic reports and personal observation to show that the modern Ch'ol make customary offerings and petitions in caves to a supernatural known as Don Juan. Ethnohistoric and archaeological evidence, including artifacts and inscriptions in the Joljá caves, and the analysis of remains in similar contexts in caves in other areas of the Maya world, indicate that such customs have been present since the Pre-Classic period. It is apparent that while the archaeological evidence adds depth to the ethnographic record, it is also true that ethnohistoric reports and the observation of modern practices inform the interpretation of prehistoric events. Before examining in detail the nature of Don Juan and other contemporary deities who are identified with caves, we will review the Classic period antecedents with the goal of relating them to historic and contemporary religious practices in chapter 8. This entails a discussion of the Classic Maya creator deities, Maya world view, and Period Ending ceremonies. An overview of these topics is necessary in order to place the contemporary Ch'ol beliefs in historical context. Here, we retain the alphabetic designations such as God A, God B, and so on when the hieroglyphic name of a deity has yet to be deciphered. These designations were coined by Paul Schellhas (1904), who categorized the various supernatural beings found in the Postclassic codices.

THE FAMILY OF CREATOR DEITIES

The Popol Vuh is the most comprehensive indigenous document to deal with the subject of Maya creation. This sixteenth-century manuscript, written by K'iche' elders, describes the activities of a family of creator deities (Christenson 2007a). These creator deities were role models for humans and represented the ideal state for humans, particularly the ruling elite, to achieve. The Popol Vuh relates the deeds of three generations of deities: the creator grandparents, named Xpiyacoc and Xmucane; their sons, named One Hunahpu and Seven Hunahpu; and One Hunahpu's four sons, named One Chouen, One Batz, Hunahpu, and Xbalanque (Christenson 2007a). Classic-period lowland parallels for all of these gods have been identified (Coe 1973, 1977, 1989; Taube 1985, 1992a; Bassie-Sweet 1996, 2008; Zender 2004b). They have similar, if not identical, names and attributes, and they appear in similar environments, performing identical actions. The Classic period inscriptions may refer indirectly to the genealogy of some of the creator deities, but the Popol Vuh states their relationships explicitly (Christenson 2007a:112–13, 130, 135; Bassie-Sweet 2008:233–34).

The Popol Vuh narrative begins before the creation of the earth and human beings. At this time, there was an elderly married couple called Xpiyacoc and Xmucane. In Mesoamerica, deities had multiple manifestations and could take the shape of such things as animals, plants, flint, obsidian, fire, water, rain, clouds, wind, lightning, thunderbolts, meteors, and other celestial objects. In addition, features of the landscape such as mountains were thought to be manifestations of certain deities. In Classic period art, it is often difficult to sort these manifestations into their respective categories, but the Popol Vuh lists some of the manifestations, or avatars, of Xpiyacoc and Xmucane and the roles associated with them. For example, in their function as healers, Xpiyacoc and Xmucane took the form of a peccary and coati, respectively (Christenson 2007a:98).

A central aspect of the family of creator deities and Maya world view in general is the principle of complementary opposition (Bassie-Sweet 2002, 2008). To order and structure their world, the Maya use such categories as male-female, senior-junior, up-down, right-left, hot-cold, and day-night. Humans are thought to be both male and female, with the right side being male and the left side being female, yet husbands and wives complement each other just as the right hand complements the left. It is believed that an adult must be married to be complete.

Xpiyacoc and Xmucane were referred to by a series of paired titles, such as K'ajolom-Alom "he who has begotten sons-she who has borne children," Mamon-I'yom "patriarch-midwife," and Tz'aqol-B'itol "framer-shaper," that reflected their harmonized nature and their embodiment of complementary opposition. The Postclassic Tzeltal and Tzotzil mythology paralleled that of the K'iche', and their old creator couple had some of the same titles as Xpiyacoc (Patol "maker") and Xmucane (Alaghom "bearer, goddess with children") (Calnek 1988:45; Núñez 1988, sec. 32; Laughlin 1988:153; Bassie-Sweet 2008:54). Like the K'iche', the Tzeltal-Tzotzil believed that this elderly creator couple made the earth, the sky, and humankind, and that they were at the head and beginning of all the other gods of each town.

According to the Popol Vuh, the creator grandparents originally lived in a pooled body of water. Above this place of duality, the sky was inhabited by a trio of thunderbolt gods called Thunderbolt Huracán, Youngest Thunderbolt, and Sudden Thunderbolt. They were known collectively as Heart of Sky. Below the place of duality was a location called Xibalba that was inhabited by a host of death deities. This underworld was ruled by a pair of gods called One Death and Seven Death. In concert with the Heart of Sky thunderbolt gods, Xpiyacoc and Xmucane made the earth rise up from the waters of the place of duality and they then set about to create humans who would honor them.

The Classic period parallels of Xpiyacoc and Xmucane are two elderly deities called Itzamnaaj and Ix Chel. The attributes of these deities suggest that Itzamnaaj was originally a god of the sky, while his wife Ix Chel had death attributes associated with the underworld. This contrast led Bassie-Sweet (2008:236) to propose that the place of duality was first formed when Itzamnaaj-Xpiyacoc of the sky married Ix Chel-Xmucane of Xibalba. In the context of the principle of complementary opposition, the creator god and, by extension, males were associated with senior, up, right, hot, and day, while the creator goddess and females were identified with junior, down, left, cold, and night.

The Popol Vuh indicates that after the creation of the earth, Xpiyacoc and Xmucane established a house for themselves at the center of the world. The spiritual center of this house was demarcated by a three-hearthstone fire just like those found in some traditional Maya houses today. As argued by Bassie-Sweet (2008:121), these three hearthstones were manifestations of the three thunderbolt deities. The surface of the earth was inhabited by a host of other deities as well. The Popol Vuh does not explain where these deities originated, but much of the story revolves around the subjugation of these beings as well as the defeat of the underworld deities.

Xpiyacoc and Xmucane's two sons, named One Hunahpu and Seven Hunahpu, lived with them. Seven Hunahpu remained a bachelor, but their eldest son, One Hunahpu, took a wife called Lady Bone Water, who subsequently died. Although the Popol Vuh does not specify how she died, circumstantial evidence indicates that she died giving birth to their sons, One Batz and One Chouen (Bassie-Sweet 2008:183). Goddesses identified with women who died in childbirth are common in Mesoamerica. The Popol Vuh does not indicate the origins of One Hunahpu's first wife, Lady Bone Water, but there is evidence that she was the daughter of a Xibalban underworld lord named Gathered Blood, and that she was a goddess identified with the corn ear and seed (Bassie-Sweet 2008:184). The Maya refer to corn seed as bone.

One Hunahpu's Classic-period parallel was a corn god named One Ixim, who is frequently illustrated with corn foliage emanating from his body. A corn plant consists of a single stalk topped by a male tassel. As the plant matures, a female ear develops on the stalk. The male tassel drops its pollen on the silk of the female ear and fertilizes it. A mature corn plant is incomplete without its ear of corn, just as One Hunahpu was incomplete without Lady Bone Water. Like the corn plant, this couple embodied the principle of complementary opposition.

In addition to being a corn god, One Ixim-One Hunahpu was also a morning-star deity and wind god (Bassie-Sweet 2008:298–301). One Ixim is most often depicted wearing jade and the long tail-feathers of the quetzal. This bird was his avian manifestation. One Ixim's attributes are similar to those of the Central Mexican deity and culture hero Quetzalcoatl "quetzal snake" of the Postclassic period, and it is likely that these two gods evolved out of the same ancient Mesoamerican mythology (Florescano 1999; Bassie-Sweet 2008:298–300). Quetzalcoatl's identification with the quetzal is seen in the description of the funeral pyre of the culture hero in the Annals of Cuauhtitlan: "And as soon as his ashes had been consumed, they saw the heart of a quetzal rising upward. And so they knew he had gone to the sky, had entered the sky" (Bierhorst 1992:36). In many regions, including Chiapas, during the Postclassic period, Quetzalcoatl was revered under the Maya name Kukulcan "quetzal snake," and 250 years after the Spanish conquest, the Tzeltal ritual specialists continued to honor Kukulcan (Núñez 1988:139).

As for the grandchildren of the creator couple, the Popol Vuh narrative indicates that One Batz and One Chouen were raised by their father, One Hunahpu, and their uncle, Seven Hunahpu, who trained them to be great sages, musicians, singers, writers, artists, and artisans of jade and precious metals. They also taught them to be skillful ballplayers. One Hunahpu owned a ball court on the road to the Xibalba underworld. The ball playing of the four gods at the edge of the underworld territory enraged the death lords, and One Death and Seven Death challenged the four gods to come down to the Xibalba underworld and play ball against them. Leaving One Batz and One Chouen behind, One Hunahpu and Seven Hunahpu journeyed through a cave passageway to the very heart of Xibalba. After failing the various tests of the death lords, the two brothers were sacrificed.

One Hunahpu's decapitated head was subsequently placed in an underworld tree. Suddenly, the tree sprouted gourds, and it became impossible to tell the difference between the fruit and One Hunahpu's skull. Fearing the power of the tree, the underworld lords commanded that no one harvest the fruit or even go near the tree. The Xibalban lord Gathered Blood told his daughter Lady Blood about the miraculous tree, and despite the restriction, she was so fascinated by the story that she could not resist visiting it. One Hunahpu's gourd skull then spit in her hand and impregnated her.

When her pregnancy became apparent, Lady Blood fled the underworld and journeyed to the household of the creator grandparents on the surface of the earth, where she gave birth to the hero twins, Hunahpu and Xbalanque. The lowland parallels for the hero twins were named One Ajaw and Yax Bolon. The attributes of Lady Blood indicate that she was a waxing moon goddess (D. Tedlock 1996:338; Bassie-Sweet 2008:203–207). The association of certain phases of the moon with females is a pan-Mesoamerican concept. Eventually, the hero twins grew up, subordinated the other deities living on the surface of the earth, including their older half-brothers, and then they, too, journeyed to the underworld to challenge the lords of death. After many contests and deceptions, the hero twins defeated One Death and Seven Death and subjugated the Xibalbans. They then adorned their father, One Hunahpu, and transformed him into the morning star (Bassie-Sweet 2008:298–301). The Venus tables of the Dresden Codex indicate that the first mythological rising of the morning star occurred on the date 1 Ajaw. Fittingly, One Hunahpu's name is the K'iche' equivalent of this calendar date.

The adornment of One Ixim (the Classic period version of One Hunahpu) by his sons is illustrated on a series of Classic period scenes on pottery. Included in these scenes are underworld goddesses who bathe One Ixim and help dress him in his jade costume. Following the appearance of their father in the dawn sky, Hunahpu and Xbalanque rose up as sun and full moon, respectively. The zenith passage of the sun in April marks the beginning of the planting season for the Maya, who traditionally sow their cornfields during the full moon. The rising of One Hunahpu, Hunahpu, and Xbalanque occurred on the April zenith passage and initiated this corn planting cycle (Bassie-Sweet 2008:219). The contrast between Hunahpu (the hot sun of the day) and his brother Xbalanque (the cold, full moon of the night) exemplifies the principle of complementary opposition. An equivalent visual opposition occurs, for the full moon rises in the east when the sun sets in the west, and the following morning the sun rises when the full moon sets. On Maya vases K1892 and K4681, the surface of the earth is represented by a turtle. One Ajaw and Yax Bolon, the Classic period parallels of the hero twins, are positioned on either side of the turtle in opposition to each other just as sun and full moon stand in opposition (Bassie-Sweet 2008, 222: fig. 8.3). These scenes indicate that One Ajaw and Yax Bolon had the same solar and lunar associations as Hunahpu and Xbalanque.

Houston (2009) has detailed some of the titles and qualities of Classic period youths and how they were contrasted with mature adult males. A particular title known as *ch'ok* was used to describe youths but was also employed to designate the future king. As an example, Kan Joy Chitam of Palenque carried this *ch'ok* title until he assumed the throne at age forty-eight, hardly a youth. This shift from a junior, youthful state to a senior, mature state is seen in the Popol Vuh in regards to Hunahpu and Xbalanque. During the creation story in the Popol Vuh, both Hunahpu and Xbalanque are repeatedly called boys. Xbalanque's name begins with the *X* diminutive/female indicator, showing his status as the junior twin. There are, however, six examples in the Popol Vuh where Hunahpu's name also carries this diminutive (Christenson 2007a:95). The name Xhunahpu occurs in the episodes when the twins jumped into a pit oven in the underworld, when they sacrificed each other and then sacrificed the underworld lords, and finally when they revealed to the Xibalbans that they were the sons of One Hunahpu. These events occurred just before they adorned One Hunahpu and rose up as sun and full moon. This climax was the moment that the hero twins made the transition from youths to adults and assumed their final destiny. The use of the diminutive *X* in Hunahpu's name appears to be a literary device to emphasize this fact.

Like the other deities, the maternal grandfather, Gathered Blood, also had a lowland Classic-period parallel (Bassie-Sweet 2008:230–35). Although the personal name for this old god has not been identified, he has been assigned the Schellhas designation of God L. Itzamnaaj-Xpiyacoc and God L–Gathered Blood, in their roles as the paternal and maternal grandfathers of the hero twins, were complementary opposites of each other. The hero twins' defeat of the underworld deities placed the maternal line of the creator deities in the subordinate position in the hierarchy of deities and established the patrilineal descent of Maya kingship. This conflict was not a battle between good and evil, but rather, an expression of the complementary opposition of life and death that reflects the cyclical renewal of the world.

At the same time that the creator deities were battling other deities on the surface of the earth and in the underworld, they were attempting to create humans. Their stated purpose was to create beings who would honor them. Their first attempts were not successful, and the resulting beings had to be destroyed, but finally they found special corn seeds buried inside Paxil Mountain. There is significant evidence that these corn seeds were the remains of the goddess Lady Bone Water (Bassie-Sweet 2008: 163–69, 201–203). One of the most prevalent stories in the Maya region concerns the discovery of corn that had been hidden within a mountain. To obtain the corn, a series of gods attempted to break open the rock containing the corn. In the Popol Vuh, Youngest Thunderbolt (Ch'i'pi Kaqulja) and Sudden Thunderbolt (Raxa Kaqulja) carry the title Ch'i'pi Nanavac and Raxa Nanavac, respectively (Christenson 2007a: 207). The Central Mexican god Nanahuatl was the deity who split open the corn mountain, and Nanavac is likely a borrowing of this name and refers to the role of these deities in breaking open the corn mountain (Schultze-Jena 1944:187; Edmonson 1971:159).

The creator grandmother Xmucane ground this corn seed into dough and mixed it with water to fashion the flesh and blood of the first humans. These first humans multiplied and created different groups that spread across the surface of the earth and established their own territories. They then climbed their sacred mountains and waited for the first appearance of the morning star and the rising sun. When One Hunahpu appeared, they rejoiced and made their offerings to the creator deities, fulfilling the desire of these gods to have beings who would worship them.

Creator Deities as Role Models

The creator deities were role models for humans to emulate. When humans donned the costume and headdress of a deity, they became the embodiment of that deity (Houston and Stuart 1996). Classic period rulers emulated both One Ajaw and his father, One Ixim. Beyond the fact that all young lords were called *ajaw* and clearly emulated One Ajaw, accession statements for Maya kings indicate that the *sak huun* "white headband" of One Ajaw was the actual crown of kingship. One Ajaw's headdress was a flexible headband of white bark cloth that was tied onto the head with a large knot in back (Schele, Mathews, and Lounsbury 1990:4–5; Schele 1992:22–24; Grube, cited in Schele 1992:39–40). It must be concluded that a young lord became specifically identified with One Ajaw when he acceded to the throne. This identification with the deity One Ajaw is most apparent in the occasional variants of the

Ajaw day sign in which the portrait of the deity One Ajaw is replaced with a portrait of the ruling king wearing One Ajaw's headdress (Stuart 1996:167; Martin and Grube 2008:108; Martin 2012:21). The association of the new ruler with One Ajaw's solar identity is reflected in the *k'inich* title of the sun god that was acquired by many lords when they became king.

As for the identification of Maya kings with One Ixim, one of his aspects was that of Venus, the morning star. The Palenque Temple of the Inscriptions sarcophagus lid illustrates the apotheosis of the ruler K'inich Janaab Pakal (Bassie-Sweet 2008:fig. 8.7). In this scene, the ruler is dressed in the costume of One Ixim as he rises into the sky. Some researchers have identified Pakal and by extension One Ixim as the rising sun, but we believe this is incorrect (Freidel, Schele, and Parker 1993:269; Taube 1994, 2004; Martin 2006; Stuart 2009). They have arrived at this conclusion because the motif below One Ixim contains a bowl marked with a *k'in* sign that has been interpreted to be a sacrificial fire vessel associated with the east and the rising sun. This motif is also the headdress of the deity GI, and he, too, has been identified as the sun based on this bowl. In hieroglyphic texts, the k'in bowl represents the verb *el* "go out, emerge" (Houston, cited in Stuart 2005a:65).

The notion that a deity could be transformed into the sun through the use of a sacrificial fire was recorded by Sahagún (1959–63, 7:3–6). He noted the Nahuatl myth in which the Aztec deities Nanahuatzin and Tecuciztecatl jumped one after the other into a primordial fire and were transformed into the sun and moon. However, the morning star was also thought to have been created by fire. As noted in the Annals of Cuauhtitlan, Quetzalcoatl dressed himself in his costume and then used a pyre to transform himself into the morning star:

> The old people said he was changed into the star that appears at dawn. Therefore they say it came forth when Quetzalcoatl died, and they called him Lord of the Dawn. (Bierhorst 1992:36)

This description is comparable to mentions of the first appearance of One Hunahpu in his morning star form in the Popol Vuh as witnessed by the first four K'iche' lords:

> They fixed their eyes firmly on their dawn, looking there to the East. They watched closely for the Morning Star, the Great Star that gives its light at the birth of the sun.

> They occupied themselves in looking for the Great Star, called Icoquih, which appears first before the birth of the sun. The face of this Green Morning Star always appears at the coming forth of the sun.

> This therefore is the dawn, the appearance of the sun, moon, and stars. Greatly they rejoiced, Balam Quitze, Balam Acab, Mahucutah, and Iqui Balam, when

they saw the Morning Star. It came forth glittering before the face of the
sun. (Christenson 2007a:207, 218, 228)

The description of the green and glittering morning star matches that of One
Ixim dressed in his green jade jewelry and iridescent quetzal feathers. If we assume
that One Ixim's final destiny was indeed as the morning star deity and not the sun,
then the death of K'inich Janaab Pakal and the subsequent accession of his son K'inich
Kan B'ahlam as the new king follow the same pattern as the Popol Vuh mythology.
The father, One Hunahpu, rose after death as the morning star and was then followed
into the sky by his son Hunahpu in his role as the sun. To become the Ajaw "king" was
to become the sun, but in his afterlife the king took on the role of the morning star.

Numerous researchers have noted that in the Classic period it is the son who is
named One Ajaw, while in the Popol Vuh it is the father, One Hunahpu, who has the
equivalent day name. (As noted in chapter 1, deities and humans alike were often named
for the day in the *tzolk'in* calendar on which they were born.) This is not a shift in
mythological roles. There is an obvious explanation as to why both these deities
carry the same tzolk'in calendar name. While the day in the 365-day solar calendar
changes at sunrise, the day in the tzolk'in calendar changes at sunset. Therefore,
both father (morning star) and son (sun) took on their final destinies on the same
day (1 Ajaw).

The Quadrilateral World Model

In the Maya world view, the surface of the earth was thought to contain a quadrilateral space constructed by the creator deities. Humans could live safely within this
space if they made the proper offerings to the gods. In metaphors that described the
quadrilateral world as a house, the center was defined by a fireplace composed of
three hearthstones that represented the hearth fire of the creator grandparents. The
Maya replicated the quadrilateral world model whenever they created human space;
thus, their household fires represented the fire of the creator grandparents. The Maya
were, in effect, creating the place of duality each time they created a house. The quadrilateral world model was also used to create ceremonial space, and a ritual performance or its climax often took place at the center of that space. In other words, they
symbolically located their ceremonies at the place of duality.

The quadrilateral world was referred to metaphorically as a cornfield (Bassie-
Sweet 2008:58–60). The Maya plant corn seeds in mounds, usually consisting of five
seeds. A corn mound and its planting hole are envisioned as a mountain with a cave.
When traditional Maya plant their cornfields, they first make a corn mound at the
center of their field and give offerings to the deities before planting the remainder
of the field.

The association of the center of the world with a cave is also found in the names
for the center of a community that include the word *ch'en* "cave" (Tokovinine

2008:160). In the context of these community place names, the word *ch'en* appears to refer to certain temples (symbolic mountains) as the center of the community.

On a celestial basis, the rise and set points of the solstice sun defined the corners of the quadrilateral world, and the center was marked by the zenith passage of the sun. Each of the world quadrants was associated with a particular color (north-white, west-black, south-yellow, east-red). The creator gods had quadripartite forms that were associated with the four quadrants and their colors. For example, an incantation in the Ritual of the Bacabs refers to a red, white, black, and yellow Itzamnaaj and Ix Chel. As noted above, each deity also had animal, meteorological, and celestial forms.

CHARACTERISTICS OF THE GRANDFATHER DEITIES

As noted above, the paternal and maternal grandfathers of the hero twins had distinct characteristics that complemented each other. Schellhas assigned the designations God D, God L, and God N to three elderly male deities who are illustrated with receding gums and wrinkles around their mouths (Bassie-Sweet 2008:figs 7.2, 7.4, 12.1, 12.2). In the hieroglyphic texts, the name glyphs for God L and God N are represented by their portraits.

The features of the maternal grandfather God L are black body paint, a jaguar ear, and a jaguar-skin cape. He also has an armadillo form, and he occasionally wears a cape woven to look like an armadillo shell. God L frequently smokes a cigar, and he carries a walking staff that reflects his role as a merchant god. This walking staff takes the form of a fire serpent and was used as a supernatural weapon. God L's diagnostic trait is a headdress composed of a nest of feathers that often has an owl perched on it (Bassie-Sweet 2008:fig. 12.1).

In the Dresden Codex, the owl is named Oxlajuun Chan Kuy "thirteen sky owl," and this owl has been interpreted as one of God L's avian manifestations (Grube and Schele 1994). The owl's call is viewed across Mesoamerica as an omen of death, which suits God L's underworld associations. In Maya art, black-tipped owl feathers are used as symbols for obsidian blades, and God L's headdress reflects his role as an obsidian merchant (Bassie-Sweet 2011). As an aside, many researchers still follow Thompson's mistaken identification of the God L bird as a *muwan* bird. The word *muwan* refers to certain falcons and hawks (Grube and Schele 1994), and the diagnostic trait of the muwan bird is that it is shown swallowing another bird (Bassie-Sweet 2008:107). Oxlajuun Chan Kuy was not a muwan.

The diagnostic trait of God N is a net headdress or waterlily headdress. An Early Classic version of God N's portrait found on a Río Azul vessel illustrates the pliable nature of the net headdress (Adams 1999:fig. 3–42). This vessel also illustrates the *mam* "grandfather/grandson" glyph that was discussed in the previous chapter. Both the God N and *mam* portrait glyphs show an old man with the sunken mouth and enlarged jaw and nose associated with old age.

God D is likewise illustrated as an old man (Bassie-Sweet 2008:fig. 7.7). His diagnostic headdress is composed of a flower infixed with an *ak'bal* "night, darkness" sign. God D and three other gods (God A, God K, and God G) appear in the Dresden Codex Wayeb pages engaged in putting the quadrilateral world in order (Thompson 1972; Taube 1988). The first identification of God D with Itzamnaaj was made because he appears in these Wayeb scenes performing functions that Bishop Diego de Landa indicated were performed by the creator grandfather Itzamnaaj.

Itzamnaaj-God D has an avian manifestation, a supernatural bird illustrated in Maya art that wears the ak'bal headdress of Itzamnaaj-God D (Bardawil 1976; Hellmuth 1987; Taube 1992a:36; Bassie-Sweet 2008:fig.7.3). The bird is based on the species *Herpetotheres cachinnans,* commonly known as the *guaco* or laughing falcon (Bassie-Sweet 2008:130–46). The name glyph for this bird is a portrait of it wearing the ak'bal headdress. As noted by David Stuart, the name glyph of God D is actually a conflation of God N's portrait and the bird (Bassie-Sweet-2008:132). In other words, God D and God N are manifestations of the same deity, the paternal grandfather Itzamnaaj.

In addition to his avian form, Itzamnaaj had opossum, peccary, and turtle manifestations (Taube 1992a:92–99; Bassie-Sweet 2008:127–47). The Popol Vuh states that the paternal grandfather Xpiyacoc likewise had opossum and peccary forms. In the etymology of the name Xpiyacoc, *kok* is a term for turtle in both highland and lowland languages, and the term *piyakok* is the name for a slider turtle (*Trachemys scripta elegans*) and for a turtle design in the weavings of Rabinal (Akkeren 2000:207, 261–64; Christenson 2007a:63). Xpiyacoc's name indicates that he had a turtle form like Itzamnaaj. In his turtle form, the creator grandfather Itzamnaaj represented the surface of the earth, and each of the quadripartite forms of Itzamnaaj represented one of the quadrants of the earth. This is evident in scenes that show the earth as a turtle shell. On Maya vase K1892, the turtle earth is shown as God N in his turtle form (Bassie-Sweet 2008:fig. 8.3).

COMPLEMENTARY OPPOSITION AND THE PLACE OF DUALITY IN THE SKY

Like many people, the Maya saw the constellations of the night sky as manifestations of their deities, and they interpreted the movements of the stars as reenactments of their mythology (Bassie-Sweet 2008:266–83). The Maya had a constellation called the three hearthstones (B. Tedlock 1985:86; 1992:29). It is composed of three stars in Orion: a star in the belt and the two knee stars (Alnitak, Saiph, and Rigel). The center of this celestial fireplace is the Orion Great Nebula M42, which appears in the sky like a smoky fire. It represents the fire of the creator grandparents' house. At the latitude of the Guatemalan highlands, the three hearthstones constellation is located about twenty degrees south of the center of the night sky when it is at its apex position. At this time, the Milky Way forms a celestial road that stretches from the southeast to the northwest, while the ecliptic forms another celestial road from the east to the west. The location where these two roads cross is just slightly north of the center of the sky.

These roads were the celestial counterparts of the four world roads that were thought to radiate out from the center of the world. As noted above, the climax of the Popol Vuh creation story occurred when One Hunahpu and his sons Hunahpu and Xbalanque rose for the first time as the morning star, the sun, and the full moon on the date of the zenith passage (late April) and began the first corn cycle. The sun's path from east to west is also a celestial counterpart to the east-west world road. When the sun passes overhead on its zenith passage, its position marks the physical center of the sky.

The pooled body of water in which the creator grandparents lived before the earth was formed, and their household on the surface of the earth, were places of duality. There are illustrations of the creator grandparents' house that include sky-bands, celestial pathways, which suggests that their house of duality was also thought to be located in the heavens. Their celestial house was likely envisioned as being directly overhead. Several Classic-period monuments suggest that this was the case. Yaxchilan Stela 1, Stela 6, and Stela 10 illustrate a ruler conducting a ritual (Tate 1992:figs. 88, 124, 130). The ruler's deceased parents, the embodiment of comple-mentary opposition, sit in solar cartouches that are positioned on a skyband above the ruler's head.

The portrait of ruler's parents on Yaxchilan Stela 4 similarly pictures the ruler's father in a solar cartouche, but in contrast to the other three monuments, his mother is situated in a moon cartouche (Tate 1992:fig. 86). The pairing of a sun and moon cartouche embodies the principle of complementary opposition (Stuart 2003). While some researchers have concluded from this Yaxchilan image that the Maya believed that the deceased ruler and his wife took on the role of sun and moon after death, we assert that this pairing is more likely a visual metonym that indicates that these ancestors were the embodiment of complementary opposition. These Yaxchilan ances-tral portraits illustrate a celestial place of duality, and they reinforce the sanctity of the Period Ending actions performed beneath them.

A metonym is a term in which two typical members of a class are juxtaposed to stand for the whole domain (Hopkins 1996). The two members of a metonym are usually the best examples of the domain and are often complementary or contrasting opposites. For example, the Maya term for ancestors is mother-father. In the Popol Vuh, mountain and valley are paired to describe the earth; sky and earth are paired to describe the world; and Heart of Sky (the three thunderbolt gods) and Heart of Earth (the creator grandparents) are paired to describe all the creator deities (Christenson 2007b:16, 19, 20). In this same manner, *cho* "lake" and *palo* "sea" are paired as a reference to all water (D. Tedlock 1987:148; Christenson 2007b:16, 157). In the Popol Vuh, the pairing of eagle and vulture contrasts raptors that eat freshly killed prey with those that consume carrion. It is a poetic reference to all birds of prey. Such complementary opposition is also found in hieroglyphic writing. The *tz'ak* "whole, complete" glyph is often replaced with a pair of signs such as day-night, sun-moon, star-moon, cloud-water, wind-water, unripe-ripe (Hopkins 1996; Hull 1997, 2003; Knowlton 2002; Stuart 2003).

Complementary couplets also occur in Río Azul Tomb 12, where the glyphs painted on opposite walls are complementary opposites of each other: day on the east wall, night on the west wall, moon on the north wall, and star on the south wall (Stuart 1985; Adams 1999:56). There is another aspect of this layout that has been overlooked. Across the Maya region, couplets are used in formal and sacred language. This poetic tradition is documented from the Early Classic to the present. The Río Azul glyphs form a narrative. Beginning with the east wall and moving in a counter-clockwise motion, the Río Azul glyphs form alternating couplets (A-B-A-B) of day-east (A), moon-north (B), night-west (A), and star-south (B).

The edge of a bench in Copan Structure 66C has the same pairs of complementary couplets carved on its edge (Webster et al. 1998). From left to right on the bench are portraits of One Ixim as a lunar patron (A), an ak'bal deity representing night (B), the sun god representing day (B), and a scorpion deity representing Venus (A). This is the well-known chiasmus or "nested couplet" form of A-B-B-A (Hopkins and Josserand 2012:29). To sanctify ritual space, prayers are said in couplet form (Gossen 1974; Joljá Cave Project field notes). The Copan and Río Azul complementary couplets transform the Copan bench and the Río Azul tomb into proper quadri-lateral ceremonial spaces for a lord to sit on and to be buried in, respectively. That is, they recreate the place of duality through their use of complementary couplets.

Period Ending Ceremonies

Period Ending ceremonies timed according to the Long Count calendar are the most frequently illustrated events in Classic-period monumental art. In the Maya calen-dar system, the Long Count records the number of days that have expired since a zero base-date. It is counted in units of 360 days that are referred to in the literature as *tuns*. While the Maya likely performed some type of ceremony at the end of each tun period, the end of a k'atun period (twenty tuns) was a particularly important event. Simply because of the mathematics, all tun dates occur on the day Ajaw in the 260-day tzolk'in calendar. It takes thirteen k'atun periods before the same coefficient and day name date will reoccur. For example, the 8.17.0.0.0 k'atun ending (A.D. 376) occurred on the date 1 Ajaw 8 Ch'en. The next 1 Ajaw *k'atun* ending occurred on 9.10.0.0.0 1 Ajaw 8 K'ayab (A.D 633).

Many Classic-period monuments mention a mythological Period Ending event that was conducted by the deities on 13.0.0.0.0 4 Ajaw 8 Kumk'u (August 13, B.C. 3114). During this event, the three hearthstones were changed or renewed (Freidel and MacLeod 2000:3; M. Carrasco 2005:126–29). The protagonists of this mytho-logical Period Ending action are named on Quirigua Stela C as the creator grandfather Itzamnaaj, the two Paddler Gods, and a deity whose name has not been deciphered. Whether this action also involved the creation of new fire that was so prevalent in other Mesoamerican calendar ceremonies is unclear, but the importance of the hearthstones is that they demarcated the fire of the creator grandparents and the center of the world. It is highly probable that part of the mythological k'atun Period Ending ceremony was the reordering and renewing of the world for the forthcoming k'atun period.

There is evidence that the mythological 13.0.0.0.0 Period Ending was the role model for human k'atun Period Ending ceremonies. This is similar to the mythological Wayeb ceremonies illustrated in the Dresden Codex, which were models for human Wayeb ceremonies (Thompson 1972). On Quirigua Stela F, a reference to the 9.15.0.0.0 Period Ending includes the statement that the hearthstones had been changed or renewed on this occasion (M. Carrasco 2005:129). While most of the historical Period Ending events do not appear to refer directly to the action of renewing the three hearthstones, the events are often framed by symbols that indicate that the ceremony occurred at the center of the quadrilateral world as demarcated by the three hearthstones.

Depictions of Period Endings often show the ruler holding a GII scepter representing a thunderbolt ax, an elaborate double-headed serpent, or another ceremonial staff with any one of a variety of deities emerging from it. The ruler is often illustrated wearing the costume of a deity and dancing. He makes incense offerings to the deities and performs personal bloodletting. The sacrifice of captives was an intrinsic part of Period Ending ceremonies, and captives are regularly displayed in a humbled position below the ruler.

We also know some of the events that preceded a Period Ending ceremony. Many narratives, such as on Dos Pilas Stela 2 and Aguateca Stela 2, refer to the preparatory events. Dos Pilas and Aguateca were twin capitals of the same polity. These two monuments have parallel texts that record the capture of the Seibal king Yich'aak Bahlam (December 3, A.D. 735), an ax event the next day, Yich'aak Bahlam's adornment (December 10), and his subsequent sacrifice by Ruler 3 of Dos Pilas-Aguateca on the 9.15.5.0.0 Period Ending (July 26, A.D. 736) (Bassie-Sweet 1991:52–54; Martin and Grube 2008:61).

Although the texts on both monuments refer to the same sequence of events, they each illustrate a different event in the sequence. In addition, each text states which particular event occurred at its site. The Dos Pilas monument specifies that the adornment occurred there, as indicated by the place names on which Ruler 3 stands, while the Aguateca text states that the Period Ending ceremony was held at Aguateca (Stuart and Houston 1994:7–12, 19). Although both scenes show Ruler 3 standing over the Seibal king, there are subtle differences in Ruler 3's costume, suggesting that these two monuments do not illustrate the same event. Indeed, the placement of the text on the two monuments reinforces the conclusion that these two illustrated events occurred at different locations and on different dates (Bassie-Sweet 1991:52–54). It is well established that a text that frames an action identifies that action. The text that frames Ruler 3 on Dos Pilas Stela 2 refers to the adornment event, while the text that frames Ruler 3 on Aguateca Stela 2 refers to the Period Ending. The framing convention was an important device used by Maya artists to indicate which of the many events of a narrative is being illustrated (Bassie-Sweet 1991:10–76, 200–37).

Landa provided detailed descriptions of the Postclassic New Year ceremonies, but unfortunately he gave far less detail of k'atun Period Ending events (Tozzer 1941: 166–69). He did note that there was a different deity for each of the thirteen k'atun periods and that an image of the ruling deity was placed in a temple and worshipped during that period. The seventeenth century priest Avendaño y Loyola (1987:39) also stated that each k'atun had its own deity, priest, and prophecy of its events. Prognostications for the upcoming period were an important component of the New Year ceremonies.

Although badly eroded, the Postclassic Paris Codex illustrates mythological k'atun ceremonies conducted by gods including the deities and priests of the k'atun (Love 1994). Each k'atun deity holds an image of God K (GII), and a bird bearing the omen of the k'atun hovers overhead. Each k'atun priest sits on a scaffold. The creator deity Itzamnaaj in his God D and God N manifestations plays a prominent role as one of the k'atun deities in these Paris Codex ceremonies. His avian manifestation also appears as one of the birds of omen. The prominence of Itzamnaaj in these depictions of the k'atun ceremonies echoes the important role he plays in the Wayeb ceremonies, where he is one of four deities conducting these rituals (Tozzer 1941). The San Bartolo murals illustrate Pre-Classic Wayeb ceremonies, and Itzamnaaj's avian manifestation appears five times in these scenes (Taube et al. 2010).

The Itzamnaaj bird also appears in many Period Ending scenes in the Classic period. The Classic period 9.15.0.0.0 k'atun ceremony illustrated on Piedras Negras Stela 11 shows Ruler 4 sitting in a scaffold niche that is similar to the Paris Codex scenes (Bassie-Sweet 1991:50–52; 1996:108; Love 1994; Stuart and Graham 2003, 9:37). The ruler performs the duties of the k'atun priest, and he even carries an incense bag that is inscribed with the Period Ending date. The avian manifestation of Itzamnaaj perches on top of the scaffold. It is likely that the ruler performed the prognostication for the coming k'atun.

Although Proskouriakoff originally identified the Piedras Negras niche scenes as the accession of the king, the texts that frame these images refer to Period Ending events, not accession (Bassie-Sweet 1991:50–52). For example, Piedras Negras Stela 6 is thematically equivalent to Stela 11; both illustrate the king in the niche (Stuart and Graham 2003, 9:36). On Stela 6, the king K'inich Yo'nal Ahk II sits on the scaffold structure, wearing the same costume elements as Ruler 4. The Itzamnaaj bird perches on the skyband above the ruler. The text that frames the scene refers only to the 9.12.15.0.0 Period Ending of Ruler 3. The text in closest proximity to a figure or action identifies that figure or explains what the event is (Bassie-Sweet 1991:10–76, 200–37).

The Pre-Classic, Classic, and Postclassic examples of Itzamnaaj mentioned above indicate the central role that the creator grandfather played in calendric ceremonies from the earliest of times. The maternal grandfather God L also played a role in Period

Ending ceremonies. Two Late-Classic pottery vessels from the Naranjo region (K2796 and K7750) refer to the mythological Period Ending event on 13.0.0.0.0 4 Ajaw 8 Kumk'u and include illustrations of God L (Coe 1973:108). The two vases illustrate God L sitting on a jaguar-draped throne within a mountain cave–house. God L gazes and gestures toward the upper left of the scene. Following the motion of God L, a viewer would rotate the vessel and see a caption text that frames a group of seated deities. Both texts begin with the date 4 Ajaw 8 K'umk'u and the verb *ts'ak* "to order." The texts then list the names of six gods, some of whom are known from other contexts. Noteworthy is the couplet referring to earth gods and sky gods. Stuart has suggested that this list of deity names does not refer to individual gods, but rather to categories of gods (Stuart, Houston, and Robertson 1999). It is unclear whether these listed gods were put in order on the Period Ending or whether they put something in order. At any rate, bringing order to the world is one of the central themes in the Popol Vuh creation myth.

Although the relationship between God L and the adjacent seated deities on the vases has yet to be established, the arm positions and gestures of these deities echo those used by visitors in human court scenes to show deference to a ruler seated on a throne. It has been suggested that these gods were secondary lords of the underworld who were ruled over by God L (Coe 1973; Freidel, Schele, and Parker 1993:68; M. Miller and Martin 2004:82–83; Martin 2006:172). But given that two of the deities are likely GI and GIII, such speculation seems unwarranted. What the scenes on K2796 and K7750 do clearly indicate is that God L had a significant role in the 13.0.0.0.0 Period Ending. Consequently he must have had a role in human Period Ending ceremonies that were modeled after these mythological actions of the gods. The role of God L in the mythological Period Ending event helps to explain the appearance of God L in the Palenque Cross Group narrative, which climaxes with the 9.13.0.0.0 Period Ending event of the ruler K'inich Kan B'ahlam. On the Tablet of the Sun of the Cross Group, God L and one of the Paddler Deities support a throne on their backs, and on the Temple of the Cross sanctuary door jamb, he stands smoking a rather large cigar (M. Robertson 1991:fig. 43). It should not surprise us that both the paternal and maternal grandfathers had roles to play in creation mythology and Period Ending ceremonies.

The family of creator deities served as models for humans to emulate. This review of Period Ending events and their associated gods demonstrates the role of the creator deities in this important ceremony. As mentioned in chapters 3 and 5, the Paddler Gods were intimately involved in these rituals as well. An assortment of other deities, including Tlaloc, is also found in association with Period Ending ceremonies. For example, Copan Stela 6 illustrates the ruler K'ahk' Uti Witz' K'awiil on the occasion of a Period Ending event. He is dressed in the costume of Tlaloc while holding a double-headed Waxaklajuun Ub'aah Chan meteor serpent that disgorges Tlaloc deities (see next chapter). Given the statements of Landa and Avendaño y Loyola that each k'atun had its own deities, it should be expected that multiple gods were associated with

Period Endings. What is consistent in these scenes is that the settings indicate that the Period Endings were conducted in spaces that replicated the place of duality.

The next chapter explores the thunderbolt and meteor characteristics of the major gods and how the Maya perceived and categorized these natural phenomena. This overview will provide a fundamental framework for understanding the contemporary Ch'ol deities that will be discussed in the final chapter.

7

ANCIENT THUNDERBOLT AND METEOR DEITIES

Karen Bassie-Sweet and Nicholas A. Hopkins

The intent of this chapter is to detail the thunderbolt and meteor characteristics of the major gods and how the ancient Maya perceived and categorized these natural phenomena. In Ch'ol and other Mayan languages, the concepts of thunder (Spanish *trueno),* sheet lightning (*relámpago*), and thunderbolts (*rayo*) are interrelated and sometimes used interchangeably. This overlap in usage and meaning derives from the common origin of all these phenomena: the deity known as Chajk in Ch'ol and as Chahk in the Classic Period. Chahk has been loaned to Yucatec Maya as Chaak, "Dios . . . del agua, de los truenos y relámpagos . . . Dios de la lluvia" (Barrera Vásquez 1980:77). The earlier Yucatec Maya term for the rain god is fossilized in the day name Cauac. Most Western Mayan languages (Yucatecan, Cholan, and Tzeltalan, but not Kanjobalan) employ cognate terms for thunderbolts and lightning, all developments of proto-Maya **kahoq* and with the same range of meanings. So do some of their neighbors (Aguacatec, Pocomam, Pocomchí, and Kekchí; Kaufman 2003:489). In contrast, most Eastern Mayan languages and Kanjobalan employ a loanword from Zoque **keyo-pa,* for example, K'iche' *kayupa'* (Kaufman 2003:473; Pocomam has both).

Specific references to the related aspects of Chajk are made in Ch'ol, such as *xu'chajk* "lightning bolt (rayo)," literally "splinter of Chajk," or *xoyob' chajk* "sheet lightning (relámpago)." *Xoyob'* is a word peculiar to Chiapas languages that in 1789 meant "rainbow" (Fernández 1892:45), as it still does in Tzeltal and Tojolabal (Kaufman 2003: 470); in Ch'ol it is now more generally "flashing, brilliance, reflection" (Aulie and Aulie 1978:151; Hopkins, Josserand, and Cruz 2010). In other Mayan languages, words for "thunder" and "lightning" are based on proto-Mayan **k'uuh* "sun" (some Kanjobalan languages), proto-Mayan **lem* "flashing, shiny" (Yucatec Maya, Chortí, Tuzantec, and Huastec), or proto-Eastern Mayan **q'a7q'* "fire" (Kekchí, Pocomam, and Cakchiquel) (Kaufman 2003).

Thunderbolt gods are ubiquitous in Maya culture. This is not surprising given the deadly intensity and frequency of storms accompanied by thunderbolts in this region. The word *Chahk* "thunderbolt" is represented in Classic period hieroglyphic texts by a portrait of a zoomorphic deity wearing a shell earring. Postclassic versions of these Chahk deities are known by the Schellhas designation of God B. The Maya believed that a thunderbolt was either the serpent form of a Chahk deity or the ax of a Chahk that had been hurled through the air. Thunder was thought to be the beating of a drum or Chahks shouting at each other.

THE THUNDERBOLT TRIAD

The Palenque hieroglyphic narratives make reference to the births and activities of a triad of mythical thunderbolt brothers at the top of the Chahk hierarchy. These brothers have been nicknamed GI, GII, and GIII (Bassie-Sweet 2008:figs. 6.2, 6.4, 6.3). It has been proposed that this triad was parallel to the three Heart of Sky thunderbolt gods of the Popol Vuh: Thunderbolt Huracán, Youngest Thunderbolt, and Sudden Thunderbolt (Bassie-Sweet 2008:107–21). Although the name of Raxa Kaqulja of the Popol Vuh has been translated as Sudden Thunderbolt, *raxa* is the highland cognate of *yax* "green-blue." The concept of colored thunderbolt gods is well attested in Mesoamerica, and it is likely that Raxa Kaqulja was a blue-green thunderbolt.

Each of three temples flanking the Cross Group plaza at Palenque focuses on one member of the thunderbolt triad. At the center of the plaza is a small platform that marks this location as the symbolic center of the world (Taube 1998:441). GI is highlighted in the northern Temple of the Cross, GII in the eastern Temple of the Foliated Cross, and GIII in the western Temple of the Sun (collectively called the Cross Group). The portrait glyph of GI is followed by the name Chahk, and some of his attributes suggest he was a god of storms (Coe 1973; Bassie-Sweet 2008:111–13: fig. 6.2). His temple in the Cross Group is oriented to the north, the dominant direction from which the storms that plague the Maya region come.

The name of GII, the youngest of the three deities, has been deciphered as Unen K'awiil "baby K'awiil" (Stuart 1987; Martin 2002). Unen K'awiil is also known by the Schellhas designation of God K. GII is depicted as a thunderbolt ax in many illustrations (Bassie-Sweet 2008:fig. 6.4). His body represents the handle, while his head has the ax blade protruding from it. One of his legs is often shown as a snake. The Palenque Cross Group narrative also states that GII was a red dwarf (Houston 1992). Red is associated with the east in Maya world view, and his temple is situated on the east side of the Cross Group plaza. It is likely that GII was the thunderbolt god who broke open the mountain containing corn.

The third thunderbolt god, GIII, has traits that indicate he was associated with fire, meteors, and warfare (Bassie-Sweet 2008:115–21). It is highly likely that the Maya categorized meteors as a kind of thunderbolt (Taube 2000:325). Both flash across the sky and can create fire and a booming sound. The diagnostic trait of GIII is a looped cord over his nose that represented the cord used to drill fire (Taube 2000; Bassie-Sweet 2008:fig. 6.7). The implication of this imagery is that the body of GIII was thought to represent the fire stick. GIII also carries the *yajawk'ahk'* title, which is held by lords with both priestly and war-related functions (Zender 2004b:195–209; Stuart 2005a:123–25). Zender noted that the term *ajaw* "lord" actually means "vassal" when it is stated in a possessed form such as *y-ajaw-k'ahk';* hence the title *yajawk'ahk'* is "the fire's vassal." The title implies that GIII and the other *yajawk'ahk'* lords were vassals of the fire god.

It has been well established that pyramids represented mountains, and that the Maya believed that mountains were manifestations of their gods. In other words, each Palenque Cross Group building represents the mountain aspect of one member of the thunderbolt triad. In addition to this mountain identification, several researchers have noted that the triadic building arrangement of the Cross Group represents the three hearthstones (Hansen 1992; Freidel, Schele, and Parker 1993). The logical extension of this identification is that the three hearthstones were thought to be manifestations of the three thunderbolt gods (Bassie-Sweet 2008:121). The identification of three hearthstones with gods is also found in Aztec mythology.

The Thunderbolt Aspect of Itzamnaaj

Whether produced by a bolt of lightning, striking flint, or drilling sticks, fire was thought to be a manifestation of the creator grandfather Itzamnaaj-Xpiyacoc (Bassie-Sweet 2008:65–67, 248–51). It was the fire of his household that was demarcated by the three hearthstones. A series of pottery scenes shows Itzamnaaj emerging from the mouth of GII-K'awiil's serpent leg (see vases K719, K1006, K1081, K1198, K1813, K2068, K2213, K2772, K3202, K3702, K3716, K4013, K5164, K5230, K6754, K7838). In the context of these scenes, the creator grandfather appears to be both the fire and the thunder of the lightning bolt (Bassie-Sweet 2008:146).

Bacab, Pauah Tun, and Xib Chac

Bishop Landa noted that there were four directional Postclassic thunderbolt gods, each known at the same time by the name Bacab, Pauah Tun, or Xib Chac (Tozzer 1941:135–49). They were characterized as brothers, and each of these three names was preceded by the appropriate directional color (red-east, white-north, black-west, and yellow-south). Landa stated that the Wayeb ceremonies were in honor of these gods: "Among the multitudes of gods which this nation worshipped they worshipped four, each of them called Bacab. They said that they were brothers whom God placed, when he created the world, at the four points of it, holding up the sky so that it should not fall" (Tozzer 1941:135). The name Bakab appears in Classic period inscriptions as an important title of Maya kings, though not in reference to deities. It is often prefixed with a directional association.

Coe (1973) proposed that the Bacab–Pauah Tun–Xib Chac deities were directional manifestations of God N, based on his reading of God N's portrait glyph as Pauah Tun. However, Stuart has since demonstrated that this reading was incorrect (see Bassie-Sweet 2008:135). Stuart has identified the Classic period Chahk deities who are specifically named as Xib' Chahks (cited in Schele and Miller 1986:60; Taube 1992:17). The illustration of the Red Xib Chak on Maya vase K1609 shows an ax-wielding thunderbolt god. Four Chahk deities are identified by their respective caption texts as the White Xib' Chahk, Black Xib' Chahk, Yellow Xib' Chahk, and Red Xib' Chahk on Codex Dresden pages 29c–30c. These illustrations indicate that Bakab–Xib' Chahk–Pawah Tun deities were not God N. There is evidence that this set of deities was a manifestation of One Ixim, who also had directional associations (Bassie-Sweet 2008:170).

THE PADDLER GODS

The two elderly Paddler Gods, as discussed in chapter 3, are named as Chahks and as *mam k'uh* "grandfather gods." These paired gods played a prominent role in Period Ending ceremonies and were intimately associated with rivers and clouds. In some inscriptions, the paired portrait glyphs of the Paddler Gods are replaced by *k'in* "day" and *ak'bal* "night" glyphs, which suggests that they are complementary opposites of each other. They are likely parallel to the aged diviners in the Popol Vuh known as Xulu and Paqam (Bassie-Sweet 2008:281–83). The words *xulu* "descended" and *paqam* "ascended" are also complementary opposites. The attributes of the Jaguar Paddler are similar to those of GIII, except that the Jaguar Paddler is aged. This old Jaguar Paddler is seen on a number of the Palenque *incensarios* and on the Tablet of the Sun, The Jaguar Paddler and God L hold up the central icon (Marc Zender, personal communication).

OTHER CHAHK DEITIES

Below these primary thunderbolt deities in the hierarchy were numerous other Chahk gods who are illustrated in Maya art and named in hieroglyphic texts and colonial documents (Grube 2002; Lacadena 2004; García Barros 2008). Many of their nominal phrases include references to age, color, rain, clouds, fire, and the sky. A sample of these names includes such descriptions as "first rain Chahk," which likely refers to the first rains of the growing season, and "cloud or mist Chahk." Chahk deities are frequently illustrated swinging an ax that represents their thunderbolt. One of the most common beliefs in the Maya area is that the stone ax-heads that are often found in the fields or forest are the remains of Chahk's thunderbolt.

One particular variant of the stone ax is wielded by a Classic period Chahk deity whose name is phonetically spelled Yopaat. What his name means is as yet unclear (Stuart, cited in Zender 2004b; Taube and Zender 2009). Yopaat is shown brandishing a stone weapon, the shape of which suggests it is an eccentric flint. Furthermore, the dotted circles emanating from the top of Yopaat's head are thought to represent sparks. Taube and Zender illustrate Classic period scenes of combat where the participants use such flint weapons to strike blows. In hieroglyphic texts, the verb *jatz'* "to strike" is composed of a hand holding Yopaat's flint weapon (Grube 2000; Zender 2004b). The verb is used in contexts where it refers to the creation of fire, which fits with the fire-making properties of flint. In ancient times, iron-containing materials such as pyrite were struck with flint to create sparks.

There are a number of scenes that show Chahk deities wielding both Yopaat's weapon and a lightning-bolt ax. Taube and Zender (2009:162, 183) noted that blows struck during ritual combat in Guerrero are compared to thunder and lightning, and they suggested that Yopaat's weapon represents thunder, while the ax is the lightning. Perhaps a better metaphor is to compare what happens when a person is hit by a thunderbolt to boxing blows. A thunderbolt that hits a tree will often split the wood just like an ax. However, when a thunderbolt hits a person, that victim becomes dazed (or dies) as though hit with a stone object. A direct blow from Yopaat's flint weapon would either daze or strike down a combatant just like a thunderbolt (see the "Our Grandfather Ty'añ Lak Mam" story in the appendix).

Humans as Thunderbolts

There is abundant evidence that the Classic Maya lords were identified with thunderbolt gods. When humans donned the mask, headdress, or costume elements of a deity, they became the embodiment of the deity (Houston and Stuart 1996, 1998). During the Classic period, rulers and young lords were often illustrated wearing the costume of a Chahk. One well-known example is the ruler Bird Jaguar, who is shown wearing a Chahk mask and headdress on Yaxchilan Stela 11. Another is the twelve-year-old K'an Joy Chitam dancing as a Chahk deity called Ox Bolon Chahk on the Dumbarton Oaks panel (Bassie-Sweet 1987; 1991:fig. 64). Furthermore, a common title held by Maya rulers is Bakab, which, as we saw earlier, was one of the names for the thunderbolt gods of the four directions.

Numerous Classic period rulers incorporated either Chahk or Yopaat into their own name phrases. For example, an eighth century Naranjo ruler was named K'ahk' Tiliw Chan Chaak, literally "fire burns sky Chaak." An eighth-century Quirigua ruler was named K'ahk' Tiliw Chan Yopaat, literally "fire burns sky Yopaat" (Martin and Grube 2008). The name K'awiil (the name for GII) was also commonly used by Maya rulers. Martin and Grube (2008) list more than thirty-four kings and queens who incorporated Chahk, Yopaat, or K'awiil in their names. This naming practice suggests that Maya elite were thought to have thunderbolt co-essences. At the very least, they were identified with these deities and their supernatural powers. Human dwarfs who act as ritual assistants to rulers are also illustrated in Maya art, and it is likely that these human dwarfs were viewed as the living embodiment of K'awiil.

An eyewitness account gives us an idea of the relevance of thunderbolt gods in the late seventeenth century. In this account, the Spanish priests Margil, Mazariegos, and Guillén describe a Lacandón Ch'ol new fire festival conducted in honor of their thunderbolt deity Macon (Margil, Mazariegos, and Guillén 1984:15). In this report on Lacandón Ch'ol religion, politics, and economics sent to President Jacinto de Barrios Leal, the priests state that during this ceremony, the leaders of Sac Bahlán were thought to be thunderbolts. With the help of four ritual assistants, these rulers prepared for their roles by becoming intoxicated on rum. Drinking was often a prerequisite for ritual activity. The leaders then ran into the town like lightning. In response, the entire population placed a pitcher of water beside each hearth and fled the town for four days. The four assistants went to every household and doused its hearth fire with the water. The rulers and their four assistants then proceeded to the temple that housed their deities. The Spanish priests did not describe the rituals conducted in the temple, but it is likely that these leaders made new fire. The four assistants maintained the temple fire constantly, feeding it copal incense while giving more drink to the Chahk leaders.

Although the Spanish priests did not mention what the town's population did for those four days, presumably they retired to the small huts that were located in their milpas and that were used as dwellings during the growing season. They returned to their houses in town on the fifth day of the festival: "The day following these four days all return to their houses, everyone killing his turkey and pouring the blood over ocote, carrying it to burn before the idols, and they ask the Caciques (rulers) whose intoxication is now over for new fire, and thence they all bring fire to their houses and cook their turkeys, and eat and drink and celebrate their great feast" (Tozzer 1984:16). The notion that humans must provide a thunderbolt deity with blood offerings in order to receive fire is seen in the Popol Vuh, where the thunderbolt deity Tohil would only grant fire if given blood sacrifices (Christenson 2007a:216–18).

METEOR MYTHOLOGY

As noted earlier in this chapter, fiery meteors and meteor showers were considered cognates of thunder and lightning in Maya world view. Meteors, or shooting stars, are frequent phenomena in the night sky; large meteors are visible even during the day. In Mesoamerica, meteors were viewed as omens of impending disaster, death, and illness. They were personified as the obsidian darts, spears, or arrows of certain deities (Köhler 1989; Taube 2000). Meteors were equated with the primordial action of drilling ceremonial fires, in which such weapons were also used. Discarded obsidian weapons and chips that the Maya find in their fields are thought to be the remains of meteors.

It is also believed that when meteors hit the ground, they can take the form of caterpillars, worms, or maggots. Prismatic blades of obsidian can resemble these creatures. Both the creatures and obsidian are referred to as the excrement of stars. The terms used for meteors in the Tzotzil, Tzeltal, and Tojolabal areas (*sanselaw, chamtzelaw, k'antzelaw, k'antzewal, sansewal, tzantzewal*) are also used to describe lightning flashes and sheet lightning as well as lights that appear in the mountains at night (Slocum and Gerdel 1965:193; C. Lenkersdorf 1979; Pitarch 2010:44). The Tojolabal characterize *sansewal* as lightning or meteors that take the form of little worms of fire or small black snakes (C. Lenkersdorf 1979:13, 312, 325, 370). In Ch'ol, the borrowed term *tzantzewal* means lightning flash (Stoll 1938:67).

Bishop Núñez described the belief that Postclassic ritual specialists in Chiapas could transform into thunderbolts and balls of fire (meteors) (Calnek 1988:46; Núñez 1988:133). He noted that one of the co-essences of ritual specialists could take the form of *tzihuizin,* which he identified as being cognate with the Postclassic Aztec fire and meteor serpent known as Xiuhcoatl (Brinton 1894:20). The identification of leaders with thunderbolts and meteors continues today in highland Chiapas (Guiteras Holmes 1961; Hermitte 1964; Vogt 1969; Nash 1970; Laughlin 1977; Spero 1987). The ancestral and current leaders are thought to use their thunderbolt and meteor co-essences to protect the community.

Tlaloc: A Classic-Period Meteor and Obsidian Deity

At Teotihuacan, there is a prominent deity whose attributes indicate he is associated with lightning, and some scholars have referred to him as a storm god. He has also been identified as the precursor of the Aztec thunderbolt deity Tlaloc. It is unknown what name the Teotihuacanos used for this deity, so we will continue to refer to him as Tlaloc. Tlaloc also appears in the Maya area, where Maya lords and ladies are often seen dressed in the costume of this god and carrying his obsidian weapons (Pasztory 1974; Coggins 1975; Hellmuth 1975; D. Carrasco 1982; Berlo 1983; A. Stone 1989; Taube 1992b, 2000; Proskouriakoff 1993; Stuart 2000, 2004a, 2004b; Braswell 2003). As noted, the Maya likely categorized meteors as a type of lightning. There is evidence that the Maya specifically associated the Teotihuacan Tlaloc with meteors, obsidian, and fire, and that this deity was incorporated into Maya world view as a patron god of war. Like other Mesoamerican deities, Tlaloc had a number of avatars including a jaguar, centipede-serpent, moth, and owl. The following is an overview of Tlaloc and some of his more prominent traits. This material is derived from a volume on Maya war deities that is currently in preparation by Bassie-Sweet.

In Maya depictions of Tlaloc, the five most common traits are skeletal form, goggle eyes, E-shaped nose element, *k'an*-cross earrings, and a headdress with a Central Mexican year sign (fig. 7.1). This year sign motif can include fire torches and bundles of *yauhtli* plants (*Tagetes lucida*) that were used as incense offerings (Taube 2000; Nielsen 2006). In the Maya region, the weapons of choice for the Tlaloc deity were obsidian darts and atlatl (spearthrower) and obsidian spears, as opposed to the flint axes and bludgeoning weapons frequently carried by the Chahk deities. For example, on Piedras Negras Stela 7 and Stela 8, the ruler who is dressed as a Tlaloc deity carries an obsidian spear (Stuart and Graham 2003:figs. 9:39, 9:44). These spears are tipped with Teoti-huacan bleeding heart symbols, indicating their lethal nature and their association with heart sacrifice. In Maya art and hieroglyphic writing, objects made from obsidian (proto-Mayan *tyaah*) are often infixed with *ak'bal* "night, darkness" signs. In contrast, objects made from flint (proto-Mayan *tyooq'*) are marked with elements also found on the *tuun* "stone" sign (Schele and Miller 1986:46; Kaufman 2003:442; A. Stone and Zender 2011:23, 83).

Another example of the Tlaloc costume is worn by Dos Pilas Ruler 3 on Dos Pilas Stela 2 and Aguateca Stela 2 (Bassie-Sweet 1991:fig. 14). This lord wears a mask composed of Tlaloc's goggle eyes and *E*-shaped nose element, and he carries an incense bag with a Tlaloc motif, an atlatl with darts, and a rectangular shield and spear. Tlaloc masks have been recovered during excavations, with the goggles constructed of either white shell or obsidian. The *E*-shaped nose elements of the Tlaloc mask are obsidian eccentrics, which have also been found in tombs. The Tlaloc gods that decorate the loincloth apron and hipcloth of the ruler have obsidian eccentrics coming out of their mouths. The hipcloth eccentrics have the bleeding heart symbol on their tips.

Despite Tlaloc's use of obsidian weapons as opposed to the flint weapons of the other Chahks, the Maya categorized Tlaloc as a K'awiil deity, that is, as a Chahk thunderbolt god. This is evidenced by a hieroglyphic text in Copan Structure 10L-26. The text has standard Maya script paired with Teotihuacan-inspired hieroglyphs (Houston and Stuart 1998:91; Stuart 2000:495–97, 2004b:388). In the Maya-style text, the word *k'awiil* in Copan ruler Waxaklajuun Ubah K'awiil's name is represented by a typical GII portrait glyph with fire (*k'ak'*) emanating from a torch in his forehead. In the parallel Teotihuacan-style text, the word *k'awiil* is represented by a Tlaloc with a torch in his forehead. Further evidence that Tlaloc was categorized as a Chahk deity is seen on Yaxchilan Lintel 25, which illustrates the conjuring of a Tlaloc and a female dressed as Tlaloc (Bassie-Sweet 2008:208–10; 2010). The main text of the lintel indicates that the conjured deity is named Aj K'ahk' (he of fire) O' Chahk, again signifying Tlaloc's identification with the Maya thunderbolt gods and the fire that they produce.

THE METEOR SERPENT WAXAKLAJUUN UB'AAH CHAN

A deity found in conjunction with meteor symbolism in Maya iconography is the serpent Waxaklajuun Ub'aah Chan. The head of the serpent, which Taube has nick-named the Teotihuacan War Serpent because of its connection to war imagery, is illustrated on the front façade of the Teotihuacan Temple of the Feathered Serpent (Taube 1992c, 2000; Grube and Nahm 1994; Boot 1999; Kettunen and Davis 2004). This serpent frequently appears in full body form in Maya art, and it is named Waxa-klajuun Ub'aah Chan in Maya hieroglyphic texts (Schele 1990; Schele and Freidel 1990; Houston and Stuart 1996:299; Stuart 2000:493). In addition to snake characteristics such as a rattlesnake tail, the Waxaklajuun Ub'aah Chan also has centipede, jaguar, and

7.1. Tlaloc from Copan Stela 6, after Fash; Copan Structure 10L–26, after Stuart; and Yaxchilan Lintel 25, after Graham.

Lepidoptera characteristics. Some examples of the snake are double-headed, such as the one on Yaxchilan Lintel 25 (fig. 7.2).

Stylized butterfly or moth wings with scalloped edges frequently adorn the body of the Waxaklajuun Ub'aah Chan, and some examples also feature lepidopteran antennae. In English, diurnal Lepidoptera are generally known as butterflies and nocturnal Lepidoptera as moths. Unlike English, the Maya use the same terms for both moths and butterflies. Large moths and butterflies are called *pejpem* (Ch'ol) and *pehpen* (Tzeltal), while smaller ones are *sulup* (Ch'ol) and *supul* (Tzeltal) (Hunn 1977:280–85; Juan Jesús Vázquez, personal communication). The lepidopteran wing elements of the Waxaklajuun Ub'aah Chan have been identified as belonging to a butterfly (Taube 2000:282–85), but as will be discussed below, they more likely belong to a specific species of moth. Taube (1992c, 2000) has noted that the Waxaklajuun Ub'aah Chan was the precursor of the Postclassic Xiuhcoatl serpent of Central Mexico, which has similar lepidopteran wings and which often takes the form of a serpent or a caterpillar (the larval form of moths and butterflies).

There are numerous examples of Maya lords impersonating the Waxaklajuun Ub'aah Chan by wearing a headdress composed of the head of this beast. Examples are found on Piedras Negras Stela 7, Stela 8, and Stela 26; Naranjo Stela 19; the Palenque Temple XVII panel; and Bonampak Stela 3. In these cases, the headdress is formed from shell platelets, and examples of such headdresses have been found in royal tombs (A. Stone 1989; Bell et al. 2004). On Naranjo Stela 2, the ruler K'ahk' Tiliw Chan not only wears the Waxaklajuun Ub'aah Chan headdress, but the snake's rattlesnake tail appears between his legs (Graham and Von Euw 1975:fig. 2:13). The loincloth apron and shield of K'ahk' Tiliw Chan are also decorated with images of the Waxaklajuun Ub'aah Chan.

Taube (1992c:63–64; 2000:294–330) noted that the Waxaklajuun Ub'aah Chan has a back-curved snout that is reminiscent of the hooked end of an atlatl, and that in turn, ceremonial atlatls are often depicted as the Waxaklajuun Ub'aah Chan, as on Bonampak Stela 3. The Waxaklajuun Ub'aah Chan is similar to the Xiuhcoatl, which is shown as the personification of an atlatl and dart. Many Postclassic representations of atlatls, such as on Codex Borbonicus 23 and 24, have a serpent form. Taube also noted that across Mesoamerica, meteors were characterized as obsidian spear darts or arrows and that they were thought to be manifestations of the Waxaklajuun Ub'aah Chan and Xiuhcoatl. Although *xiuh* means turquoise, the word also refers to meteors. The back-curved snout of Xiuhcoatl is often decorated with numerous round star signs that likely refer to a meteor shower. The meaning of the name Waxaklajuun Ub'aah Chan "eighteen are the faces or images of the snake" is ambiguous; however, several authors have noted that there were eighteen Waxaklajuun Ub'aah Chan heads on each side of the front façade of the Teotihuacan temple. Given that Waxaklajuun Ub'aah Chan represented a meteor, the conclusion we draw is that eighteen such meteors would constitute a meteor shower.

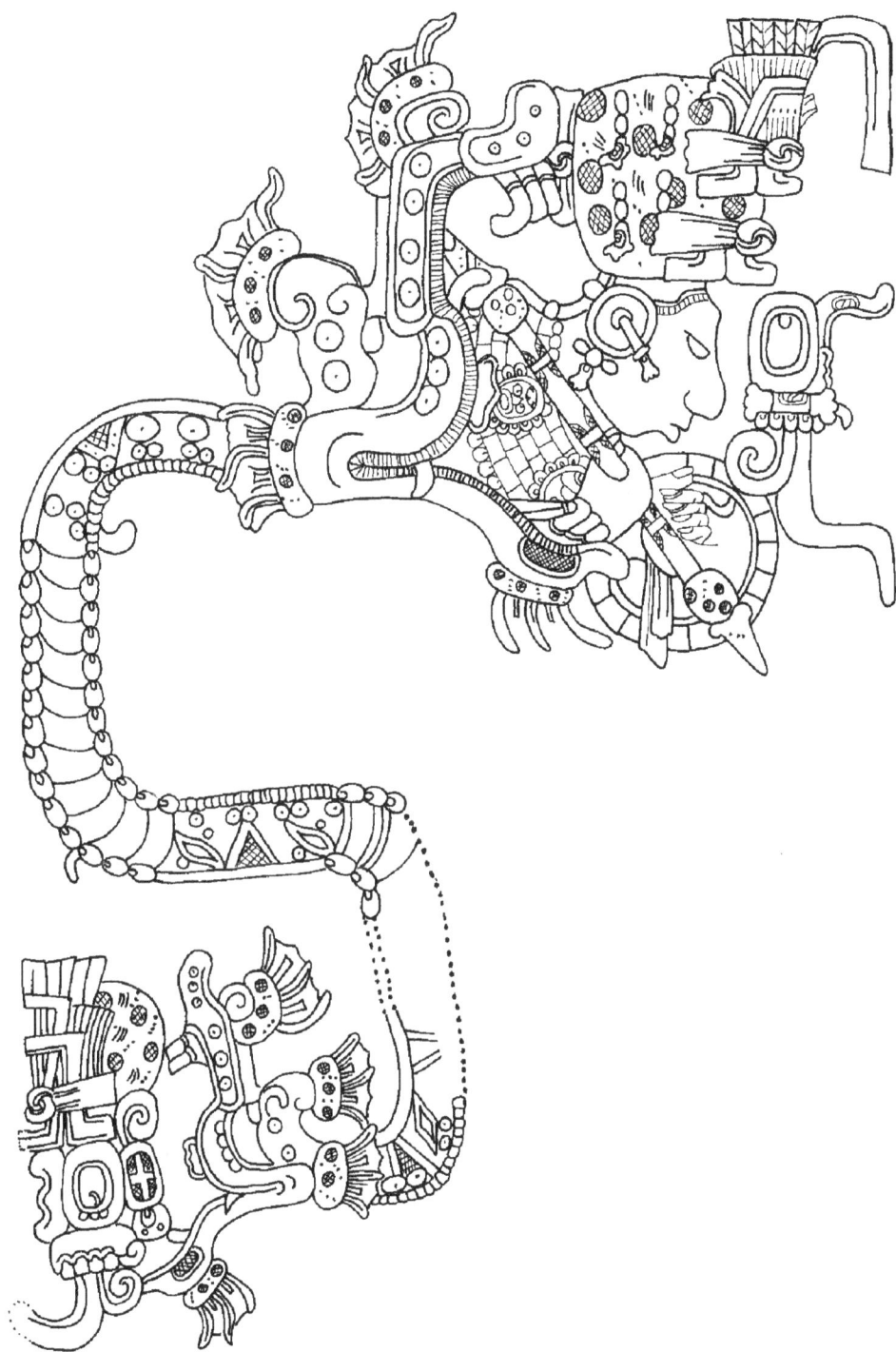

7.2. Waxaklajuun Ub'aah Chan meteor serpent, Yaxchilan Lintel 25, after Graham.

The flashes of light given off by meteor showers were associated with the drilling of fire. A reed dart or arrow frequently served as the vertical drill in Central Mexican new fire ceremonies (Seler 1990–2000, 3:213; Taube 2000). Sahagún noted that the Xiuhcoatl was a fire drill (Seler 1990–2000, 3:215), and the fire aspect of Xiuhcoatl is demonstrated in a number of scenes where fire is being drilled on the back of a Xiuhcoatl (Taube 2000:fig. 10.15). Taube (2000:274) noted that flames were frequently illustrated as feathers in Central Mexican art, and atlatls are often shown with fire-like feathers in place of the round star signs (for example, on Codex Telleriano Remensis, folios 4v and 6v). On a looted Teotihuacan-style monument from the Petén, the lord carries an atlatl with flames shooting out from its tip (Robicsek and Hales 1981:vessel 108). Many examples of the Waxaklajuun Ub'aah Chan headdress include a burning dart or torch in reference to the fire nature of this deity (Nielsen 2003; Taube 2004).

On the Teotihuacan Temple of the Feathered Serpent, the Waxaklajuun Ub'aah Chan wears a Tlaloc headdress. The close relationship between this beast and Tlaloc is also depicted in such scenes as Yaxchilan Lintel 25, Yaxhilan Stela 35, and Copan Stela 6, three examples where Tlaloc emerges from the mouth of the Waxaklajuun Ub'aah Chan. In the text of Copan Structure 10L-26, the foot of the Tlaloc god is represented by the Waxaklajuun Ub'aah Chan (Stuart 2000:495–97; 2004b:388). This depiction of the snake replacing a foot brings to mind the many portraits of the deity K'awiil (GII), which illustrate him with a serpent foot that represents his fiery thunderbolt. If the lightning serpent emerging from the thunderbolt deity GII's foot is a manifestation of GII, then it must be concluded that the Waxaklajuun Ub'aah Chan meteor emerging from Tlaloc's foot is a manifestation of Tlaloc. The inference is that the Maya viewed Tlaloc as a meteor god.

As mentioned above, meteors were thought to be the deities' spear darts or arrows, and by extension they were identified with the obsidian that forms the tips of these weapons (Laughlin 1975:99, 513; Köhler 1989; B. Tedlock 1992:180–81; Taube 2004:292, 330). In Tzotzil and Tojolabal, the term "star feces" refers to both meteors and obsidian. Several examples of the Xiuhcoatl illustrate an obsidian blade emerging from its anus. The close association between obsidian and atlatls is seen in the depictions of obsidian eccentrics with the hooked form of an atlatl. Such an eccentric is held by a Tlaloc warrior illustrated in the White Patio of the Atetelco compound at Teotihuacan. This warrior holds an obsidian blade with a bleeding heart impaled on it (fig. 7.3). The warrior also has three blades protruding from the top of his headdress. They are marked with a zigzag design that at Teotihuacan designates obsidian. Another example of the close association of obsidian and atlatls is seen in the mural at Acanceh, where a Waxaklajuun Ub'aah Chan cradles a hooked obsidian eccentric in its body (Miller 1991:fig. 35). The bleeding heart symbol hangs from the tip of the eccentric.

Rulers are often seen dressed as the Waxaklajuun Ub'aah Chan while carrying obsidian weapons that are tipped with the bleeding heart symbol. The Piedras Negras ruler Yo'nal Ahk II is dressed as the Waxaklajuun Ub'aah Chan on Stela 7 and Stela 8

7.3. Tlaloc warrior, Atetelco mural, after Von Winning.

(Stuart and Graham 2003:figs. 9.39, 9.44). The staff he holds is topped by a hook-shaped eccentric that is personified as a skull with centipede teeth. From its tip hangs the sign for a bleeding heart. On Stela 26, the ruler Yo'nal Ahk I is also dressed as the Waxaklajuun Ub'aah Chan, but in this case he holds a staff in the form of this deity.

While the Lacandón Maya and Tzotzil refer to meteors as arrows, the K'iche' specifically call them flaming arrows, and they believe that the ancient obsidian points and blades that they encounter in their fields are the remains of a meteor (Tozzer 1907:155–58; Köhler 1989; B. Tedlock 1992:180). The Tzotzil also believe that obsidian is dropped by meteors. This is in contrast to the belief that flint points and blades are the remains of Chahk's thunderbolt. The association of obsidian with the Teotihuacan Tlaloc deity is not surprising, given that Teotihuacan controlled or directed a substantial part of the Central Mexican obsidian trade.

A trapezoid element associated with Xiuhcoatl, and the obsidian zigzag pattern, also appear in Maya art in association with obsidian. The caterpillar body of the Xiuhcoatl, which represents an obsidian dart, takes the form of trapezoid segments (fig. 7.4, left). The Yaxchilan ruler Bird Jaguar IV is illustrated on Lintel 8 in the midst of a battle, and he is illustrated on Lintel 41 either preparing for this battle or returning from it (Graham and Von Euw 1977:fig. 3:27; Graham 1979:fig. 3:92). In both scenes, he carries a long spear. Long spears—as opposed to darts and spearthrowers—were the preferred weapon in the Classic period for close-contact warfare. Below the spearhead on Lintel 41, two such trapezoid segments flare out from the spear shaft, indicating that this is an obsidian spear (fig. 7.4, right). Below this pair of stylized caterpillar bodies is a series of obsidian chips embedded in the staff. The chips form the zigzag pattern that represents obsidian. The ruler's leg ornaments on Copan Stela 6 and Naranjo Stela 2 are decorated with the obsidian zigzag pattern and the trapezoid segments (Fash 2001:fig. 60). The leg ornaments of a ruler illustrated on Naranjo Stela 19 and Copan Structure 26 have similar trapezoid segments (Graham and Von Euw 1975, 2:29; Fash 2001:fig. 91). The implication of this zigzag and trapezoid imagery is that the legs of the ruler were thought to be like obsidian spears. In other words, the ruler did not just throw Tlaloc's meteor spear; he was equated with it. This is similar to the images discussed previously in this chapter that indicate that the ruler was thought to be the embodiment of Chahk and his thunderbolt.

THE MOTH TLALOC

Another manifestation of Tlaloc has the form of a Lepidoptera insect (fig. 7.5). This deity has the goggle eyes and Mexican year sign of Tlaloc as well as the same lepidopteran wings found on the Waxaklajuun Ub'aah Chan, but its distinguishing feature is a lepidopteran proboscis. A proboscis is the long, tubular mouthpart used by butterflies and moths to suck nectar. In its coiled position, the proboscis has the hook shape of obsidian eccentrics and atlatls. In some examples, the Lepidoptera Tlaloc's antennae are represented by the feathered end of an obsidian dart or by the torch found in Tlaloc's year sign (Berlo 1983:83; Headrick 2003:151; Taube 2000:fig. 10.7). Taube (2000:285) has noted that the Waxaklajuun Ub'aah Chan has caterpillar-like characteristics, and that meteors are also identified as caterpillars in Mesoamerica. Given the lepidopteran wings and caterpillar characteristics of the Waxaklajuun Ub'aah Chan, it is highly likely that the Lepidoptera Tlaloc is not only the moth or butterfly manifestation of Tlaloc, but that it is specifically the adult Lepidoptera form of the Waxaklajuun Ub'aah Chan.

The Aztec believed that the souls of warriors could take the form of five different species of birds and three different species of butterflies (Sahagún 1959–63, 3:49). Based on this evidence and the war attributes of Tlaloc, many researchers have proposed that the Lepidoptera Tlaloc was also a butterfly (see Headrick 2007 for an overview of these butterfly identifications). The fire, obsidian, and meteor characteristics of Tlaloc

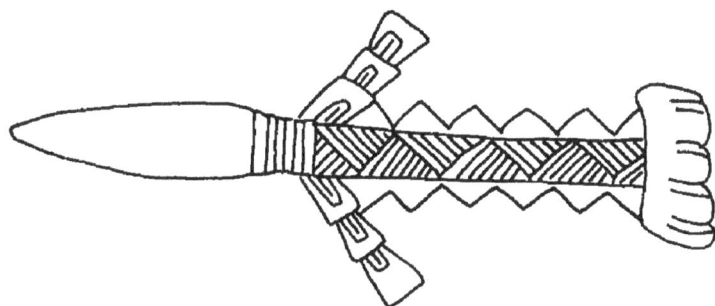

7.4. Xiuhcoatl from Codex Borbonicus, page 20, and spearhead from Yaxchilan Lintel 41, after Graham.

7.5. Moth Tlaloc from Kan Bahlam panel, after Hales; Yaxchilan Lintel 8, after Graham; and Yaxchilan Lintel 41, after Graham.

are, however, more like moths than butterflies. For example, moths are regularly found hovering around fire sources such as hearths and torches. In Central Mexico, the obsidian goddess Itzpapalotl had a lepidopteran form that was based on the *Rothschildia orizaba,* a moth (Beutelspacher 1994). This goddess is illustrated with obsidian blades on her wings like the Lepidoptera Tlaloc, whose wings are decorated with the obsidian zigzag pattern.

The meteor co-essence called *poslom* in the Tzotzil and Tzeltal areas is associated with moths. A Tzotzil shaman can perform witchcraft by sending poslom to cause disease and illness in his enemies, and this poslom can take the form of blue, green, gray, and yellow pehpen "lepidopterans" (Holland 1961:190–92). A victim of witchcraft hires another shaman to perform a curing (Robert Laughlin, personal communication; Vogt 1969:410). The moths that are attracted to the flames of the curing candles are thought to be the spies of the shaman who sent the illness, and they are killed to prevent them from returning to the witching shaman. Moths in Chenalhó are thought to belong to the nocturnal evil spirit Pukuh and are called pehpen of death (Guiteras Holmes 1961:293, 301). When Pukuh enters a home, a person becomes sick and cannot recover unless he or she moves away.

There is compelling ethnographic and iconographic evidence that the Lepidoptera Tlaloc was based on the species *Ascalapha odorata,* the Black Witch moth. The Black Witch is an impressive moth with a wingspan that can reach an astonishing fifteen centimeters. In flight, it is often mistaken for a bat because of its large size. The wings of the Black Witch have scalloped edges like the wings of the Lepidoptera Tlaloc and zigzag patterns across the wings like the zigzag design that represents obsidian. The tip of its hindwing is decorated with *E*-shaped motifs similar to Tlaloc's *E*-shaped obsidian nose element. The Black Witch moth is called *x-mahanail* "house borrower" in Yucatec, which refers to its inclination to enter the dark interiors of Maya houses at dawn to roost on the walls during the day (Hogue 1993). As noted above, meteors (the celestial manifestations of Tlaloc) were seen as signs of impending illness and death. A ubiquitous belief in Mesoamerica is that the appearance of a Black Witch moth inside a house is an omen that a member of the household will become ill or die (Hoffmann 1918; Hogue 1993, Beutelspacher 1994; Joljá Project field notes). The near-universal fear of the Black Witch moth in Mesoamerica is reflected in its Aztec name *micpapalotl* or *miquipapalotl* "death moth" (Beutelspacher 1994:22, 29, 83–84), and its Ch'ol name *pejpem xib'aj* "moth demon" (Joljá Project field notes; Juan Jesús Vázquez, personal communication). The Ch'ol kill these moths when they enter their houses, because of their death association (Joljá Project field notes; Domingo Pérez Moreno, personal communication).

The Owl Tlaloc

In addition to his moth form, Tlaloc had an owl form. An owl with Tlaloc's goggle eyes and a blood symbol hanging from its beak is featured on a Late Classic plate

(K8121) that refers to the Period Ending of the Tikal ruler Wak Chan K'awiil (Martin and Grube 2008:39). The owl's body is represented by a shield with the obsidian zigzag design and year sign motif. The zigzag motif also forms a border around the rim of the plate.

A ruler on Piedras Negras Stela 9 wears a Waxaklajuun Ub'aah Chan, or meteor serpent, headdress surmounted by a Tlaloc Owl effigy bundle (Stuart and Graham 2003:figs. 9:50, 9:51) (fig. 7.6). Effigy bundles that represent deities are well known in the Maya region (M. Carrasco 2005; Christenson 2006). Although Stela 9 is quite eroded, it is possible to see that the owl bundle is decorated with black-tipped feathers and the bleeding heart symbol. The texture of the bundle itself may be intended to represent down feathers. Atop this bundle is the head of the owl, wearing Tlaloc's goggle eyes and year sign headdress. The owl has feathery eyelids, and a single black-tipped feather appears on the brow of the bird and over each ear. The wings of the Owl Tlaloc are portrayed on either side of the bundle. Supernatural bird wings in Maya headdresses are typically composed of a serpent's head, with short secondary feathers and long primary feathers extending out from the serpent's mouth (Bardawil 1976). In the case of Stela 9, the serpent has been replaced with a Waxaklajuun Ub'aah Chan complete with a rattlesnake tail. In other words, the wings of this owl are marked with a symbol for meteors, and by extension, obsidian. Furthermore, the zigzag pattern indicating obsidian is found at the base of the owl wing, as it is on the K8121 plate.

Another owl–Tlaloc combination is illustrated on Maya vase K1463 from Motul de San José. The lord on the vase wears a Tlaloc god as a necklace (Reents-Budet 1994:60). The lord's own headdress is composed of the head of an owl with the three single black-tipped feathers protruding from its head. Even in scenes where the Owl Tlaloc itself is not visible, its feathers decorate Tlaloc headdresses. For example, the black-tipped owl feathers are included among the long quetzal feathers of the ruler's headdress on Piedras Negras Stela 7 and Stela 26. It is likely that the black marking is intended to indicate that the owl's feathers were identified with obsidian. The composition of the three feathers on the head of the Owl Tlaloc is also reminiscent of the three obsidian blades in the headdress of a Teotihuacan warrior (see fig. 7.3).

Continuing with the associations between owls and obsidian, an owl with obsidian eccentrics on its wings is pictured in the stucco façade at Acanceh (V. Miller 1991:fig. 3). A rather graphic example of an owl wing decorated with obsidian blades is found on a headdress in the Teotihuacan Tetitla Portico 11, Mural 3 (A. Miller 1973:fig. 301). The wings of this owl are composed of an open human chest with exposed heart and intestines. An obsidian blade covered with blood extrudes from the chest cavity. The close association of owls with heart sacrifice is seen also in the Popol Vuh. The duties of four members of the war council of the underworld included delivering messages and conducting heart sacrifices (Christenson 2007a:119, 132). These lords took the form of owls.

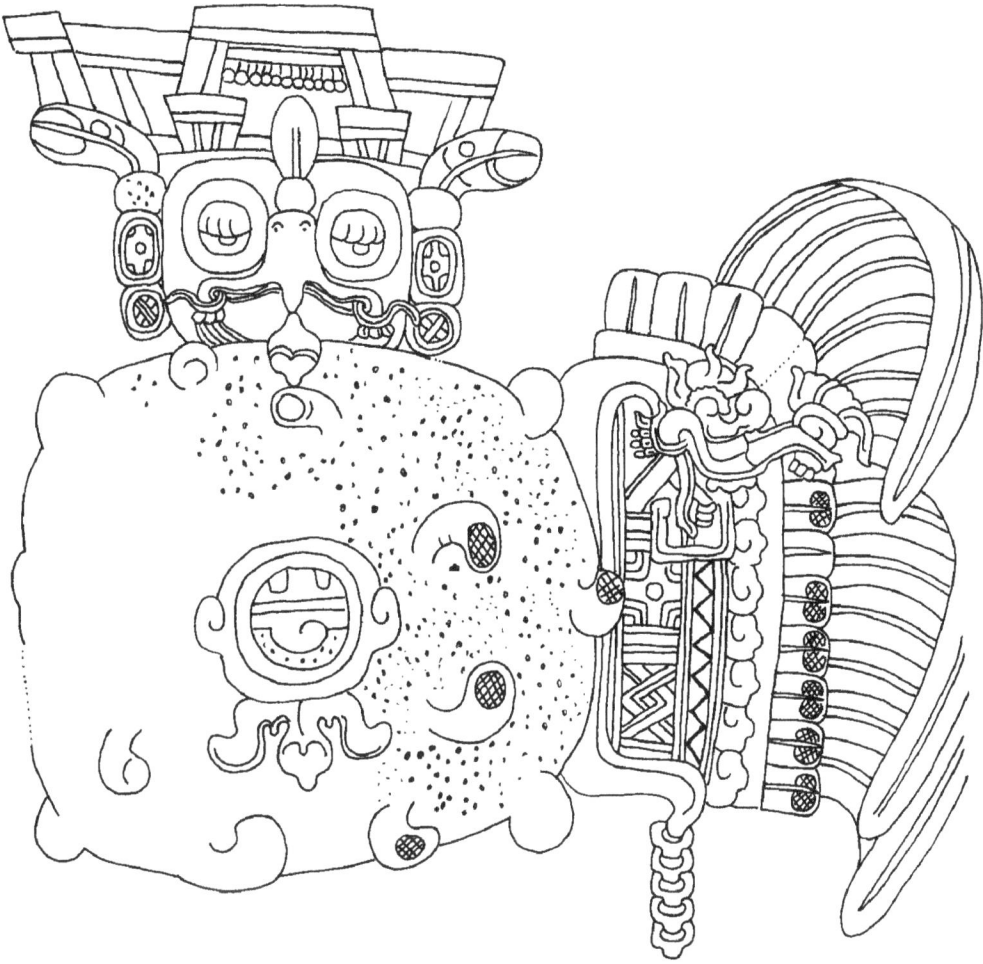

7.6. Owl bundle. Left side of bundle not shown due to erosion of monument. Piedras Negras Stela 9, after Stuart and Graham.

Obsidian-related owls are illustrated in the Teotihuacan Atetelco murals (Nielsen and Helmke 2008:fig. 3). These Atetelco owls are juxtaposed with a symbol for a mountain and function as place names. The mountain is decorated with protruding obsidian blades. Nielsen and Helmke (2008) have demonstrated that the Atetelco owl represents an atlatl. Atlatls frequently have two holes through which the warrior's fingers are inserted to hold the weapon. A comparison of the Atetelco owl atlatl with a real atlatl indicates that the Tlaloc eyes of the owl represent the two finger holes. Many examples of atlatls illustrate the finger holes as the goggle eyes of Tlaloc (Nuttall 1891). The notion that the obsidian–meteor–atlatl-dart were manifestations of Tlaloc is analogous to the flint-thunderbolt-ax being the manifestation of Chahk.

Another ubiquitous belief in Mesoamerica is that nocturnal owls are omens of illness, death, and war (Tozzer and Allen 1910; Redfield and Villa Rojas 1934:210–11;

Tozzer 1941:202; Villa Rojas 1945:157–58; Laughlin 1976:19; Scott 1988:57–58; Christenson 2007a:119). The night cry of an owl, or its appearance perched on some-one's house, indicates impending death. Like moths, owls are identified with the *poslom*, or meteor co-essence, in Tzotzil Chenalhó (Guiteras Holmes 1961:249). In Ch'ol myths, owls are the companions of witches (Josserand et al. 2003). Sahagún (1959–63, 5:161) commented that whoever heard the call of a horned owl would die in bondage or war. One can well imagine an Owl Tlaloc warrior hooting at his victims as a war cry before delivering lethal wounds with his obsidian weapons. Given the pervasive view of Black Witch moths as omens of death, the sight of a Moth Tlaloc warrior streaking toward his victim would have had the same terrify-ing effect as an Owl Tlaloc warrior.

In many illustrations, Teotihuacan warriors wear a nose plaque that has the form of a stylized lepidopteran, and a number of scholars have noted that the talud-tablero architecture characteristic of Teotihuacan has the visual form of the Lepidop-tera nose plaque (Von Winning 1947, 1979, 1987; Headrick 2003). It may be that the talud-tablero buildings that were decorated with Tlaloc imagery were intended to represent the Black Witch moth form of Tlaloc. Certainly, a Tlaloc temple decorated with moths and owls where human sacrifice was performed would dramatically rein-force the association of moths and owls with death.

THE INTEGRATION OF TLALOC WITH MAYA WORLD VIEW

Teotihuacan cultural presence in the Maya region during the Early Classic period has long been recognized in the form of talud-tablero–style architecture, iconography, ceramic vessels, and Central Mexican obsidian. While the majority of obsidian used in the Maya region seems to originate from highland Guatemalan sources, Central Mexican obsidian, particularly the green obsidian from the Pachuca sources that were controlled by Teotihuacan, is present even at highland Guatemala sites that had easy access to local sources. A number of inscriptions from the Petén region refer to three men named Spearthrower Owl, Sihyaj K'ahk', and Yax Nuun Ahiin, who had close affiliations with Teotihuacan (for an overview and summary of these texts, see Stuart 2000, 2004a, 2004b; Martin 2003; Estrada-Belli et al. 2009). The texts indicate that Sihyaj K'ahk' arrived at Tikal on the same day that the reigning Tikal king died. The following year, Spearthrower Owl's son Yax Nuun Ahiin was placed on the Tikal throne under the authority of Sihyaj K'ahk'. There has been much speculation about the identity and ethnicity of these three men. It has been proposed that Spearthrower Owl may have been a Teotihuacan ruler who sent the warlord Sihyaj K'ahk' to Tikal to overthrow the current ruler and replace him with his son, but many other scenarios are equally likely (Stuart 2000, 2004a; Braswell 2003). Both Spearthrower Owl and Sihyaj K'ahk' carry a title phonetically read as *kaloomte'* that has been characterized as "emperor" or "high ruler." Although it is beyond the scope of this book, there is evidence that the many Maya kings and queens who have this title were in reality high priests and priestesses of the cult of Tlaloc (Bassie-Sweet 2011, in preparation). Surely, in Maya belief, supplicating the deity that represented obsidian would have increased the effectiveness of obsidian weapons and the likelihood of victory in war.

What is germane for this discussion is the manner in which Teotihuacan deities and motifs were subsequently incorporated into Maya art. In many illustrations, Tlaloc is juxtaposed with imagery of the third major thunderbolt god, GIII. For example, the ruler on Aguateca Stela 2, who is dressed as Tlaloc, carries a rectangular shield emblazoned with the face of GIII. In a similar vein, the Naranjo ruler who is dressed in Tlaloc accoutrements also carries such a shield. As discussed above, GIII had meteor and fire associations like Tlaloc. In addition, Tlaloc and Chahk imagery are often juxtaposed. The implication of this imagery is that Tlaloc did not replace Maya thunderbolt and meteor deities; rather, he was incorporated into Maya world view as yet another type of Chahk.

The Popol Vuh provides a model for how foreign gods were integrated into the local pantheon during the Postclassic period. There was a long tradition in Mesoamerica of rulers and their lineages receiving validation and prestige in the form of insignia and patron deities from a foreign city. These powerful cities replicated the original place of duality and were called "place of reeds" (Tollan in Nahuatl). In the Popol Vuh, the first tribes journeyed to a city named Tulan "place of reeds" to obtain a tutelary deity (Christenson 2007a:208–27). The precise location of this Postclassic Tulan is widely debated, and suggestions have included such diverse sites as Tula, Cholula, and Chichén Itzá.

Although the various tribes received an assortment of patron gods at Tulan, it was the deity Tohil who became the dominant patron for the K'iche', Tamub, and Ilocab tribes. Tohil provided fire to the K'iche' after the initial fire was extinguished by hail and rain. He created this essential element by twisting his foot inside his shoe like a fire drill (Christenson 2007a:213, 214). In this regard, Tohil was like both GIII, who produced fire through drilling, and Tlaloc, who produced fire from his foot in the form of the meteor deity Waxaklajuun Ub'aah Chan. Like GIII and Tlaloc, Tohil was also a war god who enabled the K'iche' to overcome their enemies. The Popol Vuh narrative makes a crucial point when it states that the patron deity Tohil was the *k'exwach* "replacement" and *natab'al* "remembrance" for the deities Framer and Shaper (the creator grandparents Xpiyacoc and Xmucane) (Christenson 2007a:215). In other words, this foreign deity, Tohil, was not thought to be a separate god, but an alternative manifestation of the creator deities.

It has been suggested that during the Terminal Classic period, the cult of Quetzalcoatl and Tlaloc was spread not only through military conquest, but through traders and pilgrims (Ringle et al. 1998:214). It is likely that the Classic period worship of Tlaloc, which was intimately connected to the trade and control of obsidian, followed a similar course.

Traders and pilgrims played a dominant role in the popularity of the Black Christ cult as well. As noted in chapter 2, this cult began when the community of Esquipulas acquired a black-colored sculpture of Christ. Currying the favor of a deity with supplications and offerings was already a time-honored Maya tradition. The apparent ability of the Black Christ to heal and grant wishes drew pilgrims from increasingly distant locations. A market was developed for goods associated with the Black Christ, such as icons and stamped clay tablets for healing. Traders and pilgrims returning home not only spread the reputation of the Black Christ, but brought with them tangible proof in the form of icons and clay tablets. As the reputation of the Black Christ grew and spread, new centers of worship emerged. This decentralization of the cult provided devotees with a local alternative. These new sites developed their own reputations and supporters that were independent from Esquipulas. It is easy to imagine the worship of Tlaloc spreading from Tikal in a similar manner.

Thunderbolts and meteors were vital and central phenomena in Maya world view. In this chapter, the thunderbolt and meteor attributes of the major deities have been discussed, and the important roles of thunderbolts and meteors as supernatural weapons have been highlighted. This overview of ancient Maya deities provides a framework for understanding the contemporary Ch'ol deities who will be discussed in the final chapter.

8

CONTEMPORARY MOUNTAIN, THUNDERBOLT, AND METEOR DEITIES

Karen Bassie-Sweet, Nicholas A. Hopkins,
Robert M. Laughlin, and Alejandro Sheseña

The relevance of the previous discussion of Classic period and earlier deities lies in the fact that many of these same deities—or at the very least, deities that are strikingly similar to them—are still prominent in Ch'ol (and other Maya) religious practices. There is an oft-mentioned opinion among some Mesoamerican archaeologists that the transition between the pre-Columbian and contemporary periods was so traumatic and destructive of native culture that it is improper to assume a relationship between contemporary practices and pre-Columbian ones. In particular, the position is taken that we cannot legitimately use our observations of contemporary Maya to inform our interpretation of the archaeological evidence. This is certainly the appropriate null hypothesis: we should assume, until proven otherwise, that there is no significant relationship between the past and the present. On the other hand, if we can in fact demonstrate that there are overwhelming correspondences between the cultural elements of the past and those of the present, the null hypothesis fails and should be replaced by a new formulation. We believe that the evidence strongly supports the argument that there is considerable continuity between pre-Columbian and contemporary Maya religion in the Ch'ol area and elsewhere.

Cultural continuity has been noted in many domains other than religion. Domestic house construction depicted in pre-Columbian art (e.g., the Nunnery at Uxmal) is seemingly identical to contemporary rural housing in Yucatán and elsewhere. There are notable continuities in the patterns of narrative discourse (Hopkins and Josserand 1990; Josserand 1991), kinship systems and kin terminology (Hopkins 1988, 1991), textile design and manufacture (Morris 2011), and many other areas of culture. It should be no surprise to find continuities in religious beliefs and practices as well.

This is not to claim that there are no differences between the religious beliefs and practices of the Classic Maya and those of their contemporary cultural descendants. The former existed in the context of a highly complex society and pertained to the royalty and elite members of that society, engaged in courtly behavior and affairs of the state. The latter exists in the context of what is effectively a peasant society encapsulated within modern European-oriented states, and pertains to rural agriculturalists generally living in small, relatively unstratified villages. In his studies of the Maya populations of Yucatán, the anthropologist Robert Redfield (1941) introduced the concepts of Great and Little Traditions, and these are relevant here.

The Great Tradition is that of the elite, and involves the highly elaborated behavior of elite specialists. The Little Tradition is that of the commoners, and is significantly less elaborate in its practice. In the Great Tradition, a Catholic mass performed by the Pope involves highly symbolic choices of clothing and accessories, co-participants and supporting cast, and the details of the actions to be performed. The Little Tradition performance of a liturgically identical mass by a village priest is considerably less elaborate. Nevertheless, the two share a common belief system and involve the same core behavior, perhaps even the same language.

This contrast relates to the differences between Classic Maya religious practices and those of the modern Maya. The elite society of the pre-Columbian Maya disappeared in the turmoil of the conquest and colonial periods, and the Great Tradition went with it. The Little Tradition, on the other hand, survived, albeit not without adapting to the new circumstances. In the discussion that follows, we will point out significant survivals of pre-Columbian beliefs and practices among the colonial and contemporary Maya. Specifically, we will argue that the mountain, thunderbolt, and meteor deities attended to by the modern Maya have clear antecedents in the pre-Columbian Great Tradition.

The mythological events related in the PopolVuh were thought to have occurred at specific locations in highland Guatemala. Certain mountains were identified with each of the creator deities and the actions of these gods (Bassie-Sweet 2008:239–65). Lake Atitlán marked the center of the world, where the creator grandparents had their home. There is evidence that the three volcanoes that rim the lake were thought to represent the three hearthstones and to be manifestations of the three thunderbolt gods. To the east of Atitlán are the volcanoes Agua and Fuego that represented the hero twins. Cerro Raxón, which is situated farther east on the Río Motagua and has jade sources skirting its base, was identified with One Ixim-One Hunahpu, who is consistently shown wearing jade accoutrements. The ballcourt of One Hunahpu and the cave passageway to the underworld were located to the northeast in Alta Verapaz. In contemporary mythology, the highest and most sacred mountain in this region is thought to be the manifestation of a deity called Xucaneb, who has many of the characteristics of maternal grandfather God L-Gathered Blood of the Underworld.

While the narrative in the PopolVuh maps out the sacred landscape of highland Guatemala on a macro scale, local versions of these revered places occur in many communities. Across the highlands of the Maya region, there is still a prevalent belief in mountain deities who have the attributes of the ancient gods. This chapter examines some of these contemporary deities, and explores their correlations with the ancient gods and their relationship to lightning and meteors. As will be seen, many of the contemporary beliefs of the Ch'ol are similar to those of other Maya regions and also originated from an ancient world view.

Contemporary Thunderbolt and Meteor Gods

The identification of lightning, thunderbolts, and meteors with the primary creator deities and with the Classic-period ruling elite was discussed in previous chapters. The importance of lightning and meteors as a source of supernatural authority is high-lighted in the numerous illustrations of Classic period lords holding a GII scepter in the form of a thunderbolt ax, or the obsidian weapon of the meteor deity Tlaloc. The concept of powerful thunderbolt and meteor deities is found in most contem-porary Maya communities, and leaders are still identified with these forces. The following is a brief overview of these gods, the role of lightning in divination, and the concept that certain individuals could possess lightning and meteors as a soul.

In the Tzeltal, Tzotzil, and Tojolab'al regions, there are three deities known as Whirlwind, Thunderbolt, and Meteor (Hermitte 1964; Spero 1987; Calnek 1988; Megged 1996). As noted in chapter 6, each member of the ancient thunderbolt triad had distinctive characteristics. GI–Huracán was a storm god, GII–Youngest Thunder-bolt was a thunderbolt in the form of an ax, and GIII–Sudden Thunderbolt was a fire and meteor god closely associated with warfare. It is apparent that this pre-Columbian triad was the precursor of the contemporary deities (Bassie-Sweet 2008: 102–21). Thunderbolt deities who are similar to the pre-Columbian thunderbolt triad also appear in highland Guatemala. For example, there are many myths about red dwarf thunderbolt gods who have the characteristics of GII; these include the stories of Saki C'oxol (white C'oxol), who is described as a dwarf who moves like lightning and wears red clothes (Bode 1961:213; B. Tedlock 1986:134, 147; D. Ted-lock 1996:305; Freidel et al. 1993). Also known by the names Ajitz, Quiakacoxol (red C'oxol), and Tzitzimit, this character is thought to have struck the first K'iche' elders with his ax and awakened the sheet lightning in their blood (a description of sheet lightning and its divination qualities follows later in this chapter).

As discussed in chapter 6, it is likely that the red dwarf GII (the youngest of the three thunderbolt brothers) broke open the mountain containing corn seeds. Con-temporary myths about the breaking open of a mountain containing corn are wide-spread. In the Poqomchi' stories, the smallest or youngest thunderbolt performed this task, while the Tzeltal attribute it to their red thunderbolt deity (Slocum 1965:5; Montejo and Campbell 1993). In the Tzeltal town of Pinola, the thunderbolt deity is characterized as a small boy who is the leader of the ancestors, and he is the owner and protector of corn (Hermitte 1964). A similar thunderbolt deity called X Thup Chaak is found in Yucatán (Redfield and Villa Rojas 1934:114–15, 137). This Chaak, who dwells in the east, is the most important thunderbolt god despite being the smallest and youngest. The Ch'ol have thunderbolt spirits that they say guard their communities against evil spirits, and who use their thunderbolts to punish wrongdoers (Aulie and Aulie 1978:46, 130; Hopkins and Josserand 1990; Cruz Guzmán, Josserand, and Hopkins 1994; Joljá Cave Project field notes). The Ch'ol of Joloniel believe that the red thunderbolt spirit, who has the form of a small boy or dwarf, is the most powerful (Joljá Cave Project field notes; Felipe Pérez Montejo and Domingo Pérez Morenos, personal communication 2001.

Red, green-blue, and yellow thunderbolt spirits are well known in the Ch'ol area. The *tatuch* Miguel Arcos Méndez of Tumbalá noted that there are two powerful red thunderbolt spirits, a weaker one that is green-blue, and a yellow one that is associated with sheet lightning (Joljá Cave Project field notes). At Joloniel, red thunderbolt spirits are likewise thought to be more powerful than green-blue ones. A Tojolabal story tells of a man who was transformed into a green-blue thunderbolt and became the weakest of the thunderbolts (Basauri 1931:97–99). A disparity in power is also seen in the tools of the Ch'ol thunderbolt spirit Chajk. He has a large ax to strike trees, but he uses smaller green-blue axes to burn the centipedes that he finds in trees, and then he eats these delicacies. On the other hand, the Tila Ch'ol believe it was the green-blue thunderbolt who had the strength to crack open the corn rock (Manca 1995:226).

The color of a thunderbolt deity is often reflected in the color of his clothing. Many cautionary stories recount how a man is offered colored clothing that transforms him into that color of thunderbolt. When the man chooses the more powerful color, his inexperience at wielding this weapon causes great destruction. The notion that the costume of a thunderbolt god is the source of his power is seen in a Ch'ol story that recounts the deeds of a Chajk deity called Lak Mam "Our Grandfather" who lives in a cave near the Tulijá River (Hopkins and Josserand 1994). In one tale, a crocodile-like spirit in the river grabs onto Lak Mam's leg and won't let go. Lak Mam instructs some men fishing in the river to go to his house and ask his toad wife for his hat and shirt. Once he dresses in these clothes, he is able to strike the spirit with a thunderbolt (see "Our Grandfather Ty'añ Lak Mam" in the appendix).

Lak Mam's tools are similar to those of the ancient Chahks. The pre-Columbian ax heads that are found in the fields or forests are called *jacha lak mam* (Lak Mam's ax). Lak Mam's fingernails are believed to be made of obsidian, and he uses his fingernails to dig centipedes out of trees. The Ch'ol refer to the ancient obsidian blades that they encounter as Lak Mam's fingernails.

THUNDERBOLTS AS GUARDIANS

Thunderbolts are sometimes considered guardians of the locale. In the Tzotzil region, there is a thunderbolt deity called Anhel who protects the community. In most Tzotzil communities, Anhel is considered to be an aspect of the earth lord Yahval Balamil, but in Chenalhó he is a separate being (Guiteras Holmes 1961; Laughlin 1969, 1977; Vogt 1969:302–303, 455–61; 1981; 1993; W. Morris 1987; Köhler 1995;

Gossen 2002) (a description of Yahval Balamil follows later in this chapter). Prayers to Yahval Balamil call him holy king, holy *anhel,* holy snake, and holy thunderbolt (Vogt 1969:460). Anhel lives in the mountains surrounding the community, and he is thought to send the rains and watch over the cornfields. He creates thunder and lightning by beating his drum or by shouting. Like the thunderbolt leg of God K-GII, Anhel's thunderbolt can take the form of a snake.

Many myths record the deeds of the Catholic patron saint of the community who protects the people and the cornfields from harm, and who brings the rains. In some areas, saints are equated with the local thunderbolt deity, or these saints use thunderbolts to protect the community. In Catholic imagery, Saint Michael (San Miguel) and Saint James (Santiago) both carry swords and were associated with thunder. Saint Michael typically is shown in battle attire, slaying a dragon. The Tzeltal Thunderbolt deity in Pinola is equated with Saint Michael, the patron saint of the community, who is thought to carry a sword-like thunderbolt (Hermitte 1964). The patron saint of Tumbalá is also Saint Michael, and this saint is thought to work in unison with the Ch'ol earth lord called Don Juan (see "A Visit to Don Juan" in the appendix). In Santiago Atitlán, the sword of Santiago has the form of a thunderbolt, and this patron saint uses his weapon to protect the community (Christenson 2001: 74, 134). In addition, it is believed that when Santiago's bolt strikes the earth it breaks open the germinating corn seed and charges the earth with life-giving power.

Lighting Souls and Divination

The Maya believe that a person has several kinds of soul-like essences that are centered in different parts of the body, and that can be manifested as breath, wind, or winged beings that either leave the body after death or die with it. In addition to these body souls, humans have supernatural co-essences who share their souls and fate. These co-essences reside in mountain caves. It is believed that the spiritually strong can direct their co-essences to perform certain functions such as protecting the community from supernatural forces, and causing or curing illness. Co-essences are most often animals, but they can also take the form of natural phenomena such as whirlwinds, thunderbolts, and meteors. In the Tzeltal, Tzotzil, and Tojolab'al regions, whirlwind, thunderbolt, and meteor co-essences are the most powerful (Hermitte 1964; Spero 1987; Calnek 1988; Megged 1996). In Tzeltal Pinola and Cancuc, the most powerful co-essences of community leaders past and present take the form of thunderbolts, while in Oxchuc and Chanal they are meteors. Villa Rojas (1947:583) recorded the belief at Oxchuc that community leaders possess co-essences that take the form of red, yellow, and green balls of fire (meteors). The red meteor is considered the most powerful. The Tzeltal of Cancuc believe that red thunderbolts are more powerful than green ones (Pitarch 2010:45).

In the Tumbalá Ch'ol region, co-essences can be wind, thunderbolts, or fire (Beekman 1957). To obtain these powerful co-essences, the midwife takes the newborn baby to a cave inhabited by the earth lord called Don Juan. She sweeps the cave, makes an animal sacrifice to Don Juan, and requests that he give the child these co-essences as well as four others (jaguar, fox, hummingbird, and mole). People with these seven special co-essences are able to become shamans.

Across Mesoamerica, spiritually strong individuals are thought to have lightning as a co-essence and to be able to harness this supernatural power and use it as a weapon (Laughlin 1977:20). There are numerous stories of indigenous leaders who used their thunderbolt and meteor co-essences to protect their communities. Court testimonies regarding the 1712 Chiapas rebellion indicate that an earthquake-generated landslide that blocked the Spanish advance was thought to have been created by certain Tzeltal military leaders, using their thunderbolt co-essences (Gosner 1984:131). Gosner notes that the alleged power of such leaders to mobilize natural forces like wind, rain, and lightning was especially valued during periods of war. In Zinacantán, it is believed that the community leaders conjured a dancing pine tree to lure a menacing army off its path (Laughlin 1977:3).

The Maya also believe that lightning transmits divine knowledge. Central to the divination process used by the Maya was the 260-day *tzolk'in* calendar, which is composed of thirteen numbers and twenty day names. Each number and day name was represented by a different god, who affected the outcome of the events that occurred on his particular day. The tzolk'in day on which a person was born was thought to influence his or her destiny. Humans were sometimes named after the day they were born, while certain deities were named after the day they underwent a transformation. In the Maya system of reckoning time, each day also had several other interrelated designations that referred to its position in such cycles as the *haab*, the *k'atun*, the Supplementary Series, the Lunar Series, and the Venus cycle. The Maya believed that a different deity or combination of deities ruled each period within these cycles and that these deities influenced the fortune of the events that occurred during these periods. Prognostication was accomplished using several different techniques (see Bassie-Sweet 2008:84–101 for a discussion of these methods), but ultimately, diviners received messages or signs from the calendar deities during their prognostications, which assisted them in making their predictions.

Lightning was thought to play a key role in transmitting divination information from the deities to the diviner. The bright flash of light seen in the sky when a lightning bolt occurs inside clouds is called sheet lightning. K'iche' diviners believe that their blood contains sheet lightning. The tingling or twitching in the diviner's muscles is thought to be this blood lightning, and these movements provide him with the answer to whatever question he has asked the deities (B. Tedlock 1992:53, 110, 138). A person who survived being hit by a thunderbolt must have been viewed by the ancient Maya as a spiritually powerful individual. When a person is struck by a thunderbolt, the lightning is conducted through the veins in the body and causes a burn pattern that actually looks like a branched bolt of lightning. The concept of diviners having lightning in their blood may have initially derived from such traumatic experiences.

ANCESTRAL DEITIES

It is believed that community leaders continue their role as guardians in the afterlife. These ancestors are thought to live in the mountains surrounding the community and to use thunderbolts to defend the community. In many places, the co-essences of the community members also live in the ancestral mountain and are protected by the ancestors or the patron saint. The relationship between the ancestors and the living community leaders is well stated by Guiteras Holmes: "The authorities do not act in their own name: each one represents or is the personification of all those who preceded him back to the 'beginning of the world': they personify the gods, they are sacred. Their authority is supported by the belief in their supernatural power" (Guiteras Holmes 1961:78).

The titles employed for ancestral and current community leaders are often kinship terms. As discussed in chapter 5, the *mam* "grandfather" glyph is used in certain contexts to refer to ancestors (Stuart 2007a). The Maya also use the term "grandfather" or "father" for respected elders, lineage heads, and the earth lord. Two Ch'ol titles of respect for elders are *lac tat* "our father" and *noxix* "big powerful male" (Aulie 1979:40, 43). In the Tzotzil and Tzeltal areas, the ancestors are called the *totilme'iletik* (fathers-mothers) and *me'tik tatik* (mothers-fathers), respectively. The Tzotzil of Zinacantán believe that the ancestors, who live in the sacred mountains near the town, cause illness in wrongdoers by sending a thunderbolt that will cause fright and soul loss (Vogt 1969:301). The ancestors also release the animal co-essence of a wrongdoer into the wild, which puts the person at grave risk. In addition to thunderbolts, these ancestors also use a supernatural flaming arrow or dart to defend the community (Guiteras Holmes 1961:189). The Tzotzil, as we know, described meteors as flaming arrows.

The Tzeltal of Amatenango believe their ancestors inhabit the sacred mountain cave called Hol Shan, and they petition them for rain on the Day of the Holy Cross (Nash 1970:19–23). Until quite recently, the urns containing the burned remains of important Oxchuc community leaders were buried in a sacred cave and worshipped. Bishop Núñez of Chiapas, during the seventeenth century, described how the bone remains of powerful community leaders were preserved in caves and revered, which indicates this is a tradition with a long history (Brinton 1894:21). In some areas, patron saints are also identified with mountains and worshipped in caves. The Tzotzil of Chamula venerate their patron saint San Juan at his cave home on the sacred mountain Tzontevitz, as noted in chapter 2, while the Tojolab'al of Chiptik venerate their patron saint San Miguel at his mountain cave home called Cueva Chawal (C. Lenkersdorf 1996).

EARTH LORDS

Another group of powerful supernatural beings that are identified with mountains and caves are the earth lords. These kinds of gods are found in the Ixil, Chuj, Q'eqchi', Kaqchikel, Mam, and K'iche' regions of Guatemala as well as the Chontal, Tzotzil, Tzeltal, and Ch'ol areas of Chiapas. The names for these earth lords vary, but they share many common features. In Chuj, the earth lord is called *witz-'ak'lik* "mountain-grasslands" (Hopkins 1964–65), and in Q'eqchi' *cuul taq'a* "mountain-valley." Such terms are metonyms in which two typical members of a class are juxtaposed to stand for the whole domain (like "fathers-mothers" for "ancestors") (Hopkins 1986; Josserand and Hopkins 2005:412–13). In these cases, the earth is represented by two geographical terms that are complementary opposites.

The earth lord of the Mam community of Santiago Chimaltenango is known as Father Paxil, who is the god of Paxil Mountain and the owner of corn (Wagley 1941:34, 40). Paxil Mountain is twenty kilometers to the northwest of Chimaltenango. Petitions are made to Father Paxil to send the rain for the crop and to protect the crop from the winds. The ability of the earth lords to control the rains is their most salient attribute.

Thanks to the extensive study of the Tzotzil by the Harvard Chiapas Project, perhaps the best-documented earth lord is the Tzotzil deity Yahval Balamil "earth owner" (Laughlin 1969, 1977; Vogt 1969, 1976; Gossen 1974, 1999, 2002; Morris 1987). His name refers to his ownership of the earth and all the products generated from it. He is characterized as an extremely rich ladino who controls all sources of wealth. This description reflects the economic conditions in Chiapas, where the ladino population dominates commerce and owns the majority of land and resources. Yahval Balamil also owns and controls the rain and the water that pours out from the earth at springs and headwaters. He lives in a cave home with his toad wife, his snake son, and his corn goddess daughters. His daughters, who can also take toad form, spin cotton that turns into rain clouds when the Anhel strikes the cotton with a thunderbolt. As mentioned earlier in this chapter, Yahval Balamil can take the form of a serpent and a thunderbolt, as can his children. His seat or throne is an armadillo, and he rides on a deer. Payments in the form of ceremonial offerings must be made to Yahval Balamil for permission to use any of his resources and to entice him to send the rains. Yahval Balamil can steal the souls of people and cause illness, but he can also provide great wealth to those who honor him. Like ladino overlords, Yahval Balamil requires many workers, and he can enslave men within his cave.

In the early twentieth century, Blom and La Farge (1926–27, 2:368, 373–74) recorded a Tzeltal belief in an earth lord named Hun Ahau (One Ajaw) who was thought to be the guardian of the mountains. In Tzeltal Guaquitepec, he is called Yajwal Ajaw and the lord of the cave (Maurer 1984:114). He is thought to be the protector of the fields and wildlife. An earth lord is also found in the Tzeltal town of Amatenango (Nash 1970:24) and in Oxchuc, where he is known as Ch'ul Qui'nal and is addressed as Ch'ul Balamilal "holy earth" (Megged 1996:153, 160). The Bachajón leader Juan López was executed during the 1712 rebellion by the Cancuc leaders because he questioned their authority. In contemporary stories about this rebellion, Juan López is the primary Cancuc rebel leader, and it is he who defeats the Spanish forces (Pitarch 2010:164). Juan López and his cohort Juan García are thought to be the sons of Cancuc's patron saint, San Juan. Juan López has many of the earth lord's traits, including an association with lightning and a cave abode. The cave of Juan López is located five kilometers east of Bachajón and was visited by Karen Bassie-Sweet, Robert Laughlin, and Juan Jesús Vázquez in 2010. It is a small rockshelter on a hill adjacent to the Río Cantela (N17 1.702 W92 8.533).

Villa Rojas commented on the importance of caves in the Tzeltal region:

> In the municipio of Oxchuc, best known to the writer, each rural settlement is tied by religious bonds to a certain cave where a cross is kept as the main symbol of its sacred importance. Usually the ranchería is known by the name of the cave to which it belongs; thus the ranchería of Dzajalchen (Red Cave) is connected with the cave of that name. In addition to this main cave there are others of less importance, but also treated with respect and sanctified through one or more crosses. This mystic devotion to caves has its origin in the belief that it is from them that lightning comes to punish and to disperse the natural elements (hail, winds, storms, etc.) which frequently threaten and even destroy the cornfields. (Villa Rojas 1947)

The Tojolabal have a cave-dwelling supernatural being called Niwan Pukuj or Niwan Winik (Ruz 1982). Although he is not characterized as an earth lord, he sits on an armadillo and rides a deer. The identification of an earth lord with an armadillo is found in the Tzotzil, Q'eqchi', and Kaqchikel regions (Bassie-Sweet 2008:182, 232–33). The close association of the armadillo with riches is seen in a Yucatec song where the armadillo is compared to a rich man: "the tail of the armadillo, the cane of the rich man, the nose of the armadillo, the pipe of the rich man, the shell of the armadillo, the case of the rich man" (Burns 1973:64). As in Chiapas, the rich man is exemplified by the ladino merchant.

The earth lord, in his role as the owner of the earth and the provider of rain, parallels Itzamnaaj-Xpiyacoc. As noted in chapter 6, Itzamnaaj-Xpiyacoc, paternal grandfather of the hero twins, was the first rainmaker and healer as well as a thunderbolt deity. In his turtle manifestation, Itzamnaaj-Xpiyacoc represented the earth.

The earth lord's association with the armadillo, on the other hand, is analogous to the maternal grandfather of the hero twins, God L-Gathered Blood, who had an armadillo form (Bassie-Sweet 2008:232–33). The ability of the earth lord to steal the souls of humans and make them sick is another point in common with God L-Gathered Blood, who was the underworld lord of illness and death. The wealth of the earth lord further parallels that of God L, who was the patron god of merchants.

It is our contention that the contemporary concept of an earth lord was the result of an amalgamation of the two ancient grandfather deities Itzamnaaj-Xpiyacoc and God L-Gathered Blood.

DON JUAN-AJAW, THE CH'OL EARTH LORD

Like other indigenous groups in Chiapas, the Ch'ol have a deity who is thought to be the owner of the earth, mountains, and water (Beekman 1957; Whittaker and Warkentin 1965; Aulie and Aulie 1978; Aulie 1979; Cruz Guzmán, Josserand, and Hopkins 1980; Meneses López 1986; Alejos García 1988, 1994; Josserand and Hopkins 1996; Joljá Cave Project field notes). This Ch'ol earth lord is known by a variety of names, including Don Juan, Rowan (an assimilated pronunciation of Don Juan), Ajaw, Yum Witz "lord of the mountain," Yum Ch'en "lord of the cave," Yum Pañimil "lord of the world," and Bawitz "head of the mountain." He is addressed by the titles *lak ch'ujul tyaty* and *lak ch'ujul yum* "Our Holy Father," "Our Holy Lord," as well as the general term of address for respected males, *lak tyaty* "Our Father."

It is tempting to identify the name Don Juan with the Catholic Saint John the Baptist (San Juan) because mountain and thunder deities are identified with Saint John in other parts of Mesoamerica (Ichon 1973; Merlo Juárez 2009; John Pohl, personal communication). It is curious, though, that none of the major Ch'ol towns have San Juan as a patron. Perhaps San Juan is too universally important to be tied to any one community, and in any case, the patron saints were assigned by foreign priests, not by the local populations. Girard (1979:282) notes that the festival of San Juan on June 24 is associated with the summer solstice. San Juan is also linked with rain because his festival day occurs when the rains are intensifying. In Quintana Roo, San Juan is thought to celebrate his day by causing severe storms (Villa Rojas 1945:110). In Chiapas and highland Guatemala, it is the earth lords who cause such destructive weather, evidence that San Juan was an earth lord.

The fact that Don Juan is called Ajaw indicates his high status and importance. As noted earlier, the Tzeltal earth lord is called Hun Ahau (One Ajaw) or just Ahau. The etymology of *ajaw* is murky, but during the Classic period this name referred to lords as well as to the king. The word *ajaw* was often represented in hieroglyphic writing by a portrait of the deity One Ajaw, and Maya lords assumed the identity of One Ajaw when they became king. In the 1789 Ch'ol word list created for Charles III of Spain, the word for king is given as *ajau* (*ajaw*) while the word for prince is *yal ajau* (literally, the son of the king) (Hopkins, Cruz Guzmán, and Josserand 2008:92). In a similar manner, the seventeenth-century Lacandón Ch'ol of Sac Bahlán referred to the king of Spain as an *ajaw* (Tozzer 1984:9). Don Juan is said to look like a very old bald man or one with white hair, and he has a thunder drum. At Joloniel, Don Juan is thought to be just as powerful as the grandfather thunderbolt deity Lak Mam (Joljá Cave Project field notes). Although jaguars no longer inhabit the region around Don Juan's caves, it is believed that his caves are guarded by jaguars and fer-de-lance snakes (*Bothrops asper*), and that the ties that bind his money box are actually fer-de-lances. These snakes are the most feared because of their deadly venom and aggressive behavior. Don Juan's association with such snakes parallels that of Xucaneb (the Q'eqchi' earth lord), whose hammock is tied with these pit vipers. In addition, Xucaneb's daughter is transformed into a fer-de-lance. Some Ch'ol also believe that a giant deer guards the caves of Don Juan (Miguel Arcos Méndez, personal communication).

Although the early Protestant missionaries characterized Don Juan as the Christian devil or the companion of the devil, the origin of Don Juan is similar to that of other Maya earth lords; that is, he has the traits of the ancient grandfather gods and thunderbolt deities. In Christian mythology, the primary deity is described as a father, not a grandfather. The characterization of the earth lords and some of thunderbolt deities as grandfathers is uniquely Mayan.

Ch'ol ritual specialists such as the community elders are called *tatuches,* and curers are called *xwujty, x'ilaj,* or *tz'akayaj* (Josserand and Hopkins 1996). These specialists petition Don Juan for rain, bountiful harvests, good hunting, cures for illnesses, and protection from natural disasters such as locust plagues and volcanic eruptions. These supplications can be on behalf of individuals, families, or the entire community. Offerings of turkeys, chickens, pigs, incense, candles, and liquor are made. The prayers of the ritual specialists are not restricted to Don Juan but also include pleas directed to the ancestors, the patron saint of the community, the Señor de Tila, Jesus Christ, the Virgin Mary, Santa Cruz, and God. These prayers indicate that Don Juan is but one of the sacred beings who are thought to control or influence life.

As in other Maya regions, traditional Ch'ol believe that Don Juan is ultimately responsible for soul loss resulting in illness. This damage is thought to be retribution for inappropriate behavior. In addition, when a person falls or is shocked by some event, it is believed that Don Juan has captured or eaten their soul. Petitions and payments must be made to him to regain the soul and make the person whole again. Ritual specialists can also ask Don Juan to cause illness or death. Such requests are characterized as evil and as witchcraft. Accusations of witchcraft against ritual specialists are not uncommon. Aulie (1979:32) documents a case in 1951 of a ritual specialist from Finca Preciosa who was killed by Joloniel villagers because the villagers believed he had caused the death of their relatives.

Don Juan is thought to inhabit a number of specific caves in the Ch'ol region, such as Joljá and the Cueva de Don Juan, but there is also a widespread belief that Don Juan can manifest himself in multiple places including Ajcabalna, the highest mountain in the region (Joljá Project field notes). And obviously, the large mountain behind Palenque called Don Juan Mountain was named after this deity (fig. 8.1). Don Juan Mountain was certainly a sacred location in ancient times, considering the large pyramid, called Ha K'inna, that marks its eastern peak. The Cueva de Don Juan, as stated in chapter 3, once contained at least three Palenque-style *incensarios* representing members of the thunderbolt triad. These idols indicate that the Classic Maya thought that these thunderbolt gods inhabited the cave and could be petitioned there.

This should come as no surprise to anyone who has watched the storm clouds gathering on Don Juan Mountain and seen the thunderbolts blazing across its slopes. John Lloyd Stephens gives a vivid description of a Don Juan storm when he descended the north side of the mountain:

> At this time the sun had disappeared; dark clouds overhung the woods, and thunder rolled heavily on the top of the mountain. As we descended a heavy wind swept through the forest; the air was filled with dry leaves; branches were snapped and broken, trees bent, and there was every appearance of a violent tornado. To hurry down on foot was out of the question. We were so tired that it was impossible; and, afraid of being caught on the mountain by a hurricane and deluge of rain, we spurred down as fast we could go. It was a continued descent, without relief, stony, and very steep. Very often the mules stopped, afraid to go on; and in one place the two empty mules bolted into the thick woods rather than proceed. Fortunately for the reader, this is our last mountain, and I can end honestly with a climax: it was the worst mountain I ever encountered in that or any other country, and under our apprehension of the storm, I will venture to say that no travelers ever descended in less time. At a quarter before five we reached the plain. The mountain was hidden by clouds, and the storm was now raging above us. (Stephens 1941:276–77)

The contemporary Ch'ol Maya make pilgrimages to several caves on Don Juan Mountain to petition Don Juan, who they believe resides within. The principal cave is the Cueva de Don Juan on the white cliff face. Those who make the pilgrimage to Don Juan's caves are said to be rewarded with corn seed that will produce an abundant crop. The Ch'ol believe that the spirits of maize and beans are kept in the caves of Don Juan. In years past when there was a deer population in the region, pilgrims would also be compensated with great success at hunting them. The British traveler John Boddam-Whetham, who visited Palenque in 1877, commented on the Cueva de Don Juan: "High up in the sierra our host pointed out a white rock in which is a cavern known as the "Cueva de Don Juan." The Indians regard it as a shrine and declare that much wealth is concealed within it. Some years ago two white men determined to explore it, but on arriving at the mouth of the cave found that a landslip had blocked up the entrance. The Indians still pray there, but no attempt has been made to remove the obstruction" (Boddam-Whetham 1877:328).

This landslide is still recounted in contemporary Ch'ol stories about the cave (Cruz Guzmán, Josserand, and Hopkins 1980:123). The blockage has not, however, stopped the Ch'ol from accessing the cave. They now use ropes to climb up the cliff face to an alternate entrance (Joljá Cave Project field notes).

During the twentieth century, the Cueva de Don Juan attracted pilgrims from Ch'ol communities located on the north and south sides of Don Juan Mountain as well as the larger towns of Palenque, Salto de Agua, and Tumbalá. In times of drought,

8.1. Two peaks of Don Juan Mountain from the northern plain. Photo by Karen Bassie-Sweet.

the Ch'ol living in the vicinity of the mountain still make petitions at the cave, but most of the regular pilgrims now come from the village of Actiepa Yochib, one of the few non-Protestant communities on the mountain. The cave is within the property of Actiepa Yochib, and this village has a reputation of protecting the cave and preventing outsider visitations.

The Cueva de Don Juan is described as a large cave containing a pool of water. A cedar cross marks the location where the initial offerings to Don Juan are made during the petitions for rain. An image of the moon is said to decorate the wall. The actual house of Don Juan is thought to be farther into the cave. The ritual specialists first whistle to call Don Juan from his house, just as the Ch'ol whistle when they approach a house and wish to speak to the occupants. Don Juan relays the request for rain to San Miguel, the patron saint of Tumbalá (a taped and digitized account of a visit to one of Don Juan's caves is included in the Ch'ol collection of the Archive of the Indigenous Languages of Latin America, www.ailla.utexas.org). Many of the Ch'ol of the Tulijá Valley and Don Juan Mountain originated from Tumbalá, and consequently they have a strong affiliation with this town and its saint.

Prior to the land reforms of the 1930s, the Ch'ol were known to have made a ritual circuit from Tila to Don Juan Mountain and then to Joljá:

> En épocas de carestía, principalmente de lluvia para las siembras de mayo-junio, los ancianos llamados *tatuchob,* encargados del ritual y del culto vernáculo, realizaban una peregrinación a tres cuevas sagradas para pedir la lluvia (lo cual aún se practica). Primero visitaban la cueva de Tila, luego la cueva de *Rowan* "don Juan" en una montaña cercana a Palenque, y por último la cueva de *"Joljá,"* "cabeza del río," en lo alto de una montaña próxima a *Jolonel.*

> In periods of scarcity, principally that of rains for the plantings of May-June, the old ones called *tatuchob,* charged with ritual and popular religion, carried out a pilgrimage to three sacred caves to ask for rain (which is still done). First they visited the cave at Tila, then the cave of *Rowan* "don Juan" on a mountain near Palenque, and finally the cave of *"Joljá"* "head of the river" on top of a mountain near *Jolonel.* (Alejos García 1994:34–35)

In the middle of the twentieth century, evangelical Protestant missionaries entered the Tulijá Valley and began a vigorous campaign to eliminate ancient beliefs and convert the Ch'ol to their brand of Christianity. These Presbyterians used the same strategy used by the Catholic priests four hundred years earlier and preached that the indigenous deities were manifestations of the devil. Don Juan was characterized as the devil and as the overlord of the evil spirits called *xib'aj.* In response to these sermons, a number of their new Ch'ol converts from the village of Suclumpa went to the Cueva de Don Juan, poured gasoline into the cave mouth, and set it on fire. This desecration appears to have happened between 1954 and 1955. There is a Ch'ol story that describes how Don Juan then left the mountain and journeyed across the Tulijá Valley to Joljá Cave (see "A Visit to Don Juan" in the appendix). In this tale, men fishing in the Tulijá River see Don Juan cross the river with his wild animals following him in single file. A large flock of crested guan and great curassow (large, pheasant-like birds) was part of this parade. In another version of the story, jaguars are the prominent animals that accompany Don Juan to Joljá (Joljá Cave Project field notes).

Some traditional Ch'ol steadfastly believe that Don Juan continues to inhabit the Don Juan Mountain cave, while other Ch'ol think that Don Juan left for good. In either case, the drop in agricultural productivity experienced after this event was attributed to the loss of Don Juan's favor. As noted, three pre-Columbian incensarios were removed from the Cueva de Don Juan in 1952. A reduction in the harvest after the removal of these idols was also thought to be retribution from Don Juan (Joljá Cave Project field notes). It is said that when Don Juan now wants the rain to come, he first makes lightning at Joljá.

Don Juan as a Source of Rain

The staple crop of the Maya was and is corn. The importance of rain at the beginning of the planting season cannot be overstated. In Chiapas, there is a widespread belief that rain originates from caves. The mist that frequently hangs around the mouths of watery caves certainly contributes to this notion. For example, the central cave at Joljá contains the headwaters of the Ixteljá River, and mist is often seen lingering around the mouth of the cave even when other parts of the mountainside are clear. The Ch'ol believe that Don Juan controls the rains, and even Protestant Ch'ol are known to petition Don Juan in times of crisis.

In Catholic mythology, the Day of the Holy Cross (May 3) commemorates the date on which Santa Elena was thought to have located the original crucifixion cross. Ancient rain rituals were merged with this Catholic spring festival because the date coincides with the start of the all-important rainy season, and rain ceremonies continue to be an essential part of this festival (Blom and LaFarge 1926–27:252; Thompson 1930:55; La Farge and Byers 1931:97; Redfield and Villa Rojas 1934:84, 239; Wisdom 1940:447; Bunzel 1952:57; Mayers 1958:49; Holland 1961:129; Mace 1970:31; Aulie 1979:33, 49; Breedlove and Laughlin 1993:49, 74, 106; Faust 1998:86). The Day of the Holy Cross, which is widely celebrated across Latin America, includes masses, dances, and pilgrimages to caves, springs, and lakes. The crosses in churches and at these other sacred locations are decorated with foliage as an act of renewal.

At Joloniel, the Day of the Holy Cross ceremony is centered on a pilgrimage to the caves at Joljá to petition Don Juan to release the rain and provide the necessary moisture for the coming growing season (Joljá Cave Project field notes). In years past, pilgrims came from across the Ch'ol region for this ceremony, but today the participants are mostly current and former Joloniel community members. As in many areas, the importance of traditional ceremonies has greatly diminished. Joloniel is one of the few communities in the region whose members still have a traditional Ch'ol world view.

The following description is based on Bassie-Sweet's participation in the 2001 and 2003 Day of the Holy Cross ceremonies. The festival preparation begins with the cleaning of the path to the caves and the adornment of the Joloniel church and its doorway cross with greenery. Paper streamers are strung across the ceiling of the church, and flowers and greenery are set out on the altar. The candles, rum, and incense that will be used for the ceremony are collected and counted in the church. During the festival, a considerable amount of liquor is consumed by the ritual participants and offered to Don Juan. As is the case in other regions of Chiapas, the candles are thought to be food for the deities. More than two hundred candles are burned during the ceremony, and the beeswax candles are considered to be the most powerful.

After an all-night vigil by the Joloniel tatuch in the church, prayers are said before the doorway cross, and then a small cross and a framed picture of the Virgin, patron saint of the village, are taken in a procession up the mountain to the caves. In years past, the large statue of the Virgin that is housed in the community church was taken to the cave, but after the statue was damaged in a fall, the framed picture of the Virgin was substituted to avoid further damage. The procession includes the Joloniel tatuch; the church sacristan, who assists the tatuch; community leaders; community members; and a band of musicians. The cross and the image of the Virgin are positioned beside the river where it emerges from the central cave mouth (Joljá Cave 2). The tatuch prays and makes offerings of candles, incense, and rum before the Virgin while the band plays its guitars and violins. The rum given to the deity is poured on the ground of the cave.

A waterfall runs down the side wall of the cave just inside the mouth and feeds into the cave river (see chapter 4 for more on the cave). The waterfall creates an atmosphere of light rain in the cave. It is believed that Don Juan makes this water. In prayers, the water is called the drops of Don Juan's tears and nose. The identification of Don Juan with the river water that pours from his caves may explain an entry in the Aulie dictionary in which the Milky Way is said to be his road (*i bihlel ajaw* "the road of *ajaw*") (Aulie 1979:25). The Maya envisioned the Milky Way as a celestial river that brings the rains (Bassie-Sweet 2008:36–38, 266–77). The identification of Don Juan with the river water is expressed clearly in the language of prayer: "*kyum ktyaty, 'i jol kolem ja', ch'ujulbä kolem ja', ch'ujulbä witz, ch'ujulbä xajlel* (Our Lord, Our Father; the head of the river, the holy river; holy mountain; holy stone)" (Miguel Meneses Peñate, cited in Meneses López 1986).

After several hours of prayers at the mouth of the cave, water is collected from a pool at the base of the waterfall and used to wash the painted image of the Virgin. The washing of saint figures is common in Chiapas. For example, the statue of San Miguel in the Tumbalá church is lowered and his feet are washed during periods of drought. If rain has not fallen by May 15, the statue is taken to the river at Hidalgo and given a bath (Aulie 1979:33).

After the washing of the Joloniel Virgin, the small cross and the image of the Virgin are left at the cave mouth while the tatuch, leaders, musicians, and some of the community members proceed to Cave 1. After prayers and offerings of rum at the mouth of this cave, they enter the chamber below the Group 2 paintings. Some Ch'ol believe the left-hand figure in Painting 2 is an image of Don Juan, while others think that this painting and the other inscriptions in the cave were created by him. The Group 2 chamber is a sloped chamber with three wooden crosses near its bottom. The first cross was erected by the tatuches of Tila and Tumbalá after the burning of the cave on Don Juan Mountain (Joljá Cave Project field notes). When the first cross became worn, a second one was set up beside it. When this cross in turn became worn, the third one was erected. There was a cross in the cave as early as 1932.

Next to these three crosses is a narrow crevice from which a cool breeze blows. It is at this location that the Ch'ol believe Don Juan comes for his offerings (see fig. 4.1). Dozens of candles are set up before the three crosses and on the ledges of the chamber and lit. The band of musicians positions itself adjacent to the tatuch and the crosses, and begins to play. With the chamber ablaze in candlelight, the tatuch pours water from the pool of the waterfall on the ground before the crosses and makes offerings of incense and rum while reciting petitions to Don Juan to send rain and a bountiful harvest. He also pours rum for Don Juan into the narrow crevice. The prayers and music last until the candles are reduced to stubs.

This appears to be the same place and manner of the offerings made in 1932 by the agrarian leader Juan Guzmán Sol, as recorded in the municipal archives of Tumbalá:

> fue conducido a una cueva que se halla en la cabeza del río Yschteljá . . . viendo que Juan Guzmán y Martín Gómez entraron en la cueva a encender sus velas en una cruz bieja que ay hai y los de afuera tocaban música de guitarras y violines.

> [The witness] was taken to a cave that is located at the head of the Río Yschteljá (Ixteljá) . . . and saw that Juan Guzmán and Martín Gómez entered the cave and lit their candles at an old cross that is there, and those outside played music on guitars and violins. (Alejos García and Ortega Peña 1990, document 720)

Today, after the ceremony in the chamber below the paintings of Group 2, some individuals collect a candle stub to burn in their milpas later. Others take candles to the rear of the cave and burn them before the stalagmites and paintings there. In some years, the tatuch also prays at the stalagmites, pouring before them water from the waterfall and making offerings of candles and liquor.

The group returns to the central cave for another round of prayers and offerings, and then the entire entourage moves with the image of the Virgin to the third cave. The ritual in the third cave is only performed in years of drought when there has been little indication of rain. Placing the Virgin near the back of the cave adjacent to the stream, the pilgrims offer more prayers, candles, and rum. Individual offerings of candles are also made in the sinkhole area. Water is collected from the sinkhole area of the cave, and again the Virgin is washed. The procession then heads down the mountain, stopping at a spring close to the village. Another round of offerings is made at this location, and then the Virgin is returned to the altar in the church. At the community building adjacent to the church, a meal prepared by the village women is waiting, and the entire community partakes of this food. The men and women dance together to traditional music. In earlier times, the ritual feast was consumed at the Joljá caves rather than the community building. If the rains fail to materialize after the Day of the Holy Cross, more rain petitions are made at the Joljá caves and a larger number of candles is offered.

Petitioners from other communities also come to Joljá in times of drought and other crises. In late April 1982, the El Chichón volcano, located 150 kilometers west of Joloniel, erupted and spewed ash over the Ch'ol region. The tatuches from several communities went to Joljá and prayed to Don Juan to send the rains to disperse the ash. The rains began soon after. That year there was a bumper crop of corn and coffee as a result of the nutrient-rich ash. The disaster became a windfall.

Don Juan is also revered at Tila, but the cult of the Black Christ has taken precedence there. In celebration of the Day of the Holy Cross, the Ch'ol of Tila make a pilgrimage to the rockshelter on San Antonio Mountain with a small statue of the Black Christ that is usually housed in the church (Bernardo Pérez Martínez, in Josserand and Hopkins 1996:55–61) (fig. 8.2). At the hermitage above the cave, the Catholic priest conducts a mass. The pilgrims direct their petitions for rain, good crops, and health to the stalagmite column that is thought to represent the Black Christ. A small indentation in the top of the column contains drip water, and the Ch'ol believe that the Black Christ produces this water (see chapter 2). Ch'ol immigrants who have migrated to Campeche still travel all the way back to Tila during periods of drought to make petitions at the San Antonio cave (Stephanie Geslin, personal communication).

The Day of the Holy Cross ceremonies in the Ch'ol area are similar to those in other regions. For example, the Tzotzil of San Andrés Larraínzar perform their Day of the Holy Cross ceremonies deep within the caves that are the main source of their water (Holland 1961:130). They petition the earth lord, who is thought to release the waters. Tzotzil from Chamula go to the mountain called Tzontevitz, where they also petition the earth lord for rain at a cave near the summit (Gossen 1974:317, 2002:1047, 1067). At Lake Amatitlán near Guatemala City, pilgrims from all over Guatemala and Chiapas come to the lake on the Day of the Holy Cross to ask the Virgin and Christ to provide rain (Berlo 1980:304). There is a belief that the Virgin herself leaves the church and goes to the lake and nearby volcano to petition the cloud-gathering mountains for rain. Pilgrimages are made to sacred locations around the lake and on the mountainside; and offerings are cast into the lake. Archaeological evidence at the lake indicates a long history of ritual activities dating to at least the

8.2. Tila, with San Antonio Mountain in the background. Black dot indicates location of rockshelter with a stalagmite column, where the Black Christ is sometimes worshipped. Photo by Karen Bassie-Sweet.

Early Classic. The pre-Columbian offerings recovered from the lake indicate that pilgrims came to this location from great distances.

Malevolent Supernaturals

Don Juan and the thunderbolt deities are not the only supernatural beings that inhabit the indigenous world. Many malevolent spirits are thought to endanger the lives of the Ch'ol (Aulie and Aulie 1978; Josserand et al. 2003). The Xib'aj are a group of beings that are often referred to as devils or witches. The chief Xib'aj is thought to be a bald human-like figure (also called Tzimajol "gourd head," i.e., skull) who can take the form of a jaguar. He leads a party of skeletons and personified animals such as talking owls and foxes. *Pejpem xib'aj* "moth demon" is the name of the feared Black Witch moth that is a sign of death (see chapter 6). The tales about Xib'aj are cautionary stories that emphasize that inappropriate behavior will result in an encounter with Xib'aj and death. One cannot but wonder if Xib'aj evolved in part from the deity Tlaloc, who had a skeletal form as well as owl and moth manifestations.

One of the most common malevolent specters in the Ch'ol region is the 'Ijk'al "black man" who tries to eat humans (Josserand et al. 2003). He also carries off women and impregnates them. Another Ch'ol evil spirit is Ch'ix Wiñik "spiny man," who is described as a man with spines on his body. It is believed that Ch'ix Wiñik is a creation of God who will eat all the bad people when the world comes to an end (Aulie and Aulie 1978:54). Both 'Ijk'al and Ch'ix Wiñik are thought to live in the deep woods. Two other supernatural inhabitants of the forest who eat people are Salvaje "savage" and Kichañob "our uncles." This latter kinship name (our mother's brothers) is the same term used to denote the modern Lacandón, who are clearly the models for this class of demons.

The Tzotzil and Tzeltal have many evil spirits that are similar to those of the Ch'ol. The Tzotzil, for example, have a character of their own called Ik'al, who is thought to be a black man who eats people and carries off women (Blaffer 1972). As has been discussed in previous chapters, black-colored deities and supernaturals are well known in Mesoamerican culture. In addition, African slaves likely contributed to the belief in a menacing black man. Henri Favre (1971) observes that African slaves became the confidants of ladino overlords and often served as foremen who imposed punishment on the native population. Africans were also recruited for paramilitary activities during periods of unrest.

Maya Characters with a Christian Twist

Many of the contemporary tales that feature Christ and the Virgin Mary are fused with elements from the Maya story of creation that is found in the Popol Vuh. Before reviewing these tales, a quick summary of the relevant episodes of the Popol Vuh is in order. In the Popol Vuh, the hero twins (sun and full moon) are the children of Lady Blood (a waxing moon goddess). Their paternal grandmother is Xmucane, the creator grandmother, who is likely a waning-moon goddess. The hero twins are in competition with their older half-brothers, who are wise sages and own a productive cornfield. The older half-brothers treat the hero twins badly and try to kill them. To defeat these older siblings, the hero twins pretend that they are unable to retrieve some birds that they had shot in a tree. When the half-brothers climb into the tree, the hero twins make the tree grow so big that their brothers cannot get down. The twins instruct their brothers to unwind their loincloths, and by doing so, the brothers are magically turned into monkeys. Xmucane is offered several opportunities to rescue the half-brothers, but she cannot stop herself from laughing at them and they remain monkeys.

The hero twins then magically clear a forest to create their own cornfield, but during the night the animals of the forest instruct the trees to stand up again. The hero twins try to capture these animals. They can only grab the deer and rabbit. Although both animals escape, they leave behind their tails, which is why deer and rabbits have short tails today. Finally, the twins trap a rat and torture him by burning the fur on his tail and squeezing his head until his eyes bulge, which is why rats now have bulging eyes and hairless tails. In exchange for sparing his life and providing him with food from their house, the rat tells the hero twins that their destiny is not to be corn farmers, but to be ballplayers. He informs them that their father's ball-game equipment is hidden in the rafters of their house and he helps them retrieve it. The rat then becomes an occupant of the house and is given permission by the hero twins to eat anything that is discarded in the house, which is why rats now inhabit Maya houses and not cornfields. The hero twins become ballplayers, journey to the underworld and defeat the lords of the underworld. They then resurrect their father as the morning star and follow him into the sky as the sun and full moon. In doing so, they create the first dawning on zenith passage and begin the annual corn cycle for humans.

In Classic period art, there is a supernatural rodent who is named in the accompanying hieroglyphic text as *k'an bah ch'o*, "yellow gopher rat" (Grube and Nahm 1994:699). On the Toniná stucco facade, the yellow gopher rat carries a ball with One Ajaw's head on it. Given that gophers are the rodents that the Maya trap in their cornfields, it is likely that the hero twins trapped a gopher, which was then transformed into a rat by removing the fur from its tail, making its eyes bulge, and sending it from the field to the house (Bassie-Sweet 2008:154).

A similar theme to the hero twins' story is found in Q'anjob'al creation tales that feature Christ, who is portrayed as the sun. In these tales, Christ has two elder brothers who treat him badly and make him perform menial tasks (La Farge 1947:50–57). Although his brothers are organizing their own festival of creation, Christ sets about to perform it on his own. He creates human beings to take part in his dance to form the world, and he fashions the musical instruments and feathered bird costumes for this purpose. His older brothers jealously want bird costumes as well, so Christ takes them to the ceiba tree where he obtained his costume. The tree is full of birds, and Christ tells his brothers to climb up the tree and get their bird costumes. Christ makes the tree grow higher and his brothers are stranded. The Virgin Mary tries to help her older sons down from the tree by throwing up her hair wrap to act as a rope, but still they cannot climb down. Christ warns his mother not to laugh, but she cannot contain herself when she sees them trying to climb down like monkeys, and they then are permanently transformed into these forest creatures. In a parallel story from the neighboring community of San Miguel Acatán, it is the uncles of Christ who are the villains, and at the end of the story Christ becomes the sun (Siegel 1941: 66; 1943:120).

The Ch'ol Maya also have several versions of this tale. In his youth, the young Sun-Christ is tormented by his older brother, who has a productive cornfield (Whittaker and Warkentin 1965:13–49). The older brother attempts to kill the Sun-Christ many times. The Sun-Christ devises a plan to kill his brother instead. He creates a ceiba tree full of honey-producing beehives. He accomplishes this task by first having his mother (the moon goddess–Virgin Mary) clean some cottonseed. He places the seed in a tree, which transforms it into the kapok-producing ceiba. The Sun-Christ then tells his older brother about the tree, and the two brothers set out at dawn to collect the honey. The older brother climbs the tree to retrieve the honeycombs. While he is at the top, the Sun-Christ asks him to throw down some of the honeycombs. Using the wax and some hard wood from an edible palm, he creates a gopher to chew at the roots while he chops away at the trunk with his machete. The tree topples and kills the older brother. The Sun-Christ then transforms the blood of his older brother into animals. After this death, Christ magically clears a cornfield, but a rabbit undoes his work. Christ gives the rabbit to his mother to keep, but he grows weary of planting corn. He decides to rise into the sky as the sun, and he is followed by his mother, who becomes the moon. The moon has a rabbit on its face because Christ gave the rabbit to her.

In another version recorded of this basic story, it is the older brother who is able to magically clear the cornfield, but God sends a bird to restore the field (see "Our Holy Mother Ty'a'n Lak Ch'ujul Ña" in the appendix). The older brother wants to kill his younger brother. To turn the tables on him, the younger brother finds a tree filled with honeycombs and takes his brother there to eat the honey. While the older brother is gorging himself at the top of the tree, he throws the empty beeswax at his younger brother, who remains at the base of the tree. The younger brother models the beeswax into little gophers, and using palm wood, he creates the gophers' teeth. While the gophers gnaw on the roots, the younger brother uses his machete, which has the form of a snake, to cut down the tree. When the older brother crashes to the ground and is killed, his body is transformed into the animals of the world. When the Virgin Mary tries to grab some of these animals by the tail, their tails break off, creating all the short-tailed animals. The younger brother then becomes the sun and his mother becomes the moon.

The Virgin Mary is also featured in a number of other tales that have their genesis in ancient mythology. One of these stories involves a laughing falcon (*Herpetotheres cachinnans*) that cures her of a snakebite (Joljá Project field notes). In this Ch'ol story, the Virgin Mary is sitting in the patio of her house, preparing to spin cotton and weave the first clothing for people. Mary reaches into her box that holds her weaving supplies, and she is bitten by a hidden snake. She asks the laughing falcon to come and heal her. The bird arrives and lands in a dry tree where it begins to sing and cure her. The laughing falcon, which is also known as the waco or guaco, has two calls: "waco-waco-waco" and "ha-ha-ha." Unlike other birds of prey, the primary diet of a laughing falcon is snakes, and it has the ability to kill even the most poisonous species. The bird, which is not a rapid or stealthy flyer, usually perches in a tree patiently waiting for a snake to appear. The laughing falcon then lands beside the snake and extends its wing like a shield as it reaches out and grasps the snake by the head. After decapitating the snake, the falcon retreats to a tree to eat its headless meal. This is in contrast to eagles and hawks that often pick up a snake, fly into the sky and drop the snake in order to kill it. The Ch'ol believe that the laughing falcons can kill poisonous snakes because the birds are healers that can cure themselves if they get bitten. As indicated by the Virgin Mary story, it is the call of the laughing falcon that cures the patient. Köhler (1975:242) notes that Tzotzil healers imitate the call of a laughing falcon in order to cure a snakebite. The Tzotzil also believe that if a person can imitate the call of the bird without tiring, the person will become a bonesetter, that is, a curer who fixes broken bones (Laughlin 1975:362).

The avian form of Itzamnaaj, the creator grandfather, was based on the laughing falcon, and as noted, the creator grandfather was the first healer and rainmaker (Bassie-Sweet 2008:140–44). The Itzamnaaj bird has a hooked beak and serpent-wings, but its distinguishing feature is a headdress with a floral element that contains an *ak'bal* sign. In many examples, the Itzamnaaj bird clutches a serpent in its mouth, and several scenes show the hero twins shooting the Itzamnaaj bird with their blowguns. Examples of the Itzamnaaj bird are found in the Pre-Classic San Bartolo west wall mural, which attests to the importance of this bird from the earliest of times (Taube et al. 2010). The San Bartolo mural illustrates four trees with an Itzamnaaj bird perched in each one. In the second tree, the front head of the serpent held by the Itzamnaaj bird has had its head decapitated in a manner consistent with the hunting habits of the laughing falcon. The blood from the decapitated head and body of the serpent drips onto the deer offering at the base of the tree.

Bardawil (1976) grouped all supernatural birds with hooked beaks and serpent-wings into one category and assigned the nickname Principal Bird Deity. In their review of the Itzamnaaj bird in the San Bartolo mural, Taube et al. (2010) also lumped together all such birds and stated that this so-called Principal Bird Deity was a manifestation of Itzamnaaj parallel to Seven Macaw of the Popol Vuh and a solar eagle, although they failed to explain how the bird could be both a macaw and an eagle. Seven Macaw was a false deity who claimed to be the sun and moon. To defeat him, the hero twins shot him in the jaw, which caused him great pain. In their roles as healers, the creator grandparents, Xpiyacoc and Xmucane, convinced Seven Macaw that they could treat his pain by removing his jeweled teeth and eye adornments. In effect, they took away his status and power. He then died. While Seven Macaw and the Itzamnaaj bird were both shot by the hero twins, the similarity ends there. Equating Seven Macaw with the avian form of the creator grandfather Itzamnaaj flies in the face of logic.

There is a laughing falcon deity that *is* parallel to the Itzamnaaj bird in the Popol Vuh. His name is Wak, and he is also shot by the hero twins. In the episode concerning Wak, the creator grandmother sends a louse to deliver a message to the hero twins, who are at their father's ballcourt playing ball. On the way, the slow-moving louse is swallowed by a toad, the toad is swallowed by a snake, and the snake is swallowed by Wak. When Wak arrives at the ballcourt, he cries out to the hero twins and they shoot him in the eye with their blowguns. He then refuses to give them their message until they heal his eye. The hero twins take rubber from their ball and place it Wak's eye, which magically cures him. Given that Wak could cure himself, it seems apparent that this is one of the many tests given to the hero twins to prove that they are worthy replacements for their father. Wak then vomits up the snake and the snake vomits up the toad. The louse is found in the mouth of the toad, and he gives the hero twins their message, which is an invitation to play ball in the underworld. This sets into motion their destiny to become the sun and full moon and to start the first corn cycle. The snake eaten by Wak is named *Saqi K'as,* and from the Popol Vuh description it is most likely an indigo snake (*Drymarchon corais*) (Bassie-Sweet 2008:143–44). Such snakes are closely associated with water and thought to be the owners of springs.

The San Bartolo west wall mural has many parallels with the Postclassic New Year ceremonies, which were festivals in honor of the Chahk deities to ensure adequate rain and agricultural abundance (Stuart 2004b; Taube et al. 2010). The theme of the San Bartolo scene also seems to be rain ceremonies, given that the serpent skyband that frames the scene has motifs hanging from it that represent dark rain clouds, and a fifth Itzamnaaj bird descends from the skyband (Taube et al. 2010:46).

Parallels between the San Bartolo scene and Classic ceremonies are apparent in illustrations of Period Ending events at Piedras Negras. As discussed in chapter 6, the front of Piedras Negras Stela 6 illustrates the ruler sitting in a niche framed by a Period Ending text. The sky is defined by a Milky Way crocodile with a skyband body that arches over the ruler, spilling rain from its mouth. The Itzamnaaj bird sits perched on the skyband, clutching the double-headed serpent in its beak. A similar Period Ending scene is found on Piedras Negras Stela 11, where the ruler is again surrounded by the Milky Way crocodile with an Itzamnaaj bird perched overhead. The association of the Itzamnaaj bird with Period Ending events is also evident in the Paris Codex. In this book, a series of pages illustrate successive Period Ending ceremonies that have the same imagery as the Piedras Negras stelae (Hellmuth 1987; Love 1994). On page 4 of the codex, the Itzamnaaj bird hovers over the scene.

A similar theme is found on the front façade of the Copan Margarita panel (Bell, Canuto, and Sharer 2004:plate 2). The center of the scene is a full-figure glyph of the Copan founding ruler, K'inich Yax K'uk' Mo', with the "nine blood footprint" place name that is frequently associated with Period Ending ceremonies below it. A Milky Way crocodile frames the ruler's name, and each corner of the scene is decorated with a *bak'tun* sign. In other words, instead of showing a portrait of the ruler performing a Period Ending ceremony, the artist chose simply to use the ruler's name and the place name where the event occurred. The Copan Motmot marker illustrates this ruler seated on the same place name performing rituals for the 9.0.0.0.0 Period Ending (Stuart 2004a:fig. 11.11). The tail on most examples of the Classic-period Milky Way crocodile is decorated with the headdress of the Chahk deity who is nicknamed GI. The headdress, like the mouth of the crocodile, has water flowing from it. On the Copan Margarita panel, the tail of the crocodile takes the form of a serpent with a Chahk deity emerging from its mouth. The Chahk grasps his thunderbolt ax in his right hand. Given that the Maya believe that the Milky Way is a celestial river that brings the rain, it is obvious that these Period Ending events involved petitions to the gods for rain.

The Ch'ol story of the Virgin Mary and the laughing falcon does not overtly refer to rainmaking, but the laughing falcon is directly identified with rain (Bassie-Sweet 2008:132–49). It is said that the "ha-ha-ha" call of the laughing falcon, which sounds like the Maya word for water, brings the rain. Mary is frequently characterized as a weaver in contemporary stories, which is a role unknown in Catholic mythology. This is, however, one of the primary characteristics of the creator grandmother Ix Chel. The headdress of Ix Chel contains raw cotton and spindles of spun cotton thread (Taube 1992a, 1994; Ciaramella 1994, 1999). Cotton thread is looped around the pegs of a board to create the warp for weaving, and Ix Chel is shown performing this task in the Madrid Codex (Ciaramella 1999). In several scenes, Ix Chel also wears a tied warp-skein as a headdress, and in some examples, the skein takes the form of a coral snake. It is not a coincidence that the Ch'ol term for the coral snake is *sinta laj ko'* "our grandmother's hair ribbon" (Aulie and Aulie 1978:157). In Maya mythology, the spinning of cotton and the act of weaving are intimately associated with the production of rain, and Ix Chel is shown in the codices producing rain. Rainmaking and healing play dominant roles in Maya life. It should not be surprising then that these two areas of major concern retain numerous elements of ancient beliefs.

There is a great diversity of religious views in the Ch'ol region, with various Christian churches aggressively trying to expand their congregations. Despite the intense activities of these institutions, belief in an earth lord and thunderbolt, meteor, and wind deities is still found in the Ch'ol area as well as other Maya regions. The Ch'ol world view has numerous parallels with its Tzotzil and Tzeltal counterparts.

Although there are Christian aspects to many of these beings, their primary origins are rooted in the pre-Columbian past. There are also other characters and beliefs in Ch'ol mythology that have their genesis in ancient times, such as the Black Witch moth that announces an imminent death and the laughing falcon that announces the rain. While many researchers ignore the wealth of information contained in contemporary stories and beliefs, we believe that they are a source of important insights for understanding ancient culture. Conversely, ancient customs and beliefs reveal the deeper meaning of many contemporary stories.

APPENDIX

Ch'ol Folktales

A Visit to Don Juan

Mariano Mayo Jiménez with Ausencio Cruz Guzmán

ACG: 'Ili ty'añ mu b'u kaj käl,
'iliyi, tza 'ujtyi 'añix wäle
komo jo'lum p'e jab'.
'Alä tyo 'ili Mariano.

MMJ: Wajali che' ya tyo 'añoñ . . .
ya tyo 'añoñ b'añ kerañob'
tyi Paso Naranjoji,
'i koñ . . . en el Paso Naranjo . . .
koñ mi yälob' ke 'añ 'ab'i
San Juañ 'ab'i,
b'añ laj k'ajtyiñ chu' pejtye laj k'ajtyiñ.
'Añ wajali che' b'ajche' laj mel laj chol.
Che' b'ajche' mak mi seb' tye' [tyilel] ja'al,
mi chämel laj chol.
'I tza kub'i lojoñ
ñaxañ tzajñi juñ tyikil
jiñi jyumijel lojoñ,
'i tza juli 'i sub'eñoñ lojoñ
ke "Weñäch," che'eñ,
"Koñ laj,"
tza k'otyi 'i yäle.
'I che jiñi,

ACG: *This story I'm going to tell you,*
this, it took place now
about fifteen years ago.
Mariano was a young boy still.

MMJ: *A long time ago, when I was still . . .*
when I was still where my brothers are
in Paso Naranjo,
and so . . . in Paso Naranjo . . .
since they say that there was [a certain]
San Juan, they say,
where we asked for everything we asked for.
A long time ago that's how we made milpa.
Since the rain didn't come soon enough,
our milpa was dying.
And we heard
first one man came,
an uncle of ours,
and he came and told us
that "OK," he said,
"Let's go,"
he came and told us.
And so it was,

171

tza' 'i tyempañob' 'i b'ä

they got themselves together,

jyumijelob' yik'oty kerañob'i,

my uncles and my brothers,

"Koñ laj k'ajtyiñ ja'al chañ laj chol.

"Let's go ask for rain for our milpas.

Mañik ka laj k'ux 'ixim.

We're not going to have corn to eat.

Woli 'i laj chämel laj kixim,

Our corn is all dying,

chañ weñ kab'äl jajmel,

because there is a really big drought,

koñ weñ kab'äl jajmel ja'el.

since there is a really big drought, too.

Cha' p'e 'uj,

Two months,

pejtyelel 'abril yik'oty mayo,"

all of April and May,"

che'eñ.

they said.

Tza majliyoñ lojoñ,

We all went.

tza majyoñ [majliyoñ] ja'el,

I went, too,

koñ 'alob'oñ tyo,

although I was small,

chañ k'ajalix jcha'añ.

I still remember.

Che jiñi,

So it was,

"Jmajle ja'el," chc'oñ.

"I'm going, too," I said.

"¿Chuk 'a majl 'a mel, 'aha?

"What are you going to do, huh?

Weñ ñajty. Weñ 'añ witz,"

It's a long way. It's very mountainous,"

che' tzi sub'eñoñ.

so they told me.

"¿Che muk 'a k'otye, ma wub'iñ?"

"So you think you'll get there?"

che tzi sub'eñoñ.

so they said to me.

"Muku mij k'otyel."

"I certainly will get there."

"Koñ laj," che'eñ,

"Let's go," they said,

che 'añ kerañob'.

said my brothers.

Majliyoñ lojoñ,

We all went;

tzi mäñob' majlel

they went to buy

jum p'e litro lemb'al

a liter of aguardiente

yik'o jum p'e pakete ñichim,

and a package of candles,

yik'o juñ kojty 'i mutyob',

and a chicken,

tza majyoñ lojoñ.

and we all left.

'I sujmäch,

And it was really true,

ñajtyäch,

it was a long way,

'i puru witzäch,

and all mountains;

ñajtyäch, tza kub'i.

a long way, it seemed.

Tzäch k'otyiyoñ lojoñ,

We all arrived there,

k'otyiyoñ komo las kwatro la tarde.

we arrived about four in the afternoon.

Che jiñi,

So it was,

k'otyiyoñ lojoñ b'añ yotyoty

we arrived at the house of

jiñi sañ kristañ, mi yälob'i.

the sacristan, they call him.

K'otyi jpejkañ lojoñ.

We arrived to make our petition.

ACG: ¿B'aki 'añ 'añ sakristañ?

ACG: Where was this sacristan?

MMJ::Ya'añ tyi 'Aktyepa'Yochib',
mi yälob'. Jum p'e Yochib'.
"¿Chuki la wom?," che' 'ab'i laj tyaty ñox.
"Mañik. Tza tyili jpejkañety
mi k'el chañ ma majle 'a ñusäb'eñoñ lojoñ
'ix . . . 'ixi b'añ laj ch'uju tyaty
Sañ Roñ Juañ."
"'A, bweno. ¿Tyi la pusik'al woli la tyilel?
Ma ma wub'iñ."
"Jiñäch kuyi mi kub'iñ lojoñ."
"'A, bweno. 'Utz'aty che jiñi," che'eñ.
"¿Chuk me woli la k'ajtyiñ, ma wub'iñ?"
"Este . . . kom tyej kaj k'ajtyiñ lojoñ ja'al
chañ jchol lojoñ,
koñ woxi laj, weñ chämel jchol lojoñ.
Mach yomix kolel,
loñ tzax cha' päk'ä lojoñ,
woli 'i cha' chämel,
weñ tzax wäle jajmel.
Jiñ cha'añ tzaj peñsariñ,
yub'ili tza tyij k'ajtyiñ lojoñ
tz'itya' ja'al.
Koñ mu 'ab'i yäk' . . .
la käk'eñtyel ja'al
che' mi laj k'ajtyiñ 'ab'iyi,
'ila tyi San Ron Juañi,"
che tzi yälä jkerañ yik'o jyumijelob'.
"'A weno, yomäch che jiñi.
Weñ chapal tza tyiliyety laj'.
"Chapaloñ ku."
"Weno, weno, koñ laj che jiñi.
Pero tyi laj kuleli, laj kulel,
laj mel koleñ k'iñ 'ila tyi kotyotyi,"
che' 'ab'i 'ub'i sañkristañ."
"Chañ ku yomäch tzax ch'ämä loñ tyilel . . ."

ACG: Jiñi . . . 'a . . . ¿b'ajche 'i k'ab'a'
'añ jiñi sakristañ che tyi ty'añ?

MMJ: Este, 'i k'ab'a' jiñi bajche katekista yub'il,
koñ jiñtza' mi pejkañ cheñ.

ACG: ¿Jiñ kuyi ñusaj ty'añ?

MMJ: *There at Actiepá Yochib,*
they say. A place called Yochib.
"What do you all want?" said the elder.
"Nothing. We came to ask you
to see if you can go take us
to that . . . that place where Our Holy Father is,
San Don Juan."
"Ah, good. Do you come with your hearts?
Do you feel it?"
"We really do feel it."
"Ah, good. That's good," he said.
"What are you asking for?"
"Well . . . since we came to ask for rain
for our milpas,
since it's dying, our milpas are really dead.
They don't want to grow,
in vain we planted a second time,
and it is dying again,
it's really a drought now.
So we thought about it,
we felt that we should come ask
for a little rain.
Since they say it hasn't . . .
we haven't been given rain,
so we petition, as they say,
here to that San Don Juan,"
so said my brothers and my uncles.
"Ah, good, that's what you want.
You all came well prepared."
"We're really prepared."
"OK, OK, let's go, then.
But when we return, on our return,
we'll make a big fiesta here in my house,"
said the sacristan.
"It's a good thing we already brought . . ."

ACG: *Uh . . . What do you call*
the sacristan in Ch'ol?

MMJ: *Uh, he was called like a catechist,*
it seems, since he's the one that prays.

ACG: *He's the one that passes on the requests?*

MMJ: Nusaj ty'añ,
che b'ajche misionero, yub'il.
Che' majleloñ.
"Koñ laj che jiñi," cho'oñ,
"Mero ñajtyäch ku," che'eñ,
chañ ku mach chäkäch.
"¿Tza laj ch'eñlel [ch'äm tyilel] la poko?"
"Tza ku."
"Weno, koñ laj," chejeñ.
Majyoñ lojoñ chejax k'iñ,
majyoñ loñ ja'el, majyoñ tyak ja'el.
"Wix ma käleli," che'eñ kerañob',
'ila tyi 'otyotyi, yotyo laj tyatyi,"
che'eñ 'añ kerañob'i.
"Mañik much jkälä, jmaj ja'e," cho'oñ.
Majyoñ tyak ja'el.
'Ochiyoñ majleli.
Wox tyi b'äjlem 'aj k'iñ
tza k'otyiyoñ lojoñ.
Läpä ch'ikijach ku b'ih,
pero puro b'äjlel tzäch majyoñ lojoñ.
Che b'a tza 'ochiyoñ lojoñ
koleñ b'ujtyil, koleñ 'otyoty yilal.
Pero selekña jach, wolokña jach,
tye'el, ñuke xajlelol.
"Wex 'ilali," che'eñ 'ub'i,
"tza b'u jpejka lojoñ laj tyatyi,
mi yälob'."
"'A weno," che'eñ . . . cho'oñ lojoñ.
'Ochiyoñ loñ majlel che ya tyoktyil 'i tyi',
tza 'ochi maj ya che li,
'aya tyi mali, koleñ mal.

ACG: ¿B'ajche ñojal, 'am b'ä jum p'e metro?

MMJ: Najty mi laj xäñ majlel, che' ñajtye . . .

ACG: ¿Jiñ ku 'añ 'i tyi' ch'eñ?

MMJ: Chäch ku, tyoktyil che li,
tyoktyil che li.

MMJ: *He passes on the requests,*
like a missionary, it seems.
Thus we went.
"Let's go then," we said.
"It's really a long way," he said,
but it really wasn't so much.
"Did you bring your flashlights?"
"We did."
"OK, let's go," he said.
We all went when the sun was like this,
we all went, too, I went along, too.
"You're going to stay here," said my brothers,
"here in the house, the house of the elder,"
said my brothers.
"No, I'm not staying, I'm going too," I said.
I went along, too.
We started to go.
The sun was going down
when we got there.
The trail was full of potholes,
and it was a steep drop when we got there.
There where we entered
there was a big hill, it looked like a big house.
But it was round, circular,
with trees and big piles of rocks.
"This is it," that guy said,
"where we petition Our Father,
they say."
"Ah, good," he said . . . we said.
We entered where the mouth was open,
we went in like that,
there inside, it was big inside.

ACG: *How big was it? Would it be a meter?*

MMJ: *We walked a long way, so far . . .*

ACG: *And the mouth of the cave?*

MMJ: *Yes, it was open like this,*
open like this.

ACG: Jum p'e metro.

MMJ: Jäjä. Mi cha' ñume 'i ñup'ob' tyi jum p'e
. . . yik'o che wechtyil koleñ xajlel.

ACG: 'Aja.

MMJ: Mi ñup'ob' che tza 'ochiyoñ lojoñ majlel.
"Weno, tzuk'ux la b'ela," che'eñ.
Che kälä lojoñ, tzuk'u lojoñ jb'ela.
Tzuk'uloñ b'ela, tzaj xäñäloñ majlel,
che b'ajche 'ixi yotyo 'Umberto,
weñ k'otyiyoñ lojoñ.
'Añ ja'i ya tyi mali,
'añ 'alä pa',
ya mi jub'e tye ja',
pero tzuwañ 'a ja'i,
pero 'ik'yoch'añ tza majli.
Koñ 'añtza jb'ela,
tza majyoñ, chañetyak xajlel.
Weñ b'ojy tyak mi yajle ja'
ya tyi mal.
Che'i majliyoñ lojoñ.
K'otyiyoñ lojoñ b'añ mi mero pejkañob'
laj tyaty San Roñ Juañ.
'Ub'i sankristañ, "Wex 'ilali," che'eñ.
"Wäxka b'uchi' ya'i," che' kälälojoñ.
B'uchle lojoñ che jiñi. Che 'añ,
che li, ya wa'al 'añ krusi.
Koleñ krus 'ixi ch'ujtye'.
Mi melob' ya b'añ koleñ krus.
'I che jiñi,
tzaj tzololoñ b'ela lojoñ, tzololojoñ.
Koñ tzi ch'ämäyob' majlel
'i lemb'alob' kerañob'i,
tzaki yäk'eñob' 'ixi sakristañ.

ACG: ¿Chuki ya' 'añ ya tyi jol 'añ rus?

MMJ: Mañik chu' 'añ.
Jiñjach ñichim mi k'otye 'i tzuk'ob'.

ACG: *A meter.*

MMJ: *Uh-huh. When we came out again
they closed it with a . . . with about this size
of a big rock.*

ACG: *Aha.*

MMJ: *They closed it when we all entered.
"OK, light your candles." he said.
So they told us, to light our candles.
With our candles lit, we walked along,
it was about like to Humberto's house,
and we arrived.
There was water there inside,
there was a little stream,
there water was falling,
but that water was cold,
but it was dark where it went.
Since I had a candle,
I went on; there were a lot of big rocks.
It was slippery all over where the water fell
there inside.
So we went on.
We arrived at the place to do petitions
to Our Father San Don Juan.
The sacristan, "It's here," he said.
"Sit down over there," so we sat down.
We sat down, so. So it was,
like that, there was a cross there.
A big cross, of cedar.
They do it there where the big cross is.
And so it was,
we lined up our candles, we lined them up.
Since my brothers had brought
their liquor,
they began giving it to the sacristan.*

ACG: *What is there at the head of the cross?*

MMJ: *There isn't anything.
Just the candles we came to light.*

ACG: ¿'Añ ku tza 'uj, ma wäl?

MMJ: 'A, 'añ ku jum p'e 'uj ya'i che li.

ACG: ¿'Uj?

MMJ: Yejtyal 'uj, ya' selel che
tyi ñäk' 'otyoty, yilal.
Tzi sub'oñ lojoñ,
 much b'u 'i pejkañ sañ kristañ,
"Jiñi laj ch'uju ña' woch la käñ.
Woli ku 'aweno,
wä tyo laj b'ej majlel 'ilali."
Che' kälä lojoñ majloñ lojoñ,
tza k'otyiyoñ lojoñ.
"Wex 'ila. B'uchi laj 'ilali.
Wä tza 'añ 'i tyi' 'i yotyoty
la yum San Juañi."
"'A weno," cho'oñ lojoñ.
B'uchleyoñ lojoñ.
"'I tza tyo la ch'äñtyile 'añ laj tyäkäjib',"
 che'eñ.
"Tza ku ya witz'tyil," che'añ yumijel,
ki yäk'eñob'.
Che jiñ,
"Weno, ñich'tyañ, me ku la," che'eñ,
"'i much kaj pejkañ," che'eñ.
'Añ yalä Biblia, che ya wistyil,
ki k'ele, chejiñ laj k'ele.
B'ajche, jay p'e ty'añ mi yäk',
ki ch'uyb'añ, ki päye',
'i jatz' 'i mesa che li ki ch'uyb'añ.
Jiñjax tza kaj kub'iñ tyejchi 'a Sañ Juañi,
jiñi wäyäl, wele b'ajchex che jiñi,
tyejchi, ki . . . ki pejkañ,
ki k'äy majlel 'orasiyoñ,
jin jach tza kub'ilojoñ.
"¿Chuki la wom ma wäl," jiñi . . .
che tyilel weñ koleñ ty'añ
tyi mal tyi mali.

ACG: ¿Ch'ojla tye 'i sapato?

ACG: *Isn't there a moon, didn't you say?*

MMJ: *Ah, there is a moon there, like this.*

ACG: *A moon?*

MMJ: *The image of a moon, it's round,*
on the wall of the house, it seems.
He told us,
the one who asked the sacristan,
"That is Our Holy Mother you are meeting.
[If] you are all right,
we are going further on."
Thus they told us, and we went on,
we arrived.
"This is it. Sit down here.
Here is the door to the house of
Your Lord San Juan."
"Ah, good," we said.
We all sat down.
"And did you still bring our "warmer"
[our liquor]?" he said.
"Yes, there is a little there," said an uncle;
he began to give it to him.
So it was,
"OK, listen up, all of you," he said.
"and I'm going to start praying," he said.
There was a little Bible, small like this,
he started to read, he read it all.
How many words he said!
He started to whistle, he started to summon,
he hit the table like this when he whistled.
So just like that San Juan started to wake up,
he was asleep, perhaps, who knows,
he got up, he . . . he started to pray,
he started to sing out prayers,
that's what we heard.
"What do you say you want?," the . . .
thus came a big voice
from inside that interior.

ACG: *Did his shoes make noise?*

MMJ: 'Inki, ch'ojch'oña tyile che jiñi,
wä'le tyi tyi' 'otyoty wäleyi,
che jiñi weñ jumuk' 'i ñäch'äloñ lojoñ.
"Wenas noche, 'ijo," che tyaki.
"Wenas noches, papá," tza laj jak'älojoñ.

ACG: ¿Tyi ty'añ ma wäl 'aja papa?

MARÍA CRUZ: Laj tyaty.

MMJ: "Laj tyaty," chojoñ lojoñ.
"Weno, ¿chuki la wom, hijo?" che'eñ.
"Jiñi . . . tza' 'ab'i tyili jpejkañety lojoñ,
tyaty lojoñ, este . . .
cha'añ chañ jchol lojoñ,
woxi laj chämel,
koñ mach yoñx kolel 'ixim, kixim.
Mi käl cha'añ tzax wa'le jajmel, yilal.
Chuxka jmul loñ b'ajche jiñi,"
tzi cha'le ty'añ kerañob'.
"'A, weno. ¿Chuki la wom?"
"Mañik. Chañ kom ma wäk'eñoñloñ ja',
yilal, chañ mi koleloñ jchol.
Eske maxi koleloñ jchol loñ.
Yub'il tzax cha' päk'ä lojoñ,
mak mi kolel,
woli 'i cha' chämel,"
che cho'oñ lojoñ
tza kajiyoñ lojoñ tyi ty'añ.
'A weno, este . . .
Tzi ki pejkañob' 'i b'ä
yik'o much b'u 'i pejkañ sankristañ.
"¿B'ajche 'a wälä?
De 'akwerdojety laj,"
che'eñ, che kuyi 'ixi.

ACG: ¿"Tyeme la ty'añ," che'eñ?

MMJ: "Tyeme la ty'añ," che'eñ.
Tzi cha' sub'eñoñ lojoñ sakristañ,
"La wom chañ ja'ali."
"Komäch ku lojoñ."

MMJ: *Yes, indeed, loud footsteps came*
from there at the door of the house in there,
so for a good time we were quiet.
"Good evening, son," he said.
"Good evening, papa," we answered.

ACG: *In Ch'ol, do you say "papa"?*

MARÍA CRUZ: *Our Father.*

MMJ: *"Our Father," we said.*
"OK, what do you want, son?" he said.
"The . . . we came here to ask you,
Our Father, uh . . .
just on behalf of our milpas,
they are all dying,
since the corn doesn't want to grow, our corn.
I say that it's because of the drought, it seems.
Whatever our sin was, it's like that,"
said my brothers.
"Ah, good. What do you want?"
"Nothing. We just want you to give us rain,
it seems, so our milpas will grow.
It's that our milpas don't grow.
It seems we already planted a second time,
it doesn't grow,
it's dying again,"
so we said
when we started to speak.
Ah, OK, well . . .
They started to ask for themselves
along with the sacristan that petitioned.
"What do you say?
Are you all agreed?"
he said, really like that.

ACG: *He said, "Speak all together"?*

MMJ: *"Speak all together," he said.*
The sacristan asked us again,
"You all just want rain?"
"Indeed we all do."

Weno, tzi cha' sub'eñ ja'el,
"'A weno, weno,
'orita samoñ tyi Soyaló," che jiñi.
"Sami jpejkañ Sañ Miwel
b'ajche 'i yälä,
mi much ki chok jub'el 'añ ja'ali."
"Yoñku," cho'oñ lojoñ.
Cha' ch'ojch'oña tza letzi majlel.
Che jiñi,
"Ma pityañoñ jumuk',"
che' 'ab'i tzi sub'e,
b'uchuloñ lojoñ.
Che jiñi,
weñ ñajtye 'ora,
weno, cha' k'otyi,
cha' jujukña tyilel,
cha' ch'ojch'oña tyile.
"Weno, tzax cha' juliyoñ," che'eñ.
"Tza'ix ku papa," cho'oñ lojoñ.
"Weno, tyaläch 'añ ja'ali,"
chäch yälä 'añ San Mikel
ke tyaläch 'añ ja'ali,
"pero ma me ku la b'äk'ñañ.
Che jiñi,
tyal me ku pejtye 'ik'
yik'o tyuñi ja'
yik'o weñ ja'lel.
Ya jax tyo la majle tyi 'ojli b'ij,
maxtyo mej k'otyemety laj
tyi 'otyoty 'ixi . . . 'ili san kristañi,
b'äk' tyile ja'al,
mi tyajety laj tyi b'ij,"
che kälä lojoñ.
"Weno, kukux laj tyi lok'el,
por ke yax tye ja'al,"
che'eñ.
Che jiñi,
yorajlel tza b'äk' lok'iyoñ majlel,
lok'iyoñ loñ majlel.
Che jiñi,
ya' jpoj majle lojoñ tyi yojli b'ij,
majlel b'äk' tyili ja'al.

Well, he spoke again,
"Ah, good, good,
right away I'm going to Soyaló," he said.
"I'm going to ask San Miguel
what he says,
if he will start throwing down some rain."
"All right," we said.
Once again, his footsteps sounded as he left.
So it was,
"Wait for me a bit,"
they say he said,
and we all sat down.
So it was,
a good while later,
well, he arrived again,
he came making noise again,
his footsteps rang out again as he came.
"OK, I'm back again," he said.
"It's true, papa," we said.
"OK, the rain is going to come,"
so said San Miguel,
that the rain is going to come,
"but don't you all be afraid.
So it is,
a really big wind is coming
with hailstones
and heavy rain.
You all go out to the road,
and before you have arrived
at the house of that . . . the sacristan,
suddenly a rain will come,
it will catch you on the road,"
so he told us.
"OK, get out of here,
because a big rain is coming,"
he said.
So it was,
right then we left quickly,
we all left.
So it was,
there just as we were halfway down the road,
there came a sudden rain.

Lekoj ja'al yik'o 'ik'.
K'otyiyoñ loñ tyi yotyoty 'ub'i sankristañ,
weñ ja'lel, 'ik', 'asta tza yajli tyuñi ja', jiñi.
Pero che tyo woli 'i pejkañ jiñi sakristañ,
koñ tanto tza . . . tzi leme ja'el jyumijelob',
koñ max tz'äkäl,
wo tyi resar.
Wäle wo tyi 'orasyoñ 'añ sakristañ,
tzi b'ajb'e,
jiñ jach tzaj k'ele tyo lepelej yajlel.
"Chuk tza mele, kermañu,"
cho'oñ lojoñ.
"Mañik. Mañik. Ma jña'tyañ
b'ajche mi kujtye, 'aja," che'eñ.
"Tzi jatz'äyoñ chañ weñ yikoñix 'ab'i,
koñ 'oñatyax tza wäk'eñoñ lemb'al," che'eñ.
"Che ja'el San Juañi, yikix ja'el.
Ki jatz' 'i witara.
Tzäñtzäña kaj tyi k'aytyak.
Che jiñi, tza mich'a chañ yikix.
'I jatz'äyoñ koñ che b'ajche woj kap ja'eli.
Woch' 'ab'i hap ja'el jiñi la lemb'al
ya b'u b'utyu tyi la limetyeji.
Max 'ab'i . . . mach' 'ab'i tz'a'añix,
tzax 'ab'i 'i laj ch'ämb'e 'i ch'ujlel,"
che'eñ 'añ 'ub'i sankristañ.
"Mi laj k'otye laj kap ya tyi kotyotyi,
mañix ka laj yik'añ tyo,
che jax la kañ la wuty,"
'ab'iyi ch'eñ.
"Chañ ku. Chäch yom.
Wäle, kox la'," 'ab'i,
koñ yax 'ab'i tye ja'ali
'ojli b'ij," che kälä lojoñ.
B'äk' lok'iyoñ loñ majlel,
che jax tyo ñajtye,
che tyo ñajtye,
mach kom loñ k'otyel tyi yotyoty sankristañ,
b'ajche 'ixi b'ujtyil
ya tye ñuke 'ik', ñuki ja'lel.
K'otyiyoñ loñ tyi 'otyoty,
pero weñ koleñ ja'lel,

A terrible rain with wind.
When we got to the house of that sacristan,
a good rainstorm, wind, even hail was falling.
But when that sacristan was praying,
since so . . . he drank, as well as my uncles,
maybe it wasn't complete,
what he was praying.
There he was praying,
and it struck him down,
I just saw him fall down.
"What are you doing, brother,"
we said.
"Nothing. Nothing. I don't know
how this happened to me," he said.
"It hit me because I'm really drunk, they say,
since you all gave me a lot of liquor," he said.
"Also that San Juan, he was drunk, too.
He started to play his guitar.
He started to sing songs beautifully.
So, he got mad because he was drunk.
He hit me since I was drinking like that, too.
They say he was drinking your liquor, too,
that you had filled your bottle with.
He wasn't . . . he wasn't, they say, strong,
they say it took away his soul,"
said the sacristan.
"When we arrive to drink at the house
we aren't going to drink any more,
so you will keep your eyes open,"
they say he said.
"So be it. That's what it needs.
Now, let's go," it was said,
"since a heavy rain is coming, they say,
halfway down the road," he told us.
Quickly we left,
and about so far,
just so far,
we weren't quite at the house of the sacristan,
about where that hill is,
there came a big wind, heavy rain.
We arrived at the house,
but it was really a big rain,

pero ja'lel chalchaña jach ka yub'ili ja'le,
tyuñi ja'.

Juñ yajlel ch'ejla jach ka tyuñi ja'
tyi 'otyotyi.

Pero 'ik',
juñ yaj tzi laj k'äsätyak tye', pimeltyak.

Che jiñi,
tzi ki melob' k'iñ
ya tyi yotyoty 'ub'i sankristañ.

Ki melob' we'eläl,
tzäñsayob' chityam.

Che tyi 'ak'älel ki japob' lemb'al,
kaläyob' soñ, ñijkañob' b'iolin, witara,
che tza k'älä säk'ayoñ loñ b'ajche jiñi.

Yiktyakob' tza k'älä säk'ayob' b'ajche jiñi.

Yäktyakob' tza k'älä säk'ayob'.

'I tzi laj 'alä 'añ San Miwel
chañ jiñi Sañ Juañ, ke
"Mach la womik
chañ mi laj kom la b'äj tyi la' chol,
much majle la sewuro
ke mi ka la b'ajb'eñ me',
tyoj mi la b'ajb'eñ,
machank mi ka la säl jul,
tyoj mi la jule',"
che kä lojoñ.

'I che jiñi,
'i sujmäch.

Tza laj k'aj lojoñ,
b'ajche mi weñ mi laj chumtyil,
mi tyajoñ laj k'amijel
pejtye laj muty,
pejtye laj chityam,
'i chäch 'i laj 'ak'eñoñ lojoñ b'endisyoñ.

'i tzi yäk'eñtyakob' 'i ch'ujlel 'ixim
'a kerañob', jyumijelob',
che much'tyil, che li, che tyo,
welweltyil 'i wuty 'ixim
b'ajche 'ixim 'ib'ido, mi yälob' säk,
weñ säsäk 'ixim k'otye laj päk'
ya tyi laj chol,
jiñ 'i ch'ujlel me 'ixim 'ilili,

but rain beating down, it seemed,
and hail.

All of a sudden the hail started
at the house.

But wind!
Suddenly it shattered trees, bushes.

So it was,
they started to make a fiesta
there at the house of the sacristan.

They prepared food,
they killed a pig.

At night they started to drink aguardiente,
they made music, played the violin, guitar,
until dawn came it was just like that.

They drank until dawn like that.

They were all drunk when the sun came up.

And all that San Miguel said
through that San Juan, was
"If you don't want
to have your milpas fail,
be very sure
that when you shoot a deer,
hit it straight on,
don't just wound it,
shoot it right,"
he told us.

And so it is,
it's really true.

We asked for everything,
how we could live well,
if we encountered sickness,
all our chickens,
all our pigs,
and so he gave us all a blessing.

And he gave each one the Soul of the Maize,
to my brothers, my uncles,
like a handful, like this,
big grains of maize
like hybrid maize, they say it was white,
really white corn we were going to plant
there in our milpas,
that was the Soul of the Maize,

che kälä lojoñ.
"Jiñ la sujty'um la ñichim,
woli la ch'äm lok'el 'ilali,
majle la pul tyi la chol.
Yojli la chol mi la pule.
Che mi la xujty'um la ñichimi,
mi la ñoktyil
ya tyi yojli la choli.
Cha'leñ la resal chañ weñ 'utz'aty mi lok'el,
b'ajche jiñi,"
che kälä loñ jäjä', che jiñ.
Chäch meleyob' añ kerañob'.
Chäch tzaj mele lojoñ tyi chol lojoñ.
'I che jiñi,
poj chäb'iji tza' tzajñoñ
ya'i 'añ yumijel,
'ixi 'añ jyumijel ya'i.
B'äk' maj tyi chol,
maj tyi puleñ lumi.
Tz'äch 'i b'äk' 'ak'eñtyi 'añ me',
bäk' b'ajb'e juñ kojty koleñ tyaty me',
che k'iñ, majli che li . . .
woli k'otyel yik'o 'i me'.
"'Umb'a'añ laj we'el," che'.
K'otyel koleñ tyaty me'.
Che jiñ,
kaj tz'u lojoñ tyi 'ak'älel,
kaj k'ux lojoñ,
chäch jomokñayoñ lojoñ.
Che tyi 'ak'älel jk'ux lojoñ,
che tyo 'añ me'i.
Che b'ajche chab'i
tza majli 'ak'älelix.
Tza majliyob' yik'o yamb'u jyumijelob',
cha' kojty b'ajb'e me', koleñ me'tyak.
Cha' kojty tzi b'ajb'eyob' yorajlel.
Tzi b'ajb'e tyi cha' p'e 'ak'älel.
Tyi jum p'e 'ak'älel
che tza k'uxu loñ me' b'ajche jiñi.
'I che'äch 'añ jmuty lojoñi, chityam.
Tzäch kaj tyi poj p'ojlel ja'el jcholoñ lojoñ.
Tzäch kaj tyi kolel

he told us.
"Those ends of your candles,
you are going to take them there,
go burn them in your milpas.
In the middle of the milpa, burn them.
When you are burning your candle stubs,
kneel down
there in the middle of your milpa.
Pray that it will turn out well,
like that,"
he told us, uh-huh, like that.
Just so, my brothers did it.
Just so, we did in our milpas.
And so it was,
after about two days we went
there where my uncles are,
I have an uncle there.
He went right to his milpa,
he went to burn the land.
Right away he was given a deer.
right away he shot a big male deer,
the sun was like this, he went like this . . .
he arrived with the deer.
"Here's our food," he said.
He came with a big buck.
So it was,
we started to skin it at night,
we started to eat it,
just all of us together.
So at night we ate it,
since there was still venison.
About two days later
he went out at night.
He went with another of my uncles,
they shot two deer, big does.
Two deer they shot at the same time.
They shot on two nights.
In one night
we ate venison like that.
And thus we had chickens, pigs.
Thus our milpas began to produce as well.
Thus it started to grow

koñ tzäch ki yulmul tyi ja'a,
tyi ja'al, che jiñ.

ACG: Si, pues.

MMJ: Lekoj tza tyili 'i kuch 'añ 'iximi,
pak'akña chixka.
Chächixka b'omb'ontyil 'ixim.
Tza jpoj k'ajatyak lojoñ,
lok'otyak syento b'eynte sonte
juju p'e cholel
tzaj mele lojoñ.

ACG: 'Aja'a.

MMJ: Weñ kolen 'otyoty b'ajche 'ilili,
tza b'ujty'i,
cha' p'ej lajtz 'ixim,
pero puro ty'uñul 'ixim.
Jiñ me ku cha'añ mij ña'tyañ wäle
ke 'i sujmäch b'ajche jiñi mi yälob',
ke 'añäch b'a mi laj k'ajtyiñ ja'al,
koñ tzäch jmero yäxña k'ele ja'el.
Wajali jiñi.
Mi chäñ wox tyo,
chäñ melob' 'añ wäleyi,
b'ajchex.
Koñ wajalix b'a tza mele lojoñ,
wajali.

ACG: Che kuyi.

MMJ: 'I sujmlel.

ACG: 'I wäleyi,
mañix b'a'añ b'a
ma maj la k'ajtyiñ ja'al,
mi la wäl 'iliyi.

MMJ: B'ajchexka. 'Añtza' wäle,
pero ñajtyix, wäle, 'ilali.
Koñ maj ña'tyañ b'a' kälem,

ACG: *Yes, indeed.*

MMJ: *Fiercely came the load of corn,*
It was huge, like that.
Just like this, the ears were thick.
When we went to harvest,
we took out 120 tzontes [120 × 400 ears]
from each milpa
that we made.

ACG: *Aha.*

MMJ: *A really big house like this one,*
we filled it,
two stacks of maize,
but all big ears.
So that's why I think now
that it's true what they say,
that there is a place where we ask for rain,
since I really did see it before, myself.
It was a long time ago.
If it's still like that,
if they still do it now,
who knows?
Since it was a long time ago we did it,
long ago.

ACG: *It really was.*

MMJ: *It's true.*

ACG: *And now,*
isn't there a place
where you go to ask for rain;
do you say so, here?

MMJ: *Who knows? There might be, now,*
but it's a long way, now.
Since I don't know where it was,

since it started to get wet from the rain,
from the rain, like that.

koñ wajalix tzajñoñ lojoñ,
ma chän k'ajalix jcha'añ.

ACG: Mach ku.

MMJ: Mi yälob' ke läk'äl 'ab'i,
'i tyoje ya tyi läk'ä Wenab'ista.
'Añ mi yälob', b'ajchexka.
Yab'i 'i tyoje 'ila tyi Palenke, ja'el.
'Ila tyi che tyi 'añtza' säkjak'añb'ä xajlel,
che li.
Jiñ 'ab'i 'i witzlel jiñi.
Jiñ 'ab'i 'i witzlel Sañ Juañ.

ACG: Jiñ 'ab'i kuyi.

MMJ: Jiñ 'ab'i ku.
Pero mi yälob' ke mach 'ab'i chäñ ya
xchumul 'ab'i Doñ Juañ.
Tza'b'i lok'i ya'i.
Koñ jiñtza' tzi pulb'eyob'
jiñi xk'ayob', x'eb'anjeliko.

ACG: Chuxka 'i k'aba'ob'.

MMJ: Prespiteriano.

ACG: Jiñ 'ab'i.

MMJ: Tzax 'ab'i pulb'e 'i yotyoty.

ACG: Tza ku 'i pulb'eyob' 'i yotyoty
wajali.
Che tziji kajel 'añ tyo jiñi k'ay.

MMJ: 'Aja.

ACG: Jiñ 'ab'i tzi puluyob'.
Che jiñi, jiñ 'ab'i 'i lok'el, 'añ che jiñi.

MMJ: 'Ixku mi sujmäch.
Wäle, koñ mach mij chäñ 'ub'iñ 'i tyilel

since it was a long time ago that we went,
I just don't remember.

ACG: *Not really.*

MMJ: *They tell me that it's close, they say,*
right there close to Buenavista.
So they say, who knows?
They say it's right by Palenque, too.
It's there where there are loose white rocks,
like that.
They say that is his mountain.
They say that is Don Juan's mountain.

ACG: *That's it, all right.*

MMJ: *That's really it, they say.*
But they say that it isn't still there
that Don Juan lives, they say.
They say he left there.
Since they burned that place
those Singers, the Evangelicals.

ACG: *Whatever they're called.*

MMJ: *Presbyterians.*

ACG: *That's them, they say.*

MMJ: *They say they burned his house.*

ACG: *They really did burn his house,*
a long time ago
When the Singers were just starting out.

MMJ: *Aha.*

ACG: *They say they burned it.*
So, they say he left, and so it is.

MMJ: *That's right, it's true.*
Now, since I don't hear anyone go,

ke mi chäñ k'otyelob'.

that anyone just goes there.

ACG: Mach ku wäle.

ACG: *Not anymore.*

MMJ: Che wajali,
che ya tyo 'añoñ tyi Pasoji,
weñ kab'ä maj ki mi k'otyelob'.
K'älä ch'oyolob' tyi Tumb'ala,
k'älä ch'oyol tyi Trinida
mi k'otyelob',
mi ñumelob' wiñikob' ya'i.
Pejtye ya mi majlelob' 'ab'i,
mi k'otyelob' wajali.

MMJ: *So it was a long time ago,*
when I was still in Paso [Naranjo],
a lot of people went there.
Even those who lived in Tumbalá.
Even those who lived in Trinidad
went there,
people passed by going there.
Everybody went there, they say,
they went long ago.

ACG: Che jiñi.

ACG: *So it was.*

MMJ: Pejtye 'ab'i mi k'otyelob',
b'ajche Nuebo Mundo,
b'ajche' läk'ä ch'oyolob' tyi Palenke.
Pejtye ya mi k'otyelob', mi yälob' wajali.
Che kuyi.

MMJ: *Everybody went, they say,*
like Nuevo Mundo,
like even people who lived in Palenque.
Everybody went there, they say, long ago.
It was like that.

ACG: Tzi sub'eñoñ juñ tyikil laj tyaty ñox,
wajali 'añ,
ya tyo 'añoñ tyi San Peru',
tzi sub'eñoñ ke yax 'ab'i
tza k'axi maj tyi Jolja', jiñi 'Ichtye'ja'.

ACG: *An old man told me,*
it was a long time ago,
I was still in San Pedro,
he told me that from there, they say,
he crossed over to Joljá, that Ixtiejá.

MMJ: 'Aja.

MMJ: *Aha.*

ACG: Ya tza maj tyi 'ichtye'ja'i,
wäle, che mi yom tye ja'al,
ya ñaxañ mi tyoj meltyak jiñi chajk,
mi yälob'.

ACG: *There he went to that Ixtiejá,*
now, when he wants rain to come,
there he first makes a lot of lightning,
they say.

MMJ: Jäjä.

MMJ: *Uh-huh.*

ACG: 'I 'añ 'ab'i tzi tyajayob'
jiñi xlukb'älob'
che wo tyo 'i poj k'exe tyo majlel.

ACG: *And there was a time when*
fishermen saw him, they say,
when he was crossing over.

MMJ: Che'i.

MMJ: *So.*

ACG: Tzab'i 'i k'eleyob'.

MMJ: 'Aja.

ACG: Weñ kab'ä wu 'i k'axetyak majlel
jiñ kox chäk muty.

MMJ: 'A weno.

ACG: Yik'oty 'ab'i b'ätye'el,
che tyi 'ak'älel 'ab'i.

MMJ: 'A ja'a.

ACG: Tzolokña k'axe ya tyi kolen ja' 'ab'i,
mi yälob'.

MMJ: 'A weno.

ACG: Kox chäk muty 'ab'i,
ya tza k'axi tyi Troncha Pie, 'a mi yälob'.

MMJ: 'Aja'a.

ACG: 'Ub'i li bätye'eli,
mu b'u 'i xäñ tyi yok.

MMJ: Jäjä'.

ACG: Wä 'ab' tyi tyi'
kayejoñob'Tyemopa',
ya . . . ya 'ab'i tza laj k'axi majlel,
mi loñ 'alob'.
Bajchexka mi 'i sujm ka.

MMJ: 'A weno. 'Ixku mi sujmäch wäle.

ACG: Bajcheäch.

MMJ: Jiñi . . . pero puro wiñikax
mi yochel 'ab'i.
Ya' 'i mach 'ab'i mi yochel x'ixik.

ACG: *They saw him.*

MMJ: *Aha.*

ACG: *A lot of crested guans and great curassows
were crossing over.*

MMJ: *Ah, OK.*

ACG: *With animals, they say,
just at nightfall, they say.*

MMJ: *Aha.*

ACG: *In a line they crossed over the river,
they say.*

MMJ: *Ah, Ok.*

ACG: *Crested guans, they say,
they crossed over at Troncha Pie, so they say.*

MMJ: *Aha.*

ACG: *Those animals, they say,
walked on their feet.*

MMJ: *Uh-huh.*

ACG: *They say they were at the edge of
the little streets of Tiemopá,
there . . . there, they say, they crossed over,
so they say.
Who knows if it's true.*

MMJ: *Ah, OK. It's probably true.*

ACG: *It could be like that.*

MMJ: *It . . . but only men
entered there, they say.
There, they say, no women entered.*

ACG: ¿Mach mi yochel x'ixik?

MMJ: Mi tza 'ochi x'ixik
ya jach tyi pwerta yotyoty,
mi yajlel, mi chämel.

ACG: 'Aha'a.

MMJ: Juñ yaj mi chämel, 'ab'i.

ACG: ¿Chuki mi cha'leñ?

MMJ: Koñ b'äk' 'ora mi ch'oj lukum, 'ab'i.

ACG: ¿Lukum mi ch'oj?

MMJ: Machki b'ajlum mi k'ux 'ab'i.

ACG: 'Aja'a.

MMJ: Jiñ cha'añ puro wiñikach
mi yochelob' 'ab'i ya'i.

ACG: 'Aja'a.

MMJ: Jäjä'. Che mach laj pusik'al
mi laj majlel 'ab'iyi,
much' 'ab'i laj päs'eñtyel,
mi cha' p'e laj pusik'al laj majlel 'ab'iyi,
mu 'ab'i laj päs'entyel lukum,
b'ajlum, 'ab'i.

ACG: 'Aja'a.

MMJ: Ya hach 'a mi ch'ojoñ laj jiñi,
mi tza laj cha' 'alä,
machikax tza loñ tyiliyoñ.
B'äb'äk'echix cho'oñ laj, 'ab'i
ya jach 'a, mi laj kälel 'ab'i.

ACG: 'Aja'a.

ACG: *Women didn't enter?*

MMJ: *If a woman entered
there at the door of the house,
she would fall down, she would die.*

ACG: *Aha.*

MMJ: *All at once she would die, they say.*

ACG: *What do they do?*

MMJ: *Since right away a snake strikes them, they say.*

ACG: *A snake strikes?*

MMJ: *If not, a jaguar eats them, they say.*

ACG: *Aha.*

MMJ: *For that reason, only men
enter there, they say.*

ACG: *Aha.*

MMJ: *If not with our hearts
we go, they say,
we will be taught a lesson,
if with a divided heart we go, they say,
the snake will teach us a lesson,
or a jaguar, they say,*

ACG: *Aha.*

MMJ: *Right there they will bite us,
if we spoke with two tongues,
we shouldn't have come in vain.
If we speak in fear, they say,
right there, we will remain, they say.*

ACG: *Aha.*

MMJ: Che mi yälob' wajali.

ACG: B'ajche'äch mi sujmäch,
koñ 'añ che mi laj kub'iñ,
mi mach mi laj ñop,
pero jiñ tyo, mi laj ñop che wox laj k'el.

MMJ:: Jiñtyo kuyi.

ACG: Wox la kub'iñ.

MMJ: 'I sujmäch wäle,
koñ b'ajche wajali,
che mi kajñeloñ tyi Tila wajaliyi,
koñ tyi kok mij k'älä majleloñ,
k'älä tyi Korosal.
'Añ juñ tyikil x'ixik,
ch'oyol tyi Palenke,
'ixi mach 'a käñäyik.
Chepa, mi yälob'.

ACG: 'Aja'a. Jäjä'.

MMJ: Tza majliyoñ loñ tyi b'ih,
tyi kok tza majliyoñ lojoñ,
'i primera b'esax tza majli jiñ x'ixiki.
'I tzi ki yäl majlel
'ixtyi chañelal Perlaji,
chañ, koñ puro witz 'añ,
che jiñi, xäñ loñ majlel.

ACG: Jiñch kuyi.

MMJ: Ya tza lujb'a.
'I koñ jujp'eñjax ja'el 'añ x'ixiki.

ACG: 'Aja.

MMJ: "'Añ jlujb'oñix.
Mach k'otyoñix.
Matzax tza tyiliyoñ,"

MMJ: *That's what they said, long ago.*

ACG: *It's probably true,*
since that's what we feel,
we might not believe it,
but still, we believe because we are seeing it.

MMJ: *That's right.*

ACG: *We feel it.*

MMJ: *It's really true,*
as it was a long time ago,
when we went to Tila a long time ago,
since on foot we went the whole way,
all the way from Corozal.
There was a woman,
a resident of Palenque–
don't you know her?–
Chepa, they call her.

ACG: *Aha. Uh-huh.*

MMJ: *We went along the road,*
on foot we all went,
and it was the first time that woman went.
And she started to talk as she went
there up above Perla,
high up, it's all mountains,
so it was, we were walking along.

ACG: *Just like that.*

MMJ: *She fell down there.*
And she was really fat, too.

ACG: *Aha.*

MMJ: *"I'm falling down already.*
I won't get there.
I shouldn't have come,"

che tzi cha'le ty'añ,
b'ajche jiñi.

ACG: 'Aja.

MMJ: 'I jum p'e jach 'ora,
tza laj k'uña yoki, 'i k'äb'.
Tz'itya' ma tza yälä chämel
tyi b'ij.

ACG: 'Aja'a.

MMJ: Chañ mach jum p'e 'i pusik'al
tza majli Tila.
Tza loñ tyi tyi Tila.
"Mach 'a wäl b'ajche jiñi.
'Entonse ma ka wilañ
ke mi cha'leñ tyi kastigar Señor," cho'oñ.

ACG: 'Aja'a.

MMJ: "Mak wäle.
Mi käl mach ñajty,
läk'äl tza,"
mi loñ 'alob',
che tzi cha'le ty'añ.
'I tyik'i woj ch'äñ loñ majlel lemb'al.
woj ch'äm maj lemb'al, 'aja,
yik'o 'ixi 'Umbertoji.

ACG: Yik'o Polo.

MMJ: Yik'o Polo, 'ixi Polo.
Polo, yalob'il laj tyaty Bentura.
'I tzaj kaj käk'eñ lojoñ 'añ lemb'al.
Tza ki p'ätyañ 'i yok,
b'ajche jiñi.
Machiki, ya tza käle,
ya tza chämi, wäle.
Tza laj k'uña 'i pejtye 'i yok,
max tza mej tyi xämb'al.
Puro jach [b'uchul] tza majli,
'i sujmäch b'ajche mi yälob' wajali.

so she said,
like that.

ACG: Aha.

MMJ: And just then,
her legs got all weak, her arms.
She almost died
on the road.

ACG: Aha.

MMJ: Because her heart wasn't one
when she went to Tila.
She went in vain to Tila.
"Don't talk like that!
Don't you see
that the Lord will punish you," I said.

ACG: Aha.

MMJ: "Not here.
It's not far,
it's really close,"
they told her,
thus they spoke to her.
And since we brought aguardiente,
we brought liquor, uh-huh,
with that Humberto.

ACG: With Polo.

MMJ: With Polo, that Polo.
Polo, the son of Señor Ventura.
And we started to give her liquor.
Her foot began to get its strength,
like this.
If it hadn't, she would have stayed there,
she would have died there, then.
All of her legs got soft,
she couldn't walk.
Just so [seated] she went,
and it's true what they say, long ago.

ACG: 'I sujmku wäle.

ACG: *It's really true, now.*

MMJ: Jiñ me ku cha'añ ya tzaj ñopo ja'el,
'i sujmäch mi yälob' wajali.

MMJ: *For that reason I believe it, too,*
it's true what they used to say, long ago.

ACG: Che kuyi.
Pero 'añ 'ab'i jiñ laj tyaty, wajali,
mu 'ab'i 'i yajñel tyi Palenke 'ab'i,
mi yälob' jiñ laj tyaty Don Juañ.

ACG: *That's the way it is.*
But there was a gentleman, they say,
they say he used to come down to Palenque,
they called him Our Father Don Juan.

MMJ: 'A me muk'äch wäle.

MMJ: *He really did, then.*

ACG: 'Añ 'ab'i . . . 'añ 'ab'i juñ tyikil kaxlañ
jkäñäb'ä ya tyi Palenke,
weñ 'ab'i yujil 'ab'i lemb'al
laj tyatybäyi.

ACG: *They say . . . they say there was a ladino—*
I knew him there in Palenque—
he really liked to drink aguardiente,
that old man.

MMJ: Jäjä'.

MMJ: *Uh-huh.*

ACG: Max 'ab'i 'i b'ujk.
Max 'ab'i chu' 'añ 'i cha'añ,
wajali.

ACG: *He didn't have a shirt.*
They say he didn't have anything,
a long time ago.

MMJ: Jäjä'.

MMJ: *Uh-huh.*

ACG: Che maxtyo koleñ tyejklumik
jiñi Palenke.

ACG: *Then Palenque wasn't yet*
a big town.

MMJ: Jäjä'.

MMJ: *Uh-huh.*

ACG: Mu 'ab'i k'otyetyak
jiñ laj tyaty Juañ.

ACG: *They say Our Father Don Juan*
used to go there all the time.

MMJ: Jäjä'.

MMJ: *Uh-huh.*

ACG: Mu' 'ab'i 'i ñochtyañtyak
tyi lemb'al 'ab'i.

ACG: *He used to hang around*
the firewater, they say.

MMJ: 'A weno.

MMJ: *Ah, OK.*

ACG: Che 'ab'i, mi yälob',
jiñ tzi sub'eñoñ juñ tyikil laj tyaty ñox,
laj tyaty ya' 'añ tyi Palenke.

ACG: *So, they say,*
an old man told me this,
Our Father was there in Palenque.

MMJ: 'Aja'.

ACG: Mach weñ tza k'otyi wäle,
porke 'i yalob'ilob' mero jontyolob'.

MMJ: 'Aja.

ACG: Tzi tyajayob' 'i mul.

MMJ: 'A, jiñ wokol 'añ, che jiñi.

ACG: 'I jiñ tzi sub'eñoñ
ke mu 'ab'i k'otyetyak,
mu 'ab'i yajñetyak ja'eli
ya tyi yotyoty Doñ Juañ.
Mu 'ab'i yäk'eñtyak 'i majtyañ,
chu mi yäk'eñtyak.

MMJ: 'Aja.

ACG: 'Ab'i . . . tzab'i yäk'e 'i tyak'iñ,
chu'tyak.

MMJ: 'A weno.

ACG: Tzi yäk'e ja'el.

MMJ: Jäjä'.

ACG: Jiñ cha'añ,
much jñop 'i ty'añ ja'el,
koñ 'arapente . . .

MMJ: 'I sujmäch b'ajche mi yälob'.

ACG: 'I sujm ku.

MMJ: Che 'ab'i jiñi.
Ya tyi San Roñ Juañ
'añ mi lok'el burro 'ab'i.

ACG: ¿'Añ?

MMJ: *Aha.*

ACG: *It's not good that he came now,
because his children are really mean.*

MMJ: *Aha.*

ACG: *They found their sin.*

MMJ: *Ah, there is that problem, like that.*

ACG: *And he told me
that he would arrive frequently; they say,
he often would come down also, they say,
there to the house of Don Juan.
They say he would often give him gifts,
whatever he would give him.*

MMJ: *Aha.*

ACG: *They say . . . he gave him money,
whatever.*

MMJ: *Ah, good.*

ACG: *He gave it to him, too.*

MMJ: *Uh-huh.*

ACG: *For that reason,
I believe his story, too,
since from time to time . . .*

MMJ: *It's true what they say.*

ACG: *It's really true.*

MMJ: *They say it's like that.
There where San Don Juan is,
a burro comes out, they say.*

ACG: *It does?*

MMJ: Kuchu 'ab'i 'i cha'añ tyak'iñ.

MMJ: *Loaded with money, they say.*

ACG: 'Aja'a.

ACG: *Aha.*

MMJ: Cha' p'e' kajoñ tyak'iñ kuchul,
pero 'i ch'ajañal puro jiñ 'ab'i nabuyaka,
puro lukum.

MMJ: *Two boxes of money are loaded,*
but the ropes are all bushmasters, they say,
all snakes.

ACG: 'Aja.

ACG: *Aha.*

MMJ: 'A las dose mi lok'el tyi jum paty 'ab'i.

MMJ: *At midnight it comes out at one side, they say.*

ACG: 'Aja.

ACG: *Aha.*

MMJ: "Jijiji," che 'ab'i b'uro 'ab'i
mi lok'el tyi 'oñel.
Che 'ab'i majch mi k'el b'ajche wiñikoñlayi,
mi muy chiñwoñ 'ab'i layi,
mak laj b'äk'ñañ jiñi laso
chuk kächäl 'i cha'añ.
Mu 'ab'i maj laj kitye',
mi tzäch laj kityiyi laj cha'añ 'ab'i tyak'iñ.

MMJ: *"Heeheehee," they say the burro says*
when he comes out to bray.
When, they say, he sees a person like us,
if we are really chingón [tough], they say,
we aren't afraid of the ropes
that are tied on it.
We can go untie them, they say,
if we untie them, the money is ours.

ACG: 'Aja.

ACG: *Aha.*

MMJ: Che tzi laj sub'eñoñ lojoñ
che tzajñoñ lojoñ,
majchixiki mi jity,
che koleñ lukumächix tz'oty kächäl 'i cha'añ.

MMJ: *Thus they told us*
when we went,
if anyone should untie it,
when such big snakes were wrapped up in
knots to tie it.

ACG: Mach mi mejle laj kitye'.

ACG: *It wouldn't be possible to untie it.*

MMJ: Mach mi mejle laj kitye',
che tza sub'etyiyoñ lojoñ.

MMJ: *It wouldn't be possible for us to untie*
it, like we told you.

ACG: ¿Majki 'añ tzi sub'ety laj?

ACG: *Who was it that told you all that?*

MMJ: Jiñch'a 'ub'i sankristañ.

MMJ: *It was that sacristan.*

ACG: 'Aja.

ACG: *Aha.*

MMJ: Mu b'u 'i pejkañ laj tyaty Wa'añ.

MMJ: *The one who petitioned Our Father Juan*

ACG: Jiñ tzi sub'ety laj.

MMJ: Jiñ tzi sub'oñ loñ.

ACG: 'Ixku jiñi laj tyatyi,
¿mak chu' mi k'ajtyi,
mak chu' mi yäk'eñtyel,
'aja?

MMJ: Mañik.

ACG: B'ajche yilal 'añ tyi yotyoty.
¿Weñäch 'añ?

MMJ: Weñ ku. Koleñ 'otyoty yotyoty,
'añ 'ab'i 'i kajpelel.
Lekoj mi choñ 'ixim,
lekoj wo 'i kolel 'i chityam,
p'ulukña 'i chityam pam 'otyoty, tzajñoñ.

ACG: 'Aja.

MMJ: Che 'a kuyi.

ACG: Jiñch mi yäk'en laj tyaty.

MMJ: Jiñ kuyi. Jiñ jach mi 'añ laj tyak'iñi,
mi laj käye' cha' p'e peso,
jo' p'e peso, b'ajche'
chañ mi cha' mäñ ñichim
chañ mi tzuk' ya tyi yotyoty 'ab'i.

ACG: ¿Majki jiñ?

MMJ: Jiñ 'ixi sankristañ.

ACG: 'A, ¿jiñ mi la käk'eñ tyak'iñ?

MMJ: Jiñ 'ab'i kuyi.

ACG: *He told you all.*

MMJ: *He told us.*

ACG: *As for that gentlemen,
was there anything he asked for,
was anything given to him,
huh?*

MMJ: *Nothing.*

ACG: *What did it look like in his house?
Was it good?*

MMJ: *Really so. His house was a big
house, they say there was a coffee grove.
Abundantly he sold maize,
abundantly did his pigs grow,
they were crowded into the patio of his house,
when we went there.*

ACG: *Aha.*

MMJ: *That's the way it was.*

ACG: *That's why he gave to Our Father.*

MMJ: *Just so. Just so, if we had money,
if two pesos were left to us,
five pesos, like that,
we would just buy candles again,
we would just burn them there at his house, they say.*

ACG: *Who is that?*

MMJ: *That sacristan.*

ACG: *Ah, to him you give money?*

MMJ: *Him exactly, they say.*

ACG: 'Añ sakristañ.

MMJ: Jiñ 'ab'i kuyi,
jäjä',
che kuyi.

ACG: *The sacristan.*

MMJ: *Him exactly,*
uh-huh,
just like that.

Our Grandfather Ty'añ Lak Mam

Ausencio Cruz Guzmán

Wajali 'añ mi yälob'	*A long time ago, they say,*
ke jiñ lak mam	*that Our Grandfather*
mu 'ab'i 'i jub'eltyak 'ila tyi lum.	*used to come down here to earth.*
'Añäch 'ab'i 'i ch'ujlel.	*They say he had a soul [took human form].*
Mu 'ab'i 'i jub'eltyak tyi mäk' b'itz'	*He used to come down to eat bitz'.*
che 'i yorajlel b'itz'	*when it was the time for bitz',*
che 'i yorajlel b'uty' ja'lel	*when it was the time for floods.*
Porke jiñ jach	*Because then it is*
'añtyak 'i wuty jiñ b'itz'	*that the bitz' has lots of fruit—*
amb'ä tyi tyi' ja'	*the kind on the banks of the rivers—*
che 'i yorajlel ja'lel,	*when it's the time for rains,*
b'uty' ja'lel.	*flood rains.*
'A mañik,	*Ah, no,*
'añ 'ab'i tzi' tyajb'e 'i yora.	*it was, they say, that the time came.*
'Añob' 'ab'i xlukb'äl.	*There were fishermen, they say,*
'Ux tyikilob' xlukb'äl.	*three fishermen.*
Woliyob' 'ab'i tyi luk ch'akal	*They were fishing for macabil, they say,*
komo jiñ 'i yorajlel luk ch'akäl	*since the time to fish for macabil*
che' woli tyi yajlel 'i b'äk jiñ b'itz'i.	*is when the pods of the bitz' are falling.*
Woli 'i jub'elob' tyi luk ch'akäli.	*They came down to fish for macabil.*
Mañik,	*Ah, no,*
tza ki 'i k'elob'	*then they saw that*
k'ächäkña 'ab'i tyi ñi' b'itz'	*straddled on a limb of bitz', they say,*
jiñ lak mam.	*was Our Grandfather.*
'A mañik,	*Ah, no,*
tza' k'otyiyob'	*they arrived*
ya' b'a k'ächäli.	*there where he was astraddle.*
Tza ki' k'ajtyib'eñ:	*They started to ask him:*
"Chu' wol 'a cha'leñ, mam?"	*"What are you doing, Grandfather?"*
"Mañik.	*"Nothing.*
Woliyoñ tyi mäk' b'itz'," che'eñ.	*I'm eating bitz'," he said.*
'A che jiñi,	*So it was,*
"Kom mi la' koltyañoñ	*"I want you all to help me out*
porke 'añoñ tyi wokol 'ili."	*because I'm in trouble here."*
'A che jiñi.	*So it was.*
"Pero chuk wol 'a cha'leñ, mam?	*"But what are you doing, Grandfather?*
Chuk wol 'a cha'leñ?	*What are you doing?*
Chuk 'añ 'a chañ?" che'eñ.	*What is your problem?" they said.*

'A che jiñi.
"Mañik.
Tzi' chukuyoñ chäñil ja',
chuxka,
mi 'ajiñ,
mi chäñil ja'
wäle, chuxka,
koñ ma tza 'añ tzikil,
koñ b'uty'ul tza ja'.
Tyity, mak laj tyaj laj k'el.
Wäle, mi la' koltyañoñ,
poj koltyañoñlaj jumuk'.
Jiñ jach la' majlel;
la' poj ch'ämb'eñoñ tyilel jpixol, jb'ujk,
ya' tyi kotyoty."
"Weno, koñ,"
che'ob' ja'el 'ili wiñikob',
kom 'utzäch mi k'el,
mi k'elob'.
'A che jiñ.
Tza lok'iyob' ya' tyi tyi' ja',
'i kächäyob' 'i jukub'.
Tza lok'iyob' majlel.
  "Wäle, ma majlel
ya' tyi kotyoty,
ya' poj 'añ kotyoty 'ixixi.
Jumuk' jach ma majlel."
'Añ tza loñ majli 'añ juñtyikili.
Tza' käleyob' 'añ yamb'ä cha' tyikilob'
ya' tyi tyi' ja',
tyi jukub'.
'Añ tza majli 'ab'i 'añ juñtyikili;
tza' k'otyi
ya' tyi yotyoty.
"Pero mak majch 'añ," che'eñ.
Tza' cha' sujtyi tyilel.
"Chukoch mach majch 'añ,
si ya' 'añ
tza' k'otyiyety,
b'a tza' k'otyiyety
tyi kaj wa'tyili.
Jiñ kijñam,

So it was.
"Nothing.
A water animal grabbed me,
whatever,
maybe an crocodile,
maybe a water animal,
now, whatever,
since it can't be seen,
because the river is in flood.
It's turbid, I can't manage to see it.
Now, you all help me out,
please help me out a little.
You all just go;
please go bring me my hat and my shirt,
there from my house."
"OK, let's go,"
the men said, too,
since they saw that he was good,
they saw it.
So it was.
They went to the edge of the water;
they tied up their canoe.
They arrived there.
"Now, you all go
there to my house.
there should be a woman there at my house.
Just for a minute, you all go there."
One man went, but in vain.
The other two men stayed
there at the edge of the water,
in the canoe.
So that one man went, they say,
he arrived
there at his house.
"But there isn't anyone here," he said.
He returned.
"Why is there no one there,
if it's there
that you went;
when you arrived
she was standing there.
My wife,

jiñ kaj wa'al tyi tyi' 'otyoty.

she was standing at the door of the house.

Chañ jach mach ma käñ," che'eñ.

You just didn't recognize her," he said.

"Cha' kuku," che' tzi sub'e.

"Go again," he told him.

'A che jiñ,

So it was,

tza' cha' majli 'ub'i 'ili wiñiki.

the man went a second time.

Tza' k'otyi 'i k'el ya'

He arrived and saw there

tyi tyi' ch'eñ,

at the entrance to a cave,

tyi tyokolb'ä lum;

at a crack in the earth;

k'otyi 'i tyaj

he arrived to find

weñ koleñ ña' pokok,

a big female toad,

koleñ x'oñkoñak,

a big toad,

chuxka.

whatever.

Jiñ yijñam lak mam 'añ jiñi.

That was the wife of Our Grandfather.

Che jiñ,

So it was,

tza' ki sub'e:

he said to her:

"Wälc, mu 'ab'i 'a wäk'eñoñ majlel

"Now, they say you are to give me

jiñ 'i pixol,

that hat of his,

yik'oty 'i b'ujk jiñ kmam

and the shirt of Our Grandfather,

porke 'añ 'ab'i tyi wokol."

because they say he is in trouble."

"Chuk woli 'i cha'leñ?"

"What is he doing?"

"Chuxka!

"Whatever!

Tyik'äl mi chukul

Perhaps he is caught

tyi 'ajiñ,

by a crocodile,

tyi chäñil ja',

by a water animal,

chuxka.

whatever.

Jiñ tzi chokoyoñ tyilel.

He sent me to come here.

Ya' k'ächäl tyi 'i k'äb' b'itz'.

There he is straddled on a branch of bitz'.

Woli 'i mäk' b'itz'.

He is eating bitz'.

'A mañik,

Ah, no,

koñ 'ochem 'i yok

since his foot had gone in

ya' tyi mal ja',

there into the water,

ya' tzi' chuku."

there it caught him."

"Weno," che jach 'i yijñami.

"OK," said his wife.

Tzi' yäk'e majlel.

He took it.

Tza majli.

He left.

Che jiñ,

So it was,

tza' k'otyi ya' b'a lak mami.

he arrived there where Our Grandfather was.

Tza' ki yäk'eñ 'i pixol.

He gave him his hat.

Pero ñaxañ che' tza majli, tza' ki sub'eñ:

But before he went, Grandfather told him:

"Che ma kaj 'a ch'äm tyilel jiñ jpixoli,

"When you bring that hat of mine,

yik'oty jb'ujki,

and that shirt of mine,

ma meku kajk 'a käläx ñijkañ!

don't let it shake at all!

Ma me tzi' tz'ijiyety;
ma me 'i tzäñsañety."
Loñ che jiñi;
che jach woli 'i ña'tyañ majlel ja'el wiñiki,
porke koñ meleäch 'añ mi yäl,
koñ lak mam tza'.
'A che jiñi,
tza' k'otyi yik'oty 'i pixol,
yik'oty 'i b'ujk.
Tza' ki' sub'eñ:
"'Uxeku b'a 'añ, kmam."
"Yoñku," che'eñ.
Tza' ki' läp 'i b'ujk.
Tza' ki' läp 'i pixol.
Tzi' k'äkä 'i pixol.
Che jiñ,
tza' ki' sub'eñ:
"Wäle, kukula ya' tyi pañlum.
Kächäxla jiñ la jukub'.
Lok'eñla' tyi mal ja'.
Ya mi la maj tyi pañlum.
Ya mi la wotzañ la jol
b'a' tyokoltyak jiñ lum."
'A mañik,
tzäch 'i jak'äyob' 'añ cha' tyikili.
Jiñ 'añ juñ tyikil,
woli k'el chu' mi ki' meltyak
 jiñ lak mam.
Mak wol 'i ña'tyañ,
mi mi ki' xä'tyaj ja'el'
'i xu'il chajki.
Che jale 'ora,
k'iñlaw 'ab'i,
ñup'law 'ab'i,
tza' tyojmi jiñ chajki,
b'a' tzi' ñijka 'i b'ä jiñ lak mami.
Tza jach 'i ñijka 'i b'ä,
tza' tyojmi jiñ chajki.
Tza' tyiki jiñ ja'.
Tza säjp'i jiñ ja',
ma che' ku 'añix ja'.
K'iñlaw,

Don't let it strike you;
don't let it kill you."
In vain it was;
thus the man was thinking as well,
since what he said was possible,
since he really was Our Grandfather.
So it was,
he arrived with his hat,
with his shirt.
He told him:
"Here it is, My Grandfather."
"OK," he said.
He put on his shirt.
He put on his hat.
He lifted up his hat.
So it was,
he said to them:
"Now, go there to the riverbank.
Tie up your canoe.
Get out of the water.
Go over there to the land.
There put your heads in
where the earth is all cracked."
Ah, no,
just two of the men obeyed.
One of the men
was watching what Our Grandfather
was doing.
He didn't know
that Chajk's lightning bolt
could hit him, too.
And then it happened,
flashing, they say,
crashing, they say,
Lightning exploded,
when Our Grandfather shook himself.
He just shook himself,
and lightning exploded.
The water dried up.
The water went down,
there wasn't any water anymore.
Flashing,

ñup'law 'ab'i 'añ.

'Añ 'i chäñil ja',

tza' chämi.

'Añ che jiñ,

tza' ki' sub'eñob' 'añ 'ub'i lak mam.

"La'ix kulaj," che'ab'i tzi' sub'eñob'

yamb'ä cha'tyikil wiñik.

'Añ koñ juñtyikil

tzäch 'ab'i xä'tyaj ja'el 'ili chajki,

tza' 'ab'i jum pajk chämi.

Che jiñ,

tza ki' sub'eñ,

"Lotyoxla jiñ la' chäy.

B'uty'ux la' jukub',

chañ max tyo metza 'añik ja'.

Ch'ämä,

mero tyikiñ tyo me ja'.

Machiki,

jal tyo mi ki' tyilel jiñ ja'.

Lotyolaj!

Tyi 'ora jach mi la loty,

chañ 'ame 'i p'äyetyla majlel b'uty' ja'."

"Yoñku," che' ja'el wiñiki.

Tza' ki' b'uty'ob' 'i chäy.

Tza'ki' yotzañob' tyi jukub'.

Che tza'ix 'ujtyi 'i lotyob' jiñ chäyi,

tza' ki' k'elob' mak tzikil juñtyikil pi'äl.

Tza'ki' k'ajtyib'e 'añ lak mami:

"Ixku juñtyikil jpi'äl?

B'aki tza' käle," che'eñ.

"B'ä 'i b'ä.

Majki mi jsub'eñ ke mi' k'eloñ,

chu' ka kmel.

Tza ksub'e,

b'ajche tza ksub'etyla ja'el.

'I kom mak tzi' jak'ä,

yomäch 'i k'el chu' mi kaj kmel,

 tzi' yila.

Pero mak woli 'i ña'tyañ

mi mi kaj kxä'tyaj.

Tzäch ktyaja ktz'ij ja'el.

Machikix; la'tyo 'ajñik,

crashing, they say, it was.

The water animal

died.

So it was,

Our Grandfather told them.

"You all come over here," they say he said

to the other two men.

Since one of them

had been hit by lightning, they say.

he was half dead, they say.

So it was,

he told them,

"Gather up your fish.

Fill your canoe,

because there isn't any water yet.

Grab them,

the river is still dry.

If you don't,

the water is coming back

Gather them up!

Gather them up right now,

so that the flood doesn't carry you off."

"OK," the men agreed.

They started to fill their canoe with fish.

They started to put them into the canoe.

When they had finished gathering up the fish,

they saw that their companion wasn't in sight.

They asked Our Grandfather:

"What about our companion?

Where did he end up?" they said.

"It's his own fault.

Who did I tell to watch me,

whatever I did.

I told him,

like I told you all as well.

And since he didn't obey,

he just wanted to see what I was doing,

he watched

But he didn't know

that I was going to throw lightning.

It hit him as well.

Never mind; you all go on,

mu tyo ki' k'uñ tyejchel.
Señoñla,
lotyo la' chäy.
Tyalix me tzal ja'."
"Yoñku," che'eñ.
'Ujtyi 'i lotyob' 'añ chäyi.
Tza' ki' k'elob'
wolix 'i tyejchel yamb'ä wiñik,
k'uñ tyejchi majlel.
'Añ che jiñ,
tza'ix k'otyi b'uty' ja'.
Tza'ix meku majliyob' tyi jub'el;
k'otyiyob' tyi yotyoty.
Tza' ki' sub'eñob' pejtyel xpampañ chumtyil,
b'ajche' tza' 'ujtyityak.
'Añ mach mi ñopob',
ma tza' 'añ b'a mi laj k'el ja'el
mi jub'eltyak tyi mäk' b'itz' jiñ chajk.
'I jiñ cha'añ,
woläch 'i yixña mero ñopob' tz'itya',
porke komo tzäch 'i ñopoyob' ja'el,
koñ kab'älob' 'i chäy
tza' k'otyiyob'.
'Añ che jiñi,
che jach tza' 'ujtyi b'ajche jiñi.

he will recover after a while.
Hurry,
gather your fish.
The water is coming back already.
"OK," they said.
They finished gathering the fish.
They saw
that the other man was getting up.
he was slowly getting up.
So it was,
the flood came already.
They all went downstream;
they arrived at their house.
They told everybody in the village
how everything happened.
Ah, but they didn't believe them,
since at no time had we ever seen
Chajk coming down to eat bitz'.
And for this reason,
they really had to believe some of it,
since they had to believe it, too,
because it was a lot of fish
they came home with.
So it was,
thus it ended like that.

OUR HOLY MOTHER TY'AÑ LAK CH'UJUL ÑA'

Ausencio Cruz Guzmán

Wajali 'ab'i,	*A long time ago, they say,*
mi yälob' laj tyatyña'älob';	*our ancestors used to say—*
mi yälob', mi kub'iñ,	*they speak, I listen—*
jtyaty, jña', tzi sub'eñoñ,	*my father, my mother, told me,*
wajali.	*long ago.*
Jiñ Laj Ch'ujul Ña',	*Our Holy Mother,*
mi sub'eñoñ,	*they tell us,*
wäle, 'uj b'u,	*now, she is the moon,*
mi sub'eñob'.	*they tell us.*
Jiñi wajali	*In that age long ago*
max tyo 'ab'i 'añik majch' añ 'ila tyi pañämil;	*there still wasn't anything here on earth;*
max tyo 'ab'i 'añik 'i b'äl pañämil;	*there still weren't any things of the earth;*
max tyo 'añik muty;	*there still weren't any birds;*
max tyo 'añik chu'añ;	*there still wasn't anything;*
b'ä tye'eltyak max tyo 'añik.	*wild animals there still were none.*
Jiñ jach 'ab'i Laj Ch'ujul Ña'	*Just Our Holy Mother, they say,*
wol 'ab'i 'añ tyi lum.	*was here on earth, they say.*
'Añ 'ab'i	*It happened, they say,*
tza 'ajñi cha' tyikil 'i yalob'il.	*there came to be two children of hers.*
Juñ tyikil,	*One of them*
weñ joñtyoljax;	*was really bad;*
yamb'ä,	*the other one*
mero weñ 'i pusik'al.	*had a really good heart.*
'Añ che jiñi,	*So it was,*
mu 'ab'i 'i meltyak chol	*he would go out to make milpas, they say,*
ñaxañ b'u yalob'il;	*the one who was the first child;*
mi meltyak 'ab'i 'i chob'altyak.	*he made many clearings, they say.*
Pero max tyo 'ab'i chek wokol	*But it still wasn't such a problem, they say,*
mi lak mel lak chob'al,	*as when we make our clearings,*
b'ajche 'ilili wäleyi.	*like here and now.*
Max tyo mi laj k'äñ machity;	*The machete was still unknown;*
max tyo 'añik	*there wasn't any*
chu' mi laj k'äñ tyi sek',	*thing to use to cut down trees,*
chu'tyak.	*or whatever.*
Jiñ jach mi käch 'i yab'	*So he would just hang his hammock*
ya' tyi tye'eli;	*there in the forest;*
mi kaj tyi jäjmel.	*he would start to swing.*
Che' woli 'i jäjmesañ 'i b'äj,	*When he was swinging himself,*

woli 'ab'i yajleltyak majlel jiñ tye'.
'A ko mañik,
'añ 'ab'i 'ixi lekoj b'u 'ajtzo',
mi sub'eñob';
'ixi pavo real.
Jiñ 'ab'i mi yajñeltyak tyi 'uk'el,
tyi 'uk'el tyi 'ak'älel.
'A koñ kab'älix
chu' woli 'i mel jiñ wiñik,
mi k'el jiñ Laj Ch'ujul Tyaty.
'I komo mañik 'i wokol
b'ajche' mi yäsañtyak jiñ tye'el,
'i wolix 'i jisañtyak jiñ tye'el.
Che jiñi,
tzi k'ele
jiñ Lak Ch'ujul Tyaty,
jiñ lak Dios:
Mach 'ab'i weñik
b'ajche woli 'i mel,
mi loñ k'el.
Tzi choko tyilel jiñ lekoj b'u muty.
Mu 'ab'i 'i tyilel
che' tyi yolil 'ak'älel.
Mi kaj tyi 'uk'el;
mi kaj tyi ty'añ;
mi sub'eñtyak tyejchel jiñ tye'el.
Che jiñi,
mi tyejcheltyak.
Mi k'otyel
che' mi säk'añ jiñ wiñik.
Mi cha' k'oty 'i k'el 'i chob'al;
laj cha' tyejchemix jiñi choleltyak;
mi laj cha' tyejchel jiñ tye'el.
Mach chäñ cholob'ilix, yilal.
Mi loñ cha' mel
b'ajche' mi meltyak;
mi jäjmesañ 'i b'äj tyi yab',
pero mañix mi chäñ yajleltyak.
'I che jiñi,
pero jiñi ñaxañ b'ä 'i yalob'il Laj Ch'ujul Ña'
mach mi ña'tyañ
mi 'añ yamb'ä

they say the trees would come falling down.
Ah, but no,
there was, they say, that exotic turkey
they tell about;
that peacock.
He would come down to cry out, they say,
to cry out in the night.
Ah, since so much
that that man was doing
Our Holy Father saw.
And since it wasn't difficult for him
the way he made the trees fall,
and the forest was being destroyed.
So it was,
he saw
Our Holy Father,
our God:
It wasn't good
how he was doing it,
he saw it was wrong.
He sent down the exotic bird.
He would come down, they say,
when it was midnight.
He would start to cry out;
he would start to speak;
he would tell all the trees to stand up.
So it was,
they would all stand up.
The man would arrive
when it was dawn.
He would come and see his clearing;
all of the brush was standing up again;
all of the trees were standing up again.
There was no clearing anymore, it seemed.
He would do it again
the way he did it;
he would swing himself in his hammock,
but nothing at all would fall down.
And so it was,
but that first child of Our Holy Mother
didn't know
that there was another,

'i yijtz'iñ.

Mi yäl ke jiñ jach
'añ tyi pañumil.
Porke jiñ Laj Ch'ujul Ña'
mak mi yäk'eñ 'i k'el.
Porke koñ joñtyoljax jiñi yalob'il,
repente mi mi tzäñsañ.
Jiñ cha'añ, mi muktyak
chañ mach mi k'el,
porke koñ k'ajk'atyax,
'i repente 'añ chu' mi tyumb'eñ.
Mi yälob' ke che' ya 'añ
'añ yäskuñ,
mukb'il, 'ab'i.
Jiñ jach,
che' mi majlel tyi xämb'al
'o tyi 'e'tyel,
mu 'ab'i 'i lok'sañ tyi 'alas yik'oty.
Che' weñ wäyäl 'añ yäskuñ,
mi we'sañ, o mi chu'sañ.
Pero woli 'i b'ejb'e kolel.
Pero 'añtyak mi lok'el tyi 'alas,
'i mu tyo 'i mejlel
'i mukb'eñtyak 'i yälas.
Pero 'añ juñ yajl
max tzi laj lotyo,
'i tzi käyä tyi juñ paty
mu b'u 'i yäsiñ 'añ 'alob'.
Pero jiñi 'i yäskuñ
tzax kaji 'i ña'tyañ
ke repente 'añäch yamb'ä 'alob',
'o yamb'ä 'i yijtz'iñ,
'i mach mi sub' 'i ña'.
Pero 'añ ch'ityoñ
tzax kaji 'i ña'tyañ
b'ajche mi kaj 'i mel.
Lix tyo b'ej 'ajñik.
Pero juñ yajl tza seb' sujtyi,
'i tza k'otyi tyaj 'añ 'alob'
ke woli tyi 'alas.
Pero 'i ña', tyoj b'äk'ñijel;
max tzi tyaja chuki mi yäl

his younger brother.
They say that that one
was on earth.
Because Our Holy Mother
didn't let him see.
Because since the older brother was so bad,
he might just kill him.
For that reason, she hid him
so that he didn't see him,
because he was so hot-blooded,
and he just might do something to him.
They say that since there he was,
the older brother,
he was hidden, they say.
That one,
when he would go out walking
or to work,
she would take him out to play with her.
When the older brother was well asleep
she would feed him, or nurse him.
But he got bigger and bigger.
But many times he would come out to play
and it was still possible
for her to hide away all of his toys.
But there was one time
she didn't gather them all up,
and they were left there at one side
where the child would play.
But that older brother
began to realize
that all of a sudden there was another child,
or another younger brother,
and his mother wasn't telling him.
But the young man
started to think
how he would act.
He let some time go by.
But one day he suddenly turned around,
and he came home to find the boy
who was playing with his toys.
But his mother was really frightened;
she couldn't find words to say

tyi 'i b'äk'eñ.
'Ix ku yerañ
weñ 'utz tzi päsä 'i b'äj.
Pero chañ k'uñtye' mi ña'tyañ
b'ajche mi kaj 'i tzäñsañ 'añ yijtz'iñ.
Koñ tz'a'atyax mi k'el,
koñ 'añ 'ab'i 'i ch'ujlel.
Koñ jiñ 'ab'i laj k'iñ, 'ab'i,
mi yajñel.
Mi kaj 'i yajmel tyi pañämil,
tzi yälä.
Jiñ cha'añ,
mero tz'a mi k'el.
Mach yomik 'i k'el
'ila tyi pañämil;
'i b'ajñel jach yom 'ajñel.
'A mañik,
'i ña',
k'uxäch mi yub'iñ.
'Añ che jiñi,
'añ yijtz'iñ ñukix.
'Añ mi lok'el tyi 'alas
tyi mal tye'el yik'oty yulej.
'I 'añ tzi tyaja juñ tyejk tye'
b'a 'añ chab'.
'I tza k'otyi 'i sub'eñ 'añ yäskuñ:
"Wäle käskuñ,
koñla sek' chab';
ya 'añix tyi tye';
Koñla mäk',"
che'eñ.
"Koñla,"
che'eñ 'añ yäskuñ ja'el.
Che jiñi,
tza majliyob' tyi mäk' chab'
ya' tyi b'ij.
'Añ juñ p'ejl b'ij
b'a' 'añ juñ tyejk tye';
ya' tza majliyob' tyi mäk' chab'.
Che jiñi,
tza loñ majliyob' tyi mäk' chab'.
Tza loñ letzi 'ub'i 'askuñil b'ä.

she was so afraid.
As for the brother
he made himself be good.
But little by little he thought about
how he would kill his younger brother.
Since he looked on him with hatred,
since he had a soul, they say.
Since he, they say, was our sun, they say,
who would come down.
He would come down to earth,
they said.
For that reason,
with hatred he looked on him.
He didn't want to see him
here on earth;
and he wanted to be the only one.
Ah, no, but
his mother
she felt love for him.
So it was,
the younger brother grew up.
He would go out to play
in the forest with his slingshot.
And it happened that he found a tree
where there was honey.
And he went and told his older brother:
"Now, my brother,
let's go cut out honey;
it's there in the tree.
Let's go eat,"
he said.
"Let's go,"
said the older brother, too.
So it was,
they went to eat honey
there on the road.
There was a road
where there was a tree;
they went there to eat honey.
So it was,
they just went to eat honey.
The older brother just climbed up.

Tza letzi tyi tye',	He climbed up in the tree,
ya' woli 'i lom 'añ chab', 'ab'i.	there he chopped at the beehive, they say.
Tza kaj 'i mäk'.	He started to eat.
'Añ yijtz'iñi,	The younger brother
tza ki k'ajtyib'eñ.	started to ask him for some.
'A mañik,	Ah, no,
jiñ 'i yäskuñi,	that older brother
mach mi loñ 'ak'eñ ja'el chab'i.	just wouldn't give him any honey.
Jiñ jach 'i tya'chäb'lel,	Just the beeswax
mi loñ chokb'eñ jub'el.	he just threw it down at him.
K'oslaw,	Bam!
mi jub'el ya' tyi jol.	it came down on his head.
'A che jiñi,	So it was,
we'ekña tyi 'uk'el ja'el 'alob'i,	the child was crying and shouting,
ko mach woli 'i yäk'eñ 'i mäk'.	because he wouldn't give him anything to eat.
Jiñ jach 'i tya'chäb'lel	Only the beeswax
woli 'i yäk'eñ.	was he giving him.
'A tza ki mel 'ub'i ch'ityoñ,	So the boy began to make things,
tza ki mel 'i yaläl b'aj	he started to make little gophers
tyi tya'chäb'lel.	out of the wax.
Tza ki pajliñ b'äk ch'ib';	He carved some hard palm wood;
tzi tzäp'b'eñtyak cha' tzijty tyi cha'añ,	he inserted into them two teeth above,
'i cha' tzijty tyi yeb'al tyi yej 'añ b'aji.	and two below, in the mouths of the gophers.
Tza' ki yotzañtyak tyi lum.	He started to put them into the ground.
Che jiñi,	So it was,
tza kaji loñ paxoñ sek'jiñ tye';	he just started to pretend to chop on the tree;
tzi loñ mele jiñ 'alob'.	that's all the boy did.
Mañik,	No,
tza kaj tyi ty'añ 'i yäskuñ:	his older brother started to say:
"Ma me ku kajik 'a sek'oñ,	"Don't you go cutting me down,
porke k'ele me ku 'a b'ä	because you'll see what happens,
mi tza' yajliyoñ;"	if I fall,"
che' mi loñ sub'eñ 'i yäskuñ.	that's all the older brother told him.
'A mañik,	Ah, no,
"Kom b'ajche' mi kaj sek'ety,	"But how am I going to cut you down,
kom ma tza 'añ b'ajche' ya' k'amel	since it really isn't very big
'iliya Lukum Ch'ejl,"	this Angry Snake,"
che' mi sub'eñ.	so he told him.
'I Lukum Ch'ejl,	His Angry Snake
'i yaläl machity;	was his little machete,
mak ñoj 'añix 'i yej.	it wasn't very sharp.
Jiñ' 'ab'i woli 'i k'äñ tyi sek'.	This is what he was using to chop with.

'A mi loñ 'al:
"Pero max mi low ja' tye'."
'A mañik,
koñ jiñ 'añ b'aj,
koñ kab'älix 'añ b'aj,
tzi loñ 'otza tyi yeb'al tye',
tyi wi'tye'tyak.
'A che jiñi,
tza kaji 'i yotzañtyak wäle 'añ b'aji.
Tza kaji tyi we'el ja'el b'aji,
ki sety'b'eñ 'i wi ' 'añ tye'i.
'A mañik,
ya'ix 'añ
cha' p'ejl, 'ux p'ejl 'ora;
wäle 'añ
woli tyi 'e'tyel 'añ b'aji.
Tza ki yub'iñ 'i yäskuñi
ke tza ty'iño juñ yajl jiñi tye'
Che jiñi,
tzi yälä:
"Ma ma sek'oñ!"
Jiñ jax tza yub'i
ke wolix 'i jub'el majlel ya' tyi tye'i,
k'iñlaw, ñup'law, jub'el.
Ya' tyi ñi' tye',
ya b'a' woli tyi mäk' chab',
tza yajli.
'Añ che tza yajli,
tzax meku sujtyi majlel
'añ ch'ityoñ, 'alob'.
Tza k'otyi
b'a 'añ Lak Ña',
b'a 'añ Lak Ch'ujul Ña';
Lak Ña' b'ä
mi lak sub'eñ 'ili 'uji.
Tza k'otyi;
tza' ki k'ajtyib'eñ 'i ña':
"B'aki tza' majli 'a wäskuñ?"
loñ che' tzi sub'e.
'A mañik,
tza ki jak' 'añ ch'ityoñ,
"Majki? Käskuñi?

So he just said:
"But it doesn't hurt the tree."
Ah, no,
since those gophers,
since there were already a lot of them,
he just put them under the tree,
in all the roots.
So it was,
he started to put all the gophers there.
The gophers started to chew,
to cut away the roots of the tree.
Ah, no,
there they were
two, three hours,
there they were
working away, those gophers.
The older brother started to sense
that the tree cracked all at once.
So it was,
he said:
"Don't cut me down!"
He just felt
that he was falling out of the tree,
crashing, smashing, falling.
There from the tip of the tree,
there where he was eating honey,
he fell.
And when he fell,
running back home went
the boy, the child.
He arrived
where Our Mother was,
where Our Holy Mother was,
the one who was Our Mother,
that we say is the moon.
He arrived;
his mother began to ask him:
"Where did your older brother go?"
she just asked him.
Ah, no,
the boy began to answer,
"Who? My older brother?

Sajmäx tza' tyili.	He came in earlier.
Ñaxañ tyo tza tyili.	He came in first.
Ya' tzi käyäyoñ tyi tye'el	He left me there in the woods,
max tzi sub'u 'i b'ä	he didn't say he himself
tza tyili."	was coming."
'Añ che jiñi,	So it was,
"Ma'añik,	"No,
jatyety tza' tzäñsa.	you killed him!
'Añ chuki tza tyumb'e,"	You did something to him."
che' tzi sub'e 'i ña'.	his mother told him.
'A mañik,	Ah, no.
"Mañik,	"No,
si ñaxañ tyo tza tyili.	because he came in first.
Wi'patyoñix	Way behind
tza tyiliyoñ 'añ joñoñ."	came I."
'Añ che jiñi,	So it was,
tza majli 'i sajkañ 'i ña'.	his mother went out to look for him.
Tza ki sub'eñ 'ub'i Laj Ña', uji,	Our Mother, the moon, started to speak,
tzi sub'e:	she told him:
"Wäle, koñla k'el	"Now, let's go see
b'aki tza' käyä;	where he remained;
b'aki 'añ tza' käyä	where is it he remained,
jiñ 'a wäskuñi,"	that older brother of yours,"
che mi loñ sub'eñ.	she just said to him.
'A che jiñ,	So it was,
tza majli 'i k'elob'.	they went out to look.
Tza ki k'el 'ub'i Lak Ña',	Our Mother started to look,
Laj Chuchu'i.	That Grandmother of ours.
Ya' 'añ b'a tzi yäsañtyak	There he was where he was felled
tyi ñi' tye';	from the tip of the tree;
ya' 'añ b'a tzi yäsa.	there he was where he fell.
'I che tza yajli	And when he fell
tza laj b'ik'tyiyi.	he broke up into little pieces.
'I jiñx, b'aki tza lok'i jiñ muty,	And it was from there that the birds came out,
b'ä tye'el,	the animals,
tyi kuktyal 'i yäskuñ.	from the body of his older brother.
Pero 'i ña, mak woli 'i ña'tyañ	But his mother, she didn't know
mi chämeñix 'i yalob'il.	if her child was dead already.
Jiñ tyo tzi sub'e yamb'ä 'i yalob'il	Not until her other child told her
che tza k'otyiyob' tyi 'otyoty.	when they arrived at the house.
Pero tyi ñaxañ,	But first,
tzi jak'ä 'alob':	the boy told her:

"Wäle, mama',
'ixma 'añix 'a wixim,
chañ ma mäk'lañ 'a wälak'.
Kab'älix 'añ 'a wälak';
kab'älix 'a muty;
kab'älix 'a chityam.
K'ele chu' ma ch'äm.
Pero mach me ku kajik 'a chuk
ya' tyi ñej,
porke mach me weñik
mu mi b'ojkel 'i ñej."
'A mak tzi jak'ä ja' Laj Ch'ujul Ña'
che' tza cha' sujtyi 'i mäk'lañ.
Tza kaji loñ chuktyak 'añ xkulukab'
ya' tyi ñej.
Chityam, me', tye'lal;
yik'oty pejtyel jiñtyak b'u
mach b'ä 'añik 'i ñej,
puro 'ab'i tzi chuku jiñ Laj Ña'.
Por eso,
jiñtyak b'ä tye'el,
mach b'ä 'añik 'i ñej,
b'oroltyak 'i ñej,
porke koñ jiñ 'añ Laj Ch'ujul Ña',
tzi laj chuku ya' tyi ñej,
tzi laj b'okb'e 'i ñej.
'Añ che jiñi,
tza ki k'ajtyiñ
che' tza k'otyiyob' tyi 'otyoty:
"Peru 'a wäskuñ,
b'aki tza käle?
chuki tza tyumb'e?"
che'eñ 'añ Lak Ña'.
"Käskuñi?
B'i jiñ tza
woli b'u 'a mäk'lañ."
"Chuki tza tyumb'e?"
che'eñ.
"B'ä 'i b'äji;
mak tzi yäk'oñ jmäk' chab'.
Jiñ cha'añ,
tzak meletyak ya 'alä b'ajtyak

"Now, Mama,
shuck your corn,
so you can feed your animals.
You have a lot of animals now;
a lot of birds,
a lot of pigs.
Watch what you grab.
But don't start catching them
there by their tails,
because it's not good
if you pull out their tails."
Ah, Our Holy Mother didn't pay attention
when she went back to feed them.
She just grabbed all the tinamou
there by the tail.
Pigs, deer, pacas;
and all those that
don't have a tail,
it's because Mother grabbed them, they say.
For this reason,
any animal
that doesn't have a tail,
that has a stub for a tail,
it's because Our Holy Mother
grabbed them all there by the tail,
she pulled out all their tails.
So it was,
she started to ask him
when they arrived at the house:
"But your older brother,
where did he stay?
What did you do to him?"
said Our Mother.
"My older brother?
That was him
that you went to feed."
"What did you do to him?"
she said.
"It's his own fault;
he didn't give me honey to eat.
For that reason,
I made a bunch of little gophers

tyi tya'chäb'lel	*out of beeswax*
tza b'ä 'i mäk'b'e 'i chäb'il.	*that he ate the honey from.*
Jiñ b'aj	*Those gophers*
tzi sety'b'e 'i wi' 'añ tye'.	*chewed away the roots of the tree.*
Jiñ cha'añ	*For that reason,*
tza yajli,	*he fell,*
'i che' tza chämi.	*and thus he died.*
'I tyi kuktyal,	*And from his body*
tza lok'ityak jiñ 'a b'ätye'eltyak,	*came all your animals*
yik'oty 'a muty."	*and your birds."*
'A che jiñi,	*So it was,*
wajali 'añ tyo 'ab'i	*it was still a long time ago, they say,*
mi melob' 'i chol.	*they made their milpa.*
'Añ tyo 'ab'i	*Still, they say*
mi pulob' 'ab'i 'i pulem lum.	*they burned their fields for planting.*
Mu 'ab'i sub' 'i ña':	*They say he told his mother:*
"Wäle, mama,	*"Now, Mama,*
ma maj tyi päk',	*you are going to plant,*
päk' ñi'uk'	*plant smooth chayote,*
päk' ch'ixch'ujm,	*plant spiny chayote,*
chu' ma' päk'.	*whatever you plant.*
Jiñ jach ma sajkañ	*Just look for*
b'a weñ pulemtyak;	*where it is well burned;*
ya' ma päk'	*there you plant*
chu' ma' päk',"	*whatever you plant,"*
che' mi sub'eñ.	*so he told her.*
"'A koy,"	*"OK,"*
che jach 'i ña'.	*so said his mother.*
Tza loñ majli.	*They just went.*
Loñ päk'	*They just planted*
chu mi päk'.	*whatever they planted.*
'Añ jiñi 'ab'i ñi'uk'i;	*They say that that smooth chayote,*
jiñ 'ab'i b'a mi koleltyak jiñ ñi'uk'i,	*where that chayote grows really big,*
jiñ 'ab'i b'a mi yajñeltyak tyi pich	*that's all the places she urinated, they say,*
jiñ Lak Ña'i.	*that Mother of Ours.*
Ya' 'ab'i tza koli jiñ ñi'uk'i,	*There, they say, that chayote grows big,*
xch'ixch'ujm.	*and the spiny chayote.*
'Añ che jiñi,	*So it was,*
tzax me ku kaji tyi 'e'tyel 'ub'i 'alob'i.	*the child began to work.*
Tza kaji tyi lok'eltyak 'ab'i	*He started to go out, they say,*
tyi juñ p'ejl tyi 'otyoty.	*by one door of the house.*
Mu 'ab'i letzel	*He would climb up*

ya' tyi jol 'otyoty;
mi cha' 'ochel
che' tyi mal.
Jiñ 'ab'i k'iñ 'añ,
mi yälob'.
Jiñäch 'ab'i 'añ k'iñ,
'añ 'ili wäleyi.
Tza kaji tyi kolel majlel.
Tza kaji tyi kolel majlel.
Mi lok'eltyak tyi säk'añ;
mi ñumel ya' tyi jol 'otyoty;
mi cha' 'ochel
che' tyi juñ p'ejl tyi 'otyotyi.
Jiñ 'ab'i
che' wolix 'i yik'añtyak majlel,
jiñ che' mux 'i yochel tyi mal,
'ik'ix 'ab'i 'añ che jiñi.
'A che jiñi
tza kaj tyi kolel.
Tza kaj tyi kolel majlel.
Pero 'añ Laj Ch'ujul Ña'
mu tyo 'i pi'leñtyak tyi xämb'al.
Pero koñ wowoli 'i kolel,
chäch woli 'i ñajty'añ ja'el.
'I che jiñi,
wowoli 'i ñajty'añ,
tza b'ejb'e käle majlel Laj Ña',
'uj b'ä.
'I che jach tzi käyäyob' 'i b'äj
tyi xämb'al.

there to the peak of the house;
he would come in again
to the inside.
That one, they say, is the sun,
they say.
That very one, they say, is the sun
that is here today.
He started to grow big.
He started to grow big.
He would go out at dawn;
he would pass by the peak of the house,
he would enter again
where there was a door to the house.
He, they say,
when it was getting to be dusk,
then he would come inside again,
and it would get dark, they say.
So it was,
he started to grow.
He started to grow bigger.
But Our Holy Mother
still went out to accompany him on his walks.
But as he got bigger and bigger,
she was falling further behind.
And so it was,
she was falling further behind,
Our Mother was left behind,
the one who is the moon.
And that's the way they remained
on their walks.

REFERENCES

Adams, Richard E. W.
>1999   *Río Azul: An Ancient Maya City.* Norman: University of Oklahoma Press.

Akkeren, Ruud van
>2000   *Place of the Lord's Daughter: Rab'inal, Its History, Its Dance-Drama.* Leiden, Netherlands: Research School CNWS, School of Asian, African, and Amerindian Studies.

Alejos García, José
>1988   *Wajalix bä t'an: Narrativa tradicional ch'ol de Tumbalá, Chiapas.* Centro de Estudios Mayas, cuaderno 20. Mexico City: Universidad Nacional Autónoma de México.

>1994   *Mosojäntel, ethnografía del discurso agrarista entre los ch'oles de Chiapas.* Mexico City: Universidad Nacional Autónoma de México.

Alejos García, José, and Elsa Ortega Peña
>1990   *El Archivo Municipal de Tumbalá, Chiapas, 1920–1946.* Mexico City: Universidad Nacional Autónoma de México.

Andrews, E. Wyllys
>1970   *Balancanche Cave, Mexico.* New Orleans: Middle American Research Institute.

Andrieu, Chloé, Christophe Helmke, Harri Kettunen, Eric Taladoire, and Robert Tamba
>2012   "Maya Mural Paintings of Bolonkin, Chiapas, Mexico." *Mexicon* 34(1).

Arcos Méndez, Miguel
>2001   "Rezo para solicitar permiso de entrada a la Cueva de Joloniel." Spanish translation by Miguel Meneses López, Carlos Aracos Vázquez, and Nicolás Díaz. Manuscript in possession of authors.

Aulie, H. Wilbur
    1979   "The Christian Movement among the Chols of Mexico, with Special
            Reference to Problems of Second Generation Christianity." D. Mis.
            thesis, Fuller Theological Seminary.
Aulie, H. Wilbur, and Evelyn W. de Aulie
    1978   *Diccionario ch'ol-español; español-ch'ol.* Serie de Vocabularios y Diccio-
            narios Indígenas Mariano Silva y Aceves 21. Mexico City: Instituto
            Lingüístico de Verano. [Revised edition, 1998.]
Avendaño y Loyola, Andrés
    1987   *Relation of Two Trips to Peten.* Culver City, Calif.: Labyrinthos.
Bardawil, Lawrence
    1976   "The Principal Bird Deity in Maya Art: An Iconographic Study of Form
            and Meaning." In *The Art, Iconography, and Dynastic History of Palenque,
            Part 3,* edited by Merle Greene Robertson, 181–94. Pebble Beach, Calif.:
            Pre-Columbian Art Research, Robert Louis Stevenson School.
Barrera Vásquez, Alfredo
    1980   *Diccionario maya Cordemex.* Mérida, Mexico: Ediciones Cordemex.
Basauri, Carlos
    1931   *Tojolabales, tzeltales y mayas: Breves apuntes sobre antropología, etnografía y
            lingüística.* Mexico City: Talleres Gráficos de la Nación.
Bassie-Sweet, Karen
    1987   "Illustrated Stories: The Relationship between Text and Image." Paper
            presented at the 86th Annual Meeting of the American Anthropo-
            logical Association, Chicago.
    1991   *From the Mouth of the Dark Cave.* Norman: University of Oklahoma Press.
    1996   *At the Edge of the World.* Norman: University of Oklahoma Press.
    1998   "The Maya Earth Goddess." Paper presented at the Sixteenth Maya
            Weekend, University of Pennsylvania Museum, Philadelphia.
    2002   "Corn Deities and the Complementary Male/Female Principle." In
            *La organización social entre los mayas: Memoria de la Tercera Mesa Redonda
            de Palenque,* vol. 2, edited by Vera Tiesler Blos, Rafael Cobos, and Merle
            Greene Robertson, 105–25. Mexico City: Instituto Nacional de Antro-
            pología e Historia / Mérida: Universidad Autónoma de Yucatán.
    2008   *Maya Sacred Geography and the Creator Deities.* Norman: University of
            Oklahoma Press.
Bassie-Sweet, Karen, Julie Miller, and Alfonso Morales
    2002   "Don Juan Mountain and the Road to Palenque." *Mesoweb.* www.
            mesoweb.com.
Bassie-Sweet, Karen, Jorge Pérez de Lara, and Marc Zender
    2000   "Jolja Cave." *PARI* [Pre-Columbian Art Research Institute] *Journal*
            1(1): 5–10.

Becquelin, Pierre, and Claude F. Baudez

1979   *Tonina: Une Cité Maya du Chiapas (Mexique),* vol. 1. Paris: Mission Arquéologique et Ethnologique Française au Mexique.

1982   *Tonina: Une Cité Maya du Chiapas (Mexique),* vols. 2–3. Paris: Mission Arquéologique et Ethnologique Française au Mexique.

Beekman, John

1957   "A Culturally Relevant Witness." *Practical Anthropology* 4:83–88.

Bell, Ellen, Marcello A. Canuto, and Robert J. Sharer

2004   *Understanding Early Classic Copan.* Philadelphia: University of Pennsylvania Museum of Archaeology and Anthropology.

Berlin, Heinrich

1955   "News from the Maya World." *Ethnos* 20(4): 201–209.

1958   "El glifo emblema en las inscripciones mayas." *Journal de la Société des Américanistes de Paris* 47:111–19.

Berlo, Janet

1980   "Teotihuacán Art Abroad: A Study of Mesoamerican Style and Provincial Transformation in Incensario Workshops." Ph.D. diss., Yale University.

1983   *Text and Image in Pre-Columbian Art.* BAR International Series 180. Oxford: British Archaeological Reports.

Bernatz, Michele

2006   "The Concept of Divinity in Maya Art: Defining God L." Ph.D. diss., University of Texas at Austin.

Beutelspacher, Carlos R.

1994   *A Guide to Mexico's Butterflies and Moths.* Mexico City: Minutiae Mexicana.

Beyer, Hermann

1926   "Las dos estelas mayas de Tila." *El México Antiguo* 2:235–50.

1927   "Las dos estelas mayas de Tila, Chiapas." *Memorias y Revista de la Sociedad Científica Antonio Alzate* 47:123–43.

Bierhorst, John

1992   *History and Mythology of the Aztecs: The Codex Chimalpopoca.* Tucson: University of Arizona Press.

Blaffer, Sarah

1972   *Black-man of Zinacantan.* Austin: University of Texas Press.

Bloch, Maurice

1992   "What Goes without Saying: The Conceptualization of Zafimaniry Society." In *Conceptualizing Society,* edited by A. Keuper, 125–46. New York: Routledge.

Blom, Frans

1961   "Notas sobre algunas ruinas todavía sin explorar." In *VIII Mesa Redonda, San Cristóbal de Las Casas, Chiapas: Los mayas del sur y sus relaciones con los nahuas meridionales,* 115–25. Mexico City: Sociedad Mexicana de Antropología.

Blom, Frans, and Oliver La Farge

1926–27 *Tribes and Temples.* Middle American Research Institute Publications 1–2. New Orleans: Tulane University.

Bobrow-Strain, Aaron

2007   *Intimate Enemies: Landowners, Power and Violence in Chiapas.* Durham, N.C.: Duke University Press.

Boddam-Whetham, John W.

1877   *Across Central America.* London: Hurst and Blackett.

Bode, Barbara

1961   "The Dance of the Conquest." In *The Native Theatre in Middle America,* 203–98. Middle American Research Institute Publication 27. New Orleans: Tulane University.

Bonor Villarejo, Juan Luis

1989   *Las cuevas mayas: Simbolismo y ritual.* Madrid: Universidad Complutense de Madrid.

Bonor Villarejo, Juan Luis, and Ismael Sánchez y Pinto

1991   "Las cavernas del municipio de Oxkutzcab, Yucatán, México: Nuevas aportaciones." *Mayab* 7:36–52.

Boot, Eric

1999   "Of Serpents and Centipedes: The Epithet Wuk Chapaht Chan K'inich Ahaw." *Notes on Maya Hieroglyphic Writing* 25. Rijswijk, Netherlands.

Borhegyi, Stephen F.

1953   "El Cristo de Esquipulas de Chimayó, Nuevo Mexico." *Antropología e Historia de Guatemala* 5(1).

1954   *El Santuario de Chimayó.* Santa Fe, N.M.: Spanish Colonial Arts Society.

Borowitz, James

2003   "Images of Power and the Power of Images: Early Classic Iconographic Programs of the Carved Monuments of Tikal." In *The Maya and Teotihuacan: Reinterpreting Early Classic Interaction,* edited by Geoffrey E. Braswell, 217–34. Austin: University of Texas Press.

Brady, James E.

1989   "An Investigation of Maya Ritual Cave Use with Special Reference to Naj Tunich." Ph.D. diss., University of California, Los Angeles.

1991   "Caves and Cosmovision at Utatlan." *California Anthropologist* 18(1): 1–10.

Brady, James E., and Wendy Ashmore

1999   "Mountains, Caves, Water: Ideational Landscapes of the Ancient Maya." In *Archaeologies of Landscape: Contemporary Perspectives,* edited by W. Ashmore and A. B. Knapp, 124–45. Malden, Mass.: Blackwell.

Brady, James E., Allan B. Cobb, Sergio Garza, César Espinosa, and Robert Burnett
> 2005   "An Analysis of Ancient Maya Stalactite Breakage at Balam Na Cave, Guatemala." In *Stone Houses and Earth Lords,* edited by K. M. Prufer and J. E. Brady. Boulder: University Press of Colorado.

Brady, James E., and Pierre R. Colas
> 2005   "Nikte Mo' Scattered Fire in the Cave of K'ab Chante': Epigraphic and Archaeological Evidence for Cave Desecration in Ancient Maya Warfare." In *Stone Houses and Earth Lords,* edited by K. M. Prufer and J. E. Brady. Boulder: University Press of Colorado.

Brady, James E., and Ann Scott
> 1997   "Excavations in Buried Cave Deposits: Implications for Interpretation." *Journal of Cave and Karst Studies* 59(1): 15–21.

Brady, James E., and George Veni
> 1992   "Man-Made and Pseudo-Karst Caves: Implications of Sub-Surface Geologic Features within Maya Centers." *Geoarchaeology* 7(2): 149–67.

Brady, James E., Gene A. Ware, Barbara Luke, Allan Cobb, John Fogarty, and Beverly Shade
> 1997   "Preclassic Cave Utilization near Cobanerita, San Benito, Petén." *Mexicon* 19(5): 91–96.

Brasseur de Bourbourg, Charles Étienne
> 1866   *Recherches sur les Ruines de Palenqué et sur les origines de la civilisation du Mexique.* Paris: A. Bertrand.

Braswell, Geoffrey
> 2003   *The Maya and Teotihuacan.* Austin: University of Texas Press.

Breedlove, Dennis, and Robert Laughlin
> 1993   *The Flowering of Man: The Tzotzil Botany of Zinacantan.* Smithsonian Contributions to Anthropology 35. Washington, D.C.: Smithsonian Institution Press.

Breton, Alain
> 1988   "En los confines del norte chiapaneco, una región llamada 'Bulujib'." *Estudios de Cultura Maya* 17:295–354.

Bricker, Victoria
> 1981   *The Indian Christ, the Indian King.* Austin: University of Texas Press.

Brinton, Daniel G.
> 1894   "Nagualism. A Study in Native American Folk-Lore and History." *Proceedings of the American Philosophical Society* 33 (January): 11–73.

Brown, Linda A.
> 2000   "From Discard to Divination: Demarcating the Sacred through the Collection and Curation of Discarded Objects." *Latin American Antiquity* 11(4): 319–33.

Bunzel, Ruth
    1952   *Chichicastenago: A Guatemalan Village.* Seattle: University of Washington Press.
Burns, Allan
    1973   "Pattern in Yucatec Mayan Narrative Performance." Ph.D. diss., University of Washington.
Calnek, Edward E.
    1962   "Highland Chiapas before the Conquest." Ph.D. diss., University of Chicago.
    1970   "Los pueblos indígenas de las Tierras Altas." In *Ensayos de antropología en la zona central de Chiapas,* edited by Norman A. McQuown and Julian Pitt-Rivers, 105–33. Mexico City: Instituto Nacional Indigenista.
    1988   *Highland Chiapas before the Spanish Conquest.* Papers of the New World Archaeological Foundation 55. Provo, Utah: Brigham Young University.
Cano, Agustin
    1984   Manche and Peten: The Hazards of Itza Deceit and Barbarity. Culver City, Calif.: Labyrinthos.
Carot, Patricia
    1989   *Arqueología de las cuevas del norte de Alta Verapaz.* Cuadernos de Estudios Guatemaltecos 1. Mexico City: Centre d'Études Mexicaines et Centroaméricaines.
Carrasco, David
    1982   *Quetzalcoatl and the Irony of Empire: Myths and Prophecies in the Aztec Tradition.* Chicago: University of Chicago Press.
Carrasco, Michael
    2005   "The Incensario Stands of Palenque." Ph.D. diss., University of Texas at Austin.
Carrasco, Michael, and Kerry Hull
    2002   "The Cosmogonic Symbolism of the Corbeled Vault in Maya Architecture." *Mexicon* 24(2): 26–32.
Chamberlain, Robert S.
    1948a   *The Conquest and Colonization of Yucatan, 1517–1550.* Carnegie Institution of Washington Publication 582. Washington, D.C.: Carnegie Institution.
    1948b   "The Governorship of the Adelantado Franciso de Montejo in Chiapas, 1539–1544." Contributions to American Anthropology and History 46:163–207. Washington, D.C.: Carnegie Institution.
Christenson, Allen
    2006   "Sacred Bundle Cults in Highland Guatemala." In *Sacred Bundles: Ritual Acts of Wrapping and Binding in Mesoamerica,* edited by Julia Guernsey and F. Kent Reilly, 226–46. Barnardsville, N.C.: Boundary End Archaeology Research Center.

2007a   *Popol Vuh: The Sacred Book of the Maya.* Norman: University of Oklahoma Press.

2007b   *Popol Vuh: Literal Poetic Version.* Norman: University of Oklahoma Press.

Ciaramella, Mary

    1994   "The Lady with the Snake Headdress." In *Seventh Palenque Round Table, 1989,* edited by Virginia Fields, 201–209. San Francisco: Pre-Columbian Art Research Institute.

    1999   *The Weavers in the Codices.* Research Reports on Ancient Maya Writing 44. Washington, D.C.: Center for Maya Research.

Clark, John, and Stephen Houston

    1998   "Craft Specialization, Gender and Personhood among the Post-conquest Maya of Yucatan, Mexico." In *Craft and Social Identity,* edited by Cathy Lynne Costin and Rita Wright, 31–46. Arlington, Va.: American Anthropological Association.

Coe, Michael

    1973   *The Maya Scribe and His World.* New York: Grolier Club.

    1975   "Native Astronomy in Mesoamerica." In *Archaeoastronomy in Pre-Columbian America,* edited by Anthony F. Aveni, 3–31. Austin: University of Texas Press.

    1977   "Supernatural Patrons of Maya Scribes and Artists." In *Social Process in Maya Prehistory,* edited by Norman Hammond, 327–47. London: Academic Press.

    1978   *Lords of the Underworld.* Princeton, N.J.: Princeton University Press.

    1989   "The Hero Twins: Myth and Image." In *The Maya Vase Book,* vol. 1, edited by Justin Kerr, 161–84. New York: Kerr Associates.

Coggins, Clemency

    1975   "Painting and Drawing Styles at Tikal: An Historical and Iconographic Reconstruction." Ph.D. diss., Harvard University.

Cogolludo, Diego López de

    1955   *Historia de Yucatán.* Mexico City: Editorial Academia Literaria.

Collier, George A., and Elizabeth Lowery Quaratiello

    1994   *Basta! Land and Zapatista Rebellion in Chiapas.* Oakland, Calif.: Institute for Food and Development Policy.

Cordan, Wolfgang

    1963   *Secret of the Forest: On the Track of Maya Temples.* London: Victor Gollancz.

Cruz Guzmán, Ausencio, J. Kathryn Josserand, and Nicholas A. Hopkins

    1980   "The Cave of Don Juan." In *Third Palenque Round Table, 1979, Part 2;* edited by Merle Greene Robertson, 116–23. Austin: University of Texas Press.

    1994   "T'an Lak Mam [Story of Our Grandfather]. T'an ti Wajali." In *Chol Texts, Vocabulary and Grammar,* edited by Nicholas A. Hopkins and J. Kathryn Josserand, 44–61. Final Technical Report to the National Science

Foundation, Grant BNS-8308506, 1983–86. Tampa, Fla.: Institute for Cultural Ecology of the Tropics.

Culbert, T. Patrick

1993   *The Ceramics of Tikal: Vessels from the Burials, Caches and Problematic Deposits.* Tikal Report 25. Philadelphia: University Museum, University of Pennsylvania.

De Vos, Jan

1980a   *Fray Pedro Lorenzo de la Nada; misionero de Chiapas y Tabasco; en el cuarto centenario de su muerte.* San Cristóbal de las Casas, Mexico: n.p.

1980b   *La paz de Dios y del rey; la conquista de la Selva Lacandona, 1525–1821.* Colección Ceiba, Ensayo 10. Tuxtla Gutiérrez, Mexico: Gobierno del Estado de Chiapas. 2nd ed. Mexico City: Fondo de Cultura Económica, 1988.

1988   *Oro verde: La conquista de la Selva Lacandona por los madereros tabasqueños 1822–1949.* Mexico: Fondo de Cultura Económica.

1990   *No queremos ser cristianos: Historia de la resistencia de los lacandones, 1530–1695, a través de testimonios españoles e indígenas.* Mexico City: Instituto Nacional Indigenista.

Deal, Michael

1988   "Recognition of Ritual Pottery in Residential Units: An Ethnohistorical Model of the Maya Family Altar Tradition." In *Ethnoarchaeology among the Highland Maya of Chiapas, Mexico,* edited by Thomas A. Lee and Brian Hayden. Papers of the New World Archaeology Foundation, no. 56. Provo, Utah: Brigham Young University.

Digby, Adrian

1958   "A New Maya City Discovered in British Honduras: First Excavations at Las Cuevas and an Underground Necropolis Revealed." *Illustrated London News* 232:274–75.

Edmonson, Munro

1965   *Quiché-English Dictionary.* Middle American Research Institute Publication 30. New Orleans: Tulane University.

1971   *The Book of Counsel: The Popol Vuh of the Quiche Maya of Guatemala.* Middle American Research Institute Publication 35. New Orleans: Tulane University.

England, Nora, and Stephen Elliott

1990   *Lecturas sobre la lingüística maya.* La Antigua, Guatemala: Centro de Investigaciones Regionales de Mesoamérica.

Estrada-Belli, Francisco, Alexandre Tokovinine, J. M. Foley, H. Hurst, G. A. Ware, D. Stuart, and N. Grube

2009   "A Maya Palace at Holmul, Guatemala, and the 'Teotihuacan Entrada': Evidence from Murals 7 and 9." *Latin American Antiquity* 20(1): 228–32.

Fash, William L.
2001   *Scribes, Warriors and Kings.* Rev. ed. of 1991 publication. London: Thames and Hudson.

Fash William L., and Barbara W. Fash
1994   "Copán Temple 20 and the House of Bats." In *Seventh Palenque Round Table, 1989,* edited by Merle Greene Robertson and Virginia M. Fields, 61–7. San Francisco: Pre-Columbian Art Research Institute.

Fash, William L., Alexandre Tokovinine, and Barbara W. Fash
2009   "The House of New Fire at Teotihuacan and Its Legacy in Mesoamerica." In *The Art of Urbanism: How Mesoamerican Kingdoms Represented Themselves in Architecture and Imagery,* edited by William L. Fash and Leonardo López Luján, 201–29. Washington, D.C.: Dumbarton Oaks.

Faust, Betty
1998   *Mexican Rural Development and the Plumed Serpent: Technology and Maya Cosmology in the Tropical Forest of Campeche, Mexico.* Westport, Conn.: Greenwood Press.

Favre, Henri
1971   *Changement et Continuité chez les Mayas du Mexique: Contribution à l'étude de la Situation Coloniale en Amèrique Latine.* Paris: Éditions Anthropos.

Feldman, Lawrence H.
2000   *Lost Shores and Forgotten People.* Durham, N.C.: Duke University Press.

Ferguson, Josalyn
2001   "A Preliminary Report on the Investigations in Chamber 3B, Actun Chapat, Macal River Valley, Cayo District, Belize." In *The Western Belize Regional Cave Project: A Report of the 2000 Field Season,* edited by R. Ishihara, C. S. Griffith, and J. J. Awe, 185–94. Department of Anthropology, Occasional Paper no. 4. Durham, N.H.: University of New Hampshire.

Fernández, León
1892   *Lenguas de Centro América en el siglo XVIII según copia del Archivo de Indias hecha por el licenciado don León Fernández y publicada por Ricardo Fernández Guardia y Juan Fernández Ferraz.* San José, Costa Rica: Tipografía Nacional.

Florescano, Enrique
1999   *The Myth of Quetzalcoatl.* Washington, D.C.: Johns Hopkins University Press.

Freidel, David, and Barbara MacLeod
2000   "Creation Redux: New Thoughts on Maya Cosmology from Epigraphy, Iconography, and Archaeology." *PARI Journal* 1(2): 1–8.

Freidel, David, Linda Schele, and Joy Parker
1993   *Maya Cosmos.* New York: William Morrow.

Fuentes y Guzmán, Francisco Antonio de
    1969–72 *Obras históricas de D. Francisco Antonio de Fuentes y Guzmán,* edited by
        Carmelo Sáenz de Santamaria. 3 vols. Biblioteca de Autores Españoles,
        nos. 230, 251, and 259. Madrid: Ediciones Atlas.
Furst, Jill
    1995   *Natural History of the Soul.* New Haven, Conn.: Yale University Press.
García Barros, Ana
    2008   "Chaakh, el dios de la lluvia, en el periodo clásico maya: Aspectos reli-
        giosos y políticos." Ph.D. diss., Universidad Complutense de Madrid.
García de León, Antonio
    1979   "Algunas consideraciones sobre los choles." *Estudios de Cultura Maya*
        12:257–87.
Garza, Sergio, James E. Brady, and Christian Christensen
    2001   "Balam Na Cave 4: Implications for Understanding Preclassic Cave
        Mortuary Practices." *California Anthropologist* 28(1): 15–21.
Geoffroy Rivas, Pedro
    1961   *Toponimia nahuat de Cuscatlán.* San Salvador, El Salvador: Editorial
        Universitaria.
Gerhard, Peter
    1979   *The Southeast Frontier of New Spain.* Princeton, N.J.: Princeton Uni-
        versity Press.
Girard, Rafael
    1966   *Los mayas; su civilización, su historia, sus vinculaciones continentales.* Mexico
        City: Libro-Mex Editores.
    1979   *Esotericism of the Popol Vuh.* Pasadena, Calif.: Theosophical Univer-
        sity Press.
Gosner, Kevin
    1984   "Soldiers of the Virgin: An Ethnohistorical Analysis of the Tzeltal
        Revolt of 1712 in Highland Chiapas." Ph.D. diss., University of
        Pennsylvania.
    1992   *Soldiers of the Virgin: The Moral Economy of a Colonial Maya Rebellion.*
        Tucson: University of Arizona Press.
    1998   "Religion and Rebellion in Colonial Chiapas." In *Native Resistance
        and the Pax Colonial in New Spain,* edited by Susan Schroeder. Lincoln:
        University of Nebraska Press.
Gossen, Gary
    1974   *Chamulas in the World of the Sun.* Cambridge, Mass.: Harvard Univer-
        sity Press.
    1999   *Telling Maya Tales: Tzotzil Identities in Modern Mexico.* New York:
        Routledge.
    2002   *Four Creations: An Epic Story of the Chiapas Mayas.* Norman: University
        of Oklahoma Press.

Graham, Ian
  1979 *Corpus of Maya Hieroglyphic Inscriptions.* Vol. 3, pt. 2, *Yaxchilan.* Cambridge, Mass.: Harvard University, Peabody Museum of Archaeology and Ethnology.
  1982 *Corpus of Maya Hieroglyphic Inscriptions.* Vol. 3, pt. 3, *Yaxchilan.* Cambridge, Mass.: Harvard University, Peabody Museum of Archaeology and Ethnology.

Graham, Ian, and Eric von Euw
  1975 *Corpus of Maya Hieroglyphic Inscriptions.* Vol. 2, pt. 1, *Naranjo.* Cambridge, Mass.: Harvard University, Peabody Museum of Archaeology and Ethnology.
  1977 *Corpus of Maya Hieroglyphic Inscriptions.* Vol. 3, pt. 1, *Yaxchilan.* Cambridge, Mass.: Harvard University, Peabody Museum of Archaeology and Ethnology.

Gronemeyer, Sven
  2006 *The Maya Site of Tortuguero: Its History and Inscriptions.* Acta Mesoamericana 17. Markt Schwaben, Germany: Verlag Anton Saurwein.

Grube, Nikolai
  2000 "City-states of the Maya." In *A Comparative Study of Thirty City-State Cultures,* edited by M. H. Hansen, 547–66. Copenhagen: Royal Danish Academy of Science and Letters.
  2002 "Onomástica en los gobernantes mayas." In *La organización social entre los mayas: Memoria de la Tercera Mesa de Palenque,* vol. 2, edited by Vera Tiesler Blos, Rafael Cobos, and Merle Greene Robertson, 323–53. Mexico City: CONACULTA; Instituto Nacional de Antropología e Historia.

Grube, Nikolai, Simon Martin, and Marc Zender
  2001 "Palenque and Its Neighbors." In *The Proceedings of the Maya Hieroglyphic Workshop: Palenque and Its Neighbors, March 9–10, 2002, University of Texas at Austin,* edited by Phil Wanyerka, 1–119. Austin: University of Texas.

Grube, Nikolai, and Werner Nahm
  1994 "A Census of Xibalba: A Complete Inventory of *Way* Characters on Maya Ceramics." In *The Maya Vase Book,* vol. 4, edited by Justin Kerr, 686–715. New York: Kerr Associates.

Grube, Nikolai, and Linda Schele
  1994 "Kuy, the Owl of Omen and War." *Mexicon* 16(1): 10–17.

Guenter, Stanley
  2007 "Note on Alta Verapaz cave painting." Manuscript in possession of authors.

Guerra Ruiz, Jenny Lizeth
  2006 "Representación arquitectónica ritual maya en cuevas." Thesis, Licenciada en Arqueología, Universidad del Valle, Guatemala.

Guiteras Holmes, Calixta
    1961   *Perils of the Soul.* Glencoe, N.Y.: Free Press.
Halperin, Christina T.
    2000   "Caches in Caves: Ancient Maya Use of the *Pachychilus* Shell." Paper
                presented at the 23rd Annual Midwest Mesoamericanist Meeting,
                Urbana-Champaign, Ill.
    2001   "Report of Survey and Archaeological Reconnaissance at Jolja' Cave,
                Jolja' Cave Project, Preliminary Project Report."
    2002   "Caves, Ritual, and Power: Investigations at Actun Nak Beh, Cayo
                District, Belize." Master's thesis, Florida State University.
    2005   "Social Power and Sacred Space at Actun Nak Beh, Belize." In *Stone
                Houses and Earth Lords,* edited by K. M. Prufer and J. E. Brady, 71–90.
                Boulder: University Press of Colorado.
    2007   "Materiality, Bodies, and Practice: The Political Economy of Late
                Classic Maya Figurines from Motul de San José, Petén, Guatemala."
                Ph.D. diss., University of California, Riverside.
Halperin, Christina, Katherine Faust, Rhonda Taube, and Aurore Giguet, eds.
    2009   *Mesoamerican Figurines: Small-Scale Indices of Large-Scale Social Phenomena.*
                Gainesville: University of Florida Press.
Halperin, Christina T., Sergio Garza, Keith M. Prufer, and James E. Brady
    2003   "Caves and Ancient Maya Ritual Use of Jute." *Latin American Antiquity*
                14:207–19.
Halperin, Christina, John Spenard, and Andrés Brizuela Casimir
    2003   "Contemporary and Ancient Use of Space at Cueva Joljá." Paper pre-
                sented at the Annual Meeting of the Society for American Archaeo-
                logy, Milwaukee.
Hansen, Richard
    1992   "Archaeology of Ideology: A Study of Maya Preclassic Architectural
                Sculpture at Nakbe, Peten, Guatemala." Ph.D. diss., University of Cali-
                fornia, Los Angeles.
Headrick, Annabeth
    2003   "Butterfly Warfare at Teotihuacan." In *Ancient Mesoamerican Warfare,*
                edited by M. Kathryn Brown and Travis W. Stanton, 149–70. Walnut
                Creek, Calif.: AltaMira Press.
    2007   *The Teotihuacan Trinity: The Sociopolitical Structure of an Ancient Mesoamerican
                City.* Austin: University of Texas Press.
Healy, Paul F., Kitty F. Emery, and Lori E. Wright
    1990   "Ancient and Modern Maya Exploitation of the Jute Snail (Pachych-
                ilus)." *Latin American Antiquity* 1:170–83.
Hellmuth, Nicholas
    1975   *The Escuintla Hoards: Teotihuacan Art in Guatemala.* F.L.A.A.R. Progress
                Reports, vol. 1, pt. 2. Guatemala: Foundation for Latin American
                Anthropological Research.

1977   "Cholti-Lacandon (Chiapas) and Petén-Ytzá Agriculture, Settlement Pattern and Population." In *Social Process in Maya Prehistory: Studies in Honor of Sir Eric Thompson,* edited by Norman Hammond, 421–48. New York: Academic Press.

1987   "The Surface of the Underwaterworld." Ph.D. diss., Karl-Franzens-Universitaet, Graz, Austria. Culver City, Calif.: Foundation for Latin American Anthropological Research.

Hermitte, Esther

1964   "Supernatural Power and Social Control in a Modern Maya Village." Ph.D. diss., University of Chicago.

Hoffmann, C. C.

1918   "Las mariposas entre los antiguos mexicanos." *Cosmos* 1:18 [4 pp.].

Hogue, Charles L.

1993   *Latin American Insects and Entomology.* Berkeley and Los Angeles: University of California Press.

Holland, William R.

1961   "Highland Maya Folk Medicine." Ph.D. diss., University of Arizona.

Hopkins, Nicholas A.

1964–65 Field notes, August 1964–September 1965. San Mateo Ixtatán, Huehuetenango, Guatemala, and Vicinity. Archive of the Indigenous Languages of Latin America (AILLA). www.ailla.utexas.org.

1983   "Knowledge and Use of Dialect Variants in Lowland Chol." Paper presented at the 22nd Conference on American Indian Languages: Mayan Linguistics, Annual Meeting of the American Anthropological Association, Chicago.

1986   "Maya Languages and Maya Hieroglyphic Writing." Paper presented at the Maya Weekend, University Museum, University of Pennsylvania, Philadelphia.

1988   "Classic Mayan Kinship Systems: Epigraphic and Ethnographic Evidence for Patrilineality." *Estudios de Cultura Maya* 17:87–121.

1991   "Classic and Modern Relationship Terms and the Child of Mother Glyph (TI:606.23)." In *Sixth Palenque Round Table, 1986,* edited by Virginia M. Fields, 255–65. Norman: University of Oklahoma Press.

1995   "Ch'ol." In *Encyclopedia of World Cultures,* edited by James W. Dow and Robert van Kemper, 63–6. Boston: G. K. Hall.

1996   "Metonym and Metaphor in Chol (Mayan) Ritual Language." Paper presented at the Annual Meeting of the American Anthropological Association, San Francisco.

Hopkins, Nicholas A., Ausencio Cruz Guzmán, and J. Kathryn Josserand

2008   "A Ch'ol (Mayan) Vocabulary from 1789." *International Journal of American Linguistics* 74(1): 83–114.

Hopkins, Nicholas A., and J. Kathryn Josserand

1990   "The Characteristics of Chol (Mayan) Traditional Narrative." In *Homenaje a Jorge A. Suárez: Lingüística indoamericana e hispánica,* edited by Beatriz Garza Cuarón and Paulette Levy, 297–314. Mexico City: El Colegio de México.

1994   *Chol Texts, Vocabulary and Grammar. Final Technical Report to the National Science Foundation, Grant BNS-8308506, 1983–1986.* Tampa, Fla.: Institute for Cultural Ecology of the Tropics.

Hopkins, Nicholas A., J. Kathryn Josserand, and Ausencio Cruz Guzmán

2010   *A Historical Dictionary of Chol (Mayan): The Lexical Sources from 1789 to 1935.* Foundation for the Advancement of Mesoamerican Studies. www.famsi.org/mayawriting/dictionary/hopkins/CholDictionary 2010.pdf.

Houston, Stephen

1986   "Problematic Emblem Glyphs: Examples from Altar de Sacrificios, El Chorro, Río Azul, and Xultun." *Research Reports on Ancient Maya Writing* 3. Washington, D.C.: Center for Maya Research.

1992   "A Name Glyph for Classic Maya Dwarfs." In *The Maya Vase Book,* vol. 3, edited by Justin Kerr, 526–31. New York: Kerr Associates.

1996   "Symbolic Sweatbath of the Maya: Architectural Meaning in the Cross Group at Palenque, Mexico." *Latin American Antiquity* (2): 132–51.

2009   "A Splendid Predicament: Young Men in Classic Maya Society." *Cambridge Archaeological Journal* 19(2): 149–78.

Houston, Stephen, John Robertson, and David Stuart

2000   "The Language of Classic Maya Inscriptions." *Current Anthropology* 41(3): 321–56.

Houston, Stephen, and David Stuart

1996   "Of Gods, Glyphs and Kings: Divinity and Rulership among the Classic Maya." *Antiquity* 70:289–312.

1998   "The Ancient Maya Self: Personhood and Portraiture in the Classic Period." *Res: Anthropology and Aesthetics* 33:73–101.

Houston, Stephen, David Stuart, and Karl Taube

2006   *The Memory of Bones.* Austin: University of Texas Press.

Hull, Kerry

1997   "Poetic Discourse in Maya Oral Tradition and in the Hieroglyphic Script." Master's thesis, Georgetown University.

2003   "Verbal Art and Performance in Ch'orti' and Maya Hieroglyphic Writing." Ph.D. diss., University of Texas at Austin.

Hunn, Eugene

1977   *Tzeltal Folk Zoology.* New York: Academic Press.

Ichon, Alain
1973 *La religión de los totonacas de la Sierra.* Mexico City: Instituto Nacional Indigenista.

Instituto Indigenista Nacional
1988 *Lenguas mayas de Guatemala. Documento de referencia para la pronunciación de los nuevos alfabetos oficiales.* Guatemala City: Ministerio de Cultura y Deportes.

Ishihara, Reiko
2007 "Bridging the Chasm between Religion and Politics: Archaeological Investigations of the Grietas at the Late Classic Maya Site of Aguateca, Peten, Guatemala." Ph.D. diss., University of California, Riverside.

Jones, Grant
1998 *Conquest of the Last Maya Kingdom.* Stanford, Calif.: Stanford University Press.

Josserand, J. Kathryn
1991 "The Narrative Structure of Hieroglyphic Texts at Palenque." In *Sixth Palenque Round Table, 1986,* edited by Merle Greene Robertson, 12–31. Norman: University of Oklahoma Press.

Josserand, J. Kathryn, and Nicholas A. Hopkins
1988 *Ch'ol (Mayan) Dictionary Database.* 3 vols. Final Performance Report, National Endowment for the Humanities Grant RT-20643–86.
1996 "Ch'ol Ritual Language." Research Report to the Foundation for Mesoamerican Studies (January). www.famsi.org/reports/94017/.
2005 "Lexical Retention and Cultural Significance in Chol (Mayan) Ritual Vocabulary." *Anthropological Linguistics* 47(4): 401–23.
2007 "Tila y su Cristo Negro: Historia, peregrinación y devoción en Chiapas, México." *Mesoamérica* 49:82–113.

Josserand, J. Kathryn, Nicholas A. Hopkins, Ausencio Cruz Guzmán, Ashley Kistler, and Kayla Price
2003 "Story Cycles in Chol (Mayan) Mythology: Contextualizing Classic Iconography." Research Report to the Foundation for the Advancement of Mesoamerican Studies. www.famsi.org/reports/01085/.

Josserand, J. Kathryn, Linda Schele, and Nicholas A. Hopkins
1985 "Linguistic Data on Maya Inscriptions: The *ti* Constructions." In *Fourth Palenque Round Table, 1980,* edited by Merle Greene Robertson, 87–102. Austin: University of Texas Press.

Joyce, Rosemary
1993 "Woman's Work: Images of Production and Reproduction in Pre-Hispanic Southern Central America." *Current Anthropology* 34(3): 255–74.

Karttunen, Frances
1983 *An Analytical Dictionary of Nahuatl.* Norman: University of Oklahoma Press.

Kaufman, Terrence, with John Justeson
    2003   "A Preliminary Mayan Etymological Dictionary." Foundation for the
            Advancement of Mesoamerican Studies. www.famsi.org/reports /01051
            /pmed.pdf.
Kenward, Amalia
    2005   "Showing the Way: The Function of Three Small Caves in the Sibun-
            Manatee Karst." In *Stone Houses and Earth Lords,* edited by K. M. Prufer
            and J. E. Brady, 249–59. Boulder: University Press of Colorado.
Kettunen, Harri, and Bon V. Davis
    2004   "Snakes, Centipedes, Snakepedes and Centiserpents." *Wayeb Notes* 9.
            www.wayeb.org.
Kidder, Alfred V., Jesse D. Jennings, and Edwin Shook
    1946   *Excavations at Kaminaljuyu, Guatemala.* Carnegie Institution of Wash-
            ington Publication 561. Washington, D.C.: Carnegie Institution.
Klein, Herbert S.
    1970   "Rebeliones de las comunidades campesinas: La República Tzeltal de
            1712." In *Ensayos de Antropología en la zona central de Chiapas,* edited by
            Norman A. McQuown and Julian Pitt-Rivers, 149–70. Mexico City:
            Instituto Nacional Indigenista.
Knowlton, Timothy W.
    1995   *Chonbilal ch'ulelal-alma vendida: Elementos fundamentales de la cosmología
            y religión mesoamericanas en una oración en maya-tzotzil.* Mexico City:
            Instituto de Investigaciones Antropológicas, Universidad Nacional Autó-
            noma de México.
    2002   "Diphrastic Kennings in Mayan Hieroglyphic Literature." *Mexicon* 24:9–14.
Köhler, Ulrich
    1975   "Ein Zauberspruch auf Maya-Tzotzil zur Heilung von Schlangenbis-
            sen." *Zeitschrift für Ethnologie* 100:238–47.
    1989   "Comets and Falling Stars in the Perception of Mesoamerican Indians."
            In *World Archaeoastronomy: Selected Papers from the Second Oxford Inter-
            national Conference on Archaeoastronomy,* edited by Anthony F. Aveni,
            289–99. Cambridge: Cambridge University Press.
Kubler, George
    1977   *Aspects of Classic Maya Rulership on Two Inscribed Vessels.* Studies in
            Pre-Columbian Art and Archaeology 18. Washington, D.C.: Dum-
            barton Oaks.
    2004   "On the Reading of Two Glyphic Appellatives of the Rain God." *In
            Continuity and Change: Maya Religious Practices in Temporal Perspective,*
            edited by Daniel Graña Behrens et al. Markt Schwaben, Germany: Verlag
            Anton Saurwein.
La Farge, Oliver
    1947   *Santa Eulalia.* Chicago: University of Chicago Press.

La Farge, Oliver, and Douglas Byers
    1931   *The Year Bearer's People.* Middle American Research Center Publication 3. New Orleans: Department of Middle American Research, Tulane University.

Lacadena, Alfonso, and Soeren Wichmann
    2002   "The Distribution of Lowland Maya Languages in the Classic Period." In *Memoria de la Tercera Mesa Redonda de Palenque,* vol. 2, edited by Vera Tiesler Blos, Rafael Cobos, and Merle Greene Robertson, 275–319. Mexico City: Instituto Nacional de Antropología e Historia.

Laporte, Juan Pedro, and Vilma C. Fialko
    1990   "New Perspectives on Old Problems: Dynastic References for the Early Classic at Tikal." In *Vision and Revision in Maya Studies,* edited by F. S. Clancy and P. D. Harrison, 33–66. Albuquerque: University of New Mexico Press.

Laughlin, Robert M.
    1969   "Tzotzil." In *Handbook of Middle American Indians,* vol. 7, *Ethnology,* edited by Evon Z. Vogt, 152–94. Austin: University of Texas Press.
    1975   *The Great Tzotzil Dictionary of San Lorenzo Zinacantan.* Smithsonian Contributions to Anthropology 19. Washington, D.C.: Smithsonian Institution Press.
    1976   *Of Wonders Wild and New: Dreams from Zinacantán.* Smithsonian Contributions to Anthropology 22. Washington, D.C.: Smithsonian Institution Press
    1977   *Of Cabbages and Kings.* Smithsonian Contributions to Anthropology 23. Washington, D.C.: Smithsonian Institution Press.
    1988   *The Great Tzotzil Dictionary of Santo Domingo Zinacantán.* Smithsonian Contributions to Anthropology 31. Washington, D.C.: Smithsonian Institution Press.
    2003   *Beware the Great Horned Serpent! Chiapas under the Threat of Napoleon.* Albany: Institute of Mesoamerican Studies, State University of New York.
    n.d.   "Palenque: Mystery of the Snake House." Manuscript in possession of authors.

Laughlin, Robert M., and Karen Bassie-Sweet
    2001   "The Sacred Geography of Jolja' Cave, Chiapas." Paper presented at the 34th Annual Chac Mool Conference, University of Calgary.

Lenkersdorf, Carlos
    1979   *Diccionario Tojolabal-Español.* Mexico City: Editorial Nuestro Tiempo.
    1996   *Hombres verdaderos. Voces y testimonios tojolabales. Lengua y sociedad, naturaleza y cultura, artes y comunidad cósmica.* Mexico City: Siglo XXI Editores.

Lenkersdorf, Gudrun
    1993   *Génesis histórica de Chiapas, 1522–1532: El conflicto entre Portocarrero y Mazariegos.* Mexico City: Universidad Nacional Autónoma de México.
Leutenegger, Benedict
    1976   *Nothingness Itself: Selected Writings of Ven. Fr. Antonio Margil, 1690– 1724.* Chicago: Franciscan Herald Press.
Liendo Stuardo, Rodrigo
    2011   *B'aakal: Arqueología de la región de Palenque, Chiapas, México.* London: British Archaeological Reports.
López Bravo, Roberto
    2004   "State and Domestic Cult in Palenque Censer Stands." In *Courtly Art of the Ancient Maya,* edited by Mary Miller and Simon Martin, 256–58. New York: Thames and Hudson.
López Cogolludo, Diego
    1955   *Historia de Yucatán.* Campeche, Mexico: Comisión de Historia, Gobierno del Estado de Campeche.
Lorenzen, Karl J.
    1999   "New Discoveries at Tumben-Naranjál: Late Postclassic Reuse and the Ritual Recycling of Cultural Geography." *Mexicon* 21:98–107.
Lounsbury, Floyd
    1989   "A Palenque King and the Planet Jupiter." In *World Archaeoastronomy,* edited by Anthony Aveni, 246–59. Cambridge: Cambridge University Press.
Love, Bruce
    1994   *The Paris Codex.* Austin: University of Texas Press.
Lovell, W. George
    1992   *Conquest and Survival in Colonial Guatemala: A Historical Geography of the Cuchumatán Highlands, 1500–1821.* Montreal: McGill-Queen's University Press.
Mace, Carroll Edward
    1970   *Two Spanish-Quiché Dance Dramas of Rabinal.* New Orleans: Tulane University.
MacLeod, Barbara
    1990   "The God N / Step Set in the Primary Standard Sequence." In *The Maya Vase Book,* vol. 2, edited by Justin Kerr, 331–47. New York: Kerr Associates.
Maler, Teobert
    1903   *Researches in the Central Portion of the Usumatsintla Valley.* Memoirs of the Peabody Museum 2, no. 2. Cambridge, Mass.: Peabody Museum.
Manca, María Cristina
    1995   "De las cuevas hasta el cielo pasando a través de los colores de las enfermedades." In *Anuario IEI [Instituto de Estudios Indígenas],* edited by

M. E. Fernández-Galán Rodríguez, 5:223–59. San Cristóbal de Las Casas, Mexico: Instituto de Estudios Indígenas, Universidad Autónoma de Chiapas.

Margil de Jesús, Antonio, Lázaro de Mazariegos, and Blas Guillén
1984   *A Spanish Manuscript Letter on the Lacandones in the Archives of the Indies in Seville.* Culver City, Calif.: Labyrinthos.

Martin, Simon
2001   "Unmasking 'Double Bird', Ruler of Tikal." *PARI* [Precolumbian Art Research Institute] *Journal* 2(1): 7–12.
2002   "The Baby Jaguar: An Explanation of Its Identity and Origins in Maya Art and Writing." In *La organización social entre los mayas: Memoria de la Tercera Mesa Redonda de Palenque,* vol. 1, edited by Vera Tiesler Blos, Rafael Cobos, and Merle Greene Robertson, 49–78. Mexico City: Instituto Nacional de Antropología e Historia.
2003   "In Line of the Founder: A View of Dynastic Politics at Tikal." In *Tikal: Dynasties, Foreigners, and Affairs of State,* edited by Jeremy A. Sabloff, 3–46. Santa Fe, N.M.: School of American Research.
2005   "Metamorphosis in the Underworld: The Maize God and the Mythology of Cacao." In *The Sourcebook for the 29th Maya Hieroglyphic Forum,* edited by David Stuart, 175–90. Austin: Department of Art and Art History, University of Texas.
2006   "Cacao in Ancient Maya Religion: First Fruits of the Maize Tree and Other Tales from the Underworld." In *Theobroma Cacao in Pre-Columbian and Modern Mesoamerican Communities,* edited by Cameron McNeil, 154–83. Gainesville: University of Florida Press.
2012   "Time, Kingship, and the Maya Universe." *Expedition* 54(1): 18–25.

Martin, Simon, and Nikolai Grube
2008   *Chronicle of the Maya Kings and Queens.* 2nd ed. London: Thames and Hudson.

Martin, Simon, Marc Zender, and Nikolai Grube
2002   *Notebook for the 26th Maya Hieroglyphic Forum at Texas.* Austin: Department of Art and Art History, University of Texas.

Mathews, Peter
1991   "Classic Maya Emblem Glyphs." In *Classic Maya Political History: Hieroglyphic and Archaeological Evidence,* edited by T. Patrick Culbert, 19–29. Cambridge: Cambridge University Press.

Mathews, Peter, and John Justeson
1984   "Patterns of Sign Substitution in Mayan Hieroglyphic Writing: The 'Affix Cluster.'" In *Phoneticism in Mayan Hieroglyphic Writing,* edited by John S. Justeson and Lyle Campbell, 185–231. Albany: Institute for Mesoamerican Studies, State University of New York.

Maurer, Eugenio
  1984   *Los tseltales.* Mexico City: Centro de Estudios Educativos.
Mayer, Karl Herbert
  1980   *Maya Monuments: Sculptures of Unknown Provenance in the United States.* Berlin:Verlag Karl-Friedrich von Flemming.
  1984   *Maya Monuments: Sculptures of Unknown Provenance in Middle America.* Berlin:Verlag Karl-Friedrich von Flemming.
  1989   *Maya Monuments: Sculptures of Unknown Provenance, Supplement 2.* Berlin:Verlag Karl-Friedrich von Flemming.
  1991   *Maya Monuments: Sculptures of Unknown Provenance, Supplement 3.* Berlin:Verlag Karl-Friedrich von Flemming.
  1995   *Maya Monuments: Sculptures of Unknown Provenance, Supplement 4.* Berlin:Verlag Karl-Friedrich von Flemming.
  2004–   *Gemalte Inschriften in Höhlen der Maya.* AGST [Archäologische Gesell-
  2005   schaft Steiermark]-Nachrichtenblatt. www.wayeb.org/download/resources/mayer03.pdf
Mayers, Marvin
  1958   *Pocomchí Texts, with Grammatical Notes.* Norman: Summer Institute of Linguistics of the University of Oklahoma.
McAnany, Patricia A., Kimberly A. Berry, and Ben S. Thomas
  2003   "Wetlands, Rivers, and Caves: Agricultural and Ritual Practice in Two Lowland Maya Landscapes." In *Perspectives on Ancient Maya Rural Complexity,* edited by G. Iannone and S. V. Connell. Monograph 49. Los Angeles: University of California, Los Angeles, Cotsen Institute of Archaeology.
McGee, R. Jon
  1998   "The Lacandon Incense Burner Renewal Ceremony: Termination and Dedication Ritual among the Contemporary Maya." In *The Sowing and the Dawning: Termination, Dedication, and Transformation in the Archaeological Record of Mesoamerica,* edited by S. B. Mock, 41–51. Albuquerque: University of New Mexico Press.
Means, Philip A.
  1917   *History of the Spanish Conquest of Yucatan and of the Itzas.* Papers of the Peabody Museum of American Archaeology and Ethnology 7. Cambridge, Mass.: Peabody Museum.
Megged, Amos
  1996   *Exporting the Catholic Reformation: Local Religion in Early Colonial Mexico.* Leiden, Netherlands: E. J. Brill.
Meneses López, Miguel
  1986   *K'uk'Wits: Cerro de los Quetzales.* Tuxtla Gutiérrez, Mexico: Dirección de Fortalecimiento y Fomento a las Culturas de la Sub-Secretaría de Asuntos Indígenas, Secretaría de Desarrollo Rural; Gobierno del Estado de Chiapas.

Méndez Pérez, Marceal
    2010   *Glosas a cinco relatos de la tradición oral tseltal.* Tuxtla Gutiérrez, Mexico: Consejo Estatal para la Cultura y las Artes de Chiapas.

Merlo Juárez, Eduardo
    2009   "El culto a la lluvia en la Colonia: Los santos lluviosos." In *Arqueología Mexicana* 16(96): 64–68.

Miles, Suzanna
    1981   "Mam Residence and the Maize Myth." In *Culture in History,* edited by Stanley Diamond, 430–36. New York: Octagon.

Miller, Arthur
    1973   *The Mural Paintings of Teotihuacán.* Washington, D.C.: Dumbarton Oaks.

Miller, Julie
    2008   "Excavation and Interpretation in the Northeastern Acropolis, Copan, Honduras." Ph.D. diss., University of Pennsylvania.

Miller, Mary Ellen, and Simon Martin
    2004   *Courtly Art of the Ancient Maya.* New York: Thames and Hudson.

Miller, Virginia E.
    1991   *The Frieze of the Palace of the Stuccos, Acanceh, Yucatan, Mexico.* Washington, D.C.: Dumbarton Oaks.

Molina, Fray Alonso de
    1970   *Vocabulario en lengua castellana y mexicana y mexicana y castellana.* Mexico City: Porrúa. [Facsimile of 1571 ed.]

Mondloch, James L.
    1980   "K'e'x: Quiché Naming." *Journal of Mayan Linguistics* 1(2): 9–25.

Monroy Valverde, Fabiola
    2004   *Tila, santuario de un Cristo Negro en Chiapas.* Cuadernos del Centro de Estudios Mayas, Instituto de Investigaciones Filológicas. Mexico City: Universidad Nacional Autónoma de México.

Montejo, Víctor, and Lyle Campbell
    1993   "The Origin of Corn: A Jacaltec Tale in Comparative Mayan Perspective." *Latin American Indian Literatures Journal* 9(2): 99–119.

Morales Villa Vicencio, Juan de
    1936   "Fee de la llegada al peñol y autos de lo que en la jornada zusedio." *Boletin del Archivo General del Gobierno* 2(2): 133–84.

Morán, Fray Francisco
    1935   *Arte y diccionario en lengua ch'oltí: A Manuscript Copied from the Libro Grande of Fr. Pedro Morán of about 1625, in Facsimile,* edited by William Gates. Publication no. 9. Baltimore, Md.: Maya Society.

Morley, Sylvanus G.
    1937–38 *The Inscriptions of Petén.* Carnegie Institution of Washington Publication 437. 5 vols. Washington, D.C.: Carnegie Institution.

Morris, Walter F.
    1987   *Living Maya.* New York: Harry N. Abrams.

2010   *Guía textil de los Altos de Chiapas.* San Cristóbal de Las Casas, Mexico: Asociación Cultural Na Bolom.

Moyes, Holley

2001a   "The Cave as a Cosmogram: Function and Meaning of Maya Speleothem Use at Actun Tunichil Muknal, Belize." In *The Sacred and the Profane: Architecture and Identity in the Maya Lowlands,* edited by P. R. Colas, K. K. Delvendahl, M. Kuhnert, and A. A. Schubart. Acta Mesoamericana 10. Germany: Verlag Anton Saurwein.

2001b   "The Cave as a Cosmogram: The Use of GIS in an Intrasite Spatial Analysis of the Main Chamber of Actun Tunichil Muknal, a Ceremonial Cave in Western Belize." Master's thesis, Florida Atlantic University.

Nash, June

1970   *In the Eyes of the Ancestors.* New Haven, Conn.: Yale University Press.

Navarrete, Carlos

2000   "El Cristo Negro de Tila, Chiapas." *Arqueología Mexicana* 8(46): 62–65.

Navarrete, Carlos, and Eduardo E. Martínez

1977   *Exploraciones arqueológicas en la Cueva de los Andasolos, Chiapas.* Mexico City: Universidad Autónoma de Chiapas.

Nielsen, Jesper

2003   "Art of the Empire: Teotihuacan Iconography and Style in Early Classic Maya Society." Ph.D. diss., University of Copenhagen.

2006   "The Coming of the Torch: Observations on Teotihuacan Iconography in Early Classic Tikal." In *Maya Ethnicity,* edited by Frauke Sachse, 19–30. Acta America, no. 19. Berlin: Verlag Anton Saurwein.

Nielsen, Jesper, and Christophe Helmke

2008   "Spearthrower Owl Hill: A Toponym at Atetelco, Teotihuacan." *Latin American Antiquity* 19(4): 459–74.

Núñez de la Vega, Francisco

1988   *Constituciones diocesanas del Obispado de Chiapas.* Edited by María del Carmen León and Mario H. Ruz. Mexico City: Universidad Nacional Autónoma de México.

Nuttall, Zelia

1891   *The Atlatl or Spear Thrower of Ancient Mexicans.* Papers of the Peabody Museum 3, no. 1. Cambridge, Mass.: Peabody Museum.

Oakes, Maud

1951   *The Two Crosses of Todos Santos.* New York: Pantheon.

Ordóñez y Aguiar, Ramón de

1797   *Historia de la creación del cielo y de la tierra, conforme al sistema de la gentilidad americana.* Madrid: n.p.

1813   "Chiapas and Palenque: Notes on ancient traditions and history from documents of Ramón Ordoñez y Aguiar, MS 1813." Department of Middle American Research, Tulane University.

1817   "Informe sobre los pueblos de Tumbalá, Tila, y Bulogib." *Documentos Históricos de Chiapas,* Boletín 6:119–22.

Palka, Joel
2005   *Unconquered Lacandon Maya.* Gainesville: University of Florida Press.

Pasztory, Esther
1974   *Iconography of the Teotihuacan Tláloc.* Washington, D.C.: Dumbarton Oaks.

Pendergast, David M.
1969   *The Prehistory of Actun Balam, British, Honduras.* Art and Archaeology Occasional Paper 16. Toronto: Royal Ontario Museum.
1970   *A. H. Anderson's Excavations at Rio Frio Cave E, British Honduras (Belize).* Art and Archaeology Occasional Paper 21. Toronto: Royal Ontario Museum.
1971   *Excavations at Eduardo Quiroz Cave, British Honduras (Belize).* Art and Archaeology Occasional Paper 21. Toronto: Royal Ontario Museum.

Pérez Chacón, José L.
1988   *Los choles de Tila y su mundo: Tradición oral.* San Cristóbal de Las Casas, Mexico: Dirección de Fortalecimiento y Fomento a las Culturas de la Sub-Secretaría de Asuntos Indígenas, Secretaría de Desarrollo Rural.

Peterson, Polly Ann
2006   "Ancient Maya Ritual Cave Use in the Sibun Valley, Belize." Ph.D. diss., Boston University.

Peterson, Polly Ann, Patricia A. McAnany, and Allan B. Cobb
2005   "De-fanging the Earth Monster: Speleothem Transport to Surface Sites in the Subun Valley." In *Stone Houses and Earth Lords,* edited by K. M. Prufer and J. E. Brady, 225–47. Boulder: University Press of Colorado.

Piña Chan, Román
1967   *Atlas arqueológica de la República Mexicana.* Vol. 3, *Chiapas.* Mexico City: Instituto Nacional de Antropología e Historia.

Pincemin Deliberos, Sophia
1999   *De manos y soles: Estudio de la gráfica rupestre en Chiapas.* Tuxtla Gutiérrez, Mexico: Universidad de Ciencias y Artes del Estado de Chiapas.

Pitarch, Pedro
2010   *The Jaguar and the Priest: An Ethnography of Tzeltal Souls.* Austin: University of Texas Press.

Proskouriakoff, Tatiana
1950   *A Study of Classic Maya Sculpture.* Carnegie Institution of Washington Publication 593. Washington, D.C.: Carnegie Institution.
1993   *Maya History.* Austin: University of Texas Press.

Prufer, Keith M.
2002   "Communities, Caves, and Ritual Specialists: A Study of Sacred Space in the Maya Mountains of Southern Belize." Ph.D. diss., Southern Illinois University.

Prufer, Keith M., and James E. Brady

2005   *Stone Houses and Earth Lords: Maya Religion in the Cave Context.* Boulder: University Press of Colorado.

Pugh, Timothy W.

2005   "Caves and Artificial Caves in Late Postclassic Maya Ceremonial Groups." In *Stone Houses and Earth Lords,* edited by K. M. Prufer and J. E. Brady, 47–69. Boulder: University Press of Colorado.

Rands, Robert, Ronald Bishop, and Garman Harbottle

1978   "Thematic and Compositional Variation in Palenque Region Incensarios." In *Tercera Mesa Redonda de Palenque,* vol. 4, edited by Merle Greene Robertson and Donnan Call Jeffers, 19–30. Palenque, Mexico: Pre-Columbian Research Center.

Redfield, Robert

1941   *The Folk Culture of Yucatan.* Chicago: University of Chicago Press.

Redfield, Robert, and Alfonso Villa Rojas

1934   *Chan Kom.* Washington, D.C.: Carnegie Institution.

Reents-Budet, Dorie

1994   *Painting the Maya Universe: Royal Ceramics of the Classic Period.* Durham, N.C.: Duke University Press.

2000   "Feasting among the Classic Maya: Evidence from the Pictorial Ceramics." In *The Maya Vase Book,* vol. 6, edited by Barbara Kerr and Justin Kerr, 1022–37. New York: Kerr Associates.

Remesal, Antonio de

1932   *Historia general de las Indias Occidentales, y particular de la gobernación de Chiapa y Guatemala.* 2 vols. Guatemala: Biblioteca Goathemala, Tipografía Nacional.

Riese, Berthold

1981   "Maya-Hohlenmalereien in Nord-Chiapas." *Mexicon* 3(4): 55–56.

Ringle, William M., and George J. Bey

2012   "The Late Classic to Postclassic Transition among the Maya of Northern Yucatán." In *Oxford Handbook of Mesoamerican Archaeology.* New York: Oxford University Press.

Ringle, William M., Tomás Gallareta Negrón, and George J. Bey

1998   "The Return of Quetzalcoatl: Evidence for the Spread of a World Religion during the Epiclassic Period." *Ancient Mesoamerica* 9(2): 183–232.

Rissolo, Dominique A.

2001   "Ancient Maya Cave Use in the Yalahau Region, Northern Quintana Roo, Mexico." Ph.D. diss., University of California, Riverside.

2005   "Beneath the Yalahau: Emerging Patterns of Ancient Maya Ritual Cave Use from Northern Quintana Roo, Mexico." In *In the Maw of the Earth Monster: Mesoamerican Ritual Cave Use,* edited by James E. Brady and Keith M. Prufer, 342–72. Austin: University of Texas Press.

Robertson, John, Danny Law, and Robbie A. Haertel
 2010   *Colonial Ch'olti': The Seventeenth Century Morán Manuscript.* Norman: University of Oklahoma Press.

Robertson, Merle Greene
 1991   *The Sculpture of Palenque.* Vol. 4, *The Cross Group, the North Group, the Olvidado, and Other Pieces.* Princeton, N.J.: Princeton University Press.

Robicsek, Francis, and Donald Hales
 1981   *The Maya Book of the Dead: The Ceramic Codex.* Norman: University of Oklahoma Press.

Roys, Ralph
 1940   *Personal Names of the Mayas of Yucatan.* Contributions to American Anthropology and History 6. Washington, D.C.: Carnegie Institution.
 1965   *Ritual of the Bacabs.* Norman: University of Oklahoma Press.

Rus, Jan
 2003   *Mayan Lives, Mayan Utopias: The Indigenous Peoples of Chiapas and the Zapatista Rebellion.* Lanham, Md.: Rowman and Littlefield.

Ruz, Mario Humberto
 1982   *Los legítimos hombres.* Mexico City: Universidad Nacional Autónoma de México.
 1994   *Tabasco en Chiapas: Documentos para la historia tabasqueña en el Archivo Diocesano de San Cristóbal de Las Casas.* Mexico City: Universidad Nacional Autónoma de México.

Sahagún, Fray Bernardino de
 1959–63 *Florentine Codex: General History of the Things of New Spain.* Translated by Charles E. Dibble and Arthur J. O. Anderson. Monographs of the School of American Research and the Museum of New Mexico. 13 vols. Salt Lake City: University of Utah and School of American Research.

Saint-Lu, Andre
 1968   *La Vera Paz: Esprit Evangélique et Colonisation.* Paris: Centre de Recherches Hispaniques, Institut d'Etudes Hispaniques.

Santamaría, Francisco J.
 1959   *Diccionario de mejicanismos.* Mexico City: Porrúa.

Sapper, Karl
 1897   *Northern Central America, with a Trip to the Highland Anahuac. Travels and Studies of the Years 1888–1895.* Brunswick, Germany: Friedrich Viewig and Son.
 1907   "Choles und Chortíes." In *Congrès International des Americanistes; XVe Session Tenue à Québec en 1906,* 2:423–65. Québec: Dussault et Proulx.
 1985   *Verapaz in the Sixteenth and Seventeenth Centuries; a Contribution to the Historical Geography and Ethnography of Northeastern Guatemala.* University of California, Institute of Archaeology Occasional Paper 13. Los Angeles: University of California.

Saturno, William

2000   "In the Shadow of the Acropolis: Rio Amarillo and its Role in the Copán Polity." Ph.D. diss., Harvard University.

Schele, Linda

1990   "*Ba* as 'First' in Classic Period Titles." *Texas Notes on Precolumbian Art, Writing, and Culture* 5. Austin: University of Texas.

1992   *Notebook for the Sixteenth Maya Hieroglyphic Workshop at Texas.* Austin: University of Texas, Institute of Latin American Studies.

Schele, Linda, and David Freidel

1990   *A Forest of Kings: Untold Stories of the Ancient Maya.* New York: William Morrow.

Schele, Linda, Peter Mathews, and Floyd Lounsbury

1990   "Untying the Headband." *Texas Notes on Precolumbian Art, Writing, and Culture* 4. Austin: University of Texas, Center for the History and Art of Ancient American Culture.

Schele, Linda, and Mary Ellen Miller

1986   *The Blood of Kings.* Fort Worth, Tex.: Kimbell Art Museum.

Schele, Linda, and Khristaan Villela

1991   "Some New Ideas about the T713/757 Accession Phrases." *Texas Notes on Precolumbian Art, Writing, and Culture* 27. Austin: University of Texas, Center for the History and Art of Ancient American Culture.

Schellhas, Paul

1904   *Representation of Deities of the Maya Manuscripts.* Papers of the Peabody Museum of American Archaeology and Ethnology 4, no. 1. Cambridge, Mass.: Harvard University, Peabody Museum.

Schmidt, Peter, Mercedes de la Garza, and Enrique Nalda

1998   *Maya.* New York: Rizzoli.

Scholes, France V., and Ralph L. Roys

1948   *The Maya Chontal Indians of Acalan-Tixchel.* Washington, D.C.: Carnegie Institution.

Schultze-Jena, Leonard

1944   *Popol Vuh: Das heilige Buch der Quiché-Indianer von Guatemala.* Stuttgart, Germany: W. Kohlhammer.

Scott, Ruby

1988   *Jungle Harvest: God's Word Triumphs in Tila Hearts.* Wheaton, Ill.: Conservative Baptist Home Mission Society.

Seler, Eduard

1901   *Die alten Ansiedelungen von Chacula im Distrikte Nenton des Departements Huehuetenango der Republik Guatemala.* Berlin: Reimer Verlag.

1990–   *Collected Works in Mesoamerican Linguistics and Archaeology.* Culver City,
2000   Calif.: Labyrinthos.

Sharer, Robert

2002   "Early Classic Dynastic Origins in the Southeastern Maya Lowlands." In *Incidents of Archaeology in Central America and Yucatán,* edited by M. Love, M. Popenoe de Hatch, and H. Escobedo, 459–76. Lanham, Md.: University Press of America.

2003   "Founding Events and Teotihuacan Connections at Copán, Honduras." In *The Maya and Teotihuacan: Reinterpreting Early Classic Interaction,* edited by G. E. Braswell, 143–66. Austin: University of Texas Press.

Sharer, Robert, David Sedat, Loa P. Traxler, Julia C. Miller, and Ellen E. Bell

2004   "Early Classic Royal Power in Copan: The Origins and Development of the Acropolis (ca. 250–600)." In *Copán: The History of an Ancient Maya Kingdom,* edited by E. Wyllys Andrews and William L. Fash, 139–200. Santa Fe, N.M.: School of American Research.

Sharer, Robert J., Loa P. Traxler, David W. Sedat, Ellen E. Bell, Marcello A. Canuto, and Christopher Powell

1999   "Early Classic Architecture beneath the Copan Acropolis." *Ancient Mesoamerica* 10(1): 2–23.

Sherman, William L.

1979   *Forced Native Labor in 16th Century Central America.* Omaha: University of Nebraska Press.

Sheseña, Alejandro

2002   *Análisis epigráfico del Group 5 de la Cueva de Joloniel, Chiapas.* Tuxtla Gutiérrez, Mexico: Universidad Autónoma de Chiapas.

2004a   "El significado del Grupo de Pinturas 2 de la Cueva de Joloniel." *Anuario Centro de Estudios Superiores de México y Centroamérica,* 317–50. Tuxtla Gutiérrez, Mexico: Universidad de Ciencias y Artes de Chiapas.

2004b   "La Antigüedad del Grupo 2 de la Cueva de Joloniel, Chiapas." *Bolom* 1. San Cristóbal de Las Casas, Mexico: Asociación Cultural Na Bolom.

Shields, Karena

1959   *The Changing Wind.* New York: Thomas Y. Crowell.

Siegel, Morris

1941   "Religion in Western Guatemala, a Product of Acculturation." *American Anthropologist* 43(1): 62–76.

1943   "The Creation of Myth and Acculturation in Acatan, Guatemala." *Journal of American Folklore* 56:120–26.

Skidmore, Joel

2004   "New Ballplayer Panel from Tonina." *Mesoweb.* www.mesoweb.com/reports/Tonina_M172.html.

Slocum, Marianna

1965   "Origin of Corn and Other Tzeltal Myths." *Tlalocan: Revista de Fuentes para el Conocimiento de las Culturas Indígenas de México* 5(1): 1–4.

Slocum, Marianna, and Florencia L. Gerdel
    1965   *Vocabulario tzeltal de Bachajón: Castellano-tzeltal, tzeltal-castellano.* Mexico City: Instituto Lingüístico de Verano.

Solórzano, Sebastián
    1787   Fulgencio Solórzano to Franciso Saavedra y Carvajal. Latin American Library Manuscripts, Collection 33. Chiapas Collection, Box 1, Folder 8. Tulane Latin American Library.

Spenard, Jon
    2006   "The Gift in the Cave for the Gift of the World: An Economic Approach to Ancient Maya Cave Ritual in the San Francisco Hill-Caves, Cancuen Region, Guatemala." Master's thesis, Florida State University.
    2011   "Heading to the Hills: A Preliminary Reconnaissance Report on Pacbitun's Regional Landscape." In *Pacbitun Regional Archaeology Project (PRAP): Report on the 2010 Field Season,* edited by Terry G. Powis, 33–89. Report Submitted to the Institute of Archaeology, National Institute of Culture and History, Belmopan, Belize.
    2013   "Och Chan: A Report on the 2012 Archaeological Investigations in the Pacbitun Karstscape." In *Pacbitun Regional Archaeological Project (PRAP): Report on the 2012 Field Season,* edited by Terry G. Powis, 87–103. Report submitted to the Institute of Archaeology, Belmopan, Belize.
    2014   "Underground Identity, Memory, and Political Spaces: A Study of the Classic Period Maya Karstscape of the Pacbitun Region, Cayo District, Belize." Ph.D. diss. University of California, Riverside.

Spero, Joanne
    1987   "Lightning Men and Water Serpents: A Comparison of Mayan and Mixe-Zoquean Beliefs." Master's thesis, University of Texas at Austin.

Standley, P. C.
    1920   *Trees and Shrubs of Mexico.* Contributions from the United States National Herbarium 23(1). Washington, D.C.: Washington Government Printing Office.

Starr, Frederick
    1902   "Notes upon the Ethnography of Southern Mexico." *Proceedings of the Davenport Academy of Sciences* 9:63–172. Davenport, Iowa: Davenport Academy of Sciences.

Stephens, John Lloyd
    1841   *Incidents of Travel in Central America, Chiapas, and Yucatan.* New York: Harper and Brothers.

Stoll, Otto
    1938   *Etnografía de la República de Guatemala.* Guatemala: Tipografía Sánchez y de Guise.

Stone, Andrea
    1987   "Cave Painting in the Maya Area." *Latin American Indian Literatures Journal* 3(1): 95–108.

1989   "The Painted Walls of Xibalba: Maya Cave Painting as Evidence of Cave Ritual." In *Word and Image in Maya Culture: Explorations in Language, Writing, and Representation,* edited by William Hanks and Don Rice, 319–35. Salt Lake City: University of Utah Press.

1992   "From Ritual in the Rural Landscape to Capture in the Urban Center: The Recreation of Ritual Environments in Mesoamerica." *Journal of Ritual Studies* 6(1): 109–30.

1995   *Images from the Underworld.* Austin: University of Texas Press.

Stone, Andrea, and Mark Zender

2011   *Reading Maya Art: A Hieroglyphic Guide to Ancient Maya Painting and Sculpture.* New York: Thames and Hudson.

Stone, Doris

1932   "Some Spanish Entradas, 1524–1695: A Revision of the Data on Spanish Entradas into the Country of the Lacandon and Ahitza, containing a full translation of Antonio de León Pinelo's report, and first publication of Juan Delgado's manuscripts." In *Middle American Research Series Publication* 4, 209–96. New Orleans: Tulane University.

Stross, Brian

1988   "Burden of Office: A Reading." *Mexicon* 10(6): 118–21.

Stuart, David

1985   "The Painting of Tomb 12, Rio Azul." In *Rio Azul Reports no. 3, the 1985 Season.* San Antonio: University of Texas.

1987   "Ten Phonetic Syllables." *Research Reports on Ancient Maya Writing* 14. Washington, D.C.: Center for Maya Research.

1995   "A Study of Maya Inscriptions." Ph.D. diss., Vanderbilt University.

1996   "Kings of Stone: A Consideration of Ancient Stelae in Maya Ritual and Representation." *Res: Anthropology and Aesthetics* 29–30:148–71.

1998   "The Fire Enters His House." In *Function and Meaning in Maya Architecture.* Washington, D.C.: Dumbarton Oaks.

2000   "Arrival of Strangers." In *Mesoamerica's Classic Heritage: from Teotihuacan to the Aztecs,* edited by David Carrasco, Lindsay Jones, and Scott Sessions, 465–514. Boulder: University Press of Colorado.

2001   "A Reading of the 'Completion Hand' as Tzutz." *Research Reports on Ancient Maya Writing* 49. Washington, D.C.: Center for Maya Research.

2002   "Glyphs for 'Right' and 'Left'?" *Mesoweb.* www.mesoweb.com/stuart/notes/RightLeft.pdf.

2003   "On the Paired Variants of Tz'ak." *Mesoweb.* www.mesoweb.com/stuart/notes/tzak.pdf.

2004a   "The Beginnings of the Copan Dynasty: A Review of the Hieroglyphic and Historical Evidence." In *Understanding Early Classic Copan,* edited by Ellen E. Bell, Marcello A. Canuto, and Robert J. Sharer, 215–48. Philadelphia: University of Pennsylvania Museum of Archaeology and Anthropology.

2004b   "New Year Records in Classic Maya Inscriptions." *PARI Journal* 5(2): 1–6.

2005a   *The Inscriptions from Temple 19 at Palenque.* San Francisco: Pre-Columbian Art Research Institute.

2005b   "A Foreign Past: The Writing and Representation of History on a Royal Ancestral Shrine at Copan." In *Copán: History of an Ancient Maya Kingdom,* edited by E. Wyllys Andrews and William L. Fash, 373–94. Santa Fe, N.M.: School for Advanced Research.

2006a   "Jade and Chocolate: Bundles of Wealth in Classic Maya Economics and Ritual." In *Sacred Bundles: Ritual Acts of Wrapping and Binding in Mesoamerica,* edited by Julia Guernsey and F. Kent Reilly, 127–44. Barnardsville, N.C.: Boundary End Archaeology Research Center.

2006b   *Sourcebook for the 30th Maya Meetings.* Austin: Mesoamerica Center, Department of Art and Art History, University of Texas.

2007a   "The Mam Glyph." Posted at http://decipherment.wordpress.com/?s =grandfather.

2007b   "The Origins of Copan's Founder." Posted at http://decipherment .wordpress.com/2007/06/25/the-origin-of-copans-founder.

2009   "The Symbolism of Zacpeten Altar 1." In *The Kowoj: Identity, Migration, and Geopolitics in Late Postclassic Peten, Guatemala,* edited by Prudence Rice, 317–26. Boulder: University Press of Colorado.

Stuart, David, and Ian Graham
2003   *Corpus of Maya Hieroglyphic Inscriptions.* Vol. 9, pt. 1, *Piedras Negras.* Cambridge, Mass.: Harvard University, Peabody Museum of Archaeology and Ethnology.

Stuart, David, and Stephen Houston
1994   *Classic Maya Place Names.* Washington, D.C.: Dumbarton Oaks.

Stuart, David, Stephen Houston, and John Robertson
1999   *Notebook for the 24th Maya Hieroglyphic Forum at Texas.* Austin: Department of Art and Art History, University of Texas.

Stuart, David, and George Stuart
2008   *Palenque: Eternal City of the Maya.* New York: Thames and Hudson.

Tate, Carolyn
1992   *Yaxchilan: The Design of a Maya Ceremonial City.* Austin: University of Texas Press.

Taube, Karl
1983   "The Teotihuacan Spider Woman." *Journal of Latin American Lore* 9(2): 107–89.

1985   "The Classic Maya Maize God: A Reappraisal." In *Fifth Palenque Round Table, 1983,* vol. 7, edited by Merle Greene Robertson and Virginia Fields, 171–81. San Francisco: Pre-Columbian Art Research Institute.

1988   "The Ancient Yucatec New Year Festival: The Liminal Period in Maya Ritual and Cosmology." Ph.D. diss., Yale University.

1992a   *The Major Gods of Ancient Yucatan.* Washington, D.C.: Dumbarton Oaks.

1992b   "The Iconography of Mirrors at Teotihuacan." In *Art, Ideology, and the City of Teotihuacan,* edited by Janet Berlo, 169–204. Washington, D.C.: Dumbarton Oaks.

1992c   "The Temple of Quetzalcoatl and the Cult of Sacred War at Teotihuacan." *Res: Anthropology and Aesthetics* 21:53–87.

1994   "Birth Vase: Natal Imagery in Ancient Maya Myth and Ritual." In *The Maya Vase Book,* vol. 4, edited by Barbara Kerr and Justin Kerr, 652–85. New York: Kerr Associates.

1998   "The Jade Hearth: Centrality, Rulership, and the Classic Maya Temple." In *Function and Meaning in Classic Maya Architecture,* edited by Stephen Houston, 427–78. Washington, D.C.: Dumbarton Oaks.

2000   "The Turquoise Hearth: Fire, Self-Sacrifice, and the Central Mexican Cult of War." In *Mesoamerica's Classic Heritage: From Teotihuacan to the Aztecs,* edited by David Carrasco, Lindsay Jones, and Scott Sessions, 269–340. Boulder: University Press of Colorado.

2003   "Ancient and Contemporary Maya Conceptions about Field and Forest." In *The Lowland Maya Area: Three Millennia at the Human-Wildland Interface,* edited by A. Gómez-Pompa, M. Allen, S. Fedick, and J. Jiménez-Osornio, 461–92. New York: Haworth Press.

2004   "Structure 10L-16 and Its Early Classic Antecedents: Fire and the Evocation and Resurrection of K'inich Yax K'uk' Mo'." In *Understanding Early Classic Copan,* edited by Ellen E. Bell, Marcello A. Canuto, and Robert J. Sharer, 265–96. Philadelphia: University of Pennsylvania Museum of Archaeology and Anthropology.

Taube, Karl, William A. Saturno, David Stuart, and Heather Hurst

2010   *The Murals of San Bartolo, El Péten, Guatemala.* Pt. 2, *The West Wall.* Ancient America 10. Barnardsville, N.C.: Boundary End Archaeology Research Center.

Taube, Karl, and Marc Zender

2009   "American Gladiators: Ritual Boxing in Ancient Mesoamerica." In *Blood and Beauty: Organized Violence in the Art and Archaeology of Mesoamerica and Central America,* edited by Heather Orr and Rex Koontz, 161–220. Los Angeles: Cotsen Institute of Archaeology Press.

Taylor, Dicey

1978   "The Cauac Monster." In *Tercera Mesa Redonda de Palenque,* vol. 4, edited by Merle Greene Robertson and Donnan Call Jeffers, 79–89. Palenque, Mexico: Pre-Columbian Art Research Center.

Tedlock, Barbara

1985   "Hawks, Meteorology and Astronomy in Quiché-Maya Agriculture." *Archaeoastronomy* 8(1–4): 80–88.

1986   "On a Mountain Road in the Dark: Encounters with the Quiché Maya Culture Hero." In *Symbol and Meaning beyond the Closed Community: Essays in Mesoamerican Ideas,* edited by Gary H. Gossen, 125–38. Albany: Institute for Mesoamerican Studies, State University of New York.

1992   *Time and the Highland Maya.* Albuquerque: University of New Mexico Press.

Tedlock, Dennis

1987   "Hearing a Voice in an Ancient Text: Quiché Maya Poetics in Performance." In *Native American Discourse,* edited by Joel Sherzer and Anthony C. Woodbury, 140–75. Cambridge: Cambridge University Press.

1996   *Popol Vuh: The Definitive Edition of the Mayan Book of the Dawn of Life and the Glories of Gods and Kings.* New York: Simon and Schuster.

Thompson, Edward H.

1897   *Cave of Loltun, Yucatan.* Memoirs of the Peabody Museum of American Archaeology and Ethnology 1, no. 2. Cambridge, Mass.: Harvard University, Peabody Museum.

Thompson, J. Eric S.

1930   *Ethnology of the Maya of Southern and Central British Honduras.* Chicago: Field Museum of Natural History.

1938   "Sixteenth and Seventeenth Century Reports on the Ch'ol Mayas." *American Anthropologist* 40(4): 584–604.

1950   *Maya Hieroglyphic Writing: An Introduction.* Washington, D.C.: Carnegie Institution.

1970   *Maya History and Religion.* Norman: University of Oklahoma Press.

1972   *A Commentary on the Dresden Codex, a Maya Hieroglyphic Book.* Philadelphia: American Philosophical Society.

1975   Introduction to *The Hill-caves of Yucatan,* by Henry C. Mercer, vii–xliv. Norman: University of Oklahoma Press.

1980   "Perspectiva histórica." In *Gramática ch'ol,* edited by Viola Warkentin and Ruby Scott, ix–xiii. Serie Gramáticas de Lenguas Indígenas de México 3. Mexico City: Instituto Lingüístico de Verano.

Tokovinine, Alexandre

2008   "The Power of Place: Political Landscape and Identity in Classic Maya Inscriptions, Imagery, and Architecture." Ph.D. diss., Harvard University.

Torre Yarza, Rodrigo de la

1994   *Chiapas: Entre la Torre de Babel y la lengua nacional.* Mexico City: Centro de Investigaciones y Estudios Superiores en Antropología Social.

Tozzer, Alfred M.

1907   *A Comparative Study of the Mayas and the Lacandones.* New York: Archaeological Institute of America.

1941   *Landa's* Relación de las cosas de Yucatan. Papers of the Peabody Museum of American Archaeology and Ethnology 18. Cambridge, Mass: Peabody Museum.

1984   *A Spanish Manuscript Letter on the Lacandones, in the Archives of the Indies at Seville.* Culver City, Calif.: Labyrinthos.

Tozzer, Alfred M., and Glover Allen

1910   "Animal Figures in the Maya Codices." *Papers of the Peabody Museum* 4, no. 3:275–374. Cambridge, Mass.: Harvard University, Peabody Museum of American Archaeology and Ethnology.

Valdés, Juan A., Federico Fahsen, and Héctor Escobedo

1999   *Reyes, tumbas y palacios: La historia dinástica de Uaxactún.* Mexico: Universidad Nacional Autónoma de México, Centro de Estudios Mayas.

Villa Rojas, Alfonso

1945   *The Maya of East Central Quintana Roo.* Carnegie Institution of Washington Publication 559. Washington, D.C.: Carnegie Institution.

1947   "Kingship and Nagualism in a Tzeltal Community, Southeastern Mexico." *American Anthropologist* 49:578–87.

1961   "Los Quejaches: Tribu olvidada del antiguo Yucatán." *Revista Mexicana de Estudios Antropológicos* 17:97–117.

1967–68 "Los lacandones." *América Indígena.* Mexico: Instituto Indigenista Interamericano.

Villagutierre Soto-Mayor, Juan de

1983   *History of the Conquest of the Province of Itzá.* Translated by Robert D. Wood. Culver City, Calif.: Labyrinthos.

Vogt, Evon

1969   *Zinacantán.* Cambridge, Mass.: Harvard University Press.

1976   *Tortillas for the Gods: A Symbolic Analysis of Zinacanteco Rituals.* Cambridge, Mass.: Harvard University Press.

Vogt, Evon, and David Stuart

2005   "Some Notes on Ritual Caves among the Ancient and Modern Maya." In *In the Maw of the Earth Monster: Mesoamerican Ritual Cave Use,* edited by James E. Brady and Keith M. Prufer, 155–85. Austin: University of Texas Press.

Wagley, Charles

1941   *Economics of a Guatemalan Village.* American Anthropological Association Memoir 58. Menasha, Wisc.: American Anthropological Association.

Warkentin, Viola, and Ruby Scott

1980   *Gramática ch'ol.* Serie de Gramáticas de Lenguas Indígenas de México 3. Mexico City: Instituto Lingüístico de Verano.

Watson, Rodney C.

1982   "Nuevas perspectivas para las investigaciones geográfico-históricas en Chiapas." *Mesoamérica* 3(3): 232–39.

1983   "La dinámica espacial de los cambios de población en un pueblo colonial mexicano: Tila, Chiapas, 1595–1794." *Mesoamérica* 4(5): 87–108.

Webster, David, Barbara Fash, Randolph Widmer, and Scott Zeleznik
1998   "Skyband Group: Investigation of a Classic Maya Elite Residential Complex at Copan, Honduras." *Journal of Field Archaeology* 25(3): 319–43.

West, Robert C., N. P. Psuty, and B. G. Thom
1985   *Las tierras bajas de Tabasco en el sureste de México.* Villahermosa, Mexico: Gobierno del Estado de Tabasco.

White, William B.
1988   *Geomorphology of Hydrology and Karst Terrains.* New York: Oxford University Press.

Whittaker, Arabelle, and Viola Warkentin
1965   *Chol Texts on the Supernatural.* Summer Institute of Linguistics Publications in Linguistics and Related Fields 13. Norman: Summer Institute of Linguistics of the University of Oklahoma.

Wilson, Richard
1995   *Maya Resurgence in Guatemala.* Norman: University of Oklahoma Press.

Winning, Hasso von
1947   "Representations of Temple Buildings as Decorative Patterns on Teotihuacan Pottery and Figurines." *Carnegie Institution of Washington, Notes on Middle American Archaeology and Ethnology* 3(83): 170–77. Cambridge, Mass.: Carnegie Institution.

1979   "Representaciones de fachadas de templos en ceramica de Teotihuacan." In *Las representaciones de arquitectura en la arqueología de América,* vol. 1, *Mesoamerica,* edited by D. Schávelzon, 319–27. Mexico City: Universidad Nacional Autónoma de México.

1987   *La iconografía de Teotihuacán; los dioses y los signos.* Mexico City: Estudios y Fuentes del Arte en Mexicano; Universidad Nacional Autónoma de México.

Wisdom, Charles
1940   *Chorti Indians of Guatemala.* Chicago: University of Chicago Press.

Woodfill, Brent K. S.
2007   "Shrines of the Pasión-Verapaz Region, Guatemala: Ritual and Exchange along an Ancient Trade Route." Ph.D. thesis, Vanderbilt University.

Wright, L. E.
2005   "In Search of Yax Nuun Ayiin I: Revisiting the Tikal Project's Burial 10." *Ancient Mesoamerica* 16(1): 89–100.

Ximénez, Fray Francisco
1929–31 *Historia de la provincia de San Vicente de Chiapa y Guatemala, 1666–1722.* 3 vols. Guatemala: Biblioteca Goathemala [de la Sociedad de Geografía e Historia].

Zender, Marc
1999   "Diacritical Marks and Underspelling in the Classic Maya Script: Implications for Decipherment." Master's thesis, University of Calgary.

2000   Preliminary Report, Jolja' Cave Project.

2004a   "The Glyphs for 'Handspan' and 'Strike' in Classic Maya Ballgame Texts."
          PARI Journal 4(4): 1–9.

2004b   "A Study of Classic Maya Priesthood." Ph.D. diss., University of Calgary.

2005   "The Raccoon Glyph in Classic Maya Writing." *PARI Journal* 5(4): 6–16.

Zender, Marc, Karen Bassie-Sweet, and Jorge Pérez de Lara

2001   "Art and Ritual in Jolja' Cave, Chiapas, Mexico." Paper presented at
          the 66th Annual Meeting of the Society for American Archaeology,
          New Orleans.

INDEX

www.ingramcontent.com/pod-product-compliance
Lightning Source LLC
Chambersburg PA
CBHW081414160426
42812CB00086B/1784